W9-CWW-855

Germany in the Pacific and Far East, 1870-1914

# Germany in the Pacific and Far East, 1870-1914

edited by
JOHN A. MOSES
PAUL M. KENNEDY

University of Queensland Press

Typeset by Academy Press Pty. Ltd., Brisbane
Printed and bound by Silex Enterprise & Printing Co., Hong Kong

Distributed in the United Kingdom, Europe, the Middle East, Africa, and the Caribbean by Prentice-Hall International, International Book Distributors Ltd., 66 Wood Lane End, Hemel Hempstead, Herts., England

*National Library of Australia*
*Cataloguing-in-publication data*

Germany in the Pacific and Far East, 1870–1914.

Index.
ISBN 0 7022 1330 6.

1. Pacific area – Politics and government – Addresses, essays, lectures. 2. East (Far East) – Politics and government – Addresses, essays, lectures. I. Moses, John Anthony, 1930–, ed. II. Kennedy, Paul Michael, 1945–, joint ed.

990

TO THE MEMORY OF J. W. DAVIDSON
1915–1973
FIRST PROFESSOR OF PACIFIC HISTORY
AUSTRALIAN NATIONAL UNIVERSITY, CANBERRA

# Contents





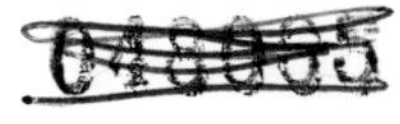

**TABLE**



**MAPS**

# Introduction

In publishing this collection of papers the editors have a twofold intention: firstly, it was thought desirable to make known the research being carried out in different parts of the world on this general topic and, secondly, the symposium is offered as a contribution to the current debate on imperialism and colonialism. There already exists an extensive scholarly literature both in English and German upon Germany's African colonies, but the coverage of the Pacific and Far East has only just begun. This symposium seeks to illustrate those fields where solid research has recently been undertaken.

Until a short while ago it was not possible for historians to examine the full range of German Foreign and Colonial Office records. These are now, happily, available for the most part to international research, and students have not been slow in taking advantage of this mine of information. Apart from scholarly curiosity concerning the little-known imperial and colonial record of a former great power in these regions, the interest in this subject is heightened by the fact that the repercussions of Germany's presence are still being felt, particularly in those Pacific areas which are in the process of being de-colonized, such as the Territory of New Guinea. The information provided here will be of obvious value not only to Western scholars and administrators but also to the historical consciousness of the emerging peoples.

Clearly it has not been possible within a limited selection of papers to do justice to all aspects of this broad subject. The balance will have to be filled later by wider and deeper monographic studies. Of course, some of these are already available, as the bibliography indicates; others will no doubt appear in the near future. However, salient issues are already taken up here. For example, the first group of papers deals with Germany's economic penetration and activity in the Pacific and

Far East, providing thereby key examples of imperialism with or without the flag. The two East German contributions are in this sphere and deserve careful reading, not least because they offer information and points of view not usually encountered in the West.

These are followed by a number of contributions upon Germany's relations with foreign powers in the Pacific and Far East, particularly focusing upon the political strategical aspects of annexation and partition, but also (as in the case of Japan) covering more general relations.

The final group of essays could be said to examine various major aspects of colonial rule and native response, a rapidly-growing field of historical and anthropological research. As can be seen from this wide selection of regional examples, the mere annexation by Germany of colonial territory in the Pacific and Far East proved to be only the beginning of its tasks: the subtle counter-measures of the Chinese in Kiautschou, Solf's dilemma regarding coolie importation into Samoa, the difficulties of understanding and influencing the native polity, and of preventing and punishing native "crimes" and revolution, were all problems of considerable magnitude and complexity to the colonial administrators. Even when the latter were assisted by the activities of missionaries, there was no guarantee of success—as the article upon the Rhenish Mission in New Guinea clearly shows.

As a general contribution to the debate upon colonialism, this symposium was stimulated to a high degree by the wide-ranging research being published on the entire question of Wilhelmine Germany. Both editors have spent a great deal of time in German archives and universities and are alive to the discussions which have been raging over the past decade on the issue of German imperialism. This would be true of every contributor to a greater or lesser extent. All have received much help and stimulus from their German professors and colleagues, both East and West. It would therefore be idle to suggest that the work presented here represents the views of any one particular "school". Each contributor was invited to submit his work without being required to conform to any kind of editorial policy other than in the questions of mechanical presentation and the general relevance to the main theme—the German presence in the Pacific and Far East. Great store has been set upon allowing contributors a completely free hand so that the highest possible degree of individuality and freedom of approach could be guaranteed.

The various papers in this collection indicate the many ways in which the German activities in the Pacific and Far East in the period 1870–1914 can be approached. Although all these aspects are now beginning to receive the attention and careful scholarship which they merit, this is not to imply that final judgements are being made in any one field; many of the contributions are in fact exploratory ventures, and the more valuable for being so. With the full knowledge that there is still much to be done, the editors felt that it would be appropriate to conclude this symposium with a select bibliographical list of what has already been published, together with a guide to archival sources to assist future scholars. In these ways it is hoped that the "pathfinding" nature of the collection may be further enhanced.

It was as we were putting the final touches to this study that we learnt of the sad death of Professor J. W. Davidson, the doyen of Pacific historians, at the early age of fifty-seven. Feeling sure that he would have approved of the multi-dimensional approach of this collection, we dedicate it to his memory.

*John A. Moses* *Paul M. Kennedy*

# Acknowledgements

In putting together the various parts which comprise this symposium, the editors have become heavily indebted to a large number of individuals and institutions, whose brief mention in the following paragraphs can scarcely hope to indicate how much is really owed them.

Ingrid Moses assisted greatly in the translation of the German manuscripts and in the compilation of the bibliographical guide; Harding Ganz kindly drew the maps for his chapter; and while virtually all the contributors gave help for the bibliographical and archival guides, special tributes should be paid to Stewart Firth and Peter Hempenstall, who provided first drafts of those parts of the latter which relate to German missionary and commercial records. Mr Robert Langdon of the Pacific Manuscripts Bureau, with his vast knowledge of Australasian records, was also consulted upon the archival guide, as were so many of the librarians and staff of those depositories: all gave generously of their time and knowledge.

We also wish to acknowledge the kind agreement of the editors of the *Australian Journal of Politics and History*, in vol.21, no. 2, 1975 of which Dr Bade's paper appeared, and of *The Journal of Pacific History* to our proposal that the copyright of the contribution of Dr Bade, as well as of those of Dr Moses and Dr Firth, which appeared in the 1973 issue of the latter journal, will be jointly held by us both.

Finally, there remains to be acknowledged that great debt which all historians owe to the holders and custodians of their documentary sources, without which their research could never have been accomplished. The list of archivists, librarians, government officials and private owners is in our case enormous, for the contributors to this symposium have used records from four continents. We can only hope to express on behalf of us all our deep thanks for the manifold assistance we received in the course of our researches.

*John A. Moses* *Paul M. Kennedy*

# Notes on Contributors

**BADE, Klaus-J.** Dr phil. (Erlangen). Published: *Friedrich Fabri und der Imperialismus in der Bismarckzeit.—Depression—Expansion.* Beiträge zur Kolonial—und Überseegeschichte, (Freiburg i. Br./Zürich 1957); "Friedrich Fabri", *Fränkische Lebensbilder*, no. 6. Veröffentlichungen der Gesellschaft für Fränkische Geschichte, Reihe 7A (Würzburg, 1975) pp 263–69; "Organisierter Kapitalismus—oder: von den Schwierigkeiten vergleichender Sozialgeschichte", *Neue Politische Literatur* 20, no. 3 (1975), pp 293–307;—,K. Manfraß, "Arbeitsmarkt und Arbeitskräftewanderung in Deutschland und Frankreich seit der Mitte des 19. Jahrhunderts. Ein komparativer Problemaufriß", *Sozialwissenschaftliche Informationen für Unterricht und Studium* 5, no. 4 (1976).
In preparation: *Neuere Imperialismusforschung*. Wissenschaftliche Buchgesellschaft, Reihe: Erträge der Forschung. (Darmstadt, 1978); Symposium *Mission und Kolonialherrschaft. Das deutsche Beispiel* 1884–1914; Migration und Arbeitsmarkt in Deutschland 1879–1929 (Habilitation thesis, for end of 1977). Currently Wissenschaftlicher Assistent at the Institut für Geschichte der Friedrich-Alexander-Universität Erlangen-Nürnberg.

**BROWN, Richard G.** B.Sc. and M.A. (Northwestern State University of Louisiana), Ph.D. (Southern Mississippi). Published: articles in *The Southern Historian*. Dissertation on *Germany, Spain and the Caroline Islands,* 1885–1899. Assistant Professor of Social Science at the Northwestern State University of Louisiana.

**FIRTH, Stewart G.** B.A. (Sydney), M.A. (Australian National University), D.Phil. (Oxon). Senior Beit scholar of the University of Oxford, 1970–71; Theodor Heuss Research Fellow of the University of Oxford, 1971–72. Published: articles in *Melbourne Studies in Education*, *Journal of Pacific History*, and *Historical Studies*. At present writing two books, *The German Colonies in the Pacific: An Economic History*, and *The New Guinean Speaks*. Visiting Lecturer in History at the Centre for South Pacific Studies, University of California, Santa Cruz, 1973;

Research Fellow in Pacific History, Department of Pacific History, Australian National University, to 1975. Lecturer, Department of Political Science, Macquarie University, Sydney, NSW.

**GANZ, A. Harding.** B.A. (Wittenberg University, Ohio), M.A. (Columbia), Ph.D. (Ohio State). NDEA (National Defence Education Act) Title IV Research Fellow, 1969. At present writing on the German navy and colonial affairs. Assistant Professor in Modern European History, The Ohio State University, Newark, Ohio.

**HEMPENSTALL, Peter J.** B.A. (Queensland), D.Phil. (Oxon). Rhodes scholar, 1970; DAAD scholar, 1970 (Hamburg). Postdoctoral Fellow, Australian National University, 1974–75. Published: articles in *Journal of the Polynesian Society*, *Journal of Pacific History*. Book forthcoming: *Pacific Islanders Under German Rule: A Study in Cultural Adaptation*. At present Lecturer in Modern History, University of Newcastle, New South Wales.

**KENNEDY, Paul M.** B.A. (Newcastle-upon-Tyne), D.Phil. (Oxon). Theodor Heuss Research Fellow of the University of Oxford, 1968–69; Research Fellow of the Alexander von Humboldt-Stiftung, 1972. Published: *Pacific Onslaught,* 1941–1943 (New York/London, 1972); *Pacific Conquest* (New York/London, 1973); *The Samoan Tangle: A Study in Anglo-German-American Relations,* 1878–1900 (Shannon/New York, 1973); articles in *English Historical Review*, *Past and Present*, *Historical Journal*, *Canadian Journal of History*, *Australian Journal of Politics and History*, *Historical Studies*, *Journal of Contemporary History*, *Journal of Modern History*, *Transactions of The Royal Historical Society* and a contribution to *Marine und Marinepolitik im kaiserlichen Deutschland* 1871–1914, ed. H. Schottelius and W. Deist (Düsseldorf, 1973); *The Rise and Fall of British Naval Mastery* (London, 1976); at present completing *The Origins of the Anglo-German Antagonism*. Reader in Modern History, University of East Anglia.

**KNIGHT, Martin P.** B.A. (Oxon), D.Phil. candidate (Oxon). At present writing a doctoral dissertation on the influence of Pacific problems on British foreign policy, 1880–87. Postgraduate student at Nuffield College, Oxford.

**MEYER, Günther.** Dr phil. (Humboldt-Universität, Berlin). Published: (with Volker Klemm) *Albrecht Daniel Thaer, Pionier der Landwirtschaftswissenschaft in Deutschland* (Halle, 1968); articles on library and information science in *Der Bibliothekar*, *Informatik*, and *Zentralblatt für Bibliothekswesen*. Vice-Director, Methodological Centre for Academic and Research Libraries, Berlin, GDR

**MIYAKE, Masaki.** B.A., M.A. (Kyoto University). Research Fellow of the Austrian Government's Scholarship (Erasmus-Preis), 1962–64; Research Fellow at the University of Heidelberg, 1964–65; teaching activity at the Friedrich-Meinecke-Institut of the Free University of Berlin, 1967–68. Published articles in the German language: "J.M. Baernreither und 'Mitteleuropa', eine Studie über den Nachlass Baernreither", and "Die Achse Berlin-Rom-Tokio im Spiegel der japanischen Quellen" in *Mitteilungen des Österreichischen Staatsarchivs*, vol. 17/18 (Vienna, 1965) and vol. 21 (Vienna, 1969); "Friedrich Naumann, das deutsche Kaiserreich unter Wilhelm II und Japan vor der Niederlage des Jahres 1945, eine Studie über Friedrich Naumann mit besonderer Berücksichtigung der japanischen Geisteswelt" pts 1 & 2 in Jimbun-Kenkyû [The Human Studies], pub. Kanagawa University, no. 56, 1973, and no. 59, 1974. Published many books and articles in the Japanese language on modern German history and German-Japanese relations. Recently published *Nichi-Doku-I Sangoku Dômei no Kenkyu* [A Study on the Tripartite Alliance Berlin-Rome-Tokyo], (Tokyo, 1975). Professor in Diplomatic History, Faculty of Politics and Economics, Meiji University, Tokyo, Japan.

**MOSES, Ingrid.** Diplom Sozialwirt (Erlangen-Nürnberg). Research Assistant in Anthropology and Sociology, University of Queensland 1967–69. M.A. student in Sociology, University of Queensland.

**MOSES, John A.** B.A., M.A. (Queensland), Dr phil. (Erlangen). DAAD scholarship holder, 1961–64 (Munich and Erlangen); Visiting Fellow in Pacific History, Australian National University, 1971; Humboldt Fellowship holder, 1972–73. Published: *The War Aims of Imperial Germany: Professor Fritz Fischer and his Critics* (Brisbane, 1968); *The Politics of Illusion* (London, 1975); articles in *Australian Journal of Politics and History*, *Historical Studies*, *New Zealand Journal of History*, *Journal of Pacific History*, and *Journal of European History*; *Geschichte in Wissenschaft und Unterricht*, *Internationale Wissenschafliche Korrespondenz*, *Jahrbuch des Instituts für Deutsche Geschichte*; and contributions to *Questioning the Past*, ed. D.P. Crook (Brisbane, 1972), and *Deutschland in der Weltpolitik des 19. und 20. Jahrhunderts*, ed. I. Geiss and B.-J. Wendt (Düsseldorf, 1973). At present writing a book *Labour and the Fatherland—The German Socialist Trade Union Struggle for Economic Democracy 1890–1933*. Reader in History, University of Queensland.

**SACK, Peter G.** Assessor (Hamburg), Ph.D. (Australian National University). Published: *Land between two Laws: Early European Land Acquisitions in New Guinea* (Canberra, 1973); ed., *Problem of Choice: Land in Papua New Guinea's Future* (Canberra, 1974); ed., *The Land Law of German New Guinea*—a Collection of Documents (Canberra, 1975), as well as various papers dealing with different aspects of the traditional and colonial history and law of Papua New Guinea. Research Fellow, Department of Law, Institute of Advanced Studies, Australian National University.

**SCHRECKER, John E.** B.A. (Pennsylvania), M.A. and Ph.D. (Harvard). Two years of study in East Asia. Published: *Imperialism and Chinese Nationalism: Germany in Shantung* (Cambridge, Mass., 1971); articles in *Journal of Asian Studies*, *Papers on China*, etc. At present working on the radical reform movement of the late 1890s in China. Associate Professor of History (East Asia), Brandeis University; Associate in Research, East Asia Research Centre, Harvard.

**STOECKER, Helmuth.** Dr phil.habil. (Humboldt-Universität, Berlin). Published: *Deutschland und China im 19. Jahrhundert. Das Eindringen des deutschen Kapitalismus* (Berlin, 1958; Chinese translation, Peking, 1961); *Kamerun unter deutscher Kolonialherrschaft*, 2 vols. (Berlin, 1960, 1968); *Handbuch der Verträge 1871–1964* (Berlin, 1968); co-editor of *Biographisches Lexicon zur Deutschen Geschichte* (Berlin, 1970); articles in *Zeitschrift für Geschichtswissenschaft*, *Wiss. Zeitschrift der Humboldt-Universität zu Berlin*, *Deutsche Literaturzeitung*, etc. At present writing a book on German imperialist expansion in Africa, Asia, and the Pacific until 1943. Professor of Modern History, Humboldt University, GDR.

# List of Abbreviations in Notes

| | |
|---|---|
| AA | Auswärtiges Amt (This applies both to the original office and to the present depository in Bonn) |
| AAHP | Auswärtiges Amt, Handelspolitische Abteilung (Potsdam) |
| AAKA | Auswärtiges Amt Kolonial Abteilung (Colonial Dept of Foreign Office) |
| *Amtsblatt* | *Amtsblatt für das Schutzgebiet Deutsch Neuguinea* |
| *ADK* | *Bericht über die Verhandlungen des allgemeinen deutschen Kongresses zur Förderung überseeischer Interessen in Berlin* |
| ADM | Admiralstab der Marine |
| Adm. | Admiralty (British) |
| *AMZ* | *Allgemeine Missionszeitschrift* |
| ARM | Archiv der Rheinischen Mission |
| BA | Bundesarchiv, Koblenz |
| BA/MA | Bundesarchiv-Militärarchiv, Freiburg |
| *BD* | *British Documents on the Origin of the War*, edited by G.P. Gooch and H. Temperley |
| *BRM* | *Berichte der Rheinischen Missionsgesellschaft* |
| Cab. | Cabinet Records, Public Record Office, London |
| CAO | Australian Archives Office, Canberra |
| CO | Colonial Office Records, Public Record Office, London |
| CPP | Commonwealth Parliamentary Papers |
| DHPG | Deutsche Handels-und Plantagen-Gesellschaft der Südsee-Inseln zu Hamburg |
| *DKB* | *Deutsches Kolonialblatt* |
| DKG | Deutsche Kolonialgesetzgebung |
| *DKL* | *Deutsches Kolonial-Lexikon* |
| *DKZ* | *Deutsche Kolonial-Zeitung* |
| DSG | Deutsche Samoa-Gesellschaft |
| DZA | Deutsches Zentralarchiv, Potsdam |

| | |
|---|---|
| FO | Foreign Office Records, Public Record Office, London |
| *GP* | *Die Grosse Politik der Europäischen Kabinette*, ed. J. Lepsius, F. Thimme, and A. Mendelsohn-Bartholdy |
| *Jahresberichte* | *Die amtlichen Jahresberichte über die Entwicklung der deutschen Schutzgebiete in Afrika und der Südsee* |
| *JbRM* | *Jahresberichte der Rheinischen Missionsgesellschaft* |
| *JPH* | *Journal of Pacific History* |
| KA | See AAKA |
| KAP | Kapuziner Mission Records |
| *KM* | *Kirchliche Mitteilungen* |
| M | The German mark, as in M 400 |
| *MB* | *Das Missionsblatt*, ed. Missions-Hilfsgesellschaft in Barmen |
| MK | Marine Kabinett |
| NARG | National Archives, Record Group (Washington) |
| NGB | Japanese Foreign Ministry Documents |
| NGC | Neuguinea Compagnie |
| *NKWL* | *Nachrichten über Kaiser-Wilhelmsland und den Bismarck-Archipel* |
| NLA | National Library of Australia |
| *NM* | *Neuendettelsauer Missionsblatt* |
| NZNA | New Zealand National Archives |
| OKM | Oberkommando der Marine |
| PAMBU | Pacific Manuscripts Bureau |
| RD | Russian Documents (Die internationalen Beziehungen im Zeitalter des Imperialismus) |
| RKA | Reichskolonialamt (This applies both to the original office and to the present depository in Potsdam) |
| RMA | Reichsmarineamt |
| *SMH* | *Sydney Morning Herald* |
| *SGB* | *Samoanisches Gouvernementsblatt* |
| STAH | Staatsarchiv, Hamburg |
| *SZ* | *Samoanische Zeitung* |

# PART 1

# Commercial Penetration and Development

1

# German Firms in the Pacific Islands, 1857-1914

STEWART G. FIRTH

German commerce was important in the Pacific for about sixty years, from the first successes of Hamburg merchants in the early 1860s to the expropriation of all German property after World War I. Like Germany's African colonies, the Pacific possessions were of little economic importance to her. Their trade was worth less than one-seventh of 1 per cent of total German trade in 1909, and accumulated capital investment, even by the most optimistic estimates, was not more than M400,000,000 by 1912, or £20,000,000 in contemporary sterling.[1] The investment was in trading, plantation agriculture and phosphate mining, dominated by a few companies based in Hamburg, Bremen and Berlin, and of minor value to the Fatherland even as a source of raw materials. Copra from Germany's Pacific colonies—their main product—provided less than 8½ per cent of Germany's copra imports in 1910 and 1911, compared to 48½ per cent from British colonies and 40 per cent from the Dutch East Indies.[2] Phosphates, the second most important export, supplied Germany with 5 per cent of her needs.[3] Significant as they were in the economy of the German Pacific, the phosphate islands of Nauru and Angaur produced a mere 3 per cent of the world's phosphate, whereas France's North African colonies—to take a contrasting example—produced 46 per cent.[4] With copra, phosphate, birds-of-paradise and cacao the list of significant exports at the end of German rule is exhausted. Economically, Germany's was the smallest of the Pacific colonial empires even after the rapid expansion of the first decade of the twentieth century. In 1911 and 1912 the exports of Fiji, Tonga, the British Solomon Islands Protectorate, Papua and the Gilbert and Ellice Islands Protectorate were

Reprinted with permission of the editors of the *Journal of Pacific History*, 1973 issue.

worth M 75,700,000, those of French Oceania and New Caledonia worth M 39,800,000, and those the German New Guinea (including the island territory north of the equator) and German Samoa worth M 33,600,000.[5]

Broadly speaking, the Germans in the Pacific engaged in three kinds of economic activity: commercial, as traders with the Pacific Islanders and general merchants in port towns; agricultural, as planters growing mainly copra and cotton; and extractive, as mine owners. While the phosphate mines were immensely profitable, the success of trading and plantation firms differed from place to place depending both on the character of the traditional Pacific Island society encountered by German firms and on the methods they used to establish dominance over it. What follows is a survey of the principal German companies active in the West Pacific before World War I, of their capital and profitableness, and of the reasons why some made more money than others.[6]

## I

The Germans began their activities in the Pacific as traders. Entering the Pacific westwards from Valparaiso, the Hamburg shipping firm of J.C. Godeffroy & Sohn established its first factor, August Unshelm, at Apia Bay in Samoa in 1857. Unshelm thought the Samoans were a "free race of men" of "lively disposition", but "unusually lazy and slow in anything to do with work and the gathering of products" because nature gave them all they needed.[7] Similar comments would often be made in succeeding years by Germans and other Europeans exasperated by the Samoans' unwillingness to work for them. In Samoa Europeans encountered a society which, for all its lack of a centralized government, nevertheless represented a single, unified culture capable of frustrating attempts at complete foreign control. The Europeans could trade with the Samoans, but they could not make labour contracts, so that any attempt at plantation agriculture had to depend on importing labourers from other, less resistant, island societies. From the beginning, then, the Germans worked within constraints on their economic activity which were imposed by the Pacific Islanders.

The capital backing of J.C. Godeffroy & Sohn enabled them to establish commercial predominance in central Polynesia within a few years. From the late 1850s onwards the tonnage of Hamburg's trading vessels visiting Apia exceeded that of Britain's. In the early 1860s resident traders tied to the Apia firm were on Savai'i, Tutuila and Manu'a in Samoa, Uvea and Futuna, and in the Lau Islands of eastern Fiji, exchanging cotton print, nails, metal tools, and other European manufactures for coconut oil, bêche-de-mer, and pearl-shell, which were then exported through Apia to Sydney, Valparaiso and Europe.[8] The network of Godeffroy agents continued to expand, especially after the company introduced a far more profitable way of exploiting the coconut than collecting the oil and shipping it in casks. Coconuts split and dried for copra were worth probably five times as much as those drained for oil, because transport in copra sacks was cheaper, the oil was purer, and what was left over could be used as cattle feed.[9] Tonga was the Godeffroys' biggest and most reliable source of copra. In 1869 they concluded a treaty with the Tongan Wesleyan Mission by which all natural produce received by the missionaries was sold to Godeffroys, giving them a virtual monopoly of the Tongan export trade.[10] The Gilbert and Ellice Islands were dotted with the company's agents, and in the Marshall Islands they had five stations by 1873. Moving southwards from their bases in the Carolines, Godeffroy agents first reached the New Britain (later Bismarck) Archipelago in 1872 and were permanently stationed on the Duke of York Islands from 1876.[11] By then Godeffroy stations were scattered across the Pacific from Tahiti to the Marianas, visited once every six or twelve months by a vessel from Apia which collected the accumulated copra, turtle-shell, pearl-shell and trepang.

J.C. Godeffroy & Sohn was not the only German firm in the Pacific. Fred Hennings set up his business in Fiji in 1863, and was joined by Ruge, Hedemann & Co., representatives of the Hamburg shipping firm Wachsmuth & Krogmann.[12] Until they became the Godeffroys' agents in the Marshall Islands, A. Capelle & Co. had operated as independent traders there.[13] And during the 1870s the brothers Eduard and Franz Hernsheim entered the Pacific trade. Eduard Hernsheim, a Rhinelander, established trading agents at Malakal in Palau in

1874, on the Duke of York Islands in the Bismarck Archipelago in October 1875, and in the Marshall Islands in 1876. By the time Eduard Hernsheim settled on the island of Matupi in the Gazelle Peninsula of New Britain in 1879, his trading interests were considerable, both in the Bismarck Archipelago and in the Marshall and Gilbert groups, where his brother Franz ran the business from the island of Jaluit.[14]

The Samoans, Tongans, Fijians, Tahitians, and Gilbertese had grown used to European goods by decades of mission and trader influence before the Germans arrived. On other island groups the Germans themselves were among the first to bring the products of Western technology to the inhabitants, and to create among them that economic dependence on the European which was the prerequisite of vigorous trade. By the end of the 1870s the Marshallese, Gilbertese and Caroline Islanders had become accustomed to ship's biscuit, beer and Schnaps, as well as the usual cotton and iron goods. Some Marshallese chiefs dressed their wives in silk, mostly bought on credit from the trader, and supplied them with sewing machines, while at Yap in the Carolines, a chief paid M 4,000 for an old machine-gun of the Bavarian army.[15] Establishing trading contacts was easier with Micronesian societies, where the chief's word was usually law, than with those of Melanesia, which, typically, were governed by fluid systems of shifting authority. When the Germans first arrived in the Bismarck Archipelago, Eduard Hernsheim recalled: "... business was restricted to barter trade of the humblest kind; the people had no needs, and even if the goods they demanded, clay beads, hoop iron and empty bottles, were also worthless, it was on the other hand quite impossible to buy any large quantity of the export articles to be found here."[16] One solution adopted was to establish smoking schools in districts which traders wished to penetrate, at which pipes and tobacco were handed out to the Islanders free of charge, so as to encourage them to demand a quickly consumable article of trade, though less success was had at first in making the Islanders feel the need for European clothes. Once useful trading contacts were made with the villagers of the Bismarck Archipelago, business was profitable, for in 1879 they were content to receive goods worth M 6 for copra which sold for M 400 in Europe.[17]

The late 1870s were the golden age of German commerce in

the Pacific. It was estimated that in 1877 German firms in Samoa, Tonga, Fiji, the Society Islands, and the Ellice, Gilbert, Marshall and New Britain groups exported products worth M 6,103,000, of which copra accounted for M 4,722,000, followed by cotton, pearl-shell, cotton-seed, coconut fibre, tortoise-shell and candle-nuts. In that year Germans had 87 per cent of the export trade from Samoa and Tonga, and 79 per cent of the import business, including the import of currency.[18] The principal source of exports was in trading with the Islanders, but cotton and a tiny proportion of copra came from the Godeffroys' plantations in Samoa and Tonga.

Plantation agriculture was always a tempting alternative to European traders in the Pacific because it left the final say about the production and price of copra to the European rather than the Islander. Given the right conditions, above all adequate supplies of labour, a high proportion of mature palms, and a favourable world price, plantation copra was much more profitable per ton than trade copra, since the benefits to the trader of a higher world price were diminished by the competition of other traders willing to pay more to the indigenous producer. This was the spur which drove Europeans to invest in coconut palm planting in the West Pacific, even though not all were to enjoy the conjunction of conditions which made profits possible. As elsewhere in the Pacific, the initial impetus to plantation agriculture in Samoa came from the high cotton prices caused by the American Civil War. The Godeffroys' first plantation in Samoa, laid out in 1865, was devoted entirely to cotton. At Vailele, near Apia, the company's second plantation (1867), coconut palms were planted between the rows of cotton in a pattern of cultivation which was to become the model for German copra plantations in the Pacific. Since coconut palms come to full maturity only after about ten years, cotton was used as a stopgap crop for three or four years while the palms were still small enough to allow it to grow. And, at least in Samoa, the practice developed of then grazing cattle among the palms so that some income was assured until the first palms began bearing.[19] By 1879 the Godeffroys' cotton and copra plantations covered an area of 4,337 acres and employed 1,210 labourers, mostly Gilbertese and New Hebrideans.[20]

German commerce would never again be as generally

predominant in the Pacific Islands as at the end of the 1870s. One by one the props upon which that predominance had rested were knocked away. J.C. Godeffroy & Sohn went bankrupt in December 1879, and although Godeffroy interests survived in the Société commerciale de l'océanie of Tahiti and the Deutsche Handels- und Plantagen-Gesellschaft der Südsee-Inseln zu Hamburg of Samoa (or DHPG), the old trading empire inevitably contracted. World commodity prices fell. After fluctuating from as high as £22 per ton at the end of the 1870s to £15 in 1881, and back to £20 in 1882, the European price of copra entered a decline from which it did not permanently recover until 1901. Foreign competition was intensified. The DHPG was driven out of Rotuma in the early 1880s by British port-of-entry regulations, and in the Bismarck Archipelago recruiting ships from Queensland and Fiji exploited the German company's source of labour, and disrupted trading contacts with the Islanders. When annexation by Germany came in 1884, it was not of the centre of German commerce, Samoa, but of New Guinea and the Bismarck Archipelago, relatively unknown territories, whose exploitation by Europeans had hardly begun. The German Solomons, added to German New Guinea after the Anglo-German agreement of April 1886, provided the Germans with little else but labourers. Germany's second colony in the Pacific, the Protectorate of the Marshall Islands, which was annexed in 1885, was the more valuable acquisition because of its flourishing copra trade.

The effect of annexation and partition was to confirm German dominance of two peripheral trading regions—the Marshall Islands and the Bismarck Archipelago, to ensure a constant flow of cheap labour from the Bismarck Archipelago to the Samoan plantations of the DHPG, and to hand over a vast tract of New Guinea tropical forest to the Berlin consortium which formed the New Guinea Company. Germany's biggest commercial interests, which were in the trade of central Polynesia, still remained without the protection of formal rule.

## II

The DHPG, capitalized at M 5,000,000, paid its first dividend of 4 per cent to holders of preference shares worth M 2,500,000 in 1884. In that year the average price of copra obtained by the company stood at over £18 a ton, but by 1886 it had dropped to £14 12s., and a loss of M 346,052 was made, followed by a further loss in 1887. H.M. Ruge & Co., the other large German firm in Samoa and Tonga, went into liquidation in 1888, and the DHPG was forced to make good a deficit of M 867,000 by halving its nominal capital and raising a loan of M 2,500,000.[21] Not surprisingly, the DHPG continued to press for German annexation of Samoa throughout the 1880s, envisaging a German Samoa in which Samoans would have provided forced labour for the plantations. In 1885 the company offered to pay for the first year's administration of the new colony; in 1886 it claimed to have invested in the belief "that the predominance of German interests must finally lead to recognised German dominion over this island group"; in December 1888 it pointed out that the English and the Americans would hardly be able to object if Germany used the current rebellion to assume power in Samoa; and in February 1889, Weber told Bismarck that the DHPG would sell out if Samoa did not become German.[22] Bismarck would not have minded had they done so—he would at least have been freed of the diplomatic irritant of Samoa—but no one would buy at the right price, either then or later in the 1890s, and the DHPG hung grimly on, blaming the lack of "ordered conditions" in Samoa for their difficulties.[23]

The situation for the DHPG was not as desperate as the directors of the company liked to paint it. The DHPG had, after all, managed to expand the cultivated area of its Samoan plantations by 85 per cent between 1879 and 1890, from 4,337 to 8,005 acres, and, despite higher labour recruiting costs and falling commodity prices, to make a small profit on these plantations every year from 1881 to 1887. So cheap was the labour employed by the DHPG that the plantations paid for their own extension, even though only about half of their area was producing crops.[24] After a peak, reached about 1887, when each labourer cost the company Chilean $79.17 for the year (about £15), the cost of labour dropped until it reached gold $46.21 (£9 5s.) per head in 1897.[25] Easier recruiting coincided with the end of plantation expansion. With an assured labour market in the new German colony in New Guinea, the DHPG obtained almost twice as many recruits from 1886 to 1890 (over

4,400) as had been obtained from 1880 to 1885 (2,289), and covered its more modest labour needs adequately during the 1890s.[26] When good prices for copra came again at the end of the decade, 65 per cent of the DHPG's planted coconut palms were already in full bearing, whereas most planters in German New Guinea were only just beginning to plant palms.[27]

The DHPG complained frequently of the Samoans' raids on its plantations during the 1890s, and there is no doubt that the thefts of taro, bananas, oranges and pineapples made by Samoans, the extra cost of feeding labourers with imported food, and the desertions by labourers which accompanied the dislocation of war, all cost the company a lot of money. The DHPG manifestly was not protected by the condominium administration against what Consul Fritz Rose called "the worst outrages" on property.[28] It is, nevertheless, significant that the company reckoned to have made a profit on its plantations every year during the 1890s except 1891, that an overall profit was made every year except 1891 and 1892, and that the first dividends paid since 1884 should have come not after the raising of the German flag in 1900, but in the midst of the "disorder" of 1898 and 1899, when the Samoan war forced the closing of two plantations for six weeks.[29] The years 1898 and 1899, it should be noted, were the first ones of relatively good copra prices since the slump beginning in May 1894. Copra prices probably had more to do with the DHPG's profitability than colonial rule.

The map of German commerce in Central Polynesia changed during the 1890s. The Germans' dominance of the Samoan economy remained—their share of imports between 1893 and 1897 was never less than 48 per cent and of exports never less than 82 per cent—but in Tonga the British replaced the Germans as the leading foreign businessmen. Whereas in 1887 Germans had held 76 per cent of Tonga's export trade and 41 per cent of its imports, ten years later those proportions had dropped to 25 per cent and 32 per cent.[31] The DHPG sold its two Tongan plantations in the early 1890s,[32] and in the Ellice Islands Germans were supplanted by the Auckland firm Henderson & McFarlane.[33]

The fundamental outlines of the European economy in Western Samoa had been drawn before 1900, and were merely confirmed, not created, by German annexation. Europeans had had to be content to trade with the Samoans, and employ them only on a casual basis. Though the Samoans knew that traders would deceive them by 30 to 50 lb in every 100 lb of copra weighed, and that traders supplied them with inferior goods for higher prices than those paid by Europeans, they nevertheless found trading with the European infinitely preferable to working for him. Every Samoan had work obligations in his village which employment away from home interrupted. To work for oneself as a paid servant rather than for the community was, in Samoan eyes, contemptible.[34] And the Samoans were not entirely at the mercy of the traders, for they would not cut copra below a certain price. As the DHPG directors commented in 1895: "The prices [offered] to the natives could not be lowered in 1895, because production would have come to a halt with inevitable certainty ... We have to submit to the experience of many years that the Samoans cut copra at no lower rate than 1 cent per lb at the very lowest."[35] In good years, moreover, competition among European traders forced up the prices offered to Samoans for copra. Any attempt to conscript the Samoans as forced labourers would have ruined the Europeans by making the Samoans stop trading, and might have led to open revolt.

Working within these limits to its own advantage, the DHPG, a single company, held the commanding position, and imposed further limits on the activities of other European firms. It had the sole right to recruit plantation labourers from the Bismarck Archipelago, who worked for a pittance. This "cheap labour-material", as Governor Wilhelm Solf described the New Guineans employed by the DHPG, created that company's "favoured position among competitors in Samoa".[36] Its trading agencies were well entrenched in Tonga and the Bismarck Archipelago, as well as Samoa. In the five years 1902–6 the DHPG received over 62 per cent of all copra made by Samoans in German Samoa, and though the proportion dropped thereafter, it averaged 49 per cent from 1902 to 1913. The Tongan agencies on Tongatapu, Ha'apai, Vava'u, Niuafo'ou, and Niuatoputapu supplied the company with more copra than those in Samoa from 1906 to 1911, and accounted for 40 per cent of total Tongan production in 1913.[37] Because of low wages and high copra prices, profits on the company's Samoan plantations quadrupled between 1900 and

1913, even though output hardly increased. The DHPG reckoned that being able to employ New Guineans instead of Chinese saved them M 125,000 a year, and while the European price of copra doubled between 1900 and 1913, the cost of labour rose by less than half.[38] The result was a succession of favourable dividends, rising from 5 per cent in 1898 to 28 per cent in 1909, and the equivalent of 36 per cent from 1911 onwards. Profits exceeded M 8,000,000 in the six years to 1914—a sum close to the total value of the DHPG's investment.[39]

Other firms in German Samoa did not fare so well. The small traders and planters, Germans, British, and Americans, who had survived the economic rigours of the 1890s, were joined in 1902 by bigger firms. The British were initially represented by Samoa Estates Ltd. and Upolu Cacao Co. Ltd., of Birmingham, the Germans by the Deutsche Samoa-Gesellschaft (1902), the Safata-Samoa-Gesellschaft (1903), and the Samoa-Kautschuk-Compagnie (1905), all of Berlin. The Deutsche Samoa-Gesellschaft, with a nominal capital of M 1,000,000, helped to cover the costs of its entry into cacao growing by exploiting the desperate need for labourers in Samoa, and charging exorbitant rates for introducing the first group of Chinese coolies in 1903. By 1912 the company had 634 acres under cacao in three plantations, a small area under rubber, and a number of trade-stores. But plant diseases, difficulty in getting labourers, and poor management led to a loss on the plantations of M 253,322 in 1913. The company was forced to close down its trade-stores at a loss of a further M 44,223, and wrote off half its paid-up capital in June 1914.[40] The other two companies, both financed by the Berlin finance group of W. Mertens & Co., did no better. They were the largest employers of Chinese coolies in German Samoa, and suffered correspondingly from the expense and delays involved in the coolie trade. An attempt to sell them to an English consortium in 1910 failed, and neither ever paid a dividend from its investments in cacao and rubber, which had a nominal value of M 2,900,000.[41] The three Berlin companies were all casualties of the restrictions imposed on European economic activity by the Samoans and by the DHPG, for without a strong base in trading, and without the underpaid Melanesian labour reserved for the DHPG, plantation agriculture in German Samoa was at best a risky enterprise.

## III

Potentially, New Guinea and its offshore islands were a much more valuable trading and plantation colony than Samoa. They were much bigger, and their inhabitants were split by language and geography into hundreds of tiny societies unable to resist the Germans collectively. New Guineans, unlike Samoans, could be attracted, cajoled, and, if necessary, forced to work on German plantations in vast numbers. Yet German Samoa's exports exceeded those of the "Old Protectorate" of German New Guinea (as the area was known after the acquisition of the Carolines and other islands in 1899, and their inclusion within an enlarged "German New Guinea") every year up to 1912, except 1907 and 1910.[42] The reasons lay in Germany's late start in New Guinea, and in the very diversity which weakened the New Guineans. Apart from a small number of coastal regions in the Bismarck Archipelago, the "Protectorate of the New Guinea Company" was *terra incognita* to the Germans in 1884, and little more than a traders' frontier when the New Guinea Company relinquished administration to the Reich in 1899. New Guineans could eventually be made to serve the European economy more than the Samoans, but it was a process which required gradual economic penetration of New Guinean societies and an expensive conquest. A diverse and splintered population could be subjected to foreign rule only slowly, district by district.

The New Guinea Company itself was a costly failure, especially during the fourteen years 1885–99 when it held an imperial charter to govern New Guinea.[43] Originally conceived as a giant speculation in land—it had exclusive rights to land, and planned to sell it to the expected flood of German settlers—the company was forced to rely on plantation agriculture when it became obvious that no settlers would arrive. The plantations were not in the Bismarck Archipelago, where traders and labour recruiters had been accustoming Islanders to the European presence since the 1870s, but on the forbidding coastline of northeastern New Guinea (Kaiser Wilhelmsland). No expense was spared, and more than M 3,000,000 were spent in the first twenty-seven months of settlement, of which 45 per cent was absorbed by the costs of the company's own shipping line.[44] More and more capital was poured into the company by its investors—a group of bankers and industrialists led by the Berlin banker, Adolph von Hansemann. Cotton, cacao, coffee, and tobacco were planted, labourers imported from the Archipelago, Singapore, and the Dutch East Indies, and two subsidiary companies established to specialize in different kinds of plantations. By 1893 over M 7,000,000 had been sunk into the enterprise—more than had been invested in any other German colonial firm—but it brought nothing except losses.[45] An epidemic of malaria forced the company to evacuate the capital of Finschhafen in 1891, half the plantation labourers died during 1891 and 1892, and the company was driven out of its Hatzfeldhafen station by superior New Guinean forces.[46] Relatively few mainland New Guineans could be made to work for the company because it lacked both a trading network, which would have made them economically dependent, and sufficient military power to force them to work. The Kaiser Wilhelmsland Plantagen-Gesellschaft, a Hamburg subsidiary formed to grow cacao, and capitalized at M 500,000, lasted less than a year.[47] The Astrolabe Compagnie was a more ambitious subsidiary with capital of M 2,400,000, but its efforts to grow tobacco were so disastrous that it was dissolved after five years in 1896.[48] The New Guinea Company itself would have been dissolved but for the 1898 agreement made on the transferral of its sovereignty to the imperial government, which gave the company a land grant of 50,000 hectares and M 4,000,000 cash in compensation for its "pioneering" work in Kaiser Wilhelmsland, and allowed it to survive as the largest firm in German New Guinea.[49]

The smaller firms, all in the Archipelago, were much more successful. Unlike the New Guinea Company, they concentrated on trading, the economic activity most appropriate to a colonial situation in which power did not lie decisively in the Europeans' hands, and unlike the New Guinea Company they worked on coastlines where there were enough coconut palms to provide the New Guineans with a trading surplus. Even trading had its difficulties: eight traders were killed in northern New Ireland between 1886 and mid-1892, for example, and, as elsewhere in the Pacific, the long slump in copra prices led to a fall in the number of trading stations from the early 1880s onwards.[50] But by 1897 the largest Archipelago firm, E.E. Forsayth & Co., was estimated to be making an annual profit of up to M 200,000, mainly from trading, and there were forty-nine trading stations spread throughout the islands in 1899.[51] E.E. Forsayth & Co. also had a plantation in the Gazelle Peninsula of New Britain, originally laid out in 1882, which grew cotton and copra on the Samoan pattern. Other plantations were laid out in the Gazelle Peninsula during the 1890s, the biggest by the New Guinea Company, and it became the centre of plantation agriculture in the colony.

Under the stimulus of rising copra prices and the more effective protection of the imperial administration, the Germans rapidly expanded their plantations after 1899, and by 1914 had transformed a trading economy into one drawing its strength from plantation agriculture. In the Bismarck Archipelago and the German Solomons the area under plantation cultivation multiplied more than ninefold between 1900 and 1914, and in Kaiser Wilhelmsland more than fivefold. The total planted acreage in 1913, 73,320, greatly exceeded German Samoa's 26,756, as did the number of labourers employed—14,990 compared to 2,118.[52] The proportion of planted acreage actually bearing was 35 per cent in the "Old Protectorate", compared with 54 per cent in German Samoa.[53]

Despite the multiplication of small business undertakings (the Chinese alone owned 207 businesses in the protectorate in 1912),[54] a few firms dominated the economy. The New Guinea Company revived itself in the Archipelago, after the disaster of the mainland plantations, by following the practice of other planters and engaging in trading. After repeated infusions of capital, as well as subsidization by the imperial government, it finally paid its first dividend, of 5 per cent, for the financial year 1912–13, its twenty-seventh year in business. The company still owned about a quarter of cultivated plantation land, and employed a quarter of the Old Protectorate's indentured labour force.[55] Apart from the New Guinea Company, there were six trading and plantation companies in 1909 which possessed capital of more than M 600,000.[56] Five were old-established: E.E. Forsayth & Co., J.O. Mouton & Co., H.R. Wahlen & Co., and the New Guinea branch of the DHPG. One was new, the Bismarck-Archipel G.m.b.H. of Berlin, founded in 1907 with a capital of M 650,000 by the same finance group which set up the Safata-Samoa-Gesellschaft and the Samoa-Kautschuk-Compagnie. Its establishment heralded the coming of what one planter optimistically called "*Grosskapital*" investment to the Old Protectorate of German New Guinea,[57] which coincided with the peak of the pre-war boom in the world price of copra. E.E. Forsayth & Co., the oldest firm of planters, was bought by Hamburg interests for M 2,750,000 in 1910, and thereby linked to H.R. Wahlen G.m.b.H. of Hamburg. Wahlen, a native of Hamburg, had built a flourishing plantation business in the depopulated North-Western Islands of the Bismarck Archipelago after leaving Hernsheim & Co. in 1903, and as head of the Forsayth firms from 1911 was the most powerful planter in the Archipelago. The two large companies he controlled were both profitable: H.R. Wahlen G.m.b.H paid 9 per cent and 12 per cent on capital of M 1,800,000 in 1911 and 1912, and Forsayth G.m.b.H. made enough money to merge with Forsayth Kirchner & Co. G.m.b.H. as an *Aktiengesellschaft*, the Hamburgische Südsee A.G., in 1914.[58] Other firms under Wahlen's control were Baining G.m.b.H., Ramu G.m.b.H., and Nambung Sägewerk G.m.b.H.[59] Hernsheim & Co. became an *Aktiengesellschaft* in Hamburg in 1909, and in the five years to 1914 made profits of over M 1,000,000 on original nominal capital of M 1,200,000 (increased to M 1,800,000 in 1911), paying dividends which averaged 10.6 per cent per year.[60] The Germans exploited the New Guinea region most profitably in those areas where long-standing trading contacts with the New Guineans provided an economic basis for investment in plantations, as in the Gazelle Peninsula of New Britain, and where depopulation by disease left abundant coconut palms available for foreign seizure, as in the North-Western Islands and the Vitu Islands. All planters benefited from the government's systematic conquest of new labour recruiting areas and its imposition of a head tax, which, as intended, increased the flow of villagers on to the plantations. In the six years 1908–14 recruiters in the Old Protectorate obtained 41,938 labourers—most of them on three-year contracts at wages of no more than M6 a month.[61] Australian valuations of German investment in New Guinea at the end of World War I put the New Guinea Company first at £1,280,000, followed by Wahlen's Hamburgische Südsee A.G. and subsidiaries at £500,000, and Hernsheim & Co. A.G. at £260,000.[62]

## IV

German firms made their greatest profits, not in Samoa or New Guinea, but in the scattered atolls of Micronesia. Following appeals from the two principal German trading firms in the Marshall Islands, Robertson & Hernsheim and the DHPG, Germany annexed the Marshall Islands in October 1885, adding Nauru in 1888.[63] Germany withdrew from an attempted occupation of the Carolines in 1885, after Spanish protests, but German trading posts remained on all the important islands of the Carolines (though not the Marianas) until these groups were bought by Germany from Spain in 1899.[64]

The German Protectorate of the Marshall Islands was administered by the Reich and the costs of administration borne by a privileged company formed in 1887—the Jaluit-Gesellschaft of Hamburg. This was a merger of the combined Micronesian interests of Robertson & Hernsheim and the DHPG, which gave it sixty trading stations stretching from Palau to the Gilberts.[65] The privileges conferred on the Jaluit-Gesellschaft by its agreement with the imperial government of 21 January 1888 included exclusive rights to take possession of unoccupied land, to fish for pearl-shell, and to exploit phosphate deposits. Other, more immediately important privileges arose from the company's special influence on the Protectorate's administration, and enabled it to drive out all major foreign competitors in the Marshall Islands. The company decided on all land purchases, for example, obtained the sole right to collect tax copra from the Islanders, and was able to determine business taxes.[66] By an agreement of 2 July 1900, its privileges were extended to the eastern Carolines.[67]

As monopolists of a trading region, the Jaluit-Gesellschaft had advantages which could be got elsewhere only by investing in plantations. The company, backed by the imperial navy, could control the prices offered to the Islanders for copra, and the wages offered to them for loading it on board ship. When the people of Mejit atoll refused in 1901 to provide workers for the Jaluit-Gesellschaft at half the previous wages, a fine of 100,000 lb of copra was imposed on them, and the price paid to them for copra was reduced by 25 per cent until they accepted the new wage rate.[68] Though the company had to reckon with occasional strikes and revolts against the authority of the chiefs, the Marshallese political structure was ready-made for foreign control through indigenous collaborators. In return for exerting their own enormous influence over the people in the company's favour, chiefs received a third of the copra tax, and sometimes a ride on a German cruiser.[69]

The Jaluit-Gesellschaft possessed a genuine trading monopoly from 1901 onwards. Competing Hawaiian and American firms had been bought out in the early 1890s, and in 1901 the English Pacific Islands Company sold all its Marshallese trading stations to the Hamburg company in return for a licence to mine phosphate in the Marshalls. High quality phosphate had been discovered by the Pacific Islands Company on Ocean Island in the British Gilberts, and on Nauru in the German Marshalls in 1899, and the new Pacific Phosphate Company, formed in London at the beginning of 1902, included both British and German capital. The Jaluit-Gesellschaft had special rights of participation, with a guaranteed free gift of 10 per cent of share capital, and a royalty on each ton mined. In all, Germans held about a third of the Pacific Phosphate Company's capital of £250,000 in 1905.[70]

Phosphate gave an added push to the Jaluit-Gesellschaft's profits—even before the Nauru field was exploited. On the proceeds of its share in the Ocean Island mine alone the company was able to expand its trading business without increasing share capital, and paid dividends of 15 per cent in 1903, 1904 and 1905, and 20 per cent in 1906.[71] Complaints from the Australian firm Burns, Philp and Co. that Germany in the Marshall Islands was breaching the free-trade provisions of the Anglo-German agreement of 10 April 1886 only helped the Jaluit-Gesellschaft, because although it lost its trading privileges in 1906 as a result of British pressure on Germany, it was granted a new ninety-four year phosphate concession as compensation. The concession, like that given to the Pacific Phosphate Company for Ocean Island, was on the most generous terms, and bound the Jaluit-Gesellschaft to an annual payment of only M 25,000 to the Reich plus 50 Pfennige on every metric ton shipped over 50,000 tons.[72]

While the Pacific Phosphate Company increased its capital to £875,000, paid dividends of between 30 per cent and 50 per cent, and made two free share issues between 1906 and 1911, the Jaluit Gesellschaft presented its shareholders with the richest dividends ever paid to German investors in the Pacific. Reckoned on the original shares, they were worth 20 per cent, 30 per cent, 39 per cent, 60 per cent, 75 per cent, 75 per cent, 78 per cent and 84 per cent from 1906 to 1913.[73]

With less spectacular success, phosphate was also mined on Angaur in Palau. A Bremen consortium, led by the Deutsche Nationalbank and including Norddeutscher Lloyd, established the Deutsche Südsee-Phosphat A.G. in May 1908, which was granted special rights to Angaur's phosphate, and began mining there in 1909. Though the terms of the concession were stricter than in the case of the Pacific Phosphate Company, and the Deutsche Südsee-Phosphat A.G. did not pay its first dividend—of 6 per cent—until 1912, the future looked bright for this company too. In 1913 it was able to pay an 11 per cent dividend, obtained additional rights to mine phosphate on Fais Island, and made a gross profit of M 1,364,280 on share capital of M 4,500,000.[74] The Japanese recognized Angaur's value when they occupied it late in 1914, and had already imported 120 labourers from Japan by January 1915.[75]

Extractive economic activity was frequently more profitable for Europeans in the Pacific islands than agriculture or commerce. A sizeable capital investment in phosphate mining paid better than one in trading or planting for a number of reasons. In the first place, the tiny populations of the phosphate islands, 1,500 in Nauru and 150 in Angaur, offered no effective resistance to the mining companies, and were powerless to exact compensation. Second, mining did not depend for its success on the attitude of the Nauruans or Angaurans, and was not threatened by competition from other Europeans seeking the same product. Third, the investor did not have to wait long for a return, because phosphate could be sold as soon as it had been dug and shipped to Europe.

Trading and planting, by contrast, involved the European in economic relationships with island populations whose wishes could not always be ignored. Though the few attempts by Islanders themselves to establish trading companies, such as the Samoan *Cumpani* movement of 1905, were quickly suppressed by colonial governments and affected European control of commerce hardly at all, the profitableness of that commerce was ultimately dependent on the Islander, for it was the

Islander who made the copra, and bought European manufactures. If the Islander was unwilling, trade was negligible: in Kaiser Wilhelmsland during the 1890s, for example, trading was either non-existent or disadvantageous for the Germans of the New Guinea Company, because the villagers were not interested in European goods as soon as they had satisfied their desire for iron. Usually, of course, the Islander was not unwilling to trade, for in most of the Pacific Islands elements of European material culture had already become indispensable in village life by the 1880s, but to the discomfiture of traders he would play them off against each other. In the Bismarck Archipelago the government had to pass an ordinance in 1900 forbidding traders from buying whole coconuts, so that the work of cutting copra would be put back into the hands of the Islanders. Competition between traders had become so fierce that they were cutting the copra themselves in order to please their "customers", the Islanders. "Really good business", the annual report commented, "is only done by traders working larger islands or smaller island groups without competition".[75] Once demand itself had been created, competition was the trader's main problem, and monopoly his best hope. This helps to explain both the relatively modest success of trading in general, and the greater profits of firms with a predominant or monopolistic hold on the trade of island groups, such as J.C. Godeffroy & Sohn in Tonga in the 1870s, the DHPG in Samoa, and the Jaluit-Gesellschaft in the Marshall Islands.

Planting, like buying out trading competitors, was a step towards rationalizing production and reducing the number of uncontrollable costs. Since cacao and tobacco had proved unprofitable, and since coconut palms require a decade to mature, profit-making plantations were long-term investments built up with the proceeds from trading. Both planters and traders suffered periodically from droughts, hurricanes and pests—scourges which the mine-owner never knew—and plantations were often beset by lack of labour. But where cheap labour, protection against pillage by Islanders, and a large proportion of bearing trees coincided with high copra prices, as with the DHPG after 1900, plantations could not fail to make high profits. By 1912 a ton of copra from the DHPG's plantation was three times more profitable than a ton of copra from its trading stations.

It is a commonplace that Germany's colonial empire failed to realize the hopes held for it by the colonial enthusiasts of the 1880s, that German investors and emigrants largely avoided it, and that it was more of an economic burden to Germany than a source of strength.[77] This applies as much to the Pacific colonies as to those in Africa: once annexed, they could not be abandoned, and their usefulness to Germany was little more than that they demonstrated her presence in the world.[78] What must not be overlooked, however, is that some individuals benefited enormously from their investment in the Pacific Islands, above all, the circle of Hamburg investors with shares in J.C. Godeffroy & Sohn, the DHPG, and the Jaluit-Gesellschaft. And that same economic process which enriched a select few in Germany was revolutionary in its consequences for tens of thousands of Pacific Islanders, for it meant access to European technology, loss of traditional lands, recruitment as labourers, and subjection to foreign rule.

1. Copy of Vereinigung der Südseefirmen to the Reichstag, Dec. 1917: "Denkschrift betr. den hohen Wert der deutschen Südsee für unsere Volkswirtschaft", Freiburg, Bundesarchiv Militärarchiv (hereinafter BA/MA), N224, Nachlass von Truppel, no. 67. Note: Throughout this article the German mark will be abbreviated to M, as in M 400.
2. Copy of Denkschrift for presentation to the Reichstag enclosed in NGC to Neuendettelsau Mission Society, 18 May 1915, in the volume of Neuguinea Company Akten Detzner 1886—1923, Neuendettelsau, Hauptarchiv Evang–Luth. Missionsanstalt.
3. 85,552 out of 1,832,404 metric tons in 1912 and 1913. *See Statistisches Jahrbuch für das Deutsche Reich 1914*, pub. Kaiserliches Statistisches Amt, 35 (Berlin), 1914: 200.
4. *Die deutschen Schutzgebiete in Afrika and der Südsee 1912/1913*. Amtliche Jahresberichte, herausgegeben vom Reichs–Kolonialamt (Berlin, 1914), Stat. pts., 370; G. Ziebura, "Interne Faktoren des französischen Hochimperialismus (1871–1914): Versuch einer gesamtgesellschaftlichen Analyse", in W.J. Mommsen, ed., *Der Moderne Imperialismus* (Stuttgart, 1971), p. 110.
5. Copy of von Grapow, "Die deutsche Flagge im Stillen Ozean" (Berlin, 1916), pp. 19–20, BA/MA, N224, no. 67.
6. The survey excludes shipping and communications companies whose major interests lay outside the Pacific Islands, such as Norddeutscher Lloyd of Bremen and the Deutsch—Niederländische Telegraphengesellschaft of Cologne, and also the Societé commerciale de l'Oceanie, which operated exclusively in Eastern Polynesia.
7. Cited in K. Schmack, *J.C. Godeffroy & Sohn, Kaufleute zu Hamburg, Leistung und Schicksal eines Welthandelshauses* (Hamburg, 1938), pp.101–2.
8. Unshelm to Merck, 31 July 1861, Hamburg, Commerzbibliothek, Consulatsberichte 1862; Schmack, *J.C. Godeffroy & Sohn*, pp. 131–2, 140.

9. G.R. Lewthwaite, "Land, Life, and Agriculture to Mid–Century", in J.W. Fox and K.B. Cumberland, eds, *Western Samoa: Land, Life, and Culture in Tropical Polynesia*, (Christchurch, 1962), p. 142.
10. D. Scarr, *Fragments of Empire: A History of the Western Pacific High Commission 1877–1914* (Canberra, 1967), p.88; Erika Suchan–Galow, *Die deutsche Wirtschaftstätigkeit in der Südsee vor der ersten Besitzergreifung 1884* (Hamburg, 1940), pp. 73–75.
11. Poppe to Merck, 12 Jan. 1874, STAH Senatsakten Familienarchiv Hernsheim. New Britain, New Ireland, New Hanover, etc., were called the New Britain Archipelago by German traders and consuls in the early 1880s. To avoid confusion, however, the term Bismarck Archipelago, which was not actually in use before 1884, will be used throughout the rest of this article.
12. Schmack, *J.C. Godeffroy & Sohn*, pp. 127, 140; R. Segebrecht, "Aus den Tagebüchern von Kapitan Nils Simson Michelsen", *Hamburger Wirtschafts–Chronik* 1, no. 4 (1956): 298–99.
13. C. Hager, *Die Marshall–Inseln in Erd–und Völkerkunde, Handel und Mission* (Leipzig, 1886), pp. 114–15.
14. "Lebenserinnerungen von Eduard Hernsheim", pp. 21–72. STAH Familienarchiv Hernsheim.
15. O. Finsch, "Über die Naturprodukte der westlichen Südsee, besonders der deutschen Schutzgebiete", *Deutsche Kolonialzeitung* (1887): 525. *Organ des deutschen Kolonialvereins.*
16. "Lebenserinnerungen von Eduard Hernsheim" p. 68 STAH, Familienarchiv Hernsheim.
17. Finsch, "Über die Naturprodukte der westlichen Südsee": 525; "Denkschrift betreffend die deutschen und fremden Interessen in dem Archipel von Neu Britannien", encl. in Stuebel to Bismarck, no. 6 of 20 Apr. 1884, Potsdam, Deutsches Zentralarchiv, R.K.A. Series AA (Foreign Office) papers–vol. 2791; Hereinafter, in order to distinguish between different periods included in the Reichskolonialamt collection, the following designations will be used, with the relevant volume number: AA (Foreign Office), for the period up to 1890; AAKA (Foreign Office–Colonial Department), for the period 1890–May 1907; RKA (Colonial Office), for the period June 1907 onwards. See also John A. Moses, "The Coolie Labour Question and German Colonial Policy in Samoa 1900–1914" fn. 3, and Marjorie Jacobs "German Colonial Archives: New Guinea and Samoa in the Deutsches Zentralarchiv", *JPH* (1970): 151–52.
18. *Drucksachen zu den Verhandlungen des Bundesraths des Deutschen Reichs* 1879, 2 no. 96: 24–27.
19. Th. Weber, *Ländereien und Plantagen der Deutschen Handels- und Plantagen–Gesellschaft der Südsee–Inseln zu Hamburg in Samoa* (Hamburg, 1888); pp. 12,14–15.
20. Bilanz pro 1881 STAH, DHPG Archiv.
21. Schmidt to Vorstand der Auswärtigen Angelegenheiten Hamburg, 21 May 1891, STAH Senatsakten Cl. 6, no. 17b fasc. 8h; Bilanzen for 1885–7, STAH DHPG Archiv; O. Riedel, *Der Kampf um Deutsch–Samoa. Erinnerungen eines Hamburger Kaufmanns* (Berlin, 1938) p. 50.
22. H. Washausen, *Hamburg und die Kolonialpolitik des deutschen Reiches 1880 bis 1890* (Hamburg, 1968), pp. 59–60. DHPG to Bisharck, 23 Mar. 1889, AA 2477.
23. *Bericht der Deutschen Handels- und Plantagen-Gesellschaft der Südsee-Inseln zu Hamburg über das Geschäftsjahr 1898* (Hamburg, 1899).

24. Bilanz pro 1881, and "Bericht der Direction der Deutschen Handels- und Plantagen–Gesellschaft der Südsee–Inseln über das Geschäftsjahr 1890", STAH, DHPG Archiv; Weber, *Ländereien und Plantagen*, p. 36.
25. Bilanz, pro 1881 and confidential reports of the board of directors 1889–1897, STAH, DHPG Archiv. The comparison is complicated, though not invalidated, by the changing value of the Chilean and the gold dollar. Chilean dollars, in use until 1892, were reckoned by the DHPG at M 4 before 1889 and M 3 from 1889 to 1892. The gold dollars which replaced them were reckoned at 4s stg or M 4.08.
26. Encl. in Foreign Office to von Kusserow, 21 Dec, 1885, and Stuebel to Bismarch, 27 Jan. 1886, AA 2316; DHPG to Colonial Dept., 10 Jan. 1891, AAKA 2301.
27. Bericht des Vorstandes der Deutschen Handels- und Plantagen Gesellschaft der Südsee–Inseln zu Hamburg an den Aufsichtsrat über das Geschäftsjahr 1899" STAH, DHPG Archiv.
28. Rose to Hohenlohe, 12 Apr. 1898 AAKA 2540.
29. Confidential reports of the board of directors 1890–1894, published company reports 1895–1899 STAH, DHPG Archiv.
30. Rose to Hohenlohe, 12 Apr. 1898, AAKA 2540.
31. Rose to Hohenlohe, 24 July 1898, based on Ibid., 2560.
32. Minutes of DHPG board meetings of 8 Nove. 1890 and 20 Jan. 1891, STAH, DHPG Archiv.
33. A.D. Couper, "The Island Trade. An Analysis of the Environment and Operation of Seaborne Trade among Three Island Groups in the Pacific", Ph.D. Thesis, Australian National University (Canberra, 1967), p. 64.
34. Solf to von Koenig (private), 30 Apr. 1904; Solf to Passarge, 29 Oct. 1906, BA, Nachlass Solf, vols. 25,26.
35. Bericht des Vorstandes an den Aufsichtsrath der Deutschen Handels- und Plantagen–Gesellschaft der Südsee–Inseln zu Hamburg über das Geschäftsjahr 1895 STAH, DHPG Archiv.
36. Solf to Colonial Department, 5 Dec. 1900, BA, Nachlass Solf, Vol.22.
37. Confidential reports of the board of directors for the years 1902 to 1913. STAH, DHPG Archiv; Couper, "The Island Trade", p. 71.
38. Confidential reports of the board of directors for the years 1900 to 1913. STAH, DHPG Archiv.
39. Published reports of the DHPG 1898 to 1913, STAH, DHPG Archiv. The total value of the company's investment was estimated at M7,743,569.71. in about 1905. See *Der Tropenpflanzer. Zeitschrift für Tropische Landwirtschaft. Organ des Kolonial–Wirtschaftlichen Komitees* (1906): 107.
40. *Geschäftsbericht der Deutschen Samoa–Gesellschaft Berlin und Apia auf Samoa für das Jahr 1912* (Potsdam, 1913): 2;ibid., 1913 (Berlin, 1914): 2–6.
41. *Adressbuch fur Deutsch–Neuguinea, Samoa, Kiautschou,* 11th ed. (Berlin, 1911), p. 37;*Pflanzungs–Betriebe auf Samoa–Auskunft über das Schutzgebiet* pubs. dem Pflanzerverein (Samoa, 1910), p. 5; Safata–Samoa–Gesellschaft, *Bericht über das neunte Geschäftsjahr 1912* (Berlin, 1913).
42. *Die deutschen Schutzgebiete in Afrika und der Südsee 1912/1913*, p. 122.
43. See S.G. Firth "The New Guinea Company, 1885–1899; A Case of Unprofitable Imperialism", *Historical Studies* 15 (1972): 361–77.
44. "Anträge an die ausserordentliche, am 30. April, 1889 abzuhaltende General–Versammlung der Mitglieder der Neu Guinea Compagnie." AAKA 2939.
45. New Guinea Company to Hohenlohe, 5 Jan, 1895, ibid.
46. NKWL (1891): pp.10–13; Rose to Caprivi, 16 Mar. 1891, AAKA 2980; Fischer to Oberkommando der Marine, 8 Feb. 1893 (copy), ibid., 2982.

47. *NKWL* (1891): 22
48. Report by the Colonial Department on the New Guinea Company directors' meeting of 21 Dec. 1897, AAKA 2404.
49. The New Guinea Company regarded the final terms as niggardly. See NKWL (1898): 2–8.
50. "Neu–Guinea nach den Berichten der dortigen kaiserlichen Beamten", report compiled in the Colonial Department in 1892 and bound in AAKA 2981.
51. Krieg to Oberkommando der Marine, 12 Feb. 1897 (copy), ibid., 2986: *Jahresbericht über die Entwickelung der deutschen Schutzgebiete im Jahre 1898 -1899*, Supplement to *Deutsches Kolonialblatt* (Berlin, 1900): 165.
52. *Die deutschen Schutzgebiete in Afrika und der Südsee 1912/1913*, p. 83; *Amtsblatt für das Schutzgebiet Deutsch–Neuguinea* (Rabaul), 15 May 1914.
53. Based on *Die deutschen Schutzgebiete in Afrika und der Südsee 1912/1913*, p. 83; and Amtsblatt für das Schutzgebiet Deutsch–Neuguinea, 1 May, 1913.
54. P. Biskup, "Foreign Coloured Labour in German New Guinea: A study in Economic Development" *Journal of Pacific History* 5 (1970): 100. The figures refer to "enterprises which paid a business tax."
55. H. Münch, *Adolph von Hansemann* (Munich, 1932), p. 243.
56. Hahl to Colonial Office, 7 Aug. 1909, RKA 2763.
57. E.E. Forsayth G.m.b.H. to Colonial Office, 21 Nov. 1912, ibid., 2313.
58. H. Schnee ed., *Deutsches Kolonial–Lexikon* (Leipzig, 1920), 1.p.650; 2.p. 13; 3. p. 656.
59. Copy of Denkschrift for presentation to the Reichstag by Pacific interests, including Wahlen's companies, May 1915, BA/MA, N224, no. 67.
60. Hernsheim & Co. A.G., *Jahresberichte*: 1909–1913, Hamburg, Welt–Wirtschafts–Archiv. Firmenarchiv.
61. Compiled from *Denkschrift über die Entwickelung der Schutzgebiete in Afrika und der Südsee in Jahre 1908–09*, F.I. pp.29–30 (*Anlage* no. 179 in *Stenographische Berichte über die Verhandlungen des Reichstages*, 2 session 1909/1910); *Amtsblatt für das Schutzbgebiet Deutsch–Neuginea*, 15 Dec. 1911, 1 Apr. 1913, and 15 Apr. 1914; and *Die deutschen Schutzgebiete in Afriha und der Südsee 1911/1912*. Amtliche Jahresberichte (Berlin, 1913) stat. pt. 65.
62. Commonwealth of Australia, Parliament, *Royal Commission on Later German New Guinea–Interim and Final Reports* (Melbourne, 1920) pp.19,67.
63. Robertson & Hernsheim to Bismarck, 23 Jan. 1885, AAKA, 3071. See also Washausen, *Hamburg und die Kolonialpolitik, p.* 63.
64. Jaluit–Gesellschaft, *Jahresbericht für 1899* (Hamburg, 1900).
65. Idem, *Jahresbericht für 1889* (Hamburg, 189).
66. W. Treue, "Die Jaluit Gesellschaft", *Tradition, Zeitschrift für Firmen–Geschichte und Unternehmer–Biographie* 7, nos. 2–3 (1962): 114–116.
67. Jaluit–Gesellschaft, *Jahresbericht für 1901* (Hamburg, 1902).
68. Von Burski to the Kaiser, 30 Nov. 1902 (Militärpolitischer Bericht, copy) AAKA 2651.
69. Treue, "Die Jaluit–Gesellschaft": 117.
70. Hernsheim to Colonial Department, 7 Dec. 1905, AAKA 2508; G. Haller, *Die Phosphat–Gesellschaften der Südsee,* 2d ed., (Mannheim, 1911), p.13.
71. Jaluit–Gesellschaft, *Jahresberichte* (Hamburg, 1903–06).
72. Treue, "Die Jaluit–Gesellschaft": 119; "Konzession", encl. in Stuebel to Reichskanzler, 18 Nov. 1905, AAKA 2508.
73. Treue, "Die Jaluit–Gesellschaft": 119–22.

74. "Bericht über das Geschäftsjahr 1913", Bremen, June, 1914, RKA 2465; *Sechster Geschäftsbericht der Deutschen Südseephosphat–Aktiengesellschaft Geschäftsjahr 1913* (Bremen, 1914).
75. Lippert to Deutsche Südseephosphat–Aktiengesellschaft, 3 June 1915 (copy), RKA 2465.
76. *Jahresbericht über die Entwickelung der deutschen Schutzgebiete im Jahre 1899-1900, Supplement to Deutsches Kolonialblatt* (Berlin, 1901), p. 178.
77. H.U. Wehler, *Bismarck und der Imperialismus* (Cologne, 1969),pp. 407–11.
78. W. Baumgart, "Die deutsche Kolonialherrschaft in Afrika: neue Wege der Forschung", *Vierteljahresschrift für Sozial- und Wirtschaftsgeschichte* 58, no. 4 (1971): 480.

# 2

HELMUTH STOECKER

# Germany and China, 1861-94

With the beginning of the relaxation of mercantilist trade policies and of the navigation laws of the sea powers in the late eighteenth century, and especially following the end of the Napoleonic Continental System in 1813, merchants and shipowners (frequently enough both in one: merchant-shipowners) of Hamburg and Bremen made their first attempts to trade directly with Latin America and the Near East. In the decades that followed they ventured on from the latter to the coasts of Southeast and East Asia, their gradual and somewhat desultory advance into these regions being much facilitated by the introduction of free trade in the British spheres of power and influence by a ruling bourgeoisie looking on its absolute commercial supremacy as a permanent feature of the world order. With the extension of free trade German shipping increased: the partial admission of foreign vessels in the ports of British colonies by the Navigation Acts of 1822–24, the abrogation of the East India Company's trade monopoly for China in 1833 and the abolition of all remaining restrictions on shipping and trade with British colonies in 1849–54 made it possible for many small sailing ships from the German North Sea and Baltic coasts to go on charter for British, Dutch and even Chinese traders in the Indian Ocean and the Pacific; especially in the cabotage on the coasts of Southeast and East Asia these vessels were prominent from the middle of the century until the eighties.

In these years a number of small and middling German trading firms established branches or subsidiaries in Bombay, Calcutta, Singapore or Hongkong, not so much to promote

This survey is based on the author's book, *Deutschland und China im 19. Jahrhundert. Das Eindringen des deutschen Kapitalismus*, (Berlin, GDR, 1958), where a full list of sources is to be found.

German as rather to participate in a very modest way in British overseas trade. The same was true of the German traders, mostly young men who had started as employees of British China merchants, who began to do business in the Chinese treaty ports after the Treaty of Nanking (1842). The dominant position and unassailable superiority of the British firms often compelled these traders to resort to small-scale sidelines and shady types of business, including the coolie trade which was looked down upon by the great "merchant princes" such as Jardine Matheson and Dent—from the morally impeccable point of view of highly successful purveyors of opium.

Most German merchants in China and other Asiatic countries until the eighties and nineties engaged in little trade with Germany, and sold British textiles and whatever other goods that would bring them profits, without regard to the country of origin. Accordingly they were accustomed to financing their transactions with trade credits given by British bankers, insured their transports with British insurance companies, and had them carried on British or other non-German ships unless, like the well-known firm of Melchers & Co., they were shipowners themselves. Direct German trade with China, in those years almost limited to the import of tea and spices and the export of woollens, remained insignificant until the seventies.

The German firms, as poor relations of sorts, were tolerated and even treated as "friendly aliens" by British consuls and other British authorities on whose support they could generally count in the frequent cases of local conflicts with Chinese officials, or outbreaks of anti-colonial emotions on the part of the Chinese population. This dependence corresponded to the virtual position of the Hanse ports as a very junior partner in Britain's world trade and shipping monopoly, to which they were grudgingly admitted on account of their importance as stations of entry for British exports to central Europe. It was rather an exceptional position, for it enabled the bourgeoisie of Hamburg and Bremen to reap some profits from colonial trade without bearing any expenses for colonial conquests, or being involved in political conflicts with other European states. In such conflicts they would have had little chance of holding their own, since they had no armed forces of any significance.

The British attitude to German commercial interests in China until the eighties was probably also influenced by the fact that German traders had no part in the opium traffic, until then the mainstay of British exports into China.

In the late fifties the "opening up" of Japan and the second opium war against China gave rise to hopes among German industrialists, suffering from the effects of the crisis of 1857, of considerably increasing exports to eastern Asia. The Prussian government of the "New Era", wishing to strengthen its position vis-a-vis Austria in the struggle for leadership in Germany, saw the chance of presenting itself as the protagonist of overseas trading expansion of all the German states except for that power. It therefore sent an expedition of four warships in 1859 to accompany the Prussian envoy Count Friedrich Eulenburg (an uncle of Philipp Eulenburg, the crony of Wilhelm II) to the Far East, where he was to obtain for the German states the same rights and privileges as had been conceded under great pressure by the governments of Japan and China to Britain, France, Russia and the United States. The fact that Prussia and Germany had hardly been heard of by these governments at that time turned out to be of some advantage to Eulenburg, who by cajolery, empty threats, and sheer bluff succeeded in getting unequal treaties of the type desired.

The treaty between China and Prussia, acting also for the other members of the Zollverein and the Grand Duchies of Mecklenburg-Schwerin and Mecklenburg-Strelitz and the Hanse cities of Lübeck, Bremen and Hamburg, signed at Tientsin on 2 September 1861, was a copy of the treaties Britain and France had concluded with China. It enabled the increasing number of German merchants in the treaty ports henceforth to claim as by right the considerable advantages of consular jurisdiction and the virtual extra-territoriality resulting from this, as well as the very low customs tariffs already enjoyed by the nationals of the Western powers. The German states had, ten years before their unification by Prussia, joined the other capitalist powers in the semi-colonial subjection of China, for which these rights and privileges created favourable conditions. The essence of semi-colonial subjection was a trade based on non-equivalence of the values exchanged under unequal conditions for the partners: relatively high prices were demanded in China for European, and low prices paid for Chinese products, compared to the price level in Europe and the United States. It was the principle applied in colonial trade the world over, and greatly harmed the economy of the peoples subjected to it.

The reduction of the "middle kingdom" to a semi-colonial condition was a process that lasted a half-century after 1842; a peculiar feature of this process was the "European solidarity" that was particularly evident whenever foreign capitalist interests in China seemed endangered. The most-favoured-nation clause in the treaties with China undoubtedly contributed to a certain degree of unity among the capitalist powers, because it made it extremely difficult for any one of them to obtain special advantages independently of the others, but the deeper reason for "European solidarity" was, of course, the common interest of all the powers in maintaining semi-colonial conditions and privileges, which would have been far more difficult under conditions of a free-for-all among them.

By the treaty with a weak Manchu government in 1861 Prussia had paved the way for the German imperialist inroads and aggressions of later years. At that time, however, semi-colonial trade expansion in China was not connected with any intentions of conquest or annexation of territory; the utmost the Prussian and later German governments under Bismarck desired was a small naval station as a base for warships in Far Eastern waters. Except for a short-lived boom of highly unpractical schemes for the founding of settlements for emigrants in various American countries during the forties, Germany's bourgeoisie and landowning class, until the turn in economic and domestic policies in 1878–79, generally showed very little interest in the idea of colonial annexation outside Europe. Often enough it was rejected outright as being out of date, too costly and incompatible with the principle of free trade. Bismarck would hear nothing of colonies in Asia or other parts of the world. There were, to be sure, naval officers, explorers, journalists, academic teachers, high ranking government officials, and members of ruling or former ruling families who, with an envious eye on British or Dutch colonial wealth and power, put forward or supported any number of proposals for the foundation of German colonies. Especially Taiwan (Formosa) was an object of colonial wishes and schemes during the sixties. But such ideas found hardly any support in commercial, industrial or financial circles; not a single political organization of any kind spoke up for colonial expansion in the form of annexing overseas territories to Prussia or Germany between 1850 and 1878. The colonial question did not exist as an issue in German politics in those years.

This rejection of colonies by no means applied to the expansion of trade under semi-colonial conditions with overseas countries. The support of such trade by the intimidation of rulers and peoples of these countries and, if it seemed necessary, by armed intervention being one of the main tasks of the very young Prussian and later German navy, North German, or else German warships were stationed in Far Eastern seas after 1869. The leading men of the navy from the very first pointed out the need for some kind of naval base there to serve as a centre for provisioning and maintenance. To this Bismarck readily agreed, and the captains of warships cruising in Chinese and Japanese seas were since 1868 repeatedly ordered to look out for suitable sites. When Bismarck instructed the North German minister in Peking in April 1870 to take up negotiations about the sale or lease of a point on the Chinese coast or an island off the coast for this purpose, he added there was no intention to place the proposed base under German sovereignty or a German protectorate, since it was hoped to preclude the danger of French attacks on it in the impending war by upholding a nominal status as Chinese territory. But nothing came of the plan: the minister, von Rehfues, had to postpone talks on it with a government which would certainly have tried to reject a scheme of this kind, and then the war in Europe put an end to it.

With the foundation of the German empire, and the negotiations for a peace treaty with France in 1871, an additional reason of great importance arose for rejecting all proposals for German colonies: the urgent need to avoid any conflicts with Britain which might lead to improved Anglo-French relations and strengthen the diplomatic position of France. Fear of Britain's probable reaction was decisive for Bismarck's strict refusal to entertain the idea of a cession of Saigon to Germany as part of the peace settlement which had been put forward by some newspapers after the victory of Sedan, and later rejected by the North German parliament. In the seventies his attitude to the establishment of German colonies remained unchanged, mainly for the same reason.

Whereas the world economic crisis of 1857 had been followed by an attack by Britain on China, with the aim of opening the vast country more fully to British trade, the deeper and more extensive crisis of 1873 resulted in a further attempt to remove all obstacles which were still impeding the full inclusion of China in the world capitalist system. The "middle kingdom", although by no means of great consumptive capacity, began to interest industrialists who were eager for new markets. Among the barriers still in the way of European exports to China after the treaties of Tientsin (Tianjin) and Peking concluded in 1858 and 1860, the most effective was probably the imposition of *likin*—i.e. more or less arbitrary inland tolls by provincial authorities—and therefore the diplomatic representatives of the powers under Britain's leadership with increasing insistence strove for the abolition or at least reduction of these imposts throughout the seventies. At the same time they demanded the opening of further ports to foreign trade, especially on the Yangtze River.

The newly-founded German empire took part in putting pressure on China with these aims in view. German policy towards the "middle kingdom", from the seventies to the diplomatic intervention of Shimonoseki in 1895, should however not be put on a par with the high-pressure imperialist expansion at the turn of the century, but it can be described as a time of transition towards full-scale imperialism. The transitional phase was personified by Max von Brandt, German minister in Peking 1875–93 and son and brother of high-ranking Prussian officers, who combined frequent assertions of friendship for China with a persistent and tenacious striving to strengthen the economic and political position of the power he represented. Brandt never missed the slightest chance in this respect; already in his first year at Peking he appealed to his home government to found and subsidize a German steamship line to the Far East, and to encourage the establishment of a German bank there. He even corresponded with German industrialists to interest them in the Chinese market—quite an unusual step for a German diplomat in those years. Hardly any of his colleagues in Peking surpassed him in the arts of blustering, scaring and blackmailing the Chinese ministers and authorities he had to deal with: among the English community at Shanghai he soon became known as the "blood-and-iron" minister.

Brandt's first important task was to obtain the assent of the Peking government to a programme of revision of the Prussian-Chinese treaty of 1861. The programme had been agreed to by the other powers, above all by Britain, for all concessions made by Peking to Germany could, by virtue of the most-favoured-nation clause, be claimed as valid for them too. The main German demands were: the opening of further ports for European trade, the opening of the Yangtze up to Itshang (Yichang) for European shipping, permission for the establishment of European settlements in the more important Yangtze ports, and the abolition of *likin*, as far as the Peking government was able to enforce it. Since only Britain's armed forces could deal China serious blows, Brandt was instructed to avail himself of British support.

The latter proved at first to be impossible, however, since the British minister in Peking, Sir Thomas Wade, disliked his German colleague intensely and preferred to act on his own. Although Brandt replied to these feelings in kind, he had no qualms in following Wade's example: the British minister had a short time before used the death of a British interpreter in fighting on the Sino-Burmese border as a pretext for pressing demands similar to those mentioned. When the Chinese crew on the German schooner *Anna* mutinied, killing the German captain and the Danish mate, Brandt acted as Wade had done, uttering ominous threats in his talks with Chinese officials.

At the suggestion of the German Foreign Office Britain and Germany agreed to co-operate against piracy in Chinese waters, the real purpose being not so much co-operation against the 'distinctly scarce pirates as rather against the recalcitrant Chinese government. While the German naval command was concentrating six men-of-war with 1,380 men near Hong Kong, Brandt demanded from the government in Peking the opening of a considerable number of ports on the coast and the Yangtze to foreign trade and negotiations on *likin*. At the same time—the summer of 1876—Wade was continuing to exert pressure for the same purposes. Success was finally achieved by an unmistakable threat of war: in August Britain, France, Germany, and the United States, by drawing together parts of their Far Eastern naval forces near Chefoo (Yantai), managed to frighten the Peking government to such an extent that it decided to give way. By the Convention of Chefoo of 13 September 1876 it conceded the more important demands of Britain and Germany, except for those relating to *likin*. To this result Brandt had contributed not a little by repeatedly intervening behind the scenes.

The treaty thus obtained was a further important step in the process of reducing China to a dependent position; it shows very clearly the extreme helplessness and incompetence of the Manchu government, which had not even realized to what extent British forces were tied in Europe on account of the eastern crisis.

In subsequent negotiations on the revision of the treaty of 1861 Brandt tried, by means of constant threats and extortion, to get some results in the matter of *likin*, but to no avail. Germany alone proved incapable of breaking the resistance of the Peking regime in this important question, and so the German-Chinese supplementary treaty of 31 March 1880 only provided for the opening of Woosung (Wusung) near Shanghai as a landing place, not as a treaty port, and for some other unimportant concessions in matters of trade and shipping for Germany and, therefore, for the other "treaty powers" too. The British trading community in Shanghai which had placed great expectations in Brandt did not hide its disappointment.

The blustering methods of its representative were not, after 1879–80, always looked on with approval by the Berlin Foreign Office, for Bismarck did not wish any serious deterioration of German-Chinese relations. He knew that the ministers at Peking, curiously enough, hoped for political aid from the only European great power (except for Austria-Hungary, of no account in the Far East) which had not annexed territories in China or adjacent countries, and he meant to exploit this illusion in order to gain new markets in China—more especially for the products of Germany's heavy and armament industries. Bismarck also wanted to keep the door open for an alliance with the "middle kingdom" in case of a European war, for its armies, although no match for European forces, could tie down some enemy units in the Far East.

It was for these reasons that Brandt was temporarily recalled to Berlin in early 1883. He had felt impelled to demonstrate German power in China by twice having small detachments landed by German warships in southern Chinese ports in order to compel local authorities there to give way in petty quarrels with German traders, and thereby incurred Bismarck's displeasure. Brandt was not expressly reproved, but received strict instructions to act carefully in future and avoid all friction.

Shortly afterwards the two leading Berlin banks, the Disconto-Gesellschaft and the Deutsche Bank, submitted a carefully prepared offer to the Chinese government of capital, materials and experts for railway construction. Although the offer expressly referred to "Chinese" railways, it found no favour with a government well aware of the implications of railway building by "Western barbarians". But the banks and some important iron and steel firms such as Krupp held on to their intention, and vainly tried during the years following to reach an agreement with British banks and industrialists on a division of loans to China and of the ensuing orders. (It was only in 1895, when Germany's position had become much stronger, that British banks consented to a division of Chinese business on a large scale with a group of German banks.) The promotion of these plans was Bismarck's main aim in inaugurating in 1885 a steamship line to East Asia with Reich subsidies. Subsidies for shipping were a novelty in German economic policy and played an important part in pushing exports in overseas countries.

At the same time the chancellor secretly encouraged France, and subsequently Russia (powers which were not dangerous as trade rivals in the Far East) to colonial expansion in Asia in order to draw their forces away from Germany's borders and embroil them in conflicts with Britain—an extremely simple line of tactics, which corresponded to Bismarck's policy in North Africa and the Middle East, and undoubtedly stood in the forefront of his political calculations regarding China in the eighties.

During the French-Chinese War of 1883–85 especially, Bismarck supported France's colonial aggression in Indochina in the diplomatic sphere, because France's advance up to the southern borders of China inevitably would bring about a worsening of Anglo-French relations. By his assistance given to French colonial expansion in East Asia and Africa—without which this expansion would have been impossible—he increased France's diplomatic isolation, and bought her consent to German colonial expansion in Africa and the Pacific. The German-French "colonial entente" in general, and Bismarck's attitude and conduct during the French aggression in the Far East in particular, contributed not a little to Ferry's successes and the conquest of Tonking by the French bourgeoisie.

France's aggression in Tonking gave rise to optimistic expectations in the other leading Western countries. Not a few newspapers predicted that China would soon be fully thrown open for railway building, and as a market for vast quantities of modern industrial products of all sorts. The fantastic idea of three hundred million customers began to excite the imagination of large numbers of people with something to sell. Influential bourgeois groups began pressing their respective governments and diplomatic services for steps to help them secure as great a share as possible in the enormous business deals now hoped for. When peace had been restored, a sharp tussle set in, between British, German, French, and—less forcefully—American banks and their partners in heavy industry, for loans and contracts with Chinese authorities, in which diplomats played a very active part. Britain's predominance and decisive voice in all matters relating to China was no longer accepted without question.

The international struggle for loans and contracts saw the Germans as very active participants; it can be safely stated that none of the governments involved worked so closely hand-in-hand with its bankers and industrialists as the German government did. On behalf of a syndicate founded in 1885 by the Disconto-Gesellschaft, the Deutsche Bank, Fried. Krupp and some other powerful industrial undertakings, Brandt extorted a declaration from the Peking government to the effect that China would give preference to Germany when ordering armaments, warships, and railway materials, or when taking up loans. (For this he was promoted Wirklicher Geheimer Rat, with the title, Exzellenz, shortly after.)

In the year following the sending out by this syndicate of a three-man commission to study Chinese conditions caused still more nervousness and hectic activity on the part of British and French commercial representatives and diplomats, but the whole fracas did not result in breaking the strict refusal of government circles in the Chinese capital to permit railway building on a larger scale. All hopes in this direction had to be postponed until the resistance of the Manchu regime to "modernization" was finally overcome in the last years of the century.

A very important part of the inter-capitalist struggle for contracts concerned the arms trade. There were heavy and persistent attacks by British and French manufacturers on Germany's almost monopolist position in this field, especially as regards artillery and warships. To support French efforts a general Chanoine was appointed French military attaché, and Jardine Matheson sold Armstrong cannon at a loss in an attempt to squeeze the British into the market, but Krupp of Essen, who predominated in the German armament exports, enjoyed the very active support of German diplomacy in China, as in other countries, and until the Sino-Japanese War of 1894–95, succeeded in warding off the attacks of all rivals and selling artillery and other armaments worth many millions to the Peking government, various other governments, and to governors-general. (In 1888–89, for example, orders totalled fourteen million marks.) The firm was quite unscrupulous as regards the methods employed to achieve this result: they extended from diplomatic interventions by Brandt, and the employment of German officers as advisers and instructors of Chinese military units, to pro-Krupp propaganda in Chinese newspapers, and handsome bribes for high-ranking Chinese officials. For the most eminent of the latter, the governor-general in Tientsin and virtual minister for foreign affairs, Li Hung-chang (Li Hongzhang), the grateful Friedrich Alfred Krupp had a monument erected near Shanghai after the Sino-Japanese War, in which both sides had used weapons manufactured by the firm. The highly cherished customer had "seemed glad about it", Consul v. Seckendorff reported, after he had submitted a design for the monument to Li in 1893.

Not that there were no qualms about selling arms to China, since it was naturally feared that they might sooner or later be used not only against France, Russia, or Japan, but against the European powers in general. But warnings of such dangers were disregarded, since the profits were very high and the arms sold, in many cases, obsolete. There were also considerable and fully-justified doubts among German diplomats and officers as to whether the thoroughly corrupt and incompetent Chinese autocracy and bureaucratic officialdom would ever be able to build up a properly functioning modern army. The experiences of military advisers and instructors had been anything but encouraging in this respect. But the fears occasionally voiced were not entirely groundless, as events in 1900 showed, when German units landing near Tientsin were fired upon by Krupp batteries.

Before 1895 very few Europeans succeeded in founding factories or industrial enterprises of any kind outside Shanghai. The treaties imposed on China had not clearly provided for such activities on the part of foreign nationals, and even Li Hung-chang strictly refused to permit any attempts in this direction. Industrialization, if ventured upon at all, was to be the prerogative of high Chinese officials. When a dispute on this question between the Peking office and the European diplomatic corps arose in 1888, Brandt wrote in one of his reports that he was not at all sure if "we should be much interested" in breaking the resistance of the Chinese authorities against the founding of mixed firms or companies, which was the only feasible way of rapidly developing industrial production. Such a development would "artificially create new competitors for many of our manufactures". His point of view was shared by his superiors. The director of the commercial department (Handelspolitische Abteilung) of the Berlin Foreign Office, Reichardt, emphatically propounded official policy: "In our opinion the development of industry in such countries as are promising markets for our own products should not be encouraged. For it is evident that we would thereby assist in rearing competitors." (May 1889) The German consuls in the treaty ports were instructed to discourage all Chinese attempts at erecting plants or workshops for industrial purposes.

The markets thus prophylactically being guarded were gradually growing in importance for some German export industries. During the years between the Sino-French and the Sino-Japanese wars Britain's primacy in China's foreign trade began to decline in favour of Germany, the United States, Japan, and the Chinese trading bourgeoisie, German trade totals increasing not only absolutely, but also relatively when compared to British trade totals.

The increase in German cotton exports to China was the subject of emphatic complaints by British industrialists; at the same time London ceased to be an important centre for the sale of Chinese raw silk. Japan's trade with China rose considerably, resulting in sharp competition with German trading houses, who found seriously threatened their leading position in the import into China of cheap mass consumption goods. Besides armaments, Germany in those years exported to China woollens, dyestuffs, metal wares (especially sewing needles), beers and liquor, copper, brass, lead, lamps, glassware, stationery, and toys; from China it imported tea, spices, feathers, bristles, skins and hides, unrefined gold, straw and bast wares, furs, and camphor. Except for tea and spices, the imports were virtually all raw materials for various German industries; the German trading firms, mainly established in

Hamburg, Hongkong and Shanghai, in their exports to China obviously favoured such goods as had a chance of withstanding British competition.

At the end of the period here considered (1892–94) German exports to China amounted to 0.9–1.0 per cent of Germany's total exports; China was Germany's most important market for cannon and sewing needles. German-Chinese trade totalled 43.1 million marks in 1892, 48.7 million in 1893, 49.2 million in 1894—a sum far higher than trade with all German colonies in Africa and the Pacific put together.

Finally there were preparations for financial penetration. After the Deutsche Bank had been compelled to close its branches in Shanghai and Yokohama in 1875, the idea of founding a German bank for eastern Asia had been put forward repeatedly, especially by Brandt, and was finally taken up by the government, which since 1881 intermittently urged the leading Berlin bankers and the Hamburg Chamber of Commerce to take the initiative in this respect. But neither the bankers nor the chamber showed much interest in a venture they obviously regarded as unpromising in view of the British monopoly in Far Eastern trade banking, and of fluctuating silver prices. Discussions and negotiations dragged on from 1883 until late 1887, when representatives of the Disconto-Gesellschaft, the Deutsche Bank, Bleichröder and the Norddeutsche Bank agreed jointly to found a German-Chinese banking institute on condition that the German government handed over silver "at a certain price" from the stocks of the Reichsbank. Bismarck gave his consent to this arrangement, which was, however, rescinded when it was realized that it had to be put before the Reichstag.

After years of wrangling the bankers declared themselves prepared to act if the Prussian state bank (Seehandlung) participated and if the emperor officially confirmed the chairman of the board of directors in his position after every election. These terms were accepted and the Deutsch-Asiatische Bank was thereupon founded in February 1889, the Disconto-Gesellschaft (like Bleichröder well-known for its close association with the Bismarck regime) taking the greatest number of shares. Virtually all German banks of any importance took part in the foundation. Most of them were represented on the board of directors, of which Hans Jencke of Krupps was also a prominent member. In China the new bank acted very cautiously during its first years, to Brandt's disgust; only after 1895, when the grip of the powers on China was tightening, did it succeed in negotiating Chinese loans of greater significance.

The persistence with which Bismarck encouraged the reluctant bankers over such a long period must be seen in the context of the chancellor's policy of promoting overseas commercial interests. The purpose of overseas banks and especially the bank in the Far East, was to break the German dependence on British trade credits and currency transfers, which inevitably hampered German economic expansion. One might fittingly conclude this survey, therefore, by quoting a letter of his to Boetticher in 1888 which summarizes his policy:

> If I lay particular stress on the foundation of a strong German finance institute in China I do so because I am convinced that sooner or later that spacious and densely populated country will be generally opened to European commerce and then offer new and lucrative markets to foreign industry, above all to railway building. According to numerous and unanimous reports the foreign office has been receiving for years, it can be regarded as certain that whenever this occurs those nations represented in China by influential banks will be destined before all others to exploit the favourable opportunity of securing the lion's share of the great transactions to be expected there for their commerce and industry.

# 3

GÜNTHER MEYER

# German Interests and Policy in the Netherlands East Indies and Malaya, 1870-1914

The history of German policy towards the European colonial territories in Southeast Asia in the years prior to World War I reflects a series of typical traits in German imperialism. At the same time, however, there are a few tactical peculiarities in this policy of so-called peaceful penetration which was applied chiefly in the territories occupied by foreign colonial powers.

The German bourgeoisie, until far into the nineteenth century, had not succeeded in achieving any worthwhile share of the direct exploitation of the rich East Indian colonies. On the other hand Germany was becoming an ever-growing market for the products of Netherlands East Indies. This aroused more and more the desire of the German bourgeoisie which with growing economic strength demanded access, previously denied, to the direct exploitation of the Southeast Asian markets. Projects for territorial conquest of Southeast Asian territories were not lacking, though initially there was no real basis for these. The reason for this was the absence at that time of German economic and political unity. Nevertheless, even the young Prusso-German Reich was not able immediately to take up an active colonial policy. Those groups of the German bourgeoisie who were interested in colonies were not yet sufficiently significant to be able to force a colonial policy. Further, Germany lacked the tools of maritime power to secure any territorial acquisitions in Southeast Asia. Although the Netherlands at this time exercised scarcely more than a nominal rule in many areas of the East Indies (the population

This contribution, translated by Dr John A. Moses, provides a survey of the most important findings of the author's dissertation, "Das Eindringen des deutschen Kapitalismus in die niederländischen und britischen Kolonien in Südostasien von den Anfängen bis 1918". This dissertation was defended in September 1970 at the Humboldt University, Berlin, GDR. It contains an extensive list of sources and literature on the theme.

over the years had been bravely resisting the consolidation and extension of the Dutch colonial power), the German government was not in a position to exploit this situation for a territorial foothold in the area. Instead it had to content itself with the indirect support of the Dutch by allowing the recruitment of mercenaries, and supporting missions there. In this way the Germans sought to protect their trade in and with the East Indies, which had been growing since the founding of the colony and their first capital investments there.

The attempts of individual German entrepreneurs to get established in Southeast Asia and to develop their possessions into German colonies, as, for example, the concessions of Baron von Overbeck in North Borneo,[1] failed because of the reluctance of German capital to take up concessions and the lack of government support, chiefly because of the greater financial power of the British merchants and the British policy of "preventive" seizure of possession. The stronger presence and perceptibly growing competition of German commercial firms in Southeast Asia in the 1870s and 1880s, and finally the beginning of a German colonial policy in the South Seas and in New Guinea caused the British government to activate its policy towards the Southeast Asian territories, and to extend their rule both directly and indirectly over further Malayan territory and North Borneo.[2]

"Peaceful" penetration of German capital in the Dutch possessions in the East Indies was made possible when the Dutch abandoned the colonial policy of privileged companies, which were mostly in the hands of the aristocracy and the old commercial bourgeoisie, to go over to a "liberal" colonial policy in the interests of industry and banking capital, a policy which suited more the conditions of freely competitive capitalism. This stage of Dutch colonial policy had begun already in the 1860s when the first Dutch capital was invested in the plantation economy of Sumatra. The outward sign of this new period was the agricultural law of the Dutch colonial minister, de Waal, in 1870, which allowed foreign capital to enter plantation enterprise in the colony.

Whereas Dutch and British capital had the advantage of their own banks in the colony, German capital in the Dutch East Indies, in spite of initial successes, was with the advancing development of monopoly capitalism not strong enough to withstand the competition of Dutch and British companies.

German capital was until the 1880s mostly represented by small or medium sized firms. As such it was unable to meet the requirements which developing large plantation enterprises demanded. For this reason the German plantations were much more vulnerable to crises in the colonial economy, as was the case in the sugar crisis of 1884 and the tobacco crisis of 1891.[3]

Only in connection with the penetration of German enterprises into the Far East did Southeast Asia assume greater importance in the framework of German politics. Bismarck's move to advocate an imperial subsidy for a postal steamship line to the Far East—thus creating better conditions for German capital with regard to its competitors in the expansion of trade in China and Japan—centrally affected Southeast Asia, which became increasingly more significant for German maritime trade, with its important ports on the route to China, particularly Singapore. Following the main line of the Imperial German Steamer Service to the Far East and the branch line to the German South Seas colonies, the German shipping lines based in Singapore built up an entire network of coastal lines. With those the German shipping companies came to dominate coastal navigation in this area.

At the same time the process of monopolization within German capital in Southeast Asia had advanced. German trading and navigation interests in the East Indies and Malaya towards the end of the nineteenth century were being concentrated more and more in the large monopolistic shipping firms, particularly Norddeutscher Lloyd, and those trading firms which were closely bound to it through capital or business connections.

The discrepancy between the growing economic and military strength of German imperialism on the one hand, and the political position of the German Reich as well as the minor significance of its colonial possessions on the other hand, of which the Junker and middle class groups were becoming more and more aware since the mid–1890s, found expression in demands for a strengthening of the territorial share of Germany in overseas possessions.

Towards the end of the nineteenth century, Southeast Asia assumed an independent importance in the politics of German imperialism as a source of raw materials, besides its role as a station on the way to the Far East; this resulted from the growing expansive power of German capital and the increasing demand for raw materials by the German economy. For this reason the demands of expansionist circles in Germany were directed not only to the Far East but also to Southeast Asia. These areas were in the possession of less powerful colonial states, and seemed, therefore, virtually to offer themselves for partition among the stronger imperialistic powers. But Germany had to abandon her hopes in the Philippines in favour of the United States in 1898–99, and the convention with Britain on the partition of the Portuguese colonies, 30 August 1898, was only an apparent success with regard to Southeast Asia. In reality it was precisely the rivalry of the great powers which kept the colonies of the smaller states in Southeast Asia from being directly annexed by one of the large powers.

This line of approach by the German Reich did not lead to acquisitions in Southeast Asia. But neither did the other line bring any success. The first one was chiefly an expression of the goals of commercial and naval capital and of the navy. The second line was determined by the heavy industry of Rhineland-Westphalia. Their goal was the incorporation of the Netherlands in a customs association with Germany, and by this means to exert stronger influence on the Dutch colonies. Their efforts to bring about a customs association with Holland were linked with the new commercial treaty policy which emerged under the aegis of the so-called *Sammlungspolitik* (policy of collective interests) at the end of the 1890s. This seemed to offer some promise of success because the security of the Dutch colonies was endangered by the American presence in the Philippines and the continuing Atjeh war. In May 1898 the Auswärtiges Amt outlined in two drafts its policy towards a customs association with Holland. It was assumed by the Auswärtiges Amt that the Netherlands would only enter a customs association if they were accorded complete equality as partners in determining the customs tariffs and commercial treaties, and if Germany would assume responsibility for the security of the Dutch colonies. Their protection could "under circumstances become a serious responsibility and bring with it military complications". For such a "reduction of our national security" the Netherlands would have to pay a "compensation by conceding some of their colonial possessions".

It was decided to make, first, suitable suggestions in the Dutch press in order to test and influence public opinion. The demand for ceding Dutch colonial possessions was not to be made public so as not to arouse "mistrust against Germany" again through premature press reports.[4] However, the German press itself did not exercise restraint. It wrote, for example, that with the customs association, "the first and most important step is taken ... which enables the completely rational exploitation of the Indian lands ... in co-operation with Germany".[5] The Pan-German *Rheinisch-Westfälische Zeitung*, the organ of West German heavy industry, pointed to the strong growth of the population in the Dutch East Indies, the significance of which as a "market for our export industry was not to be under-estimated". In order to force the Netherlands into a customs association they urged the extension of German North Sea ports to challenge the Dutch transit trade.[6]

A section of the Dutch press at first welcomed a customs treaty. They saw in an increasing economic and political involvement of Germany in Southeast Asia a guarantee for Dutch colonial possessions, in view of American and Japanese expansion which was just beginning.[7] However, the vast majority of the Dutch commercial and industrial bourgeoisie rejected the idea of a customs union; it judged the real German intentions quite correctly. Also, the Dutch colonial bourgeoisie began in the course of the months to feel secure once more in their possessions. The Japanese danger did not yet seem to threaten them immediately. The American competition was, because of the continuing struggle against the Filipinos, unable to direct its attention to the Netherlands East Indies. And beyond this the core of the 1896 rebellion under Tunku Oemar in Atjeh had been successfully suppressed. In the light of these developments the possible German protection appeared more of a danger than a great advantage. In the final analysis, such a customs association did not fulfil the basic requirements of the customs policies of both sides. Above all, the Dutch commercial bourgeoisie could not accept the high German protective tariffs without endangering their chief profits from commerce and transit trade in East Indian colonial products.

A third avenue of trying to gain influence in Southeast Asia lay in a political approach to the Netherlands. Such an approach was made favourable by the policies of the Dutch prime minister, Abraham Kuyper, whose Christian-Conservative government came to power in 1901. Against the resistance of many, Kuyper sought to cultivate relations with Germany. The most significant result of this policy was the treaty of 24 July

1901 which led to the founding of a German-Dutch Telegraph Company in 1903.[8] This company finished, in 1905, the construction of a cable connection with the Dutch East Indies, the German colonies in the Pacific, and Kiautschou independently of the British cable firms. These cables were considered in Germany to be, in the first place, of strategic importance for the connection of German East Africa with Sumatra or Java.[9] This was economically of great significance for the German electrical industry, since it was a breach in the monopoly of the Eastern Extension Australasian and China Telegraph Company. The German-Dutch Telegraph Company was dominated by Allgemeine Elektrizitätsgesellschaft (AEG). At the same time as the installation of the cable, AEG and those firms associated with it, Siemens and Telefunken, penetrated the Dutch colonies, where they established numerous enterprises in the electrical industry.

The German Admiralty Staff also directed stronger attention to Southeast Asia at the beginning of the new century. In the winter of 1900–01 naval exercises had indicated that the German Far Eastern Squadron would have been ineffective in a real naval engagement. In order to improve the conditions of the squadron the Admiralty Staff required the setting up of an extensive network of agents in China and Southeast Asia, and the construction of adequate coaling stations.[10] Whereas the first requirement was achieved with the help of German nationals living in foreign colonies, the construction of coaling stations ran into serious difficulties. Requests by German entrepreneurs for concessions to build depots in the Dutch East Indies, for example, in 1901 on the Anambas Islands some 175 nautical miles from Singapore, were rejected by the Dutch government.[11] Germany even attempted to go through diplomatic channels. In April 1902 Kuyper was in Berlin for talks with the secretary of state in the Auswärtiges Amt, Baron von Richthofen. According to German newspaper reports negotiations were conducted, among other things, on a German coaling station in the East Indies.[12] However, in September of the same year Kuyper declared, after his round of talks in Berlin, Vienna, and Roma, that all rumours about the Netherlands joining the Triple Alliance, or concerning the cession of a coaling station to Germany, were without foundation.[13]

Nevertheless, the question of a coaling station was re-opened when Kuyper was again in Vienna, Rome, and Berlin during the Russo-Japanese War. But to date no documents have been revealed on Kuyper's talks in Berlin. Herre assumes that the content of the talks was that Kuyper had given assurances that his government would fulfil its obligation to maintain neutrality in this war.[14] It appears, however, very likely that Kuyper, in private conversations with von Richthofen in Berlin in January 1905, had also discussed the question of a coaling station or a guarantee-treaty between Germany, with possibly Russia, Austria, and the Netherlands, for the latter's East Indies colonies.[15]

Kuyper's policy vis-à-vis Germany was strongly influenced by the growing presence of Japan in Southeast Asia. Imperialistic circles there had been showing increased interest in the Netherlands' colonies. Indeed, after Britain had signed the Anglo-Japanese Treaty of 30 January 1902 (on which power and security of the Dutch colonies to a great extent depended), an approach to and a re-insurance in the Triple Alliance as a balance may have appeared useful to the Kuyper government.

On the other hand the anti-German section of the Dutch bourgeoisie was growing stronger, so that the government was unable to make any decisive steps in this direction. This group felt that Kuyper had already gone too far in his approaches to Germany. The opposition to both domestic and foreign policy turned against his policy, since with a view to the British attitude they rejected an abandonment of Dutch neutrality in favour of Germany. The absorption of the Dutch colonies into the German sphere of influence would not have been tolerated by the other powers interested in the area. In the autumn of 1902 the British minister in the Hague, Sir Henry Howard, declared to his French colleague, Baylin de Monbel, in reply to the latter's question concerning the fate of the Dutch colonies in the event of the Netherlands joining Germany, that that would be the end of Dutch independence and of their colonial empire. The Germans would not be quick enough to be able to take over the colonies in the East Indies. Further, the fate of the Dutch colonies in the next twenty years depended, above all, on the political and economic development of Australia. This open declaration of the British diplomat that Britain would under certain circumstances take over the East Indies caused the French minister to comment: "De là on pourrait aussi conclure que l'Allemagne et l'Angleterre protègent réciproquement la Hollande contre leurs propres ambitions".[16]

Fear of the loss of the colonies was mainly in the background of the opposition to Kuyper's German policy. This opposition was even present in government ranks and in Kuyper's own party. The unpopularity of an approach to Germany led to his election defeat in the summer of 1905, and to his replacement as head of government.[17]

The German navy, in its efforts to establish coaling stations for German war-ships in co-operation with the large shipping firms, was proceeding on the assumption that such supply bases in the Dutch East Indies could only exist under the protection of Dutch neutrality. The Admiralty Staff, therefore, did not presume German occupation of Holland in their operational plans.[18] Above all, the navy had no interest through hostile action against Holland to give Britain the chance of fully cutting the connection by sea via the Netherlands to and from the East Indies and elsewhere, which was important for German industry. This idea of the German Admiralty Staff was, however, quite illusory. There were already signs in 1905–6 that none of the powers was predisposed to adhere to international law and permit the transport of goods to Germany through a neutral Holland.[19]

The plans of the General Staff for waging war in western Europe were at first contrary to the navy's plans. A march through Dutch territory was part of the Schlieffen Plan. Such violation of neutrality would simultaneously endanger the security of German coaling stations in the Dutch colonies in the event of war. The intention of a march through the Netherlands was undoubtedly connected with the tentative approach of the Kuyper government to Germany. Kuyper's defeat, the recognition that the Dutch colonies were largely dependent on Britain, and the increasing significance of raw material imports from the Netherlands East Indies for German industry finally caused the General Staff to revise their idea of violating Dutch neutrality.[20]

Then, however, a proposal from the German minister in Holland, von Schlözer, met half-way the efforts of the navy and also those of the shipping firms, as well as of the electrical and engineering industries whose share in the Southeast Asian trade was growing quickly. In November 1907 Schlözer suggested extending the guarantees of the status quo at the coasts to the colonial possessions of the signatory powers in the projected North Sea Convention. What German diplomacy had in mind must have been the security of the neutral protection from the desired coaling depots in the East Indies.

In January 1908 the Dutch government noted this proposal with approval. They believed that the obligations of such a status quo guarantee gave them an important argument with which they could refuse future requests for concessions to build coaling stations in the East Indies. Particularly after the governments of Japan and the United States, in an exchange of notes, had come out for the maintenance of the status quo in the Pacific, the Dutch foreign minister, van Swinderen, considered at the end of 1908 taking similar diplomatic steps.[21] His first attempts in this direction with President Taft, during a holiday in the United States in the summer of 1909, made it clear that the American government, for foreign policy reasons, did not wish to take the initiative in promoting such a South Seas convention.[22]

Apart from the operational plans of the German Admiralty Staff, which were also supported by the lessons in naval warfare from the Russo-Japanese War, it was chiefly the developing rivalry with Britain which was behind the stronger interest in investing German capital in neutral areas in Southeast Asia instead of in British dominated territories. The Anglo-German rivalry was intensified here mainly by the activity of German interests in the northern Malay states, which were among the more sensitive areas of the British position in Southeast Asia. The Anglo-Siamese Treaty of 1909, in which Britain took over the four states of Kelantan, Trengganu, Kedah, and Perlis, was the British reaction to German efforts to gain concessions in this region.[23]

A detailed report by the German consul-general in Singapore, Kiliani, to the Reich chancellor at the beginning of 1906 admitted quite openly that Anglo-German rivalry in Southeast Asia was intensifying and was virtually beyond repair. The German merchants in the area would therefore be confronted with the question whether the Straits Settlements and Singapore were secure enough for their investments in view of this rivalry, or whether they should not better concentrate, for example, on the Dutch East Indies.

Behind these reflections was the fact that the Dutch East Indies, not least as a consequence of the activity of the German shipping monopoly, were no longer dependent on the port of Singapore for a market or for the transportation of their products to Europe, because the direct route Europe-East Indies was being extended continually. For some time it had been no longer possible for East Indian products to be purchased in Singapore, but only on the spot in the archipelago itself. "Perhaps our interests which are established here should attempt to profit from this present trend", the consul-general suggested.[24]

The main reason for the increased interest of European capitalists in the Netherlands East Indies in the first decade of the new century was that the colony offered favourable investment possibilities because of the growing demand for rubber, the improvement of the situation for Javanese sugar production on the world market after the Brussels convention of 1902, and the relaxation of the state monopoly on natural resources which had been begun in 1899.

The economic development of Southeast Asia then aroused the controllers of large capital to listen to the plans and appeals of those who had experience of the area. A pamphlet of decisive significance in this regard was composed by Emil Helfferich and Franz Heinrich Witthoeft; it appeared as a confidential memorandum in Hamburg in 1910 under the title, "German Economic Policy in South East Asia". Both authors belonged to the group of Behn, Meyer & Co. This trading firm had been operating in Singapore since 1840. It had developed towards the end of the century to become the most important German commercial firm in Southeast Asia. And through its connections with the larger German shipping firms it had become the focal point of German economic expansion in this area. Witthoeft had been in Singapore working for the firm since 1885, and in Hamburg since 1900 to become finally head of the enterprise. Helfferich, a brother of the director of the Deutsche Bank, Karl Helfferich, had been a merchant in the Netherlands East Indies.

From 1901 on Behn, Meyer & Co. had been extending their activity to Macassar and Menade and later to Batavia, Surabaya, Telok Betong and Semarang. This extension of the Behn Group into the East Indies doubtlessly promoted the desire to win further German capital to strengthen their position in Southeast Asia. An opportunity to do this was offered on the occasion of a study trip of Duke Johann Albrecht von Mecklenburg, the chairman of the German Colonial Society, to the Netherlands East Indies. It was then given out that the above-mentioned pamphlet had been produced for the Duke's background information.

Helfferich and Witthoeft based their argument on the fact that up until that point German commerce in Southeast Asia had suffered from lack of support of national capital, and that it could not keep up its present position if German capital "did not involve itself more than it has done in the past in the opening up and development" of Siam, Malaya, Singapore, and the Dutch East Indies. German economic policy in Southeast Asia would have in future to concentrate "on creating new capital, expanding the metropolitan markets and opening up new possibilities for the surplus energy of sixty million people".[25]

German capital in Southeast Asia had been previously represented mostly by smaller and medium-sized commercial firms. German entreperneurs had also operated largely in mixed companies with foreign capital. Now high finance was to be attracted in order to make possible an extension on the basis already established. For the practical realization of his plans Helfferich proposed the founding of an investment-trust on the Anglo-Dutch model. The basis of his plan was to get German capital not only into commerce and shipping, but also into plantations within the country itself, thereby actively participating in the exploitation of the Dutch East Indies and the Malayan states. It was not sufficient merely to control the importation of such important raw materials as tobacco, tea, coffee, and rubber; it was necessary to bring the production itself under the control of German capital.[26]

The projected investment trust was founded in October 1911 as the Straits-und-Sunda-Syndikat. Those firms associated in it were the Commerz- und Disconto-Bank in Hamburg, the Deutsche Bank and particularly the Hamburg banking house of M.M. Warburg, as well as a number of Hamburg commercial firms. The syndicate was also joined by the Société commerciale et financière Belge of Antwerp. Under the managership of Albert von Bary it represented fifteen mainly German firms in Antwerp, and one London firm. Ever since 1889 Bary had been in close touch with the Disconto-Gesellschaft. Besides Witthoeft and Max Warburg, the board of directors of the syndicate included the well-known Belgian Congo investor, General Albert Thys.[27]

The growing economic and political interest of German imperialism in the Netherlands East Indies and indeed in all Southeast Asia was paralleled by a simultaneous penetration of Holland itself by German capital. Leading German monopolists such as Hugo Stinnes had set up daughter firms in Holland. Then, in close co-operation with Dutch firms, German concerns sought footholds in third countries.

At the same time as German firms were establishing themselves in Holland, the economy of the country was being penetrated by German banking capital. There was immediate involvement in and/or connections with such Dutch banks as the Algemeene Maatschappij voor Handel en Nijverheid, the Amsterdam Bank and the Handelsbank van Nederlandsch Indie. The two last-named ones in particular were involved in the financing of colonial enterprises. The Berliner Handelsgesellschaft, which in addition shared an interest with Dutch capital in South African railways, was a shareholder in the Bank Labouchère, Oyens & Co. in Amsterdam. And Labouchère had interests in many German companies in the Netherlands East Indies. By taking over, and through sharing capital, the Germans eventually controlled 141,900,000 marks worth of Dutch currency. In this way, "the economic annexation had basically been prepared ..., when the Pan Germans ... took it up in their political propaganda".[28]

Parallel to the founding of the Straits-und-Sunda-Syndikat as the focal point for an even stronger and directed penetration of German capital in the East Indies there began a more intensive political activity for German expansion in Southeast Asia. In June 1912 there appeared in the conservative-agrarian newspaper, *Deutsche Tageszeitung*, an article, "Germanism and German Trade in Southeast Asia" under the pseudonym, Viator. This article caused a great deal of consternation in Batavia when it became known there. Viator had actually proclaimed a programme of open annexation, the goal of which was not only the economic but also the ultimate political-territorial establishment of Germany in Southeast Asia. Viator, arguing from Helfferich's basic conception, urged the creation of an exclusively German production in the area with the aid of large capital aiming at achieving a wider market for German goods. He proposed that the political ministries of the German Reich should direct finance capital to such countries "in which the political power of the German Reich is able to exert actual pressure if German interests are damaged". In these areas commerce and capital had to create "moral capital" which ultimately would transform itself into political privileges and form "the firm bases for Germanism".

As future German spheres of influence besides areas in China, the most advantageous were considered to be Siam, the Dutch East Indies and Portuguese Timor: "These countries do not only offer rich and certain gains but they are also open to the influence of our political power." Viator emphasized particularly the so-called peaceful conquest of the Dutch East Indies. Here one had to combat British influence in particular. The creation of a secure basis for German capital must prevent Holland herself becoming "a base for operations by Britain against us" through the back door of British influence in the Indies. As one of the most important instruments for this, the establishment of a large German colonial bank in the Dutch East Indies was demanded, which would operate in close touch with the Auswärtiges Amt.[29]

Further, the Anglo-German compromise over armaments and colonial questions being sought at this time was to be used to promote Germany's advance into Southeast Asia. The imperial chancellor, Bethmann Hollweg, declared in January 1912 to the chiefs of the civil cabinet, von Valentini, and the naval cabinet, Admiral von Müller, that in the event of an agreement with Britain in the naval question Germany would create a large colonial empire into which the Dutch colonies would be integrated.[30] Both the plans of the Straits-und-Sunda-Syndikat and of Viator leave little doubt that they were thinking mainly of the Dutch East Indies and not simply of Dutch New Guinea, which was neighbouring the German colony of Kaiser Wilhelmsland. Dutch New Guinea had only been a desired object of annexation in the early period of German colonial acquisitions.

The Viator pamphlet occupies a special position in the writing on this subject since it prescribed the future steps in Southeast Asia with the emphasis on the Dutch East Indies. And in the period up to the outbreak of World War I significant advances were made in fulfilling this programme. For industrial activity in China a Far Eastern syndicate was formed in Hamburg at Helfferich's instigation, whereas a Siam syndicate under the leadership of the Frankfurt Metal Company began activity with the acquisition of tin mine concessions in Siam. In both syndicates the managing director became Emil Helfferich, and the Hamburg banking house of M.M. Warburg had a significant share.[31]

The extension of the German sphere of influence to Portuguese Timor which had also been proposed was not, however, taken up at that time. Indeed, that which had apparently been achieved through the Anglo-German pact of 1898 concerning the Portuguese colonies was actually abandoned *de jure* when Germany, in the pact of 13 August 1913 with Britain, exchanged its claims on Timor for interests on the African islands, Sao Thomé and Principe.[32] German capital had been penetrating the cocoa business on these islands since 1907. And because those most interested in southern Asia, such as M.M. Warburg, were themselves involved in the expansion of German capital in Portugal's African colonies, this exchange by no means ran counter to their interests.[33]

Towards the end of the pre-war period German capital was involved in the Netherlands Indies to the extend of 120 million to 180 million marks. This represented about one-fifth to one-third of German capital in East Asia. Germany was thus in fourth place behind Dutch, British and Franco-Belgian capital in the colony. However, in the final years before the war German capital encountered increasing American competition. Within the Dutch East Indies the German enterprises were concentrated on Java (trading firms and plantation companies), Sumatra (mining companies), and Celebes (trading firms). The infiltration of German capital showed a similar pattern to its expansion in other colonies of semi-colonial regions—that is, chiefly in the spheres of interests or territories occupied by other imperialistic powers. In this process the German interests availed themselves of the economic aid of foreign capital, or tried to hide their activities under the flags of other companies. On the other hand they were able, by means of such linking of their own economic interests with those of other powers, to gain more political security. The effectiveness of these expansion tactics has been demonstrated already in China and Egypt.[34]

The explanation for this form of activity in the Dutch colony lies partly in the fact that the colonial government only admitted firms which were registered in Holland or her colonies. For this reason a number of German enterprises were registered in the Netherlands as *Naamlose Vennootschapp* (shareholding company). This measure which was originally introduced as a safeguard against German competition proved to be in some instances a useful disguise enabling the penetration of German capital. However, the German enterprises sought to strengthen their position in that they in part relied on foreign capital or on their own daughter companies in England. By means of these daughter companies they were able to exploit the advantages which English companies received as a result of the Anglo-Dutch treaties of 1824. These treaties, by virtue of the concession of most-favoured-nation and the elimination of all discrimination in trade between Britain and the Dutch East Indies, had given Britain a more advantageous starting position for sharing in the exploitation of the colony than other countries.

Germany's foreign trade with the Dutch East Indies had developed with extraordinary energy in the ten years prior to the world war. While exports to the Netherlands Indies between 1904 and 1913 rose from 27.3 million to 98.6 million marks, imports in the same period increased from 99.3 million to 227.6 million marks. So, for the German economy the Dutch colony was in the first place a supplier or raw materials and only secondly a market. But even the latter aspect of the overseas trade developed particularly towards the end of the pre-war period and gained increased significance. The growth in exports was due to the expanding share of heavy industry, but above all to the new electrical and chemical industries. This sector alone accounted for twice the value of the entire German export to the colony in the year 1905.[35] Here those industries in which Germany was in advance of Britain, and which were in a leading position within Germany, made rapid progress in the markets. The imbalance of raw material imports with regard to exports was characteristic for the raw material hunger of German economy. In this respect the Dutch colonies in Southeast Asia were more important as suppliers than Germany's own colonies. In 1913 the Netherlands Indies supplied something of the order of three-and-a-half times the value of the imports from German colonies. Also the exports of Germany to her own colonies were behind those to the Netherlands Indies both in extent and in the rate of development.

From the beginning of the century German capital in Britain's Southeast Asian possessions did not develop as strongly as in the neighbouring Dutch possessions. However, in terms of commercial politics these areas—Singapore, Malaya and North Borneo—were just as important as suppliers of raw materials for the German economy. Rubber and tin comprised in 1913 about half the value of imports from these areas to the sum of 24.3 million marks. (1900: 13.3 million marks).[36] The German capital invested there was concentrated chiefly in Singapore and Penang trading houses. From 1897 to 1905 it rose from 10 million to 35 million marks.[37] In contrast to the development in the Dutch colonies during the decade prior to the outbreak of war German capital made only little investment in the Malay states, in spite of the growing opportunities there. In the face of strong British competition, the share of German capital, for example, in industrial enterprises, receded. By 1911 the capital of the two large tin smelters of Malaya, which had been predominantly in German hands, was completely in British possession.[38]

The strongest position of German capital was in Singapore, chiefly in coastal shipping in which it dominated since the turn of the century, when two British lines were taken over by the Germans. The same thing was true for the British possessions in North Borneo. The two most important shipping connections here were the lines operated by Norddeutsche Lloyd between Singapore, North Borneo and the Philippines, as well as between Hong Kong, the Philippines and North Borneo. In 1911 another British shipping firm was taken over by the German firm of Behn, Meyer & Co. Thus the shipping lines to North Borneo were almost completely in German hands. "The ports are British, but the only steamers which carry the trade fly the German colours!" lamented the British Borneo investor John Dill Ross.[39] At the outbreak of war in 1914, North Borneo found itself to be suddenly cut off from all sea connections, and experienced for a time a serious shortage of supplies because all German vessels had fled into the neutral harbours of the Philippines.[40]

Even in 1906 the German consul-general, Kiliani, had recommended that economic expansion in the face of British competition should concentrate more in the Dutch colonies. In the years following, the strengthening of the German economic position in the Dutch Indies created the base for a renewed attempt to penetrate Malaya. Of course, the Straits-und-Sunda-Syndikat had acquired a few plantations in the Malayan states. However, although the new German consul-general in Singapore, Feindel, had urged in mid–1912 further expansion of German trade and capital in Malaya, this did not take place in the years before the outbreak of war.[41]

By 1914, then, German capital in Southeast Asia, particularly in the Dutch East Indies, had undoubtedly a firmly established position. However, in contrast to the advances in the Portuguese colonies, in China, or in Persia, German finance capital in the Dutch Indies was not able to divide this area into spheres of interest with its strongest rival here, British finance capital. Although the East Indies were in the possession of one of the weaker colonial powers, Dutch finance capital was strong enough to prevent the colonial administration from becoming dependent upon foreign loans. Further, the economic and political ties of the Netherlands to Britain still outweighed those to Germany. In addition, the organization and territorial concentration of German capital in the colony was not so far advanced as to enable it to lay claim to spheres of interest of its own. Nevertheless, the founding of the Straits-und-Sunda-Syndikat indicated that such a concentration was beginning. In this syndicate a group representing German finance capital became the most important of all German interests in Southeast Asia and these were in the main connected with the Deutsche Bank as well as Hamburg bank and Bremen shipping capital. This syndicate, which also had connections with the Disconto-Gesellschaft via a Belgian-German finance group, was identical (in its chief shareholders) with the mainstays of the finance capitalist group which had begun to implement the German *Mittel-Afrika* concept through its advances in the Belgian Congo and in the Portuguese African colonies during the five years prior to the outbreak of war.

With its assets in Java the syndicate formed the base for an expansion of the economic and political interests of German imperialism in the Dutch East Indies. The intention was that this should strengthen the voice of German diplomacy in the affairs of Southeast Asia. Directed against Britain, the economic and political expansion programme of this group in Southeast Asia which, apart from the Dutch Indies, encompassed Portuguese Timor and Siam, adumbrated the war aims of that section of the German bourgeoisie interested in this area in World War I.[42]

1. R. Pape, "Gustav Freiherr von Overbeck (1830–1894)", *Lippische Mitteilungen aus Geschichte und Landeskunde* 18 (1959): 163–217. This work on Overbeck, which is the only one on the subject to date, considerably overestimates his significance.
2. cf Wong Lin Ken, "Western Enterprise and the Development of the Malayan Tin Industry to 1914", *The Economic Development of South–East Asia* (London, 1964), p. 134; G. Irwin, *Nineteenth Century Borneo* (The Hague, 1955), p. 213.
3. AAHP, no. 5871, Generalkonsul Letternbaur in Batavia to AA, 9/2/1914.
4. Ibid., no. 9872, note of May 1898.
5. *Berliner Börsenzeitung*, 25/8/1899.
6. *Rheinisch–Westfälische Zeitung*, 21/9/1899 and 27/9/1899.
7. For example, the *Haagsche Courant*, cited in *Leipziger Neueste Nachrichten*, 13/9/1899.
8. *Bescheiden betreffende de buitenlandse politiek van Nederland* 1848–1919, 3d Period, vol. 1 (The Hague, 1957), no. 436.
9. R. Hennig, "Die deutsche–niederländische Telegraphenallianz im Fernen Osten", *Grenzboten* 65 (1906, second quarter): 292.
10. W. Hubatsch, *Der Admiralstab und die obersten Marinebehörden in Deutschland 1848–1945* (Frankfurt a.M., 1958), p. 106.
11. *Bescheiden,* no. 508, Colonial Minister van Asch van Wijk to Governor General Rooseboom, 17/1/1902.
12. *Neue bayerische Landzeitung,* 26/7/1902.
13. Schulthess: *Europäischer Geschichtskalender* N.F. 18 (1902): 277.
14. P. Herre, *Die kleinen Staaten Europas und die Entstehung des Weltkrieges* (Munich, 1937), p. 163.
15. C. Smit, *Hoogtij der Neutraliteitspolitiek* (Leiden, 1959), pp. 62–63. Smit, the editor of the Dutch publication of records, represents this view in the light of his knowledge of the relevant Dutch official and private archives.
16. *Documents diplomatiques francais* [*1871–1914*), ser.2, vol. 2 (Paris, 1931), no. 393.
17. Smit, *Hoogtij,* p. 63.
18. Hubatsch, *Admiralstab*, pp. 247–48.
19. J. Ellis Barker, "The Absorption of Holland by Germany", *The Nineteenth Century and After* 60 (July 1906): 36–37.
20. G. Ritter, *Der Schlieffenplan* (Munich, 1956), p. 180.
21. *Bescheiden* vol. 3 (The Hague, 1961), nos. 141 and 148.
22. Smit, Hoogtij, pp. 103–5.
23. K.G. Tregonning, *A History of Modern Malaya* (London, 1964), p. 171.
24. AAHP, no. 9860.
25. E. Helfferich and F.H. Witthoeft, *Deutsche Wirtschaftspolitik in Südost–Asien* (Hamburg, 1910), pp. 10–11.
26. E. Helfferich, *Ein Leben*, 1 (Hamburg, 1948): 191–92.
27. Ibid., p. 224; AAHP no. 1105, Prussian legation in Hamburg to AA, 17/1/1912.
28. Z. Jindra, "Über die ökonomischen Grundlagen der Mitteleuropa–Ideologie des deutschen Imperialismus", *Probleme der Ökonomie und Politik in den Beziehungen zwischen Ost– und Westeuropa vom 17. Jahrhundert bis zur Gegenwart* (Berlin, 1960), pp. 148–49.
29. Viator (pseud.), "Deutschtum und deutscher Handel in Südostasien", *Deutsche Tageszeitung*, Supplement: *Zeitfragen*, 10/6/1912.
30. G.A.V. Müller, *Der Kaiser . . . Aufzeichnungen des Chefs des Marinekabinetts über die Ära Wilhelm II,* ed. W. Görlitz (Berlin/Frankfurt/ Zürich, 1965), p. 107.

31. Helfferich, *Leben*, p. 256.
32. GP 37/1, no. 14, p. 681, draft of the treaty of 13/8/1913.
33. H. Mayer, *Das portugiesische Kolonialreich der Gegenwart* (Berlin, 1918). p. 23; A. Vagts, "M.M. Warburg & Co. Ein Bankhaus in der deutschen Weltpolitik 1905–1933", *Vierteljahresschrift für Sozial- und Wirtschaftsgeschichte*, 45 (1958): 346–47.
34. A.S. Jerussalimski, "Das Eindringen der deutschen Monopole in China an der Wende vom 19. zum 20. Jahrhundert", *Zeitschrift für Geschichtswissenschaft*, 8 (1960):1838–1839; L. Rathman, "Zur Ägyptenpolitik des deutschen Imperialismus vor dem ersten Weltkrieg", *Geschichte und Geschichtsbild Afrikas* (Berlin, 1960), p. 89.
35. *Statistisches Jahrbuch des Deutschen Reiches*, vol. 26. (1905) and vol. 35. (1914).
36. Ibid., vol. 35 (1914).
37. AAHP, no. 8598, consulate in Singapore to AA 14/12/1897; RMA *Die Entwicklung der deutschen Seeinteressen in letzten Jahrzehnt* (Berlin, 1905), p. 155.
38. AAHP, no. 1081, consul general Kiliani in Singapore to AA, 27/9/1910: Kiliani to AA., 20/5/1911.
39. J.D. Ross, *Sixty Years: Life and Adventures in the Far East*, Vol. II, (London, 1911) p. 196.
40. O.Rutter, *British North Borneo* (London/Bombay/Sydney, 1922), p. 343.
41. AAHP, no. 3294, consul general Feindel in Singapore to AA, 20/7/1912.
42. RKA, no. 2444, memorandum by the Board of Commerce, Hamburg, Kolonialpolitische Friedensforderungen of 6/8/1915, pp. 94–97.

# PART 2

# Annexations and International Relations

# 4

**MARTIN P. KNIGHT**

# Britain, Germany and the Pacific, 1880-87

In 1880 the Pacific was not an important area in the calculations of Whitehall. It was a frontier zone of the empire, where the issues raised were irritating, unimportant—indeed, the same as those of the period 1865–75 which W. D. McIntyre has examined.[1] The variables of Anglo-German relations in the Pacific remained the need to reconcile Australasian demands with German interests in places where the local situation was getting out of control. The frontier still created problems, but as seen from Whitehall they were problems of the periphery, solvable at the periphery for the time being, and solvable within the local situation and the local demands. But by 1886–87 Pacific issues were dealt with at the highest political level. Far from being isolated, peripheral disputes, Pacific matters had become an integral, and at times important, part of the perspective of statesmen whose scale of priorities was founded on the realities of *Weltpolitik*, of the diplomatic power game. This essay is an examination of the changing nature of Anglo-German relations in the Pacific in the period 1880–87, of the effects of the adoption of a colonial policy by Germany on the conceptual framework of Whitehall for dealing with Pacific problems, and of the cathartic effect of this change on the process of the partition of the Pacific.

The obvious centre of Anglo-German contact in the Pacific was Samoa.[2] The treaties of 1879 had safeguarded the interests of the two parties concerned, but the problems of the local polity, for which these treaties were in part responsible, demanded a decision on the degree of intervention by British officials in Samoan affairs.[3] The debate on the line to take on Samoa in 1880 mirrored the debate which had taken place in the period 1870–75. Withdrawal was one suggestion which the Admiralty favoured: it opposed the policy lines laid down by

Salisbury in January 1880 as "unnecessary and impolitic interference". According to admiral Wilson, the commodore on the Australian station at the time, it was "a great mistake" to mix with the unstable politics of local factions in areas where Britain had no real interest. Kimberley was even more explicit: "Our interest in Samoa is not considerable and the sooner we leave to those who have large interests the duty of taking the chestnuts out of the fire the better".[4] But withdrawal never became likely because of the interests at stake. Maudsley, acting consul-general while Gordon was on leave, wrote that "Fiji, Samoa and Tonga are so close relatively that anything in one affects the other". Thurston later stressed "the reversionary interest" of Fiji in Tonga, and Gordon explicitly stated that Britain could not afford to allow any foreign Power "to acquire a degree of authority within and control over our colony of Fiji" through influence over Tonga. The Australasians, to Thurston's annoyance, also claimed an interest in Samoa and Tonga. Auckland merchants and New Zealand politicians were to the fore in this respect. The official line became increasingly an assumption that "We can't drop out altogether", or "No retreat is possible now".[5]

But this refusal to withdraw was not allowed to lead to annexation. Herbert, who had a slight preference for annexation, acknowledged that the question was "out of the field of practical politics", while Kimberley stated, when Gordon, the high commissioner and governor of Fiji, and Russsell, the British ambassador in Berlin, suggested annexation: "We have got quite enough on our hands already." Instead, the officials chose a *via media*. What was wanted was "a strong, native government which would be able to maintain peace and afford security to foreign traders".[6]

In Tonga, the Baker regime, it was increasingly appreciated, provided just such a satisfactory framework. Once the treaty of 1879 had been ratified in 1882, Tonga posed no problems for the Foreign Office for a time.[7] When Des Voeux, high commissioner at the time, asked for a warship to aid in Baker's deportation, Pauncefote, the permanent under-secretary of the Foreign Office, refused: "We must take care we get into no trouble by deporting Mr. Baker." As far as he was concerned, Foreign Office responsibility and interest in Tonga had ceased with Gordon's acceptance of the situation as the best available.[8]

But in Samoa, the problem was less easy to solve. In the state of the collapse of the local polity, foreign aid to the native government was considered essential to ensure peace, security and reliability. Co-operation at a governmental level, in the hope that the governments would have sufficient, even if not total, control over the officials on the spot to ensure consular unity, which might provide that aid, was only part of the answer. For the real problem, once annexation or withdrawal had been discounted, lay in finding that degree of intervention and co-operation which was neither so great as to lead to disputes with foreign powers, or even annexation, nor so little as to lead to chaos and therefore the need to intervene to salvage the situation. Given that the United States stayed aloof, the only other interested power was Germany, and the question resolved itself into what degree of co-operation the government should pursue with Germany. The Liberal government rejected Salisbury's line as going too far. Partly this can be seen as a reaction from the forward policy of the Conservative government, but largely it was the result of naval officers' rejection of this degree of intervention, and partly a rejection by the Foreign and Colonial Offices of the Executive Council set up by the officials on the spot in March 1880. Hill, a clerk in the Consular Department of the Foreign Office, wrote two memoranda on this question to provide the basis for the 7 September 1880 dispatch which attempted to lay down the degree of intervention which the British government was prepared to allow.[9] Thereafter, until the crisis of 1884, the Foreign Office was extremely reluctant to become involved in Samoan tangles. Given Gordon's own opinion that "unless we are prepared to face all the difficulties of a Protectorate, I am sure the less we interfere with the internal affairs of the country the better", the Foreign Office stood back and left matters to the High Commission, merely keeping a supervisory check over the developments at Samoa to ensure that nothing "should mar the existing harmony of opinion among the Powers in Samoa". The only times the Foreign Office became at all active over Samoan affairs were when this harmony was threatened; for example, when Zembsch, the German consul, was thought to be prepared to back a rival to Malietoa in the succession question in 1881, Lister had a dispatch sent to Ampthill "to get the German Government to instruct their

Consul not to separate from the others and recognise the old party government". In general, this negative policy had some degree of success in the years 1880–83: "the greatest cordiality existed between German and British Consuls and Governments and very little was heard of Samoa".[10]

But the situation at the periphery did not remain satisfactory. The reason for this lay in the vicious circle of two local sub-imperialisms. On the one hand, the DHPG, which dominated the Pacific islands' trade, feared that the developments in the Samoan situation, the labour trade and the Australasian demands would fatally prejudice its future; on the other hand, the Australasians, though by no means consistently united, were felt to have become more extreme and virulent in their demands for wholesale British annexation of the islands.[11] The inter-reaction of these two expansionist elements was the central reason for the crisis in the Southwest Pacific which took place in 1883–85.

But the importance of these developments should not be exaggerated. The causal connection between German commercial demands for protection and the adoption of a more active colonial policy by Bismarck is still a contentious issue. If the endogenous forces which H. Wehler emphasizes were the primary motivating factor, short and long term, then on the German side it can be argued that a mere crisis at the periphery was not of overriding importance.[12] From the British side, it seems plausible to argue that the colonial demands and actions of 1883–84 did not create a significant change in official thinking about Anglo-German relations in the Pacific or about Pacific problems in general.

Queensland's annexation of New Guinea is the obvious case to examine: the story is well known, but the findings of M. G. Jacobs show that a colonial initiative was hoped for. Indeed, the reason for the Colonial Office's rejection of the Western Committee Report was precisely that they were looking for such an initiative in Pacific affairs. Derby's statement in July was not born of the Queensland annexation, but of the established Colonial Office views on the matter.[13] The main problem concerning New Guinea in the 1870s and the early 1880s had lain in the difficulties of jurisdiction. The Foreign Office role in this problem before the German annexation lay simply in ascertaining the degree of foreign interest there, and of attempting to establish, on Colonial Office demand, the assertion of British paramountcy. By mid-1883, Lyons had obtained assurances from the French government "that the French Government had no intention of interfering with the island of New Guinea". Similarly, the Italians, anxious to please Britain at this stage, were "bullied" on behalf of the Australian colonies into agreeing that they would not disturb the established British pre-emptive right to New Guinea, even if as yet no decision on annexation had been reached by the British government.[14] But a more germane problem was the German interest. It was certainly true, as the Foreign Office asserted in its later quarrel with the German government, that the Germans had no establishments in New Guinea. But the Foreign Office had not, up to the news of the Queensland annexation, obtained from the German government the same categorical denial of interest in relation to New Guinea as it had received from the French and Italians. The assurances received from Ampthill, if at least consistent in their tenor that Bismarck had no intention of pursuing a more active colonial policy, were vague and often unofficial. This fact was realized with some concern by the Colonial Office, for it wished, in refusing the annexation, to be able to give such an assurance that there was no danger of foreign intervention. For two months the Foreign Office refused to give that assurance. In the end, Granville agreed only to the phrase "H.M.G. have no grounds for believing that it is the intention of any Foreign Powers to annex New Guinea". As an apology, Lister wrote to Herbert that "The phrase I suggested had the merit of being true, but I own it had no other and that it is not likely to allay Queensland's anxieties".[15] The Queensland annexation was simply a variation on the theme of the initiative of the man on the spot, but this time the action had been checked.[16]

It is perfectly true that when, in March 1884, the Anglo-French negotiations reached something of a deadlock, the Colonial Office instructed the British commissioners that "the altered position of all questions relating to the Pacific since the recent strong expression of feeling by the Australasian colonies with regard to their interests in that ocean, render it extremely difficult for H.M.G. to deal with the Islands of the Pacific without having special regard to those objects to which the Australasian colonies attach a special importance".[17] But this altered position cannot be said to have started any scramble for the Pacific. The importance of the combined—as it was largely seen in Whitehall—Australasian pressure as evinced in the 21 July 1883 dispatch from the Agents-General and the Intercolonial Convention Resolutions was that it increased the attention paid to that variable in any Pacific matter. If Australasian demands stimulated German fears of the *Torschluss*, then indirectly they can be seen as a possible part of the cause of the scramble. But to the officials in Whitehall, the combined pressure of the Australasians was a continuation of the peripheral initiative, and one which was alarmingly demanding in its scope; a change of degree not of kind.

This increasing tension at the periphery was reflected in several areas of Anglo-German contact in the Pacific. The labour trade was one of these. At first, the problems arising from the trade were seen as High Commission ones; but this altered somewhat with the question of "foreign flags" and the complaints that the High Commission regulations put British traders at a disadvantage as compared with foreigners. Attempts at an international agreement were to be a recurring theme in the 1880s.[18] But far more important for Anglo-German relations was the danger of clashes between Queensland and Fijian labour traders, and German labour traders and other commercially interested parties. This became possible when developments in the labour trade between 1882–83 led to a situation where Queensland and Fijian vessels moved to the more northerly islands of the New Guinea Archipelago and the New Britain Archipelago from the New Hebrides and the Solomons. For it was in these islands that the firm of Hernsheim had its stations and from where the DHPG, was increasingly hoping to recruit its labour force.[19] The clash at Laughlan Island was not unforeseeable. In forwarding the complaint by Hernsheim, Plessen, the German chargé, told Granville of the moves to regulate the German labour trade. It was during this period that Bismarck was moving towards his policy of protecting German commerce.[20] But to the Foreign Office, the problem was a routine one which, as was by now quite normal, was passed on to the Colonial Office. Between September 1883 and August 1884, when the issue was closed for a while, the Foreign Office was lucky not to create for itself another issue like the Fiji lands question. Only the election of Griffith, and his determination to end labour trade abuses, saved the Foreign Office. The Colonial Office did nothing pending the Western Committee Report until March 1884, when a dispatch was sent to Fiji and Queensland requesting details of the colonies' reaction. When the reply was received from Queensland giving the news of the grant of 500 dollars' compensation and a determination to end all recruiting if no means could be found to end abuses, Pauncefote and Anderson, the head of the Consular Department, were keen to forward the information to the German government. July 1884 was not a good moment to delay gaining a bit of German goodwill.[21]

In Samoa, governmental co-operation was being undermined. Malietoa's leanings towards England, the antics of Lundon, the Intercolonial Convention Resolutions (particularly the Land Resolution, in the light of the Fiji question) and Churchward's damaging exposé of the treatment of labourers on DHPG plantations, were stimulating fears of a British annexation and of the dangerous consequences for the German commerical position.[22] The fact of the matter was that governmental co-operation removed none of the fundamental weaknesses of Samoa which had been so apparent to all British officials since the 1870s. But when the warning signals reached the Foreign Office, there was no realization of a changing situation. Lundon was another beach politician, and Thurston's analysis, to dismiss him as a land speculator, was accepted.[23] The 21 July 1883 dispatch from the Agents-General was dealt with summarily; Grey's Confederation Bill and the Inter-colonial Convention Resolutions on Samoa and Tonga received similar treatment at the Foreign Office. But Thurston regarded the situation as more serious. Expressing his views on Malietoa's petition of November 1883, he thought "a continuation of non-intervention will not much longer be possible". Given the increasing commercial and landed interest in Samoa, if the government continued its present policy, it would "incur many of the obligations and collateral responsibilities of dominion without any of its rights and advantages". His remedy was annexation to Fiji or to a foreign power other than Britain.

The Colonial Office recognized that the situation needed some corrective: it suggested, given that annexation was out of the question, a greater degree of control over Samoan affairs by the Treaty powers. Anderson and Lister were put out by this turnabout from the decision of 1880, and thought that "strong grounds would have to be adduced for such an entire reversal of policy".[24] In fact, the Colonial Office suggestion for a united Protectorate was hardly "an entire reversal of policy"; rather it was a mere increase of the degree of intervention. Two more disturbing accounts were received about Samoa, one of which recorded the seizure of Mulinu'u Point by the Germans. When the Colonial Office gave reasons for their change of tack, the arguments were that changes at the periphery, that is, Malietoa's petition and the Australasian agitation, had necessitated the measures suggested. But nothing more was heard of the suggestion: when Hill went over to the Colonial Office to check up on it, he was told it had been shelved. Between 27 May 1884 and 5 August 1884, something had happened at the Colonial Office to give pause for stocktaking.[25]

The Fijian lands question provides the explanation: it presents the most clear-cut example in Pacific affairs of the change in dealing with peripheral issues after Bismarck had made it clear that he was in earnest about his adoption of a more active colonial policy. Until the summer of 1884, there is no indication that the Foreign or Colonial Offices felt that the problem needed to be dealt with in any terms of reference, but simply as a local dispute. The parellel with the Angra Pequena dispute is, as it was then to the *Standard* and the *Times*, very obvious. In both cases, the Foreign Office merely passed on German enquiries and complaints to the Colonial Office until it became clear that the German government was prepared to embroil these colonial issues with major political ones in order to get its own way.[26]

The disallowance of about half the settler land claims in the first instance led to a howl of protest. British complaints could be crushed by a sharp negative from Whitehall; American complaints were fobbed off.[27] But not so German ones, given that the German government became the increasingly enthusiastic vehicle of these protests. The details need not concern us, except to say that the German arguments followed closely those used by the law officers in the debate leading up to the ordinance of October 1879. The crown, it was asserted, had arrogated to itself, in defiance of Article 4 and International Law, the right to judge by administrative authority the *bona fides* of German claims. Given the necessary lack of impartiality of the crown and hence of the Land Commission, it was argued that the procedure and basis of the colonial actions was "altogether illegal and arbitrary, not founded upon any established right and precedent". Rebuttals of German arguments by those very men about whose partiality the Germans complained, were hardly likely to restore German confidence in the assertion by Selborne, the lord chancellor, that the crown was the fount of all justice and had to be trusted. The Germans did not simply want a rehearing of cases; they required a mixed commission to establish what compensation should be given to those German complainants who, in the eyes of the German Foreign Office, had suffered unjustly.[28]

Appreciation of the validity of the German cause in the Foreign Office was limited: Dallas alone had reservations: on the communication of 26 April 1883 from Count Münster, the German ambassador, Dallas wrote "The Germans seem to me to make out a very plausible case". However, the Foreign Office was given warning that the question was an issue over which Bismarck was becoming irate: on 28 April 1883, Granville noted that Count Bismarck had specifically called his attention to the question; Ampthill, on 9 May 1883, stated that Bismarck had expressed great disappointment at the small amount of interest which the British government had given to it; in a private letter of the same day, Ampthill noted: "Bismarck is said to feel strongly in the matter and to intend to press those claims steadily, so as to show Germany that he can protect German interests all over the world."

That Bismarck was becoming impatient can be seen by the fact that Count Münster had been instructed on 16 April 1883 to "express a hope that H.M.G. in return for services rendered to England by Germany on other questions would take the legitimate wishes of the German Government on this question into favourable consideration". In fact, Count Münster made no such comment to Granville, but the German persistence appeared to have had some effect, for Ashley, the parliamentary under-secretary at the Colonial Office, told Count Münster that the government would have no objection to the suggestion of a mixed commission, even if it were impossible to reverse the final decisions of the Land Claims Commission. However, the official reply from the Colonial Office was a blunt refusal to contemplate a mixed commission.[29]

Bismarck's patience was running out: he complained at being passed on to the Colonial Office. That department's refusal in December 1883 to yield an inch coincided with Bismarck's increasing suspicion of Britain. The developments of early 1884 reinforced his view that Britain met his complaints "not only with indifference but with severity and deliberate injustice".[30]

The problem with regard to Fiji was that there was no unilateral action that Bismarck could take, unlike the position in Southwest Africa or the Cameroons. He was, in a sense, dependent on British co-operation. The difficulty was that the legal arguments used by the two sides shared no common ground, and the Colonial Office argument that the Germans had nothing to complain about brooked no dispute. Bismarck, as the complainant, had therefore to resort to extra-legal tactics, and in default of a willing co-operation he was prepared to force that co-operation. The main charge that can be levelled against the Foreign Office is that it did not insist on being more accommodating earlier. In March 1884, Ampthill warned that Bismarck was faced with a General Election "in which the Opposition may raise the popular cry of Colonies for Germany" Unless a mixed commission was granted, "We must make up our minds to a phase of ill humour on the part of the Chancellor, whose sensitiveness has become proverbial". On 8 April 1884, a quite specific threat was received from Count Münster: it was hoped that the British government would stop viewing the question solely in the context of colonial interests, and begin to look to "political considerations". Count Münster's instructions were even more explicit: "an unfriendly and in our view unjust treatment of our subjects must necessarily react on our political relationship towards England".[31]

Dallas immediately realized that the question had taken on a different complexion: "The German Government hold very tenaciously to their views and it might possibly be advisable from motives of policy to endeavour to find some means of satisfying them." Pauncefote was ambivalent: "As a question of international law, the complaint is inadmissable. But there is something to be said on grounds of international comity".[32]

A conference ensued, involving Pauncefote, Granville, Derby, and Count Münster. It revealed the partial control which Granville exerted over foreign relations at such a crucial time. Contrary to W. P. Morrell's views, Granville was most unwilling to oppose Germany. It was Derby who proved something of a block. Pauncefote, ever legalistic, shared Derby's doubts that concessions to German complainants would raise difficulties with British and American settlers.[33] The Colonial Office, with no clear lead from the Foreign Office, had failed to realize the full significance in political terms of the 8 April 1884 dispatch from Count Münster. For whereas the Foreign Office appreciated that Bismarck was irritated about the question, there was still an incomplete awareness that Bismarck was determined to have a full settlement of German land claims, whatever the Colonial Office's and Pauncefote's legal arguments. For the first time, a Foreign Office official drafted the reply, yet its actual terms continued to uphold the legalistic rejection of German demands: the British government was prepared to re-examine German claims and, if necessary, refer them to a mixed commission. This was a defeat for the Foreign and Colonial Offices in that they had had to retreat from the position that no re-examination was allowable. But the Colonial Office communication enclosing a memorandum removed all possibility that such a reply to the German government would serve to placate an increasingly distrustful Bismarck. Essentially it consisted of a defence of the legal system used, concluding that a re-investigation was unnecessary. Pauncefote defiantly wrote on the Colonial Office letter: "We shall see how far the German Government will be able to substantiate their complaints."[34] Whitehall had still not realized that Bismarck intended to exploit his strong diplomatic political position in his attempts to gain his point in colonial peripheral disputes.

This slowness to appreciate the reality of Bismarck's change of mind can be attributed to the assumptions of Whitehall. It was accepted that Anglo-French relations at the periphery were ones of conflict. But not so Anglo-German ones. It was inconceivable to the Foreign and Colonial Offices that any such Anglo-German dispute could have any lasting importance. All the more then did it come as a shock when, contrary even to the pattern of Anglo-French colonial rivalry, Bismarck began to associate peripheral conflicts with political issues. The latter days of June 1884 radically altered the officials' conceptual framework for dealing with such Pacific problems. On 7 June 1884, Bismarck categorically rejected the offer of 9 May 1884. Herbert Bismarck laid bare the weakness of Granville's diplomatic position: "While Prince Bismarck still entertained the same friendly feeling towards H.M.G. and was desirous of supporting their policy in Egypt, His Highness thought it right that I should be warned that ... with the best wishes he felt he should be unable to afford us the same friendly assistance as hitherto, unless he could give some satisfaction to public opinion on the subject." On 15 June 1884 Granville suspended action on the reply to the latest German complaints about Fiji. By 19 June 1884 Count Münster had told Granville that Bismarck accepted the "new" arrangements of a mixed commission to be appointed to examine and report on the Fiji land claims. Bismarck's tactical manoeuvre had forced the British government to accept that Egypt and the forthcoming conference required a complete retreat; a mixed commission had been granted, and with the almost simultaneous backdown over Angra Pequena and the Anglo-Portuguese Treaty, the success of Bismarck's tactics was resounding.[35]

The period from July to December 1884 can be seen as one during which Whitehall adjusted to the facts of a more active German colonial policy. It is characterized largely by Anglo-German estrangement, by the Colonial Office's reluctance to yield to German demands, and the Foreign Office's and cabinet's unwillingness to antagonize the German government. The failure to gain the expected goodwill from the agreement over Fiji and Angra Pequena can be seen partly as a result of the Foreign Office's inept handling of the Angra Pequena matter, as Aydelotte has shown, and partly because of the generally bad diplomatic climate between the two countries.[36] The Colonial Office's antagonism towards Germany had several outlets: one was its initial reluctance to accept the climb-down over Fiji. It wanted a strict definition of the extent of the concessions from the outset, given that these had been granted on political grounds in the first place. Pauncefote and Dallas sat on that demand. Although Pauncefote reacted angrily to the news of the German annexation over a large part of Southwest Africa—it was, he thought, rather an abrupt proceeding and "would seem to remove the objection to our taking the remaining part ... and also of the northeastern coast of New Guinea".—Granville and the Foreign Office in general sought to placate Germany. When the Colonial Office refused to allow New Guinea to be discussed in a commission, Granville used it as an excuse to offer Germany "large concession", stating that if informal discussions were started the British approach would be "in a large and liberal spirit".[37]

But all these efforts in this period of the "Cementing of the Franco-German Entente" were in vain. On 27 September 1884 two notes were delivered by Plessen: the first on Southwest Africa was "in all sense short", and the second on New Guinea led the cabinet to limit the Protectorate to the south coast of the island. Still the Colonial Office tried to press forward: on 15 October 1884 it suggested the establishment of a Protectorate over the south coast, but together with the d'Entrecasteaux Group and the coast up to Cape Vogel. The reason for this attempt lay in the fact that "there will be great and well-founded complaints from the Australian colonies if arrangements are now made such as would enable foreign Powers to establish themselves in close proximity to the British stations". When Granville finally returned the dispatch to the Foreign Office one month later, his department replied that they could not agree to the extension up the coast.[38] Bismarck had refused consistently to take account of the British government's difficulties with her colonies' own expansionist aspirations. But these difficulties were real enough: the variable of Australasian demands in this period had reached a tension point, at the same time that Bismarck rejected the notion that the government should pay attention to such demands in dealing with him.

Pacific affairs were at this stage overshadowed by the Berlin Conference, which had opened on 15 November 1884, and seen something of an Anglo-German rapprochement.[39] Although there is no evidence that Pacific issues impinged on the conference discussions, the presence of several senior civil servants was seen as a good opportunity to settle matters of Anglo-German dispute elsewhere. Meade, assistant under-secretary at the Colonial Office, who had once been Granville's private Secretary and still "enjoyed his special confidence", was entrusted with the job of attempting some kind of overall exchange of views with the German government.[40] On 8 August 1884, Granville and Count Münster had had an important talk on Pacific affairs. Granville's view was that it had been of a "general and preliminary character": in order to facilitate an agreement on their respective areas of interest, he would have liked "a more distinct idea of their views and further explanations as to particular islands and parts of islands referred to as being those where German trade is largely developed and is daily increasing". The Foreign Office had not yet received any such information. Meade's task was to obtain that information and try to defuse a series of embryonic problems before a real altercation blew up. Accordingly, on 7 December he had a talk with Busch, a senior German Foreign Office official, in which he presented a scheme "for a general settlement of all colonial questions affecting the two countries", of which only Pacific ones need concern us.[41] Meade's plan was for Britain to have non-Dutch New Guinea, including all the islands within twenty-five miles of the coast, and specifically Rook and Long Islands, and the Louisiade Archipelago. Germany was to have the New Britain Archipelago, New Ireland, York Island, and those islands where German trading concerns were established, recognizing at the same time British traders' rights, and agreeing that no convicts should be sent to the Pacific. There was also to be mutual agreement on the suppression of labour trade outrages. Samoa and Tonga were to be internationalized by mutual agreements to respect the independence of the Islands—New Zealand's pleas in this respect were thus ignored.

But the most significant part of his whole plan was the acknowledgement that France should be allowed the New Hebrides, as it was part of the New Caledonian system. This statement was savaged in the Commons on 12 March 1885 by Bourke and Wolff, the latter a member of the notorious Fourth party, the former having once been parliamentary under-secretary at the Foreign Office in the last Convervative government. It was Bourke who stated that it was "a monstrous piece of imprudence for a British Government to permit a statement to be made to Prince Bismarck that France was to be allowed to take the New Hebrides Group". This attack on Meade's proposal forced Ashley to state that the government would never agree to any foreign control of the New Hebrides without the agreement of the Australasian colonies.[42] The importance of Meade's scheme for the partition of the Pacific is that it was a tacit acknowledgement that Anglo-German affairs in the Pacific now impinged on Anglo-French conflicts in that area; and at this point we must therefore widen the discussion to include France. Anglo-French difficulties in the Pacific centred on the Leeward Islands and the New Hebrides. Until the German intervention in colonial affairs, these were simply Anglo-French questions, which had, as in West Africa, a rationale of their own. It is perfectly true that the French forward movement in West Africa in 1880 was paralleled in eastern Polynesia, with the annexation of Tahiti and the illicit Protectorate at Raiatea.[43] The question of the abrogation of the 1847 Declaration was thereupon linked to the attempt to secure a general settlement of the Newfoundland question. In 1881 negotiations broke down; between August 1881 and January 1884 there was something of a stalemate, partly as a result of Kimberley's disillusionment at the linking of the 1847 Declaration with Newfoundland, and partly because of French obstructionism (as it was largely considered in the Foreign Office) after the Egyptian crisis.[44] But the negotiations of early 1884 had resulted in an agreement in which it was acknowledged by Pauncefote that the French had given more than they received. There were two clouds on the horizon: one was the law officers' opinion that colonial legislation would be needed to implement the agreement: the precedent of 1857 loomed up. The second was pressure from the Australasians to secure Rapa if Borabora were given up.[45] On 28 May 1884 Ferry had called for his *quid pro quo*; no reply was sent to this request until the unofficial meetings recommenced in late September. When negotiations restarted, the British had two additional proposals: the Newfoundlanders had demanded two modifications, and in return for the total abrogation of the 1847 Declaration, Rapa was required. This was not seen as a major departure in Anglo-French relations in the Pacific. Indeed, the British commissioners were sure that, totally within the framework of this Anglo-French colonial rivalry, a settlement was near completion.[46] But when the negotiations began in November 1884, the German intervention had altered the perspective in dealing with Pacific problems.

Similarly, the negotiations over the New Hebrides became affected by the change in German colonial policy. There were two main issues in the dispute: the *Récidivistes* question, and possible French annexation in defiance of the 1878 and 1883 agreements. The relative importance of these two factors fluctuated according to circumstances. Lyons, the British ambassador to Paris, and Bell, the New Zealand agent-general who had important political contacts in the French government circles, were particularly active in attempting to persuade successive French governments to agree not to send any relapsed criminals to the Pacific.[47] The Foreign and Colonial Offices backed the Australasians on this issue. All the more, then, did Meade's remarks to Busch come as something of a surprise to the colonies.

The German intervention provided that variable which had hitherto been missing in all Anglo-French rivalries at the periphery. But the nature of the added variable is the important factor, if any attempt is to be made to answer the question of who were those responsible "for the enlargement of the game". The scramble was not simply caused by the arrival on the scene of other rivals. According to H. Brunschwig, "What was new was essentially the shift from dual rivalry to multinational rivalry". But this simple "multinationalization" is not enough to explain the phenomenom of the scramble. Indeed, Brunschwig goes on to talk about "This internationalization of Africa" and "the entry of black Africa into the realm of international affairs". This is the vital point.[48] Once Bismarck showed he was prepared to use his strong diplomatic position in Europe to force other countries, dependent on his support in the important high political questions of the day, to kotow to him, peripheral disputes were subordinated to the demands of foreign policy as a whole. Bismarck's determination to support German colonial enterprises, and his willingness to use political weapons to get his own way, created a different situation for those officials who were attempting to establish a satisfactory solution to other colonial rivalries in the Pacific. The developments of the summer months of 1884 had placed Britain in an isolated diplomatic position, but it should be noted that while, by August, Ferry and Bismarck had an arrangement over West Africa, the French had no illusions as to the meaning of the adoption of a colonial policy by Bismarck in the Pacific. C. W. Newbury has stated that French energies in the Pacific from 1880 onwards were geared towards the removal of those diplomatic constraints in the Leeward group and the New Hebrides. But those very diplomatic restraints were, it is important to note, bilateral not multilateral. There was nothing to stop Germany from annexing either group, possibly in agreement with Britain, and Bell appreciated that this was a factor in French official thinking at the time. Bell's analysis of the development of French policy in the Pacific was particularly acute. He thought that the French would push ahead in the New Hebrides in the same way as they had done in the Leeward Islands. Wary of the danger of being left with only New Caledonia and the Loyalties, while the rest was partitioned by Britain and Germany, and given the German annexations in

New Guinea and the neighbouring island groups, France would soon advance in the Pacific.

The influence of the German intervention on Anglo-French relations was stated quite explicitly by Meade in his talk with Busch: "Any arrangement which embraced the Pacific would have to be in some degree of a tripartite nature, as France has claims which would have to be considered".[49] The obverse of this argument was that any arrangement with France would have to be in some degree of a tripartite nature, as Germany might have interests as well. In fact, Anglo-French areas of rivalry in the Pacific were not areas of German interest. German trade in the Leeward Islands was not large, and since 1880 German companies had centred on Samoa and the more north-easterly islands in the Southwest Pacific. Unlike Fiji and Queensland, the Samoan labour requirements were met by a system which had been set up without any dependence on the New Hebrides. Germany certainly had no territorial ambitions there either. But as early as August 1883, Weber, alarmed at Australian pressure in Samoa and the increasing competition for labour in the New Britain Archipelago, had petitioned the Chancellor in order to make him realize that the whole question of German interests in the Pacific was at stake at that time. The Queensland annexation in New Guinea was but one part of the problem, for Anglo-French negotiations over the New Hebrides could lead to a partition whereby one power, that is, France, would get the New Hebrides, and the other would get New Guinea and the surrounding islands. Such a partition would, it was argued, be disastrous for German commerce in this area, for Germany had a vested interest, if a general one, in any Anglo-French dealings in the Pacific.[50] The distribution of coaling stations and strategic outposts on the route from the Panama Canal across the Pacific was a case in point. Once Bismarck became an open adherent of an active colonial policy, the German interest had to be considered in any Pacific dispute or negotiation, not necessarily because of any positive demand by Bismarck, but on account of the negative (but given the European situation) extremely important value of steering clear of "complications" with Germany. The Foreign Office had experience of such matters over Angra Pequena, the Fiji lands claims question and, at this stage, New Guinea. The fear of such complications was as important as this reality in stimulating the scramble.

One should not then look for direct German intervention in Anglo-French disputes in the Pacific. As has been said, Germany in fact had no real interest in the Leeward Islands or the New Hebrides. But Anglo-German and Anglo-French negotiations henceforth could not be entirely separated. While French claims had to be considered on the one hand, Bismarck's shadow was ever-present on the other. By raising the stakes, Bismarck had introduced a new dimension into the whole question of peripheral rivalry, and in so doing had provided the spark to the scramble for the Pacific. In the course of 1885 it looked to all those who came across Pacific problems in the Foreign Office as if the Pacific was about to be partitioned once and for all.

When negotiations re-opened over the Leeward Islands question, the French made no secret of their fear of German expansion in the Pacific. The argument that the French might simply have been playing a bargaining card in fact strengthens the hypothesis, for it can then be asserted quite accurately that it was an extremely good card to play. Pauncefote's reaction, indeed, was to hasten a settlement if possible, and grant the abrogation of the 1847 Declaration *in toto* before the Newfoundland legislature accepted the April Agreement, an argument which had been vigorously opposed by the Foreign and Colonial Offices earlier in 1884. Both departments in fact realized that the German intrusion involved a major departure from the essentially friendly Anglo-French rivalry. In the official communication from the Colonial to the Foreign Office (which the latter department had helped to draft) this realization was explicitly stated: the German government had indeed proposed a commission to look into Anglo-German interests in the South Seas. But the British interest in the Leeward Islands would cease only if Britain were ceded Papa by France, for thereby any German interests in the group would become a bilateral Franco-German affair. In other words, the two departments realized for their own best interests that it was important to settle the issue soon. If the question were not resolved, it was feared that "complications"[51] might arise.

The negotiations of the early months of 1885 established a set of terms at Whitehall which were regarded as acceptable. On 2 July 1885, Waddington, the French ambassador in London, presented the French proposals: France was, in effect, to take over those two areas which had been kept independent through the agreements and declarations of 1847, 1878 and 1883. Britain, in return, was to receive the French island of Rapa as compensation for the loss of Borabora, one of the Leeward Islands, which the Admiralty and informed opinion agreed was of great strategic importance, given its position and potential as a fine safe harbour. The French were also to agree that as well as granting certain commercial and religious safeguards to Britain, they would end the plans they had for the transportation of *Récidivistes* to the Pacific. Certainly, such an arrangement would have pleased Bell, with regard to New Zealand's interests in those areas where they clashed with French interests. New South Wales would similarly have been prepared to accept it. Certainly, also, the Foreign Office was thoroughly satisfied with this proposal, for the unofficial and official negotiations between Britain and France ever since mid-1884 had established just such a set of priorities.[52] The spur to partition created by the threat of German complications seemed to have pushed France and Britain to agreement.

Anglo-German negotiations were also nearing a conclusion. On 15 December, after the Foreign Office had received news of another petition from Malietoa, Count Münster asked Pauncefote to send a communication to the Samoan government disavowing any attempt at British annexation. Warburton, a clerk in the Consular Department, drafted a dispatch in which the governor of Fiji was asked to make such a communication. This dispatch was not sent until 16 February 1885, and Count Münster was only told on 13 March 1885. The reasons for this delay were, first, the association of Samoan and Tongan affairs with the New Guinea dispute, and second, the elevation of these disputes to cabinet and diplomatic level. On 16 December 1884 Warburton minuted that Herbert had told him that as far as the Colonial Office was concerned "they would not be sorry if Germany took Samoa and perhaps Tonga also". Derby wrote to Granville on the same day along similar lines. On 19 December 1884 the Foreign Office received Churchward's long account of the events of which Bismarck had complained on 1 December 1884. Far from revealing any British or colonial pressure on Malietoa, it showed that the antics of Weber and Stuebel had caused the difficulties. But neither Warburton nor Lister showed any inclination to alter the first draft of the dispatch for Fiji. The turnabout came when the Foreign Office got news of the German annexation in New

Guinea. Together with the publication of the White Book on Angra Pequena, it was too much. However, after Pauncefote's initially harsh response of "This is an extraordinary proceeding—we ought to take the rest", the Foreign Office was less hostile than the Colonial Office, which even contemplated throwing over the proposed commission.[53]

January and February 1885 were months of extreme aggravation between Britain and Germany. The White versus Blue Book controversy was one manifestation. Anglo-German disputes in the Pacific were affected. The cabinet now dealt with these questions, and Gladstone began to take an interest in them. The result was that Australasian pressure received scant attention. When Pauncefote minuted "It is silly of the Australians to hold such language .... This calls for no reply", he voiced the views of Granville, Gladstone and the Foreign Office in general.[54] Australasian interests were by no means ignored, but they were subordinated to the needs of foreign policy, for Bismarck now associated all his colonial disputes in dispatches whose tone was highly antagonistic and whose purpose was essentially to blackmail the British government over Egypt. It therefore required an overall thawing of relations to allow a settlement of each individual dispute. The Egypt question, Gordon's death and the Pendjeh crisis forced a détente from the British government. The realities of the political situation meant that, as Gladstone pressed, the Foreign and Colonial Offices would have to agree to yield everywhere at the periphery to prevent the counter-strokes at the diplomatic level.[55] Herbert Bismarck's arrival early in March 1885 signalled the détente. The backdown on New Guinea was arranged privately by Pauncefote and Krauel. Similarly, news from Samoa of the further antics of Weber and Stuebel were not allowed to interfere in the general move towards harmonious relationships. The Colonial Office reply to a New Zealand petition for annexation put the matter in perspective. There were three grounds for refusing: "the explicit understanding" with Germany; the extent of German interests in Samoa, and "the importance, no less to Australasia than to other parts of the Empire, of recognising frankly the good claims of a Great friendly Power". Indeed, given Thurston's recommendation that German interests in Samoa were predominant enough to warrant that power being allowed to annex Samoa on certain conditions, it was by no means inconceivable that when Germany asked for official British acceptance of a German annexation of the group, it would be granted.[56]

However, the proposed general détente failed: the Colonial Office rejected suggestions of a German annexation, and proposed British annexation instead. Anglo-French negotiations similarly collapsed when Waddington went back on his proposals of 2 July 1885. His Anglophile approach had led him to exceed his instructions and offer too much. When Rapa was withdrawn from the French proposals, the terms were deemed insufficient, and the wholesale division, which had seemed feasible since the end of 1884, faded.[57] The interests of the Australasians had prevented agreements which would have seen the general partition of the Pacific.

But once these negotiations had failed, Pacific affairs did not slip back into the anonymity of purely isolated disputes. Between mid-1885 and the end of 1887, when the pattern of partition was finally laid out, three developments took place: the Anglo-French convention of 1887, the Anglo-German Agreement of 1886 and the Samoan negotiations. These showed no change in their essential character from those of the period 1884–85.

Over the New Hebrides and Raiatea, it is perfectly true that Rosebery resented the idea of backing down to the French, particularly after the events of the spring of 1886. But after Salisbury returned to the Foreign Office, it was felt that the needs of foreign policy demanded a decrease in tension in relations with France. Despite the attacks of colonial ministers at the Colonial Conference, Salisbury felt that he had secured a satisfactory settlement in relation both to the demands of local interested parties and the needs of his *Weltpolitik*.[58]

A similar process was at work in Anglo-German disputes in the Pacific. The agreement of 1886 was a continuation of the negotiations of April 1885 between Thurston and Krauel, the German Foreign Office official with responsibility for Anglo-German colonial disputes. Matters were settled satisfactorily regarding the Marshalls, Gilbert, Ellice and Solomon Islands.[59] Together with the agreements with Spain over the Carolines and the Sulu Islands, this represented the pattern of partition of the northern corner of the Southwest Pacific. Also involved was the question of the neutral areas, in which French interests had to be taken into account. This was partly the result of the wish to "prevent France from having grounds for saying Germany and England have divided the South Seas without reference to her interests". The German government was opposed to involving the French by sending the French government the Anglo-German correspondence on the matter and asking France to join in an agreement on neutral regions. In fact, the Franco-German Agreement of 1885, which Thurston described as "an unfriendly attitude to British interests in the New Hebrides", ended official French interest in the Anglo-German disputes in the Pacific, apart from the episode of the revival of the French Tongan Treaty in 1887.[60]

This continued inter-reaction of Anglo-French and Anglo-German disputes was also partly caused by the sustained Australasian demand for satisfaction of their own aspirations. There was a flood of protests over New Hebrides from colonial governments, Presbyterian missions and colonial enthusiasts in the first half of 1885, the most important of which was Paton's article in the *Pall Mall Gazette*. Robertson, in a minute, revealed the cause and effect relationship between these protests and Meade's indiscretion: "These increasing numbers of protests against French control of the New Hebrides are the result of Meade's unofficial and, as far as I know, unauthorised references on this to Dr. Busch."[61] But the Foreign Office was becoming increasingly sceptical: "The time has gone by when Great Britain can assert a Munro [*sic*] Doctrine in every part of the world. We have settled ourselves nearly everywhere that is suitable to European colonisation and it is more than we can with propriety assert or safely claim that no other subjects of civilised Powers can found colonies, wherever our own may in some future time expand themselves."[62]

The Foreign Office's perspective gave diplomatic relations priority over Australasian interests. P. M. Kennedy has shown how, in the period 1885–99, Anglo-German relations in Samoa and Tonga were affected by and mirrored the demands of Anglo-German relations on the diplomatic level.[63] This is not to say that local interests were ignored: both Rosebery and Salisbury admitted the importance of the colonial stake in Samoa and Tonga, and if Rosebery was more reluctant than Salisbury to accept German demands for a German annexation of Samoa, Salisbury too demanded a *quid pro quo* in January 1886.[64] But the demands of foreign policy required certain concessions. The advice of Thurston was sound: "Our actual interests in Samoa are not sufficient to make it worthwhile being on unfriendly terms in respect of them with a neighbouring Power having such intimate relations with us as Germany." In fact, Pauncefote, Hervey, the Foreign Office's head of the Western Department, and Fergusson, the parliamentary under-secretary, had all reached the same conclusion earlier, and Salisbury was prepared to concede Samoa and try to secure Tonga.[65] When that *quid pro quo* failed to materialize, the scale of priorities necessitated agreement without it.[66]

The problem was now that the United States was not prepared to accept this neat Anglo-German division. In the same way that France had reacted against a supposed bilateral division of the Pacific, so did the United States. On 27 February 1886, Bayard instructed the United States minister in London to represent against such a division. The complaint was renewed on 20 March 1886. Thereafter the United States was intransigent in defence of its Samoan interests.[67] But it needs to be added that once the United States took a stand on Pacific issues, the process of embroilment could not be stopped. In 1887, Salisbury declined to restart the contentious negotiations over Samoa while Britain was still involved in lengthy discussions with the United States over the fisheries question. The reasoning behind this refusal was that it "might hamper our negotiations" if the United States were given the chance to take umbrage over the Anglo-German "agreement" over Samoa.[68]

In conclusion, it is most obvious that the nature of Anglo-German relations in the Pacific changed fundamentally in the period 1880–87. In his determination to get his own way after his adoption of a more active colonial policy, Bismarck had shown himself prepared to take the extreme step of mixing Pacific affairs with high policy matters. The result was that Anglo-German disputes in the Pacific, from being isolated, peripheral ones, which were regarded as being of no lasting significance, had become, by mid-1884, matters to be treated within the framework of the demands of *Weltpolitik*. This had a vital impact on the process of the partition of the Pacific, which, by 1887, had, in all its essentials, been completed. The simple intervention of another power into the field of colonial rivalry would not have led to this scramble. Instead it would merely have made it more difficult to solve the peripheral problems in the context of the local situation. By raising the level of these local disputes into the pattern of *Weltpolitik*, Bismarck's tactical manoeuvres not only changed the whole nature of Anglo-German relations in the Pacific, but also thereby provided the spark to the process of the scramble.

1. W.D. McIntyre, *The Imperial Frontier in the Tropics* (London, 1967). At this point I would like to thank D.K. Fieldhouse and Dr. A.F. Madden for their help in the writing of this article.
2. A great deal has been written on the Samoan affairs in the nineteenth century: S. Masterman, *The Origins of International Rivalry in Samoa: 1845–84* (London, 1934); J.W. Davidson, *Samoa mo Samoa* (Melbourne, 1967); J.W.Ellison, *The Opening and Penetration of Foreign Influence in Samoa up to 1880* (Oregon State monograph, Corvallis, Oregon, 1938); R.P. Gilson, *Samoa, 1830–1900: The Politics of a Multi–Cultural Community* (Melbourne, 1970); P. M. Kennedy, "The Partition of the Samoan Islands, 1898–1899," D. Phil. thesis, (Oxford, 1970); G.H. Ryden, *The Foreign Policy of the United State in Relation to Samoa* (Yale, 1928).
3. The promise of Maudsley's analysis of the Samoan situation in 1880 was: "European intervention has forced responsibilities on the Samoans which they have no means of adequately discharging." FO 58/171, Maudsley memorandum, 20/10/1880.
4. Ibid., Admiralty to FO, 31/7/1880; ibid., Wilson to Key, recd. at the FO, 31/7/1880; CO 226/6, Kimberley minute of 18/9/1880 on FO to CO, 7/9/1880.
5. FO58/171, Maudslev memorandum, 20/10/1880; FO58/225, CO to FO, 1/1/1887 enclosing Thurston to Stanhope, secret and confidential, 8/10/1886, FO58/168, Gordon to Granville, 31/7/1880, FO58/167, CO to FO, 17/7/1879, enclosing Gorrie to Beach, 28/4/1879; A. Ross, *New Zealand Aspirations in the Pacific in the Nineteenth Century* (Oxford, 1964), pp. 173–205; FO 58/225, CO to FO 10/1/1887, enclosing Thurston to Stanhope, 27/10/1886; FO58/169, Hill minute on Graves to Salisbury, 24/3/1880, CO 225/6, Mercer minute on FO to CO, 12/7/1880.
6. CO 225/5, Herbert and Kimberley minutes on FO to CO, 17/5/1880; FO 64/968, Granville to Brinken, 7/9/1880.
7. For an analysis of Baker's position and importance in this period in Tonga, see N. Rutherford, "Shirley Baker and the Kingdom of Tonga," (Ph. D. thesis, ANU Canberra, 1966), pp. 251–426.
8. FO 58/185, Des Voeux to Granville, 1/8/1883; ibid., Pauncefote note on draft, Granville to Derby, 2/11/1883; FO 58/177, Gordon to Granville, 15/7/1882.
9. FO 64/968, Granville to Brinken, 7/9/1880; FO 58/170, Admiralty to FO, 10/3/1880, enclosing Wilson to Admiralty, 5/1/1880, ibid., Granville minute on Admiralty to FO, 10/5/1880; FO 58/171, Admiralty to FO 8/6/1880; FO 58/ Lister minute on Gordon to Salisbury, 28/4/1880; FO 58/171, Hill memorandum of 31/7/1880; FO 58/169, Hill memorandum of 11/8/1880.
10. FO 58/168, Gordon to Granville, 13/9/1880; FO 58/199, Hill memorandum of 24/12/1884; FO 58/174, Graves to Granville, 22/1/1881; ibid., Granville to Walsham, 25/6/1884.
11. See P. M. Kennedy, "Bismarck's Imperialism: The Case of Samoa, 1880 –1890", *Historical Journal* 15 (June 1972); Ross, *New Zealand Aspirations*, pp. 145–156, 211–229; and R.C. Snelling, "British Policy towards Australian and New Zealand Ambitions in the Pacific, to 1919" D.Phil. thesis, Oxford, (1972) pp. 21–22 and especially p. 32.

12. H.U. Wehler, "Bismarck's Imperialism 1862–1890", *Past and Present*, no. 48 August, (1970); H. A. Turner, "Bismarck's Imperialist Venture: anti–British in Origin?", R. Gifford and W.R. Louis eds; *Britain and Germany in Afrika*, Yale/London (1967); P.M. Kennedy, "German Colonial Expansion in the Late Nineteenth Century: Has the 'manipulated Social Imperialism' been Ante–Dated?", *Past and Present*, no. 54. (February, 1972).
13. M.C. Jacobs, "The Colonial Office and New Guinea, 1874–84", *Historical Studies, Australia and New Zealand*, vol. 5 (May 1952); D. Scarr, *Fragments of Empire* (Canberra, 1967), p. 132.
14. FO 64/1144, Lyons to Granville, 7/7/1883; W.L. Langer, *European Alliances and Alignments, 1870–1890* (New York, 1950), pp. 217–50; FO 64/1144, Sanderson note of 28/5/1883, and Granville's minute on Pauncefote's note of 14/6/1883.
15. See Kennedy, "Bismarck's Imperialism", p. 270; FO 64/1144, Staveley, Pauncefote and Granville minutes on CO to FO, 18/6/1883, and Lister to Herbert, 21/5/1883. (These dispatches and letters were collected together on Granville's order: FO 64/1149, Hervey Note of 7/2/1885.)
16. See Jacobs, "The Colonial Office and New Guinea", pp. 112–14.
17. FO 27/2700, CO to FO, 8/3/1884, enclosing CO to commissioners, 8/3/1884.
18. See Scarr, *Fragments of Empire*, pp. 115–27; and O.W. Parnaby, *Britain and the Labor Trade in the Southwest Pacific* (Durham, NC, 1964) pp. 176–79.
19. Kennedy, "Bismarck's Imperialism", p. 266. For a detailed analysis of German labour recruitment and labour–trade policy, see S.G. Firth, "*German Recruitment and Employment of Labourers in the Western Pacific before the First World War*" D. Phil.thesis, Oxford, (1973), especially pp. 24–32; also P. Corris, "Blackbirding in New Guinea Waters", *JPH* 3 (1968).
20. FO 58/192, Plessen to Granville, 4/9/1883; FO 58/193, Plessen to Granville, 13/9/1884; Turner, "Bismarck's Imperialist Venture", pp. 53–62.
21. FO 58/192, FO to CO, 24/9/1883; ibid., CO to FO, enclosing Derby to Thurston and Derby to Kennedy, 8/3/1884; ibid., CO to FO, 27/6/1884, and Anderson and Pauncefote minutes thereon.
22. See D.J. Routledge, "Mr. Lundon in Samoa, 1883–85", *Historical Studies, Australia and New Zealand*, 11 (1964); Kennedy, "Bismarck's Imperialism':,pp. 267–68; for an examination of Churchward's statements, see Firth, "German Recruitment", pp. 62–66.
23. FO 58/185, Admiralty to FO 3/9/1883, and FO to CO, 12/9/1883; FO 58/188 Thurston to Granville, 28/1/1884, enclosing Churchward to Thurston, 6/12/1883.
24. Ross, *New Zealand Aspirations*, pp. 141–48; FO 58/199, CO to FO, 23/2/1884, enclosing Des Voeux to Derby, enclosing Thurston to Des Voeux, 1/12/1883; ibid., Anderson and Lister minutes thereon.
25. FO 58/189, Admiralty to FO, 7/3/1884; FO 58/188, Thurston to Granville, 28/1/1884; FO 58/199, CO to FO, 27/5/1884, and Hill memorandum of 5/826.
26. See W.O. Aydelotte, *Bismarck and British Colonial Policy–the Problem of South–West Africa, 1883–85* (Philadelphia, 1937).
27. W.P. Morrell, *Britain in the Pacific Islands* (Oxford, 1960), pp. 378, 388–89; J.K. Chapman, *The Career of Arthur Hamilton Gordon, 1829–1912* (Toronto, 1964), pp. 202–11; FO 5/2537, CO to FO, 21/8/1880, enclosing Gordon to Kimberley, 25/5/1880; ibid., Lowell to FO, 27/10/1880.
28. FO 64/1107, Münster to Granville, 1/7/1882; ibid., Ampthill to Granville, 9/5/1883; FO 64/1108, Münster to Granville, 8/4/1884.

29. FO 64/1107, Dallas minute on Münster to Granville, 26/4/1883, and Granville minute on CO to FO, 26/4/1883; Ampthill to Granville, 15/3/1884, in E. Fitzmaurice, *The Life of Lord Granville*, 2 vols (London, 1906), 2:338; FO 64/1108, Hatzfeldt to Münster, 16/4/1883, and Münster to Hatzfeldt, 2/5/1883, both enclosed in Malet to Granville, 28/1/1885; FO 64/1107, CO to FO, 19/2/1883.
30. FO 64/1107, Münster to Granville, 18/10/1883; Turner, "Bismarck's Imperialist Venture", p. 65.
31. Ampthill to Granville, 15/3/1884, in Fitzmaurice, *Granville*, 2:339; FO 64/1108, Münster to Granville, 8/4/1884; Morrell, *Britain in the Pacific*, p. 390.
32. FO 64/1108, Dallas minute on Münster to Granville, 8/4/1884, and Pauncefote note of 14/4/1884.
33. See Langer, *European Alliances*, chap. 9; R. Robinson and J. Gallagher, *Africa and the Victorians* (London, 1961), pp. 138–44; A.J.P. Taylor, *The Struggle for Mastery in Europe*, 1884–1918 (Oxford, 1954), chap. 13; Morrell, *Britain in the Pacific*, p. 391; FO 64/1109, Münster to Hatzfeldt, 10/4/1884, enclosed in Malet to Granville, 28/1/185; FO 64/1108, Pauncefote note of 14/4/1884.
34. Ibid., Pauncefote draft, in FO to CO, 8/5/1884; ibid., CO to FO, 8/5/1884; ibid., Pauncefote minute on CO to FO, 29/5/1884.
35. Ibid., Granville to Ampthill, 14/6/1884; FO 64/1102, Pauncefote note of 15/6/1884, and Granville to Ampthill, 19/6/1884. For the Angra Pequena episode, see Aydelotte, *Bismarck and British Colonial Policy*, p. 96; for the Anglo–Portuguese episode, see S.E. Crowe, *The Berlin West Africa Conference* (London, 1942), pp. 23–33.
36. Ibid., pp. 34–71; and Aydelotte, *Bismarck and British Colonial Policy*, chap. 6.
37. FO 64/1108, CO to FO, 10/7/1884, with Dallas and Pauncefote minutes thereon; FO 64/1103, Pauncefote minute of 16/8/1884; FO 64/1144, Granville to Plessen, 25/9/1884.
38. Crowe, *Berlin Conference*, chap. 6; FO 64/1103, and FO 64/1144, Plessen to Granville, 27/9/1884, with Lister minute on former; FO 64/1145, CO to FO, 15/10/1884; ibid., Pauncefote minute on CO to FO, 20/11/1884.
39. Crowe, *Berlin Conference*, pp. 72–77, 95–104.
40. Fitzmaurice, *Granville*, 2:372.
41. FO 64/1144, Granville to Ampthill, 9/8/1884; FO 64/1147, Meade to Granville, 13/12/1884.
42. The *Times*, 1/3/1885.
43. See J.D. Hargreaves, *Prelude to the Partition of West Africa* (London, 1963). For the interpretation of the French forward movement, see C.W. Newbury and A.S. Kanya–Forstner, "French Policy and the Origins of the Scramble for West Africa", *Journal of African History* 10 (1969).
44. See F.F. Thompson, *The French Shore Problem in Newfoundland: an Imperial Study* (Toronto, 1961).
45. FO 27/2700, CO to FO, 8/3/1884, enclosing law officers to CO, 3/3/1884, and CO to commissioners, 8/3/1884.
46. FO. 27/2701, Lyons to Granville, 28/5/1884; FO 27/2702, CO to 2/8/1884, enclosing CO to commissioners, draft, and commissioners to CO, 24/7/1884.
47. Childers and Rosebury were also very much involved and interested in the question of the *Récidivistes*. For Lyon's attitude, see Newton, *Lord Lyons, a Record of British Diplomacy* (London, 1913), p. 373.
48. See J. Stengers, "L'Imperialisme coloniale de la fin du XIX Siecle: myth ou realité", *Journal of African History 3* (1962); H. Brunschwig, "Conclusion", in P. Gifford and W.R. Louis eds, *France and Britain in Africa* (Yale/London, 1971), pp. 404–5.

49. Crowe, *Berlin Conference*, p. 63., C.W. Newbury, "Aspects of French Policy in the Pacific, 1853–1906", *Pacific Historial Review* 27 (1958); Ross, *New Zealand Aspirations*, pp. 213, 217; FO 64/1147, Meade to Granville, 13/12/1884.
50. FO 64/1147, Hatzfeldt to Münster, 2/8/1884, enclosing Promemoria, enclosed in Malet to Granville, 7/2/1885; ibid., Weber to Stuebel, 6/8/1883.
51. FO 27/2703, CO to FO, 22/11/1884, with Robertson and Pauncefote minutes thereon; FO 27/2700, CO to FO, 8/3/1884.
52. FO 27/2766, Salisbury to Walsham, 2/7/1885; FO 27/2702, CO to FO, 24/6/1884, and same to same, 24/7/1884, enclosing Admiralty to CO, confidential, 14/7/1884; Ross, *New Zealand Aspirations*, pp. 211–12.
53. FO 58/199, Granville to Malet, 19/12/1884; ibid., Warburton draft, and Warburton minute of 16/12/1884; M.C. Jacobs, "The Colonial Office and New Guinea", p. 117; FO 58/199, Churchward to Granville, 11/11/1884, wth Lister and Warburton minutes thereon; FO 64/1145, Admiralty to FO, 17/12/1884, and Malet to Granville, tel. of 19/12/1884; The *Times*, 13/12/1884; FO 64/1105, Malet to Granville, 13/12/1884; FO 64/145, Pauncefote minute on Malet to Granville, tel. of 19/12/1884; ibid., CO to FO, 31/12/1884; FO 58/19 CO to FO, 31/12/1884.
54. FO 64/1145, Granville minute on CO to FO, 29/152/1884; S. Gwynn and G.M. Tuckwell, *The Life of Sir Charles W. Dilke,* 2 vols. (London, 1917), 2:80–84; A. Ramm, *The Political Correspondence of Mr. Gladstone and Lord Granville, 1876–86*, 2 vols. (Oxford, 1962), 2: 309, 330–33; FO 64/1145, Pauncefote minute on CO to FO, 29/12/1884. For Gladstone's views on the general question of foreign Powers setting up colonies near British colonies, see A.B. Cooke and J.R. Vincent, *Lord Carlingford's Journal* (Oxford, 1971), p. 47; and D.W.R. Bahlman, *The Diary of Sir Edward Walter Hamilton, 1880–1885* (Oxford, 1972), p. 761.
55. See M.C. Jacobs, "Bismarck and the Annexation of New Guinea", *Historical Studies, Australia and New Zealand* 5 (November 1952), 25; Ramm, *Gladstone and Granville*, 2:343.
56. FO 64/1149, Granville to Münster, 16/3/1885, and Krauel to Pauncefote, 19/3/1885; FO 64/1150, FO to CO, 21/4/1885, and Granvilie to Münster, 25/4/1885; FO 58/200, Churchward to Granville, 27/1/1885, 28/1/1885 and 4/2/1885; FO 58/207, CO to FO, 2/4/1885; FO 58/201, Thurston to Granville, 29/4/1885.
57. FO 58/203, CO to FO, Immediate, 7/8/1885; FO 27/2766, Salisbury to Lyons, 8/7/1885.
58. For Salisbury's attitude to the French in the New Hebrides, see Crewe, *Lord Rosebery,* 2 vols. (London, 1931), 1:268; and Lady Gwendolen Cecil, *The Life of Robert, Marquis of Salisbury*, 4 vols. (London, 1921–32), 4: 51–52.
59. FO 64/1152, Malet to Granville, tels. of 6/4/1886 and 10/4/1886.
60. This idea of involving the French in the Anglo–German negotiations was a constant in the period from May to the end of 1885, as the documents in FO series 27, 58 and 64 show.
61. FO 27/2755, *Pall Mall Gazette*, 5/1/1885, and Robertson minute on Rogers to Gladstone, 7/2/1885.
62. FO 58/219, Ferguson memorandum of 27/11/1886.
63. See P.M. Kennedy, "Anglo–German Relations in the Pacific and the Partition of Samoa, 1885–1899", *Australian Journal of Politics and History*, 17 (April 1971).
64. For Rosebery's attitude, see especially FO 343/2, Rosebury to Malet, 17/3/1886, in which he states that in return for a German annexation of Samoa a *quid pro quo* would be needed, for example the Northeast of

New Guinea, which was absolutely worthless but would be a satisfaction to Australian feeling. In January 1886 Salisbury also asked for a *quid pro quo*.

65. FO 58/225, CO to FO, 1/1/1887, enclosing Thurston to Stanhope, secret and confidential, 8/10/1886; FO 58/205, Hervey and Pauncefote notes; FO 58/211, Pauncefote minute of 16/3/1886 on Malet to Rosebury, 11/3/1886; FO 58/219 Ferguson memorandum of 27/11/1886.
66. The Colonial Office had been very reluctant to accept the proposed agreement with Germany over Samoa: FO 58/219, CO to FO, 23/11/1886; but in the face of Foreign Office insistence, as well as Churchill's and Salisbury's support for the latter department, they had to accept: FO 58/219, Salisbury, Churchill and Stanhope to Pauncefote, tels. of 21/12/1886; but it should also be noted that the Foreign Office still clung to the idea of securing Tonga: e.g., FO 58/223, Pauncefote minute on CO to FO, 14/10/1887; FO 58/231, Salisbury minute on Mitchell to Salisbury, 28/8/1887; and Thurston also retained his hopes; FO 58/231, CO to FO, 19/9/1887, enclosing Thurston to Stanhope, 13/9/1887.
67. See Ryden, *Foreign Policy of United States*, pp. 302–404; FO 83/1084, Phelps to Rosebury, 25/3/1886; FO 58/211, West to Rosebery, 20/3/1886.
68. FO 58/223, Salisbury minute on CO to FO, 14/10/1887.

5

PAUL M. KENNEDY

# Germany and the Samoan Tridominium, 1889-98: A Study in Frustrated Imperialism

In the ten years between 1889 and 1899 the Samoan Islands were administered by three great powers, Britain, Germany and the United States, through a unique tripartite system of government. This unusual experiment in shared political control is worthy of attention in itself, occurring as it does in an age when most of the previously unclaimed territory of Africa and the Pacific was falling under the exclusive possession of one or other of the imperialist nations. Certainly, as their reports indicate, most of the officials and statesmen responsible for the administration of the Samoan tridominium recognized its peculiar situation and groaned at the special problems it presented. Nowhere could the awareness of this be seen more clearly than in Germany, where government and public alike came to regard it with increasing frustration throughout the 1890s. It is the intention of this paper to examine those ten years of mixed control in Samoa as seen through German eyes, and at the same time to illustrate the general rise of imperialist sentiment in Germany during the final decade of the nineteenth century.

That this aberration of tripartite rule should have been created at all was a matter of considerable resentment and regret to many Germans, who had looked upon Samoa for decades as the "pearl of the South Seas" and as the natural centre of their economic and political activities in the Pacific. It was as early as 1857 that the famous Hamburg firm of J. C. Godeffroy & Sohn had established a trading depot in the Samoan capital of Apia on the main island of Upolu. Under the drive of its successive managers, August Unshelm and Theodore Weber, the firm was quickly built up to be the largest in the Pacific, with Apia becoming a major entrepôt for trade in oil, trepang, tortoise-shell, pearl and copra. From 1865 onwards, Germans also secured and developed large amounts of land in the group for plantation purposes. Although European mining speculations caused the Godeffroy company's collapse in 1879, its Samoan interests were secured by the formation of the Deutsche Handels– und Plantagen-Gesellschaft der Südsee-Inseln zu Hamburg (hereafter DHPG), which continued to dominate commerce in the Southwest Pacific, its chief rivals being other German firms rather than English ones.[1]

Although secure commercially, the German traders encountered an increasing number of difficulties in Samoa in the early 1880s. The DHPG was threatened by the drying up of labour supplies from New Britain and New Ireland, upon which their plantations so desperately depended, by the vigorous incursion of recruiting vessels from Fiji and Queensland. In addition, a strident agitation for annexations in the Pacific arose in the Australasian colonies, with Queensland going so far as to attempt to acquire New Guinea, while New Zealand agitators sought to persuade the Samoans to petition for annexation to Great Britain. Samoa itself was plagued with native rivalries between the two leading families, Tupua and Malietoa, with the head of the latter, Malietoa Laupepa, in uneasy possession of the so-called "kingship". However, his Anglophile proclivities, inefficient government, and absolute inability to prevent depredations upon the German plantations alienated the Godeffroy manager, Weber, and the German consul, Stuebel, and in November 1884 they attempted to eliminate both the internal and external threats to their interests by forcing Malietoa to sign a treaty which turned Samoa into a de facto German protectorate.[2]

Although this action came as a surprise to the German government, Bismarck was inclined to abandon his earlier negative stance towards the acquisition of Samoa, not only because of the urgings of the DPHG but also because he was in the midst of establishing a colonial empire in Africa and New Guinea to protect German commerce there and to secure his domestic position. Nevertheless, while urging Stuebel to defend German rights and interests in Samoa, the chancellor could not sanction the immediate annexation of the group because of a further factor—the existence of British and American treaty rights. All three powers had individually secured privileges there from the native government in the years 1878–79 and this obviously prevented any unilateral annexation without due consultation with the other interested nations. In fact, following the signing of these treaties and the joint Apia municipality treaty of 1879, it would scarcely be an exaggeration to say that Samoa was under the tripartite control of the powers from that time onwards, although it was admittedly a vague and very irregular form of supervision, and one that was much disliked by the home governments themselves. Diplomatic niceties and a respect for treaties necessitated an approach to London and Washington before Berlin could establish controls in Samoa, therefore.

The British government offered no great obstacle to Bismarck's plan. Despite pressure from the Australasian colonies and although at first seeking (unsuccessfully as it turned out) to obtain compensation in the form of the Tongan Islands, Lord Salisbury required German diplomatic support in the more important Egyptian and Eastern questions, and to obtain this he agreed to a German "mandate" for Samoa in a secret treaty of 23 April 1887.[3] On the other hand, the United States government, advancing the right to uphold the independence of the group by virtue of the American-Samoan treaty of 1878, resolutely opposed the solution desired by Berlin. While Bismarck endeavoured for several years to persuade the State Department to abandon its stand, the situation in the islands further deteriorated. The de facto German rule by that country's consular and naval officials provoked strenuous reactions from the settlers of other nationalities and from the Samoans themselves, which even the deposition of Laupepa and his replacement by the puppet regime of Tamasese Tupua could not quell. A native rising at the end of 1888 under a chief named Mata'afa, and the ambush of a German naval landing party, led to a proclamation of annexation by the enraged consul, Dr Knappe, at which the American public and government, which had been watching these developments with growing disquiet, vigorously criticized Berlin, and appeared to be moving towards a showdown on the issue.[4] Bismarck, by this stage completely disenchanted with colonialism, and aware that both his domestic and foreign policies were near to collapse, could hardly afford to call the American bluff, and swiftly abandoned Germany's claims to any special predominance in the group. Seeking solely to extricate himself from this irritating problem, he invited the other two governments to partake in a conference in Berlin which would restore law and good government in Samoa on the basis of the equality of all three powers concerned.[5]

The elaborate and formal system of tripartite rule was thrashed out by the delegates in a series of meetings in the late spring of 1889, and on 14 June the Final Act of the Berlin Samoan Conference was signed. Under it the ageing Malietoa was to be restored to the throne; the purchase of land by whites, and the sale of arms and intoxicating liquors to natives was forbidden; all land disputes were to be settled in a special court; a variety of taxes were to be imposed to raise revenue for the Samoan government; the municipality of Apia would be ruled by a council of six members and would be chaired by a president who would also act as "adviser" to the king, particularly in financial matters; and the extraterritorial jurisdiction of the consuls was to be maintained, but on the other hand the post of chief justice was to be created as final appellate judge in non-national cases, and as "umpire" in the case of future monarchical succession disputes where the natives themselves could not agree.[6]

By any criterion, the establishment of the tridominium was an advance upon the four years of chaos and internal rivalry which had preceded it. In the long term, however, it was an unsatisfactory settlement. Despite the first article of this act, which was "A declaration respecting the independence and neutrality of the islands of Samoa", the powers had reduced that independence to nothing. They had kept separate the key township of Apia; they had retained consular jurisdiction outside the municipality; they had imposed a king of their own choosing upon the Samoans and ignored the fact that by 1889 the majority supported Mata'afa; they had given this king a supervisor of revenues and a permanent "adviser"—controller might be a better word; they had created a Supreme Court to be the final body in all appeals, including contested elections to the kingship which the natives themselves could no longer settle in their customary way; they had, upon insufficient evidence, decreed a tax system which was soon to prove to be a gross miscalculation; they had ignored all dubious land sales before 1879; and by establishing a monarch bereft of all strength—he had to call upon the three powers if he required military aid—they had made the kingship into a figurehead, for the Samoans themselves to scorn. Moreover, the twin rivalries, those between the native factions and those between the various white nationalities, had in no way been eliminated, and could indeed flourish in a system which relied for its efficacy upon so many balancing influences and jurisdictions.

Some of these difficulties were appreciated; others emerged only later. But even when the weaknesses were seen at the conference, the delegates either thought them to be the best of a number of bad solutions, or were often reluctant to tackle them at all. As Herbert Bismarck remarked during the discussions, the whole thing "was the result of a series of compromises and that, if he attempted to dislodge a brick, others might do the same and the foundations might be shaken".[7] For him and for his father, the main task had been to mend an American-German quarrel rather than to provide a lasting solution to the Samoan question. Indeed, due to diplomatic exigencies the chancellor had completely reversed his earlier policy of affording full protection for German interests in the group; when, in March 1889, the DHPG pleaded once again for rule by Germany, Bismarck savagely minuted "the old song!", and later in the year he willingly forwarded to the United States the news that the firm would sell out if a suitable offer for it were made.[8]

Yet although the chancellor was willing to abandon Germany's colonial strivings for the sake of his European policy, many of his countrymen were not. Public opinion, which had long shown an interest in Samoa as the place of Germany's first overseas ventures, and had been greatly moved by the death of her sailors in the fighting of 1888, and by the loss of the German warships in the famous hurricane of 1889, was now led by a monarch who displayed a similar interest. Within a year of the signing of the Final Act, Bismarck had been replaced in office by men whose first major move in the colonial field was to conclude the Heligoland-Zanzibar treaty with Britain, an act which provoked much regret in Germany, and led to the founding of the extremely chauvinistic Pan-German League.[9] Bismarck himself had endured many attacks upon his policy of colonial retrenchment in the years 1888–89, although he was able to brush most of these aside[10]; but whether his successors, lesser mortals who were more sensitive to the charge that they were ignoring Germany's overseas interests, could withstand pressure was an open question.

If critics in Germany (and to a lesser extent in Britain and the United States) considered the 1889 Samoan settlement to be unsatisfactory, the inhabitants of the group regarded it as much more so; they, after all, had to live with this compromise arrangement, which they could easily perceive was nothing more than a collection of the various ideas upon which the powers had managed to agree. Nevertheless, the restoration of peace and the prospect of regular government was welcomed by all. By June 1889 the situation in the islands was slowly improving, though an immediate implementation of the act was impossible because nothing could be done *officially* until the United States Senate had discussed and ratified the agreement. In fact, the ratifications were not exchanged until 12 April 1890, much to German annoyance. While this prevented steps against the purchase of land, and other actions for which American citizens were not yet legally liable, the three governments felt justified in proceeding with the kingship decision. Unwilling to see Mata'afa enjoy the fruits of his victory in Samoa any longer, Germany requested that the consuls be instructed to recognize Malietoa as king unanimously, and to announce the decisions of the conference. As soon as the old monarch was restored to power, he should be informed of the clauses concerning land alienation, arms and liquor sales, etc. To speed his return, a German naval vessel had already left for the Marshalls to bring the king back to Apia.[11]

On 11 August 1889, Malietoa landed in Upolu. The captivity and journeys had greatly weakened the former ruler, and he willingly resigned the kingship to Mata'afa at a large native assembly, which met in early October. Bismarck, although reprimanding the newly returned consul, Stuebel, for his obsession about Anglo-American backing for this development, nevertheless became very uneasy at it and pressed Salisbury for his support, warning that Mata'afa's succession even to the vice-kingship would "render it impossible for the German government to ratify the Convention recently agreed to at Berlin".[12] Since nothing could have annoyed Salisbury more than a revival of the diplomatic squabbles over Samoa, the British consul was instructed to join his fellows in recognizing Malietoa as quickly as possible. Their proclamation to this effect was issued on 9 November. On 5 December Malietoa hoisted his flag and assumed control of the Samoan government, receiving at the same time the official recognition of the powers.[13] Faced with this unanimous stand by the signatory nations, the Samoans received these decisions quietly and the expected troubles did not occur.

Yet satisfying though this was for the relations of the powers, it did not greatly help the situation in Samoa. There the very negation of government existed; for while the pre-1889 system had been demolished by the Berlin Act, the new structure had not yet been raised in its place. Moreover, it was to take many months, even years in some cases, before the specific provisions for the better regulation of affairs in the group were carried out. Had the new structure been immediately set up in all its aspects, there would probably have been a readier acceptance of the scheme of government drawn up in Berlin. Instead, it was constructed piecemeal, which aroused the suspicions of the Samoans and the vitriolic criticism of the group's most famous resident, R. L. Stevenson.[14]

The chief justice, a Swedish judge named Conrad Cedercrantz, was not nominated until 1890; while the appointment of the German candidate for the presidency of the municipality, Baron Senfft von Pilsach, was not settled until December 1890, and he did not arrive in Samoa until May 1891. Until then, the newly elected municipal council could hardly function. Cedercrantz himself only assumed his post in Apia in the January of that year. Moreover, the British consul reported that the Samoan government had neither influence nor money, since the native districts were refusing to pay the capitation tax; and that the Supreme Court was not yet open and Cedercrantz was asking for an advance of money from the three powers to pay for a Samoan constabulary, without which little could be done.[15] Throughout the year matters continued to go from bad to worse. The chief justice quarrelled fiercely with the land commissioners over the latters' expenses, refused to pay any taxes upon his salary and then left for an eight-week tour of Fiji. The president adopted a dictatorial attitude towards the Samoan government, became involved in a quarrel over the use of German currency in the group, and, in October, resigned when he learnt that a German member of the municipal council had corresponded with the king without his knowledge. While these petty arguments were developing, Mata'afa moved away to Malie, where he was crowned king by his followers.[16] By the beginning of 1892, therefore, Samoa still lacked any form of peace, order and effective administration.

The three powers were acutely embarrased by the reappearance of difficulties which they had hoped the 1889 act had eradicated. Senfft's resignation was angrily declined by the

German government and he was urged to show co-operation, but the squabbles of the officials continued. The chief justice and the land commissioners still quarrelled about their respective powers, while the whole municipality complained when an attempt was made to take away the customs revenues from it and give them to the Samoan government; yet without this move, the native administration would be crippled by a lack of finances. Salaries, which consumed $28,520 from the budget, were in arrears, and taxes were unpaid. Senfft also clashed with the consuls. Moreover, action against Mata'afa was repeatedly postponed and Malietoa's prestige sank further. Faced with this chaos, the Americans proposed a further conference, which would modify sections of the act and perhaps abolish the post of municipal president altogether. Naturally enough, the German government opposed this reduction in their influence, and preferred instead to replace both the chief justice and president.[17] The internal reason for this attitude was made clear to the British ambassador, who was informed that "in view of the severe attacks in the Reichstag whenever the slightest opportunity was given to the opposition, it would be impossible to abstain from appointing a President of the municipality because to do so would be held to be weakness and abandonment of German interests".[18]

The new Chief Justice Ide did not arrive until the November of 1893, while President Schmidt assumed office on the penultimate day of that year. Only in the work of the Land Commission was an improvement gradually taking place. Suffering repeated delays due to the illness and absenteeism of the German and American members, the commission's inquiries only really got under way in 1893. Its task was enormous, with some 3,942 claims demanding investigation; and, as the British commissioner pointed out, the area claimed by the many applicants totalled 1,700,000 acres, which was "some 900,000 more acres than there is supposed to be acreage in Samoa".[19] By the end of 1894, after further delays and a great deal of work, the commission had finished. The findings can be summed up in the accompanying table.[20]

The result was a very gratifying one for the Germans, who had possession of most of the DHPG's lands confirmed, while seeing the extravagant claims of their rivals (including one Frank Cornwall, who claimed 414,000 acres in Savai'i) rejected.

**Table 1. Relationship between Acreage Claimed and Confirmed**

| Nationality | Acreage Claimed | Acreage Confirmed | Percentage Confirmed |
|---|---|---|---|
| German | 134,419 | 75,000 | 56 |
| British | 1,250,270 | 36,000 | 3 |
| American | 302,746 | 21,000 | 7 |
| French | 2,307 | 1,300 | 57 |
| Various | 2,151 | 2,000 | 95 |
| Totals | 1,691,893 | 135,300 | 8 |

On the other hand, the years 1893–94 also saw the outbreak of a native civil war, followed by the capture and deportation of Mata'afa. Despite the pleas of Malietoa's government, action by naval forces had been postponed throughout 1892, and the advent of the hurricane season again forced its delay until the spring of 1893. By that time, Mata'afa had unfurled his standard, rejected the warrants of the Supreme Court to come to Apia, and war had been officially declared. His main support now came from the powerful inhabitants of the Aana and Atua districts, who were traditionally opponents of the Malietoan house, and who had turned to Mata'afa after the death of Tamasese in 1891. Malietoa's forces then managed to defeat the rebels and drive them on to the small island of Manono. At that stage, a British warship arrived on the scene and joined two German vessels in "persuading" Mata'afa to surrender. The chief was soon taken away with some of his main supporters to the Union Islands, and thence to the Marshalls.[21] However, unrest among the Samoans was not crushed by these deportations and only the continual presence of warships prevented further serious disturbances.

The constant chaos in Samoa, with its inevitable consequences for German property and commerce, was immensely irritating to the men of the "new course" in Berlin and to their impulsive monarch. Pressed by political difficulties at home, they would take any reasonable opportunity to achieve control of the islands and thereby a diplomatic success to strengthen their internal position. Moreover, there was now much less fear of arousing American antagonism, for the Foreign Ministry was assured by successive secretaries of state in the early 1890s that the United States government regretted Bayard's previous policy, and privately desired to withdraw from the group when the time was ripe.[22] Even this proved to be too negative and slow a policy for the kaiser, though; learning in January 1893 of the annexation of Hawaii by the American minister there (temporarily as it turned out), he minuted "We must just so act in Samoa! It is a good moment."[23] Ambassador Hatzfeldt was asked to sound out Rosebery as to suggesting once again to Washington Salisbury's old idea of a Samoa-Tonga-Hawaii "split". However, reports from the United States indicated that any German action regarding Samoa would be frowned upon by Congress and, in any case, Rosebery's policy towards Hawaii "was to ignore the whole matter".[24] After attempting to secure an assurance of future British support for the German plan, Marschall encountered some reluctance in London and decided to let the matter drop, fearing that rumours of such discussions would annoy the United States just at a time when Germany was hoping for some tariff concessions from the incoming administration.[25]

By April 1894, American discontent at the tridominium became more open than before, and it seemed as if the German dream of gaining Samoa might come true. Their minister at Washington was again told by Gresham of America's private wish to withdraw, Cleveland had been critical of the tripartite rule in his December 1893 message to Congress, and even members of Senate were promising to get the question reviewed. All the signs were that America, while taking over Tutuila where it had rights to a naval station, might well step out of the remainder of the Samoan group.[26] Within a few days, Marschall had suggested a Samoa-Tonga deal to the British ambassador, and a week later he ordered Hatzfeldt to do the same at London. "The object of our policy there is the establishment of a German administration", the state secretary wrote, adding that "this would not only present a solution satisfying to our considerable local interests there, but it would mean a political triumph at home the effect of which should not be underestimated. As Your Excellency is aware, public opinion in Germany has occupied itself for years over the Samoan question and it would therefore be of great value to the Imperial Government to bring a final settlement of this affair in a manner according with German wishes".[27]

To Berlin's disappointment, the Liberal government refused pointblank to accede to the German wishes. A fear of provoking both New Zealand and the rising imperialist sentiment at home, gradual changes in the relative diplomatic position of Britain and Germany, and a whole series of disputes in the colonial sphere—all eroded London's desire to buy German support through concessions overseas.[28] Rosebery's own problems were of little concern to Marschall and Caprivi, however, who were forced to stand firm themselves because of the public agitation in Germany. When New Zealand inopportunely commenced a fresh newspaper campaign for the annexation of Samoa by London or Wellington, this provoked fear, some denunciations, and violent abuse from the German press. The *Weser Zeitung, Kölnische Zeitung*, and the official *Norddeutsche Allgemeine Zeitung* strongly denounced the idea, while the *Börsen-Courier* declared that the English press "by its hypocritical and overweening treatment of the Samoan question will not contribute to lessen the deep distrust which prevails towards England in Germany". The *Post* demanded the dispatch of a regiment to Samoa to protect German nationals and their property, and the colonial pressure groups commenced a large-scale campaign for annexation with the Pan-German League at their head.[29]

Moreover, throughout 1894 native disturbances on Upolu continued to plague the DHPG. Fresh conflicts between rival Samoan groups occurred, and although Malietoa's forces were again successful, this did not put an end to the troubles; by May, the civil war was renewed in a more formidable manner, for the late Tamasese's son (also called Tamasese) was now leading the Atua people against the government.[30] The white residents were believed to be threatened, the plantations once more suffered heavily, and Malietoa renewed his appeals for assistance, but the British and American governments remained cool to the idea of military action. Despite this, local Germans pressed most insistently for disarming the natives and for rigorously enforcing that control over the sale of arms and ammunition for which the Berlin Act had made provision.[31]

Faced with the possibility of further native disturbances, the hostility of the British to their wishes, and the rumours of possible action by New Zealand, certain circles in Berlin began to advocate a swift seizure of the group by a squadron of cruisers and a strong landing force. Pan-German and colonial pressure groups demanded such an action and the kaiser, influenced by his military advisers and by his wish for an exciting overseas policy, seems to have been attracted by the idea; but Caprivi, who intensely disliked colonial entanglements, was not, and he rejected the plan put forward by the colonial expert Dr Kayser for taking Samoa and presenting Britain with a *fait accompli*. Nevertheless, the navy continued its planning for operations to take over the group and disarm the natives, insisting that this could only be properly done if the German flag was hoisted, a protectorate declared, important buildings and all arms seized, and the group blockaded.[32] It is difficult to know whether this was to be done with the consent of the other two powers or not, since it was sometimes stated in the operations documents that there would be no hindrance from Britain or America, and yet the strength of the other two navies in the Pacific was also carefully calculated. Perhaps the idea was to suddenly seize the group and disarm the Samoans in the belief that the British and Americans would, although complaining, see the good side of this action and do nothing about it.[33]

With his opinions challenged by these more aggressive views, Caprivi sought Hatzfeldt's advice.[34] The ambassador replied in a long dispatch, suggesting that the best solution might be to seize the opportunity—offered by the recent Anglo-Belgian treaty over the Congo—to join up with France in Africa, and to make difficulties in Egypt. Hatzfeldt also suggested an alternative solution, but this section of his dispatch has been completely omitted from *die Grosse Politik*. The ambassador recommended that if German public opinion made action imperative, the cruiser squadron should go ahead and occupy Samoa. If the international circumstances were favourable to Germany, the British would probably swallow their pride and accept this as a *fait accompli*: "But if they will decline to come to an agreement, our task would then be to make it clear to them that we would consider as an unfriendly act any attempt to drive us out again and that, since we are not strong enough at sea, we would answer it by placing our entire influence completely at the disposal of England's foes, both in Europe and elsewhere."[35] Hatzfeldt did not hide from his superiors the fact that public opinion in Britain might push the weak Liberal government into decisive counter-measures, and he therefore advocated pressure in Egypt and the Congo as the first tactic, but should this prove fruitless and should internal political considerations make further delay impossible, then there would be nothing left to do but to adopt this more extreme measure.

It should be noted that it was the entire dispatch—and not just the first, published, part—which the kaiser found to be "Excellent. Exactly corresponds with my views and we must arrange our policy as recommended here, starting with the first way suggested—Egypt".[36] Planning for the seizure and pacification of Samoa therefore continued into the following year, although the operation was never implemented.[37] The reasons for its postponement and final abandonment are not hard to find. America's attitude to such an action was unpredictable and Washington was taking no further steps to withdraw. A British warship remained in the group and undertook some small joint actions with the two German vessels there. Finally, the British gave way over the Congo treaty, though with reluctance, and the tactic of pressure in Africa was preferred to a rash step in the Pacific. Nevertheless, these discussions indicated how far a German government, split internally and needing to recoup some of its lost popularity, might go should public opinion press it, and should the obstacles to the success of such a daring venture become less formidable. Indeed, at one stage in the quarrel Marschall wrote in his diary: "The Samoan question worries me. The reputation of the New Course depends upon it."[38]

The concern in Berlin to maintain German interests in Samoa was so great and the suspicion of England so deep that the Foreign Ministry refused to let German warships leave the area during the hurricane season, and ignored the navy's protests until the kaiser himself was persuaded to agree to a withdrawal.[39] In the following spring, however, German vessels were once more directed to Samoa, since, as the Foreign Ministry noted, the "previous intervention of the warships has only had a temporary influence upon the political situation".[40] But a remedy to the troubles remained impossible to achieve while the United States declined the German plan of searching all vessels for arms, and the German Admiralty preferred to act alone in pacifying the islands, in case it had to surrender operational control to a British or an American admiral.[41] The High Command, for its part, did not like the Samoan burden at all, and was particularly opposed to stationing warships there all the year round, insisting that "the expenditure of means for this purpose is far too great. In the current Budget year the activities of both cruisers of the Australia Station, whose crew maintenance takes 310 men (therefore almost the crew of a battleship) and who burden the maintenance funds by 414,000 Marks, have been *completely* absorbed by the rather small and still not very valuable Samoan Islands".[42]

Furthermore, the commander-in-chief of the Australia station felt it completely unnatural that his ships should act in favour of the pro-English Malietoa and that they were always being summoned by the United States consul (as the doyen), while that country never provided any vessels. In view of all these factors, the Foreign Ministry was by 1896 compelled to abandon its attempts to eliminate the native unrest.[43] Since the Samoan government was not strong enough to act by itself and Malietoa's health was deteriorating, the opposition party was left unmolested in the years following.

There was also little of encouragement to discover in the affairs of the white officials after 1893. Schmidt, as a former German vice-consul, already had many enemies in Apia, and quickly proved himself to be as capable as his predecessor of arguing with the chief justice.[44] He also provoked many objections, including those of the United States government, by trying to take control of the Samoan finances, and early in 1895 Malietoa petitioned for his removal. "The usual monthly bulletin of squabbles and paralysis of government in Samoa" was how one Foreign Office official described the consul's reports on these matters. Schmidt further annoyed Washington by assuming the chief justice's powers when that officer took a vacation. Even the German naval officers found him impossible to work with, while the white residents wanted his post abolished entirely.[45] Moreover, Ide himself clashed with the consuls over his assertion that he could attend political discussions. The American and German consuls also quarrelled over legislative matters.[46] By 1896 things were no better, for Schmidt attempted to get everything done in German, and the government of the group was almost non-existent: out of an anticipated capitation tax of $30,000 only $10 was collected. The only gleam of hope came with Schmidt's resignation, at which the German government quickly put forward a replacement candidate, having "just regard for the prevailing German interest in Samoa ... ".[47] No objections being raised to this by the other powers, a Dr Raffel was appointed as the next president. Soon afterwards Ide also resigned his post and was replaced by another American, William L. Chambers.

In view of the continuous chaos and trouble in the group, which naturally caused a decline in its trade and prosperity, all powers manifested great dissatisfaction with the system they had created. The American secretary of state, Gresham, publicly regretted that his country had not adhered to "the wise policy that had previously preserved us from such engagements as those embodied in the general Act of Berlin" while the British attitude was summed up by Buxton's minute that "This rotten little island gives more trouble than it is worth".[48] In Germany this frustration was mixed with a certain worry. The DHPG had lost 400,000 marks worth of goods and produce in the 1888–89 troubles, and was not in a very healthy position despite the managerial reorganization of 1890. The company operated at a loss in 1889, 1891, and 1892, and the profit of the following two years was solely due to better copra prices in Europe; but by 1895 and 1896 the bottom had dropped out of the market and a much smaller profit was made. The government-subsidized steamer service lost heavily in the early 1890s, too, and was withdrawn. The DHPG had also definitely surrendered their commercial predominance in Tonga to the British.[49] Moreover, while the German consul was worried about the growing influence of the London Missionary Society missionaries by 1895, the naval commander reported that the DHPG was being hard pressed by Australasian commercial rivals, and that English influence, in the form of more teachers, traders and shipping connections, was growing rapidly: as a sure sign of this, he mentioned that cricket had been re-introduced for the first time since it was banned by the Tamasese-Brandeis regime in 1888. Pointing out that the Reich had in the past twenty years spent in the region of 15 million marks in naval expenditure, solely for the protection of this now decrepit firm, the commander-in-chief urged that something drastic needed to be done.[50]

An attempt was, in fact, made to buy out the DHPG, and therefore the German interests in Samoa, at the close of 1894. It was an idea which the New Zealanders had repeatedly urged—without, however, offering the money themselves. But in November a British consortium, Messrs J. Arundel & Company and Messrs John Morrison & Company, began to make approaches to Hamburg about forming a joint Anglo-German company. The DHPG declined to do anything other than to sell out completely, demanding in return the large sum of

£750,000. At this, the negotiations collapsed, for the British firms could not possibly raise that amount without a government guarantee—and this was so dim a prospect under a Liberal cabinet that serious explorations in this direction were never begun. Besides, the German Foreign Ministry did not look kindly upon these talks, seeing in them a threat to their claims to a major say in the administration of Samoa. If the firm fell into British hands, it was realized, Germany's interests in the group would be negligible. With the abandonment of these talks, the DHPG was compelled to soldier on, hoping and pressing for a drastic alteration in Samoa—above all for a German annexation.[51]

The truth of the matter was that all sides realized that the 1889 settlement had proved to be a failure, and that order and prosperity would not return to the islands until some major change occurred. Not only did Samoa's native social and administrative structure possess disintegrating and disunifying tendencies, but the whole concept of a tridominium appeared false to nations who were then so used to straightforward territorial annexations and rule by one power. In an age when imperialist agitation was steadily rising, fanned by certain press organs and pressure groups, no government felt strong enough to disentangle itself from the Samoan troubles—even Cleveland was hesitant about that. Yet there was little hope of this unique structure of government functioning smoothly when the vast majority of the participants and observers looked forward to its future demise. Of course, the advent of the new chief justice and president might serve to postpone the event indefinitely should those officials prove capable of co-operating in a friendly and impartial manner with each other for the good of the island; but they might also prove to be the catalysts to a further crisis, leading to the breakdown of the 1889 structure altogether.

Changes inside Germany, too, were slowly causing events to move towards a climax. In 1897 that country's internal and foreign policy took a decisive turn, the significance of which has perhaps only recently been fully appreciated.[52] For in that year the men of the *persönliches Regiment* of Kaiser Wilhelm II manoeuvred themselves into the key positions of state; and with Bülow as foreign secretary, Tirpitz as navy secretary and Miquel as Prussian minister of finance and vice-president of the Prussian Council of Ministers, the government turned deliberately towards *Weltpolitik, Flottenpolitik* and the "mobilisation of the masses". From that time onwards, Wilhelm at last possessed the politicians he needed to assist his ambition of playing a leading role in world politics, of constructing an enormous battlefleet, and of creating internal unity and a stabilization of the political status quo. The country was directed towards the twin aims of reaction at home and an extravagant, expansionist policy abroad. It was to be a feature of this *Weltpolitik* that any gains in the colonial field, however small, were trumpeted before the nation as a great addition to the German empire and an outstanding diplomatic achievement. A case in point was the acquisition of the Caroline Islands, which the navy privately thought worthless. Bülow, in contrast, enthusiastically told the kaiser that "This gain will stimulate people and navy to follow Your Majesty further along the path which leads to world power, greatness and eternal glory".[53]

As a natural consequence of these internal changes, the acquisition of Samoa became an even more important object in the eyes of Germany's leaders. For the next year or so, though, they were doomed to disappointments. In the same year the American annexation treaty with Hawaii caused deep discontent among Pan-German and colonial advocates and, as Chancellor Hohenlohe put it, "aroused a general wish to use this opportunity to bring about a final settlement of the unsatisfactory conditions in Samoa".[54] As a result, Hatzfeldt was ordered to find out if Salisbury was disposed to join Berlin in persuading the United States to withdraw from Samoa, thus redressing the balance in the Pacific which it had upset. The ambassador was also to discuss once again the possibility of a Samoa-Tonga agreement. Salisbury, naturally enough, baulked at the idea of upsetting America for the sake of Hawaii, although he proposed to cede British rights in Samoa for the whole of German New Guinea. Such a suggestion brought an immediate rejection from Berlin, and the prime minister then managed to have the matter postponed.[55]

When the question of the future of the Portuguese colonies arose in 1898, the German Foreign Ministry included Samoa in the list of "compensations" which they would expect in return for allowing Britain a free hand at Delagoa Bay. It was soon made clear, however, that neither Samoa nor Tonga could be given up, due to the strong objections this would raise in

Australasia.[56] Only a short while after the signing of this secret Anglo-German agreement over Portugal's colonial possessions, the Germans were persuaded to inquire again about Samoa on learning that Malietoa had died and that the succession could prove troublesome; and once again the British refused to be interested in any scheme which involved their withdrawal from the group.[57] In 1898, too, Berlin had tried a different course, suggesting to the American government that Germany "should be left unhampered in Samoa" in exchange for allowing the United States to retain the Philippines; but this suggestion received only hostility in Washington, where it was regarded as little short of blackmail by McKinley's imperialist-minded administration.[58]

During the course of these diplomatic negotiations, the state of affairs in the group had further deteriorated. Malietoa had become feebler and more indecisive than ever, and there was a growing campaign by many of the chiefs to press the king to appeal to the powers for the return of Mata'afa and his followers from Jaluit. This movement, the British and American consuls reported, was inspired by the Germans, who had kept the exiles under close supervision and who obviously reckoned that they were now friendly to German aspirations in Samoa. Feeling that Mata'afa would be "a pawn in German colonial policy", they therefore opposed the return.[59] Unfortunately, both were replaced by the beginning of 1898 by consuls who lacked knowledge of the group, and this changeover closely followed upon the arrival of Chief Justice Chambers and President Raffel. Only the German consul, Rose, remained, and he favoured the return of the Jaluit exiles. Moreover, in October 1897 the Mata'afan family and clan had joined the native government, and the threat of a rebellion receded; but once within the Malietoan camp, they pressed even more strongly for the release of their leader until the king himself agreed to it and persuaded the consuls to appeal to the powers to this effect.[60]

After some discussions by the home governments, the consuls were told in July 1898 that the return of Mata'afa and his followers had been agreed to, and the German warship *Bussard* was dispatched to the Marshalls to bring them back. Shortly after the vessel left, however, the king's condition worsened rapidly, and he died on 22 August. Although the consuls and the president joined together in a proclamation enjoining peace and order, there was some doubt whether the state of comparative tranquillity would last very long now that the succession question had occurred at such an inopportune moment. The only way to avert trouble, the British consul believed, would be a swift and unanimous decision on the kingship by the treaty powers.[61] This idea of interfering in Samoan affairs met with a cold reaction in the State Department, which pointed out that the Berlin Act provided for an election by the natives themselves "according to the laws and customs of Samoa". Although this reply undoubtedly represented the correct legal position, the refusal to consider even joint advice to the consuls was soon seen to have been an impolitic move. Left without instructions, the white officials in the group quickly arrived at varying interpretations of the clauses of the 1889 treaty concerning elections.

The opportunity thus presented of arranging the election of a native candidate favourable to one's own national interests attracted many of the white residents, especially the Germans, who were by now very worried about the decline of their commercial paramountcy and all that that implied. Although the 1898 harvest gave the DHPG the opportunity to pay its first dividend for many years, and although the company was still the greatest landowner and taxpayer in Samoa, it remained beset with labour difficulties, and the extent of its land under cultivation had shrunk; the German navy referred to it sarcastically as the "once promising but now ever-decaying company".[62].

But the chief concern, at least of the German officials in the group, remained the extent of the influence exerted upon the Samoans by the London Missionary Society. How effective this really was is difficult to judge, but the belief that Malietoa was in the hands of the English was a constant thought upon the German side, and a source of annoyance to colonial circles. In 1897, though, representatives of the Roman Catholic missionaries, the Marists, secretly urged Berlin to press for the release of Mata'afa, who was of their profession, and promised in return that they would influence him to be pro-German. It was an idea which attracted members of the Centre party, some of them being friends of Bülow; which was strenuously advocated by tbe consul, Rose, as a means by which to combat English influence; which attracted the official dealing with Samoan affairs in the Foreign Ministry, Schmidt-Dargitz, who was pressing for financial help for the teaching of German studies by the Marist school to the tune of 12,000 marks from the secret funds; and, finally, which persuaded the DHPG to drop its earlier opposition by 1898.[63] There is, however, little concrete evidence that Berlin was planning anything other than a defensive move, aimed at halting the decline of German influence in the group, rather than a plot leading directly to their exclusive control, with Mata'afa as their puppet.

What does seem clear, is that some of the local German officials interpreted their instructions to imply that a positive policy was intended. Rose, whose reports revealed a constant obsession about the preservation of *Deutschtum* in the group, had advocated since 1896 the use of Mata'afa as a "tool" with which to combat the *Anglisierung* of Samoa, and he thus automatically assumed that Berlin had agreed to his scheme without reservation. Nor did the Foreign Ministry's directions dispel such ideas, for the Admiralty was asked to bring back Mata'afa and his followers in a German warship "for political reasons", and was informed that the magnanimity of the pardon and the sanctity of the oath of good behaviour the exiles must take should be reinforced by celebrations.[64] As a result, the officials at Jaluit, the crew of the *Bussard*, and the German colony in Samoa made much of Mata'afa, stressing also, however, that his release was solely due to the wish of the kaiser. It is further worth noting that the same Dr Irmer, who had charge of the Samoans in the Marshalls and who was the first German to press for their recall, later boasted to Saunders, the *Times* correspondent in Berlin, "that he had trained Mata'afa, when a German prisoner, for the role he was afterwards to play in Samoa".[65]

The story after the return of Mata'afa to Samoa is well known. Assisted by his German supporters but still more by his commanding personality, he rapidly became the most powerful contender for the kingship—and was then debarred from that office on technical grounds by the American chief justice, who awarded it to the dead king's teenage son. Following a civil war which broke out on New Year's Day, 1899, Mata'afa's forces gained control of the group, but his actions alienated the British and American officials and their governments, who for the following four months endeavoured to implement the chief justice's ruling by naval force.[66] These bombardments and landings in turn infuriated the German public, and Bülow managed to secure the dispatch of an international commission to Samoa, which restored peace and recommended rule by one power as the only real means to avert future troubles. Fortified by this advice and taking full advantage of the British diplomatic weakness during the approach and early stages of the Boer War, Bülow pressed London to agree. After a Herculean tussle with the stubborn Salisbury, this was eventually accomplished—though not perhaps for the reasons Berlin believed—and Britain stepped out of the group for compensations elsewhere while the Americans were content to pick up the more distant Samoan island of Tutuila, where they were constructing a naval station. Consequently, the main islands of Upolu and Savai'i became German possessions through the partition treaties of November and December 1899.[67]

At long last, therefore, the tridominium had come to an end and the Germans had achieved their aim, although by that time Bülow and the kaiser were far less interested in Samoa's intrinsic value than in the effect of its acquisition upon domestic opinion and the campaign for the second Navy Law. Throughout the 1890s, and especially after 1897, German policy towards Samoa provides a superb example of the *Primat der Innenpolitik* at work, of the sensitivity of the government to commercial pressure and public opinion, regard for which seems to have overridden all other considerations, including Chamberlain's tempting offers to buy Germany out of Samoa by more valuable territories elsewhere during the 1899 negotiations.

With regard to the group itself, this interesting experiment in shared political rule had exposed more disadvantages than advantages. It cannot be denied that the tridominium, despite its drawbacks, had been a distinct improvement in many ways: land disputes were settled, the sale of alcohol to the Samoans was virtually eradicated, some roads were built, litigations were settled in the Supreme Court and—until 1899—a full-scale native civil war was averted. But the three major weaknesses—the powerlessness of the Samoan monarchy, the deeply-rooted rivalries of the white nationalities, and the lack of a unified and effective executive—were left uncorrected and as strong as ever. Were one power unchallenged in the group, as had been the case in Fiji, matters would have been regulated by annexation long before the late 1890s; but with three nations claiming rights in the islands, Samoa had to be given a patched-up, temporary settlement—if only to avoid the anarchy and international tension of the 1880s. Yet herein lay a further basic weakness; everyone, whether in Samoa or in the offices of the metropolitan governments, was aware that the 1889 Final Act, despite its title, was only a provisional measure which had been hastily devised to solve a diplomatic crisis.

If the white settlers and their governments suffered from this patched-up series of regulations for the administration of the islands, so too did the Samoans. Yet never at any time was it thought proper or even advisable to consult the native inhabitants about the form of government they might desire; in the age of "new imperialism" such a suggestion would have been considered ridiculous. "Uncivilised" or "dying" peoples were simply expected to accept what was decided for them in the chancellories of Europe and, given the temper of the times, the natives might be considered fortunate if a protectorate was established over their lands in one swift, uncomplicated movement. Where great powers quarrelled over the possession of a particular territory, its inhabitants were often ground between the rival pressures, and probably suffered the more. In a sense, therefore, the partition treaties of 1899 were an advantage for the Samoans, too; neither their economic or political development had been much furthered by the rivalries of the white groups, which had assisted and intensified the Samoan dynastic struggle for the kingship. If actual Samoan independence could not be recovered, was it not better for the islands to be ruled by one responsible and paternalistic government than to be subjected to the pressures of various, often irresponsible, influences? Although we must await a native historian's judgement on this point, to Western eyes this seems certainly to have been the case; and while the cry of "Samoa for the Samoans" never fully disappeared, at least the interests of the islanders were better protected under individual German and American rule than they had been in the days when Samoa was the cockpit of international rivalry in the South Pacific.[68]

1. On German trade in the Pacific, see E. Suchan-Galow, *Die deutsche Wirtschaftstätigkeit in der Südsee vor der ersten Besitzergreifung 1884* (Veröffentlichung des Vereins für Hamburgische Geschichte, Vol 14, Hamburg, 1940); R. Hertz, *Das Hamburger Seehandelshaus J. C. Godeffroy und Sohn* (ibid., vol g4, Hamburg, 1922): K. Schmack, *J. C. Godeffroy und Sohn, Kaufleute zu Hamburg* (Hamburg, 1938).

2. On the background to the German coup of 1884, see P. M. Kennedy, "The Partition of the Samoan Islands, 1898–1899" D.Phil. thesis (Oxford, 1970), pp. 21–31; idem., "Bismarck's Imperialism: The Case of Samoa, 1880–1890", in *Historical Journal* 15 (June 1972). On the state of native politics, see J. W. Davidson, *Samoa mo Samoa: The Emergence of the Independent State of Western Samoa* (Oxford, 1967); and especially, R. P. Gilson, *Samoa 1830 to 1900: The Politics of a Multi-Cultural Community* (Melbourne, 1970).
3. Kennedy, "The Partition", pp. 47–52; and, more briefly, idem., "Anglo-German Relations in the Pacific and the Partition of Samoa, 1885–1899", in *Australian Journal of Politics and History* 17, no.1 (April 1971): 57–58.
4. On the American policy towards Samoa in the late 1880s, see G.H. Ryden, *The Foreign Policy of the United States in Relation to Samoa* (New Haven, 1933), pp.264–521; C.C. Tansill, *The Foreign Policy of Thomas F. Bayard 1885–1897* (New York, 1940), pp.1–185; Graf Otto zu Stolberg-Wernigerode, *Deutschland und die Vereinigten Staaten von Amerika* (Berlin/Leipzig, 1933), pp.247–98.
5. Kennedy, "The Partition", pp.61–70.
6. The text of the Final Act is in *Accounts and Papers* 81, 1890 (c.5911).
7. FO 58/252, British Plenipotentiaries to Salisbury, tel. no. 15 Samoa, 7/6/1889.
8. RKA 2477, DHPG to Bismarck, 23/3/1889, and minute thereon; ibid., Berchem to Arco (copy), private, 26/12/1889.
9. M.S. Wertheimer, *The Pan-German League, 1890–1914* (New York, 1924), pp.25ff. M.Sell, *Die deutsche öffentliche Meinung und das Helgoland-Abkommen im Jahre 1890* (Berlin/Bonn, 1926).
10. H. Pogge von Strandmann, "Domestic Origins of Germany's Colonial Expansion under Bismarck", in *Past and Present*, no. 42 (February 1969); P.M. Kennedy, "German Colonial Expansion in the late nineteenth century: Has the 'Manipulated Social Imperialism' Been Ante-Dated?" in ibid., no.54 (February 1972).
11. FO 58/249, Hatzfeldt memorandum of 5/7/1889; ibid., Cœtlogen to Salisbury, no.33 of 15/7/1889; RKA 2905, memorandum of 26/6/1889.
12. RKA 3024, Stuebel to Bismarck, no.854 of 16/7/1889, and Rothenberg to Berchem, 24/8/1889; FO 58/249, Salisbury to Beauclerk, no.296 conf. of 5/9/1889; ibid., Sanderson note of 3/9/1889.
13. Ibid., Salisbury to Cœtlogen, tel. of 16/9/1889, and Cœtlogen to Salisbury, nos 45 and 46 of 8/11/1889 and 6/1/1889; Ryden, *Foreign Policy of United States*, pp.513–14.
14. Following his more famous *A Footnote to History: Eight Years of Trouble in Samoa* (London, 1892), Stevenson's criticisms can also be seen in his *Valima Letters* (London,1895), in his many letters to the *Times*, and in his letter to Rosebery (Rosebery Papers, National Library of Scotland, Box 91, letter of 2/1/1894). The tridominium is sympathetically treated in Gilson, *Samoa 1830 to 1900*, pp.396–424, but is given a more critical appraisal in A. Vagts, *Deutschland und die Vereinigten Staate in der Welpolitik*, 2 vols (London, 1935), 1:681–797.
15. RKA 3026, Steubel to Caprivi, no.75 of 4/11/1890 and no.24 of 28/3/1891; FO 58/260, Cusack-Smith to Salisbury, no.35 of 23/5/1891.
16. On these difficulties, see Cusack-Smith's dispatches, nos 36,45,47, 50,51,53,57,60, and 71, throughout the latter half of 1891 in FO 58/vols 261–62; and vice-consul Schmidt's reports, nos 51,55,67,80, and 95 of the same period in RKA 3027.
17. FO 58/265, Senfft von Pilsach to Salisbury, 29/2/1892, and Cusack-Smith to Salisbury, nos 8 and 10 of 13/1892 and 10/3/1892; FO 58/266,

same to same, no.13 of 26/4/1892; FO 58/267, same to same, nos 24 and 34 of 3/8/1 and 11/10/1892; FO 58/268, Herbert to Rosebery, no.312 conf. of 3/11/1892, Malet to Rosebery, no.283 of 31/12/1892, Sanderson memorandum of 18/11/1892; Ryden, *Foreign Policy of United States*, pp.530–33; Vagts, *Deutschland und die Vereinigten Staaten*; I: pp.713–19.
18. FO 58/274, Malet to Rosebery, no.17, conf., of 14/1/1893.
19. FO 58/262, Haggard to Salisbury, 8/12/1891.
20. FO 58/287, Haggard to Kimberley, 5/12/1894, reviews the work of the commission. The German side is covered in great detail in RKA 2918–24.
21. Gilson, *Samoa 1830 to 1900*, pp.421–23; Vagts, *Deutschland und die Vereinigten Staaten* 1: 719–21; Ryden, *Foreign Policy of United States*, pp.590–94.
22. The private hints of Blaine and Gresham can be found in R.K.A.2867–68.
23. AA (Auswärtiges Amt Archiv-Bonn) *Südsee-Inseln I*, vol.1, minute on Bremen to AA, 29/1/1893.
24. Ibid., AA to Hatzfeldt, no.42 of 30/1/1893, and his reply, no.14 of same date; AA to Washington, tel. no.2 of 31/1/1893, and reply, tel. no.5 of 2/2/1893. The quote is from Rosebery's minute on Wodehouse (Hawaii) to FO, tel. of 5/4/1893 in FO 58/279.
25. AA *Südsee-Inseln I*, vol.1, AA to Hatzfeldt, no.45 of 2/2/1893, and his reply, no.20 of 6/2/1893; AA to Hatzfeldt, tel. no.23 of 21/2/1893, and Hatzfeldt to the chancellor, no.159 of 3/3/1893. On the British side, see FO 343 (Malet Papers) 3, Rosebery to Malet, 8/2/1893; FO 343/11, Malet to Rosebery, private and conf., 11/2/1893; and FO 343/13, Malet to Rosebery, 18/2/1893.
26. RKA, 2867, Saurma (Washington) to Caprivi, nos 136, 141, and 142 of 3/3/1894 and 3/4/1894.
27. *GP*, 8, no.2024. Marschall's own soundings are recorded in FO 58/285, Malet to Rosebery, no.70, conf., of 2/4/1894.
28. Kennedy, "Anglo-German Relations in the Pacific", pp.60–62.
29. BA/MA 5078, *Samoa*, vol. 1, copies of *Weser Zeitung* (24/4/1894), *Kölnische Zeitung* (26/4/1894), *Norddeutsche Allgemeine Zeitung* (26/4/1894 and 29/4/1894), and *New Zealand Herald* (17/4/1894 and 10/4/1894); FO 58/285, Gosselin to Kimberley, nos 83 and 86 of 4/5/1894 and 10/5/1894.
30. FO 58/284, Cusack-Smith to Rosebery, no.3 of 2/1/1894 and tel. of 22/3/1894; FO 58/285, tel. of 17/5/1894, and German embassy communications of 17/5/1894 and 4/6/1894; BA/MA 5166, *Geheime-R-Angelegenheit Samoa*; Ganz Geheim, vol. 1. Adm. memorandum of 1/5/1894; RKA 3033, Biermann to Caprivi, no.27 of 26/3/1894.
31. FO 58/277, Malet to Rosebery, no.210 of 18/9/1893, Currie note of 20/9/1893; RKA 3032, Biermann to Caprivi, no.84 of 30/11/1893.
32. RKA 2868, Caprivi to Hollmann, 5571 of 28/4/1894, and Kayser memorandum of 1/5/1894; BA/MA 7577, *Hauptakten der Australischen Station*, vol. 1, Oberkommando to *Bussard*, Ganz Geheim, 17/5/1894 and 29/5/1894, and *Bussard* replies, Geheim, of 17/7/1894 and 30/10/1894.
33. Ibid., memorandum on British and American naval strengths in the Pacific, 29/5/1894.
34. *GP*, 8, no.2035.
35. AA *England* 78 Secret, vol. 2, Hatzfeldt to Caprivi (private), secret, of 1/6/1894, and compare with *GP*, 8, no.2039.
36. Kaiser's closing minute on the same.
37. BA/MA 7577, *Hauptakten der Australischen Station*, vol. 1, Oberkommando to *Bussard*, 19/2/1895, replying to the operational proposals encl. in Scheder (*Bussard*) to Oberkommando, no.53, Ganz Geheim, 30/10/1894.

38. H. Pogge von Strandmann, "The Kolonialrat, its Significance and Influence on German Politics 1890–1906" (Oxford D. Phil. thesis, 1970), p.293.
39. BA/MA 624, *Die Entsendung S.M.Schiffe nach der Südsee Station*, vol 2, AA to RMA, 20/10/1894; vol. 3, Oberkommando to RMA, 21/1/1895, and AA to RMA, 12/2/1895.
40. BA/MA 5166 *Geheim-R-Angelegenheit Samoa*, Ganz Geheim, vol. 1, AA to Adm., 9/7/1895.
41. Ibid., Adm. to AA, 23/7/1895; Ryden, *Foreign Policy of United States*, pp.543–45.
42. BA/MA 2023, *Bestimmungen über Immediatberichte u. Vorträge*, vol. 3, Oberkommando Promemoria of 19/1/1895.
43. BA/MA 624, *Die Entsendung S.M. Schiffe nach der Südsee Station*, vol. 3, Oberkommando to RMA, 10/12/1895, encl. c-in-c's report; AA to RMA, 12/6/1896. The documents concerning the German attempt to stop the sale of arms and give the right to *all* warships of searching merchantmen are collected in FO 58, vols. 305–7.
44. FO 58/277, Cusack-Smith to Salisbury, no.46 of 15/3/1893, and Rosebery minute thereon; FO 58/285, Cusack-Smith tel. of 17/5/1894; RKA 3035, Biermann to Caprivi, no.59 of 5/8/1894.
45. FO 58/297, Dallas minute on Woodford to Kimberley, no.12 of 25/2/1895; ibid., FO to Malet, no.42 of 9/2/1895; Ryden, *Foreign Policy of United States*, pp.543–47.
46. BA/MA 624, *Die Entsendung S.M. Schiffe nach der Südsee Station*, vol. 3. AA to RMA, 25/10/1894; BA/MA 7577, *Hauptakten der Australischen Station*, vol. 2, AA to Adm., 24/2/1896, encl. Schmidt-Leda report of 30/12/1895.
47. FO 58/302, Hatzfeldt communication of 22/6/1896.
48. Ryden, *Foreign Policy of United States*, p.554, quoting Gresham to the president, 9/5/1894; CO 225/46, paper 2383, FO to CO, 7/2/1894, with the minute of Buxton, then parliamentary under-secretary for the colonies.
49. STAH, DHPG Archiv, *Bericht der Direktion an den Aufsichtsrat*, for the years 1889–96; Vagts, *Deutschland und die Vereinigten Staaten*, 1: 686–96, 718.
50. BA/MA 624, *Die Entsendung S.M. Schiffe nach der Südsee Station*, vol. 3, Oberkommando to RMA, 10/12/1894, encl. Scheder's report; ibid., Scheder's report of 9/4/1896; RKA 3038, Schmidt-Leda to the chancellor, no.81 of 6/9/1895.
51. Details of the negotiations are in CO 537/136, paper 475, secret, 1895; STAH, DHPG Archiv, Abt. 26, Sitzungs-Protokolle, 20/11/1894 and 10/1/1895; RKA 2478, Kayser to Meyer-Delius (DHPG), 26/5/1894, and replies of 30/5/1894 and 28/12/1894.
52. J.C.G. Röhl, *Germany without Bismarck* (London, 1967); D. Stegmann, *Die Erben Bismarcks* (Cologne/Berlin, 1970), pp.63–75, 97–113.
53. F. Fischer, *Krieg der Illusionen* (Düsseldorf, 1969); p.93, quoting Bülow to the kaiser, 25/2/1899; compare with the navy's unenthusiastic view in AA *Südsee-Inseln* 3 secr., vol. 2, Oberkommando to AA, 10/12/1898.
54. AA Südsee-Inseln I, vol. 5, Alldeutscher Verband to Hohenlohe, 19/6/1897; *GP* 13 no.3409.
55. Kennedy, "The Partition:, pp.141–42.
56. BD 1, no.78.
57. FO 58/316, Salisbury minute on Balfour to Lascelles (draft), no.189a of 2/9/1898.
58. Kennedy, "The Partition", p.147.
59. FO 58/310, Cusack-Smith to Salisbury, nos 1 and 4 of 11/1/1897 and 25/1/1897; NARG 84, Apia Consulate dispatches (C38–8a), vol.1, Churchill to State Dept, no.45 of 11/1/1897.

60. FO 58/311, Cusack-Smith to Salisbury, nos 40 and 43 of 5/10/1897 and 1/11/1897; FO 58/315, Maxse to Salisbury, nos 3 and 13 of 16/4/1898 and 16/5/1898; NARG 59, T-27, roll 24, Churchill to State Dept., nos.108 and 115 of 29/9/1897 and 28/10/1897; ibid., Osborn to same, nos 21, 36 and 38 of 18/2/1898, 14/4/1898 and 16/5/1898.
61. Ibid., same to same, nos 50 and 55 of 9/8/1898 and 31/8/1898; FO 58/315, FO to Maxse, tel. of 13/7/1898; FO 58/316, Maxse to Salisbury, nos 40 and 43 of 24/8/1898; *Papers relating to the Foreign Relations of the United States* (Washington, 1900), pp.604–7.
62. BA/MA 697, *Akten der Kreuzer-Divison*, vol. 6, Diederichs to Oberkommando 29/10/1898.
63. AA *Akten der Missionen—Botschaft Rom*, vol. 1, Bülow (Rome) to Hohenlohe, 12/2/1897, and Marschall to Bülow, 10/3/1897; RKA 3041, memorandum of 19/3/1898; Vagts, pp.779–801.
64. BA/MA 5097, *Samoa*, vol. 2, AA to Admiralstab, 19/7/1898; RKA 3040, Rose to Hohenlohe, no.150 of 29/12/1896; RKA 3041, same to same, no. 109, secret, of 1/11/1897.
65. BA/MA 3419, *Kolonien*, vol. 1, Knorr to Wilhelm, 8/11/1898; Saunders Papers (Times Archives, Printing House Square), Saunders to Chirol, 10/11/1899.
66. On this, see P.M. Kennedy, "The Royal Navy and the Samoan Civil War, 1898–1899" in *Canadian Journal of History* 5, no.1 (March, 1970).
67. Kennedy, "Anglo-German Relations in Pacific", pp.64–72.
68. On Samoa after 1900, see Davidson, *Samoa mo Samoa*, pp.76ff.

# The German Navy in the Far East and Pacific: The Seizure of Kiautschou and After

A. HARDING GANZ

Late in the evening of 1 November 1897, two German missionaries of the Roman Catholic Steyl Society, Fathers Nies and Henle, were murdered in their sleep by a band of Chinese in a small village in the Chinese province of Shantung. In 1890 Pope Leo XIII had put the Steyl Society missionaries under the protection of the German Reich; and whatever Germany's "obligation", the murder of the missionaries prompted the arrival of a German naval force and the occupation of Kiautschou Bay two weeks later. But the martyrdom of the missionaries was the justification, not the reason, for the seizure of Kiautschou. As Foreign Secretary von Bülow in Berlin instructed his ambassadors abroad: "The idea of securing the multifarious German interests in East Asia by the acquisition of a Chinese harbor for a territorial *Stützpunkt* (base), both for docking the numerous German ships and for facilitating trade with the interior, had already been the subject of thorough examination here, as well as in East Asia, for years."[1]

German trade with China had been steadily increasing following the emergence of the German Reich, and by the 1890s three German firms, including Norddeutscher Lloyd of Bremen, maintained regular sailings to the Far East.[2] The volume of German business in China was second only to that of Great Britain—though much less.

To protect the growing German mercantile activity in the Far East was the Cruiser Squadron, which had periodically been formed for specific purposes ever since the 1870s. After Bismarck's acquisition of a colonial empire the Cruiser Squadron remained in existence, and by the 1890s was usually located east of Suez.[3] Yet it had no base of its own for the necessary overhauling, maintenance and repairs, hospitalization of sick or wounded crew-members, and coal re-supply. The squadron was instead dependent on Nagasaki in Japan and

British Hong Kong. Its own requirements were hence low-priority in those foreign dockyards; and at Hong Kong berthing space had to be reserved some nine months in advance, and even then might be cancelled at short notice.[4]

Nonetheless, the navy had not been especially concerned about acquiring a base in the Far East before the 1890s. The development of the navy itself had been retarded while Leo von Caprivi, an army general and later chancellor who had little interest in naval matters, was head of the Admiralty from 1883 to 1888; and the navy's requirements played no role in Bismarck's overseas acquisitions in Africa and Asia in 1884 and 1885. Then too, the steam-sail warships that Germany had no foreign station, sailing ships with auxiliary steam propulsion, were not yet tied to coaling stations and bases.

By 1890, however, the navy's attitude had changed, and this was caused by three factors: the eagerness of the young Kaiser Wilhelm II to build a more impressive navy, the formulation of a strategy for that navy, and the technological transition from sail to steam, making coaling stations distant from home waters mandatory.

Decisions regarding naval policy and strategy were complicated by the fact that on 30 March 1889 the Kaiser had dissolved the Admiralty office into three separate but equal departments: the Reichsmarineamt (RMA) or Imperial Naval Office, under a state secretary appointed by the chancellor, with responsibility for the administrative and technical development of the navy; the Oberkommando der Marine (OKM) or High Command of the Navy, under a commanding admiral appointed by the Kaiser, with responsibility for operational planning and exercising operational control over all naval forces; and the Kaiserliches Marinekabinett (MK) or Imperial Naval Cabinet, which controlled personnel appointments and promotions, and served as an advisory cabinet to the Kaiser. Wilhelm's motive was the "divide and rule" concept, but the system assured constant friction between the three departments.[5]

The Kaiser's enthusiasm for his navy was greatly stimulated by Captain Alfred Thayer Mahan's *The Influence of Sea Power Upon History,* 1660–1783, published in 1890, in which the American naval historian maintained that in the history of the world it was sea power that had always decided the destiny of nations. But what kind of a navy to build?

It was patently obvious that a German fleet could never hope to match the leading fleet (the Royal Navy) in size, and consequently a decision by battle-fleet action must be avoided. The solution appeared to be a strategy advocated at that time by a French school of thought, the *jeune école* or "Young School", a commerce-raiding strategy (*la guerre de course*) of cruiser-warfare. While torpedo boats prevented a close blockade of home ports, commerce-raiders would prowl the trade routes of the enemy, sinking ships and disrupting maritime commerce—"Shamelessly attack the weak, shamelessly fly from the strong".[6]

Cruiser-warfare (*Kreuzerkrieg*) was attractive to the German navy, for it implied an active role by a small fleet. Its chief advocate was Vice-Admiral Victor Valois, but Admiral von Hollmann, state secretary of the Reichsmarineamt from 1890 to 1897, also favoured the idea. The OKM and the MK heads, however, as well as Alfred Tirpitz who succeeded Hollmann at the RMA in 1897, argued for a battleship building programme for decisive fleet action in home waters, and opposed cruiser-warfare abroad.[7] Nonetheless a cruiser-warfare strategy was in vogue, if not officially adopted, for a good part of the decade.

But no longer could commerce-raiders like the Confederate *Alabama* keep to the seas for months at a time. The transition from sail to steam meant that bases overseas were now necessary, and warships engaged in cruiser-warfare would have to replenish their coal supply at least once a week.[8]

If Germany was to pursue a strategy of cruiser-warfare then, it was obvious that the commerce-raiders would have to operate from fortified naval bases abroad (*Flottenstützpunkte*). Thus by the early 1890s, the possession of a naval base in the Far East would be more than a mere convenience for the warships stationed there; it was now necessary for coal re-supply, and might even be a vital link in a strategic network of fortified bases for cruiser-warfare around the world.

The opportunity to acquire such a base seemed to present itself in 1894 during the Sino-Japanese War. Kaiser Wilhelm believed that the imminent collapse of a decadent China would initiate a scramble for the spoils by the other major powers. He urged chancellor Hohenlohe that if this should occur, "we should not permit ourselves to fall short or to be taken by surprise. We also require a base in China, where our annual trade is valued at 400 millions". The kaiser proposed that Germany prepare to take Formosa by entering into a secret understanding with Japan, and by issuing the necessary directives to the Cruiser Squadron.[9] But no action was taken.

With the military defeat of China there was much speculation during the late winter of 1894–95 as to what Japan's peace terms would be, and what "compensation" Germany, like the other powers, might be able to claim. On 11 March 1895 Foreign Secretary Marschall von Bieberstein wrote to Admiral von Hollmann, state secretary of the Reichsmarineamt, requesting a memorandum setting forth the reasons why the navy desired a base in China and what locations might be suitable; the acquisition of Formosa, he added, would only lead to difficulties with other powers, and would require a disproportionate amount of strength to secure.[10]

On 17 April (the same day that the Treaty of Shimonoseki was signed), Hollmann replied in a long report with the conclusions at which the RMA, as well as Admiral von Knorr's OKM, had arrived.[11] From the first, Hollmann believed that a Far East harbour should have great commercial possibilities; and this consideration was to be a major factor in the ultimate selection of Kiautschou Bay. As German trade in Asia extended from Singapore in Malaya north to Hakodate in Japan, he favoured *two* bases, one in the north and one in the south, "which must be on the main trade routes, and must themselves already possess significance in a commercial respect; dead places, not capable of development, are worthless". Commercial considerations would locate the Cruiser Squadron where its presence was most advantageous, and port facilities mutually beneficial to business interests and the navy should encourage political co-operation between the two.

Hollmann named three pairs of locations in the order of their desirability. The first were the Chusan Islands in the north, close to the Shanghai area and the mouth of the Yangtze, and Amoy in the south, favourably located regarding the maritime traffic that funnelled through the Formosa Strait. On the other hand, he pointed out, the English might be sensitive about a German naval presence near Shanghai, and as a treaty port, Amoy presented certain diplomatic difficulties.

Secondly, there was Kiautschou Bay with its small fishing village of Tsingtao on the Shantung peninsula, which could tap the resources of the area, principally coal; and in the south Hollmann suggested Mirs Bay near Hong Kong. Kiautschou,

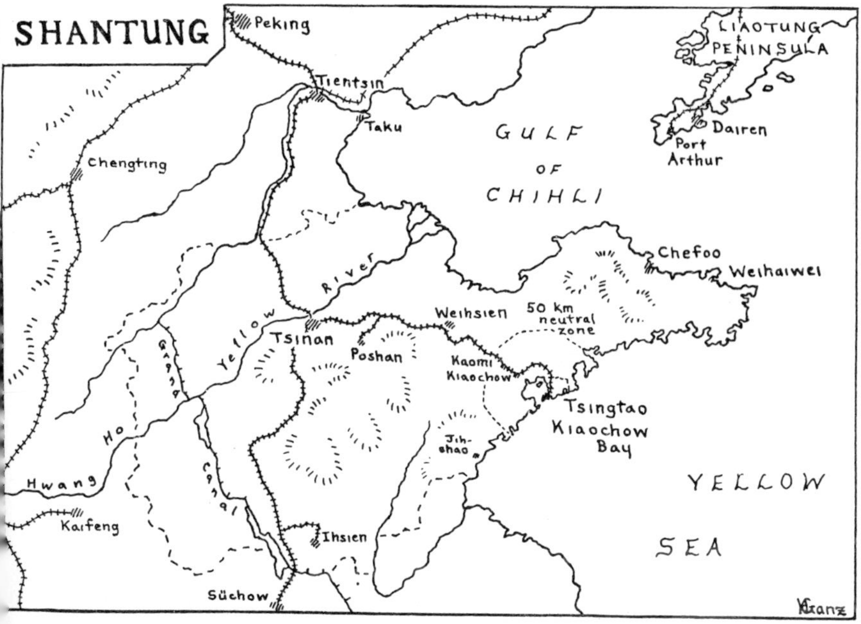

## SHANTUNG

Peking
Tientsin
Taku
LIAOTUNG PENINSULA
Dairen
Port Arthur
GULF OF CHIHLI
Chengting
Chefoo
Weihaiwei
Yellow River
Weihsien
50 km neutral zone
Tsinan
Poshan
Grand Canal
Kaomi
Kiaochow
Tsingtao
Kiaochow Bay
Hwang Ho
Jih-shao
YELLOW SEA
Kaifeng
Ihsien
Süchow
Kranz

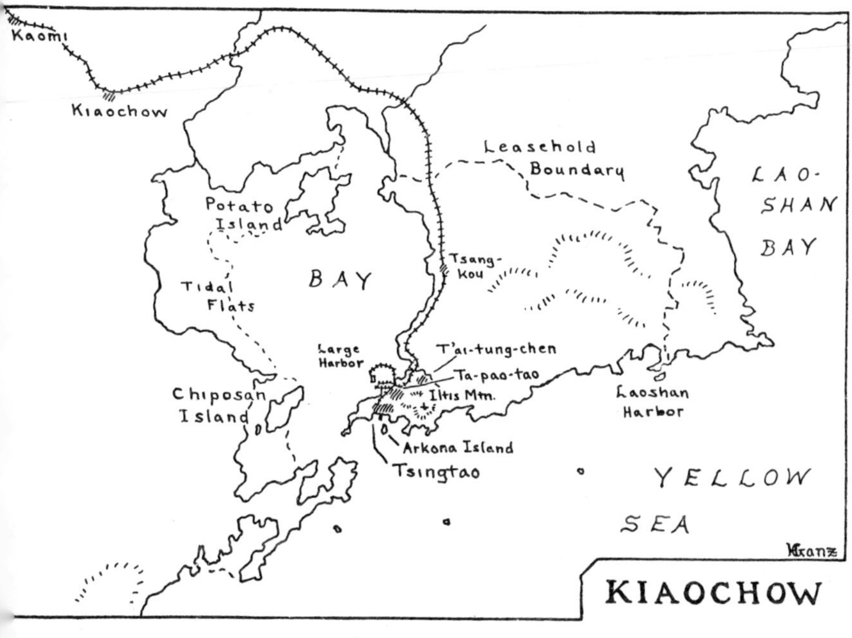

Kaomi
Kiaochow
Leasehold Boundary
Potato Island
LAO-SHAN BAY
Tsang-kou
Tidal Flats
BAY
Large Harbor
T'ai-tung-chen
Ta-pao-tao
Iltis Mtn.
Chiposan Island
Laoshan Harbor
Arkona Island
Tsingtao
YELLOW SEA
Kranz

## KIAOCHOW

however, was reputedly blocked by ice in the winter, and Mirs Bay could not compete with British Hong Kong, Portuguese Macao, and the treaty port of Whampoa, already serving maritime trade with Canton and the rich province of Kwangtung.

Lastly, there was Montebello Island (near Korea), which was in both the Russian and the Japanese spheres of interest, and the Pescadores Islands off Formosa which, however, had no hinterland. There was, Hollmann noted, insufficient information to draw conclusions regarding other possible localities. The real result of the memorandum was to stimulate further investigation.

The Kaiser was impatient, however, and when a band of Chinese destroyed a German mission house at Swatow on the South China Sea in September 1895, he had the OKM order Admiral Hoffmann's Cruiser Squadron to seize Wei-hai-wei (temporarily substituted for Kiautschou) on the Shantung.[12] But the ships were scattered and could not gather for several days; and since the missionaries at Swatow had not been personally harmed, there was insufficient excuse for intervention. Nor was the navy satisfied about Wei-hai-wei. Located on the northern coast of the Shantung, it was isolated from the interior by mountainous terrain and thus lacked the necessary commercial potential the navy desired.[13]

Nonetheless, Envoy Schenck presented the German demand for a coaling station on 29 October, but the Chinese successfully resisted this.[14] In the end, after the European powers had pressured Japan into moderating the peace settlement and had then taken "compensation" from China, Germany received only two minor trading concessions: in Hankow at the confluence of the Han and Yangtze rivers, an inland port, and in Tientsin, the treaty port for the Peking region.[15]

The idea of a base was now firmly established, however, and for the next two years, until the necessary "moral" pretext for the seizure of Kiautschou in November 1897, the German navy and the German government made a thorough study of the question of acquiring a base in China. In particular, the criterion had been established that the base must feature a harbour capable of commercial development which would facilitate trade with the interior, to which naval requirements would be secondary. Yet the navy never did want to *control* the hinterland, for an indigenous native population forcibly subordinated to German rule, as was the case in the African colonies, posed more problems than plaudits. Then too, the navy recognized the diplomatic dangers in entering the spheres of influence claimed by the British, the Russians, and the Japanese, and consciously sought to avoid antagonizing them. It was Kiautschou that ultimately met these requirements.

While there was agreement in principle regarding the need for a Far East base, however, location after location was analysed and discarded for one reason or another. Kiautschou unexpectedly came up again when Russian warships, with Chinese permission, wintered there in 1895–96. It was now obvious that the waters of the bay did *not* freeze over during the winter months. But the apparent Russian interest in Kiautschou deterred the Foreign Office in particular; and when Knorr at the OKM favoured Chusan near Shanghai, Marschall feared antagonizing England, and suggested Quemoy or Amoy or "some other place of minor importance, suitable for strictly naval purposes".[16]

In the spring of 1896 the dynamic Rear-Admiral Tirpitz went to the Far East for a tour of duty with the Cruiser Squadron. He made perfunctory stops at the places under consideration, all of which confirmed him in an opinion he later claimed to have formed before leaving Europe, that only the "unset pearl Tsingtao" at Kiautschou would do.[17] But Baron von Heyking, who had come out that same spring to succeed Schenck at Peking, was opposed: the bay, he felt, had officially been granted to the Russians as a wintering station for their ships. The Kaiser was exasperated at Tirpitz's reports favouring Kiautschou. "We could have had the bay last summer", he noted, "but the Navy didn't want it then. I was certainly for it!" And he added, "That we have nicely trifled away!"[18]

But Tirpitz doubted that the place was of any lasting value to the Russians, especially as there was no possibility of a railroad connection with their Siberian line. This belief was confirmed when he sounded out Admiral Alexiev, the senior Russian naval commander, at Vladivostok.[19]

Tirpitz's final conclusions favouring Kiautschou were sent in a long thirty-one page report to Berlin from Hakodate on 5 September 1896.[20] In his analysis he stressed the commercial factors, and particularly suggested a railroad that would tap the coal resources at Weihsien and Tsinanfu. Regarding the bay itself, winter ice posed no problem and harbour installations were quite feasible. Chinese military defences could be discounted, and Kiautschou's geographic location did not encroach on any major power's sphere of influence. Kiautschou, Tirpitz ended, thus adequately fulfilled the commercial, military, and political requirements for a Far Eastern base.

Tirpitz's report apparently only confused the Kaiser as to what the navy wanted, but it did rekindle his impatience. He finally demanded action. "We must act now, swiftly and resolutely."[21] Orders were dispatched to Tirpitz to concentrate the Cruiser Squadron off—Amoy! Tirpitz was thunder-struck, and immediately wired Heyking at the Chinese capital for an explanation. "In reply to my astounded inquiry", Tirpitz related in his memoirs, "Heyking wired back that Berlin had asked whether an understanding had been reached between him and me; and he replied, 'Yes, Amoy!'"[22]

In any case the OKM now favoured Kiautschou, and the Foreign Office was cool to any such venture; in a meeting of his officials the kaiser received no support regarding Amoy, and the orders to Tirpitz were cancelled. Then Kiautschou it would be, and the OKM was ordered to draw up an operations plan for the seizure of the bay. This was submitted to the kaiser two weeks later and, with only minor change, was the plan ultimately put into effect.[23]

Tirpitz was suddenly depressed, meanwhile, to read a story in the Hong Kong *North China Daily News* that Kiautschou had been leased to Russia for fifteen years. "The seizure of Kiautschou Bay", he wrote to Berlin, "doubtless means the expansion of the Russian sphere of influence over all of North China to the Yangtze territory". No other port seemed appropriate, and Tirpitz suggested a settlement of colonists in the Yangtze valley or at Wusung near Shanghai. "If we want to accomplish something really great out here, we must get in there, as Your Excellency has already said."[24] But it soon became apparent that the Russo-Chinese agreement merely reconfirmed permission to winter at Kiautschou, and that German ambitions had not been seriously jeopardized.

The selection of Kiautschou had thus been agreed upon, and its potential was confirmed by Georg Franzius, director of the harbour works at Kiel, sent to the Far East in January 1897. Tirpitz escorted him to the bay on board his flagship, all of which activity caused the Foreign Office to complain that

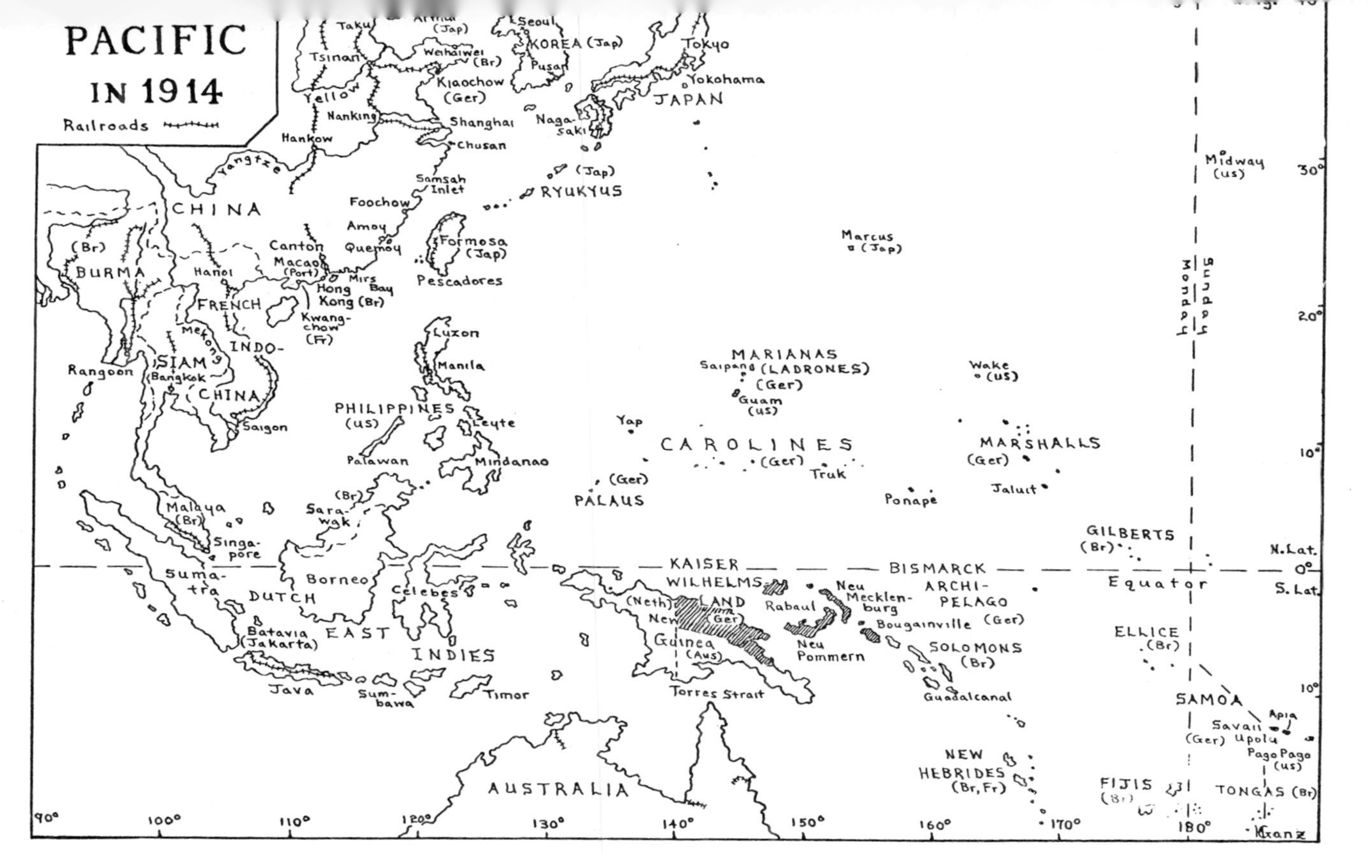
PACIFIC
IN 1914
Railroads
Taku
Tsinan
Yellow
Nanking
Hankow
Yangtze
Weihaiwei (Br)
Kiaochow (Ger)
Shanghai
Chusan
Seoul
KOREA (Jap)
Pusan
Tokyo
Yokohama
JAPAN
Naga-saki
(Jap)
RYUKYUS
Samsah Inlet
Foochow
Amoy
Quemoy
Formosa (Jap)
Pescadores
CHINA
(Br)
BURMA
Canton
Macao (Port)
Mirs Bay
Hong Kong (Br)
Kwang-chow (Fr)
Hanoi
FRENCH
INDO-
CHINA
Mekong
SIAM
Bangkok
Rangoon
Saigon
Marcus (Jap)
Midway (us)
Sunday
Monday
MARIANAS
Saipan
(LADRONES)
(Ger)
Guam (us)
Wake (us)
Luzon
Manila
PHILIPPINES (us)
Leyte
Palawan
Mindanao
Yap
CAROLINES
(Ger)
Truk
(Ger)
PALAUS
MARSHALLS (Ger)
Jaluit
Ponape
GILBERTS (Br)
N. Lat.
0°
S. Lat.
Equator
Malaya (Br)
Singa-pore
(Br)
Sara-wak
Borneo
Celebes
Suma-tra
DUTCH
EAST
INDIES
Batavia (Jakarta)
Java
Sum-bawa
Timor
KAISER
WILHELMS-
LAND
(Neth)
New
Guinea
(Ger)
(Aus)
Torres Strait
Rabaul
Neu Mecklen-burg
Neu Pommern
BISMARCK
ARCHI-
PELAGO
(Ger)
Bougainville
SOLOMONS (Br)
Guadalcanal
ELLICE (Br)
SAMOA
Apia
Savaii
(Ger)
Upolu
Pago Pago (us)
NEW HEBRIDES (Br, Fr)
FIJIS
TONGAS (Br)
AUSTRALIA
30°
20°
10°
10°
90°
100°
110°
120°
130°
140°
150°
160°
170°
180°
Kranz

snooping around Kiautschou "may easily arouse suspicions on the part of the Russians and prove a political danger under the circumstances".[25] But these obstructions were to no avail.

Tirpitz had played a significant role in choosing Kiautschou. But the Chinese bay was of only secondary importance to him at this time, for in June 1897 he took office as the state secretary of the Reichsmarineamt, replacing Admiral von Hollmann. His appointment was the victorious culmination to a power struggle within the ranks of the navy that had been continuing for several years, and represented the official adoption of a battleship building programme for decisive fleet action in *home* waters, and the end of the cruiser-warfare concept of commerce-raiding *abroad*.[26] Tirpitz's building programme was signed into law on 10 April 1898, and expanded in 1900.

What then of Kiautschou, for which Tirpitz had so persuasively argued? Such a base on the other side of the world would now be strategically irrelevant and a constant drain on funds, men, and material, to the detriment of a home battle fleet. Aware, however, of the Kaiser's obvious desire for a Far East base, did Tirpitz perhaps advocate its acquisition only for political advantage? Indeed, he did apparently object to the actual seizure when it occurred several months later, after he was well ensconced in the RMA. This has caused Steinberg, at least, to wonder if Tirpitz were indeed sincere in later maintaining that he always favoured Kiautschou.[27] Certainly no detailed plans for acquiring a network of strategically located bases around the world was ever drawn up, and no bases of any value were ever developed in Germany's other colonies.[28] The cruisers and gunboats on foreign stations were only maintained there to placate certain commercial and political interests.

The situation in the Far East, however, was significantly different. As long as imperial Germany was to participate in political decisions there, as long as commercial interests were increasing their trade, the navy would have to maintain a squadron of warships in the area, although they would not have to be of the latest design. Given that political fact, and the technical difficulties of servicing and provisioning that squadron some 10,000 nautical miles from the nearest German naval base, the advantages of a base in the Orient were obvious. Irrespective of interdepartmental rivalries and differences regarding strategic and administrative policies, then, the leaders of the navy, Tirpitz included, were all agreed on the need for such a base. That base was to be Kiautschou.

The Foreign Office, now headed by Bernhard von Bülow, was less disposed to thwart the project; but the question of Russian opposition remained, for Russian warships still apparently had Chinese permission to winter at Kiautschou. The Kaiser raised the matter himself when he visited the tsar and Foreign Minister Muraviev at Peterhof in August 1897, and was encouraged by their non-committal replies. On 9 September the Germans informed the Russians that in accordance with the Peterhof talks they were considering anchoring vessels in Kiautschou Bay during the coming winter, and got little reaction.[29] On 1 October Heyking informed the Chinese government: "We reserve the right during the coming winter to anchor, in case of need, German vessels of war temporarily in Kiautschou Bay."[30] The Chinese reaction was to continue fortifying the area, planning for which had been initiated at the beginning of the year.

Continuing Chinese exasperation at the relentless encroachment of the European powers resulted in incidents which the German government could utilize as pretexts for securing its objectives. On 30 October a Chinese mob in Wuchang stoned officers and sailors from SMS *Cormoran*, which had brought Heyking up the Yangtze to visit the German concessions there. Vice-Admiral Otto von Diederichs, who had succeeded Tirpitz in command of the Cruiser Squadron, pressed Berlin: "May Wuchang incident be utilized for the pursuance of our broader goals through high demands for satisfaction, or should usual satisfaction be enough?"[31] The Kaiser felt the time for action had come, but the Foreign Office stalled.

Then, scarcely a week later, came the news that the two Roman Catholic missionaries had been murdered on the Shantung peninsula. Three years of frustration determined the Kaiser's orders for Diederichs: "Proceed immediately to Kiautschou with the whole squadron, seize suitable points and villages there, and in such manner as may appear best to you, compel full satisfaction."[32] This Diederichs proceeded to do enthusiastically.

Russian Foreign Minister Muraviev now, however, sent a pointed reminder that Russia had a "prior right of anchorage" at Kiautschou and was also dispatching ships.[33] The Russian reaction upset Berlin. Tirpitz, distressed that the political repercussions in the Reichstag might jeopardize the passage of his battleship building programme, objected to Chancellor

Hohenlohe: "Consider the action against China as unfavorable for the Navy Bill, and in the intended form very risky; the result of this sort of action must lead to a serious threat of hostilities. Request by return permission an audience with your Highness."[34]

The OKM now also demonstrated timidity, and joined with the RMA, the chancellor, and the Foreign Office in successfully urging the Kaiser to modify his orders to Diederichs.[35] All to no avail. Diederichs was—conveniently—out of wire communication with Berlin. He gathered three of his ships and steamed into Kiautschou Bay on 13 November, and went ashore with a landing party the next morning. The Chinese garrison evacuated its defences without resistance, and Berlin was faced with a *fait accompli*.[36]

The actual occupation had been carried out smoothly and without bloodshed, which relieved the German government immensely, and in a crown council meeting on 15 November it was agreed that the occupation should continue. Ultimate acquisition of the bay would take the form of a ninety-nine-year lease, to be negotiated with China later.[37] Reinforcements were dispatched in the form of the 3d Naval Infantry Battalion on two transports, and three more cruisers, commanded by Rear-Admiral Prince Heinrich, the Kaiser's brother.[38]

Fears that Russia, England, or Japan might intervene proved groundless. Russia was more interested in Port Arthur on the Liaotung Peninsula, which it leased on 27 March 1898. Great Britain was more concerned with Russian ambition than German, and on 1 July leased Wei-hai-wei on the other side of the Gulf of Chihli "for as long a period as Port Arthur shall remain in the occupation of Russia".[39]

Germany had thus finally acquired her long-sought base in the Far East. It was somewhat ironic, however, that Kiautschou's strategic potential had already diminished with the abandoning of the cruiser-warfare strategy upon Tirpitz's accession to the R.M.A. This shift in German naval strategy was soon corroborated by the Spanish-American War, in which a world-wide colonial empire dramatically changed hands, primarily as a result of decisive fleet action in Manila Bay, and the blockade and destruction of Spanish units in Santiago Harbour. "Cruiser-warfare", emphasized the naval journal *Nauticus*, "is a utopia!"[40]

Nonetheless, Kiautschou would be of tremendous importance in its own right as a peace-time naval base. Tirpitz himself was insistent that the new possession should be administered by the navy, and not the Colonial Department.[41] It was true that if Kiautschou were a civilian protectorate, the navy budget would only have to cover naval installations such as dock facilities. Commercial and native problems would be the responsibility of a civilian governor, problems concerning which the navy had been glad to avoid in the case of the African colonies. But the Kiautschou protectorate itself was primarily a naval base; and while the navy felt commercial development essential, such commercial enterprises would pursue their activities under Chinese concession, rather than within the protectorate or while exercising dominion over Chinese soil and populace. If the navy were to administer the base itself, then a separate civilian administration would appear unnecessary and would only cause duplication and friction.[42]

In any case, however, it would seem that the Colonial Department was content to let the navy have the responsibility. "I have no objection from the standpoint of my office", Foreign Secretary Bülow told Tirpitz, adding only that he assumed that "the various political and commercial affairs like railroads and mining established outside the leasehold, would remain under the Foreign Office as previously ... ".[43]

More difficult to resolve was the question *which* navy department should administer Kiautschou. Knorr of the OKM argued that as the Cruiser Squadron was subordinated to the OKM its base should be also, like the naval squadrons and bases in home waters.[44] But Tirpitz insisted that the Kaiser place the protectorate under the RMA, and he prevailed.

The civil and military administration of Kiautschou was to be under a naval officer serving as military governor. He would be assisted by a civil commissioner and a special commissioner for Chinese affairs, and three advisers from the German civilian community. The RMA (Tirpitz) had ultimate responsibility for the protectorate.[45]

The first permanent governor was Captain Rosendahl, who assumed his duties on 15 April 1898. His task was a formidable one that included surveying and auctioning the land while preventing speculation, charting, dredging, and opening the harbour, establishing licenses and harbour fees, and co-ordinating import and export activities with the Chinese Imperial Maritime Customs (IMC) service. It was inevitable that visiting newspaper correspondents and impatient businessmen would find details of the navy administration to criticize; and perhaps an undue sensitivity to adverse publicity led Tirpitz to replace Rosendahl with Captain Paul Jaeschke in February 1899.[46]

Germany's base at Kiautschou enhanced her presence in the Far East, but German activities in the area reflected the confusion of objectives and policies within the German government. With the outbreak of the Spanish-American War in 1898, the Kaiser ordered Diederich's Cruiser Squadron to Manila Bay—but for what purpose is still not clear. Knorr at the OKM subsequently prepared a memorandum considering a naval base in the Philippines, particularly at Palawan Island, but Foreign Secretary Bülow had already told Tirpitz that the Kaiser rejected the idea of a German protectorate in the Philippines.[47]

If, instead, the Germans hoped to gain American support elsewhere in the Pacific by backing American annexation of the islands, then Diederichs's actions had the reverse effect. The movements of his warships around Manila Bay, in apparent disregard of the American blockade, finally caused Admiral Dewey to retort to one German complaint: "Why, I shall stop each vessel whatever may be her colors! And if she does not stop, I shall fire at her! And that means war, do you know, Sir? And I tell you, if Germany wants war, all right, we are ready."[48] But Germany did not want war; Diederichs had received only ambiguous instructions from Berlin, and in the end Germany only gained American ill-will.

In December 1898 Germany purchased the Carolines, the Palaus, and the Marianas or Ladrones (except Guam) directly from Spain. But these Pacific islands were of little economic value; and while they might have had a certain strategic use as coaling and cable stations, the German navy never did show any real interest in developing them.

Similarly, when the Samoan question arose again that same autumn, German intervention was prompted by political and economic, rather than naval, motives. Tirpitz indeed argued against giving up the German claim for meagre compensation elsewhere.[49] But he also realized that the best harbours—Pago Pago at Tutuila in the Samoas and Vavau in the Tongas—would go to the United States and Britain respectively. In the final treaty Germany received the islands of Upolu and Savai'i where her traders had been established, and neither island was ever of any use to the German navy.

At Kiautschou, Captain Jaeschke not only had to continue the work begun by Rosendahl, but was also faced with the Boxer Rebellion which broke out early in 1900. The coolies employed by the Germans became increasingly restless and construction work was interrupted, and when a number of missionaries were murdered in the interior, the garrison was put on a war footing. A small detachment of fifty troops was dispatched to protect the German embassy at Peking, but the Europeans in the city were soon besieged. An international relief expedition under English Vice-Admiral Seymour, including a German contingent from Admiral Bendemann's Cruiser Squadron, marched on Peking in June, but was stopped beyond Tientsin and forced to retreat.[50]

The major powers all competed now in dispatching warships to the scene—though their presence would be more ostentatious than effective. The United States, France, and Japan were represented by one battleship each, England by three, and Russia by five. Not to be outdone, the Kaiser sent his four latest *Brandenburg*-class battleships, the First Division of the First Battle Squadron, under Rear-Admiral Geissler, accompanied by numerous cruisers and smaller vessels. Their five-week, 10,000 mile voyage out from Wilhelmshaven, however, once again vividly demonstrated the German dependence on the coaling ports of the British empire: Gibraltar, Port Said, Aden, Colombo, and Singapore.[51] A reinforced international expeditionary ground force had already marched on Peking, entering the capital on 14 August 1900, and the officers and men of the battleships had little to do but savour the delights of cosmopolitan Shanghai for the next several months. The German battleships returned to Wilhelmshaven a year later.

In January 1901 Captain Jaeschke was stricken with illness, and on 27 January he died. He was succeeded as governor of Kiautschou by Captain Oskar Truppel, who was to retain that office for the next ten years, and whose name almost became synonymous with the protectorate. Under him Kiautschou continued to develop at a rapid pace.

Tirpitz himself, who had not only been instrumental in acquiring Kiautschou but also in organizing its administration, took a special interest in this development. The Deutsch-Chinesische Hochschule, a college for Chinese in Tsingtao, was his personal project; for Tirpitz realized the importance of influencing the rising giant of China with German ideas. Yet

Governor Vice-Admiral Truppel opposed the concept, and after the school opened in 1909 friction with the civilian faculty ensued.

There was no compromise, and Tirpitz again desired to avoid a public controversy; on 28 December 1910 Truppel was informed that he would be relieved in the spring.[52] Yet Truppel did not have to suffer the humiliation of being publicly fired, but was instead promoted to full admiral on 27 January 1911 in recognition of his services, and was ennobled shortly thereafter. His able assistant, Captain Meyer-Waldeck, was a man more agreeable to the civilian community and was picked by Tirpitz as Truppel's successor. Meyer-Waldeck remained as governor until Kiautschou was surrendered in 1914. The Hochschule prospered, and went far to reconcile the Chinese to a German presence in China, and to justify the administration of an overseas protectorate by the German navy.

When Tirpitz's 1900 Navy Bill had become law, it had reinforced the 1898 act in committing Germany to the construction of a battle fleet in home waters. The Cruiser Squadron was now superfluous to any battle-fleet strategy, and in fact generally received only older ships that were expendable in wartime. In addition, the Japanese blockade of Port Arthur in 1904 confirmed what the American blockade of Santiago in 1898 had demonstrated—that a fortified naval base might only prove a trap for warships confronting a major naval power. While Kiautschou was later fortified against a land attack, the Cruiser Squadron was not to be caught in harbour in the event of major hostilities. In the years that followed, operations plans for the squadron in time of war called for rendezvousing in isolated Waworada Bay at Sumbawa in the Dutch East Indies, rather than operating from Kiautschou itself. Cruiser-warfare would be undertaken until hostilities ceased.[53]

But a general European war seemed remote to the Europeans in East Asia, and the Cruiser Squadron pursued its more mundane duties of charting coastal waters, combating piracy in the South China Sea, and assisting merchant vessels that were stranded or stricken by storm.

On 25 December 1910 the light cruiser *Emden*, at Tsingtao for repairs, received orders to rendezvous with SMS *Nürnberg* from Hong Kong and proceed to the island of Ponape in the eastern Carolines, where District Magistrate Boeder had been killed in a native revolt.[54] The rebels were of the Jokoi tribe, and under their leader, Jomatau, holed up on their island of Jokaj, separated from the northern part of Ponape itself by a small canal. After the little steam-sail cruiser *Cormoran* from the Australian station and the survey vessel *Planet* had sounded the off shore reefs, *Emden* and *Nürnberg* bombarded the rebels on 13 January 1911 with their 10.5 cm guns. Simultaneously a landing party of marines and native police-soldiers went ashore and, guided up a jungle trail by a loyal native, emerged on the rebel-held plateau and scattered the Jokois.

Nonetheless Jomatau and some of his followers escaped to the mainland, and for the next four weeks German columns tracked them through the steaming jungle until the exhausted leader finally surrendered. The 254 Jokoi captives who had been interned on Yap Island were now returned. Jomatau and sixteen other ringleaders were executed by black police troops from New Guinea on 24 February.

In tracing the origins of the uprising, Commander Vollerthun of the *Emden* was disgusted by the whole affair. "Seldom indeed", he angrily reported to the Kaiser, "has a half-civilized native people been handled so without purpose and so illogically as have the Ponapese."[55] Vollerthun probably expressed the sentiments of most naval officers who were called on to suppress native uprisings, in Africa as well as in Asia, incited by the activities of overzealous missionaries and rapacious and callous civilian colonial officials and entrepreneurs.

At the Reichskolonialamt (Imperial Colonial Office) Dr Bernhard Dernburg and his successors gradually realized that with its emphasis on a battle-fleet strategy in home waters, the navy could not be depended on to protect the colonies if a major war broke out. In October 1912 the colonial secretary, Dr Solf, finally wrote to von Heeringen of the Admiralty Staff asking what plans the navy had to secure important colonial coastal locatities against hostile warships. Von Heeringen replied on 6 December, lamely suggesting that the individual governors confer with the senior naval officer on the appropriate station.[56]

The naval officers on the African stations were frankly pessimistic; and for Samoa Lieutenant Commander Zuckschwerdt on the Australian station could only suggest destroying the wireless station, extinguishing the harbour entrance lights, and entering into negotiations with the enemy commander—and advised the governor of New Guinea that he was equally helpless.[57] The naval base at Kiautschou, of course, was garrisoned and fortified; it would hold out as long as possible, in the hope that a European war would be short. The activities of the Cruiser Squadron would depend upon the extent of hostilities. But for the rest of the colonies, there was little the navy was willing or able to do; and the colonial defence measures in turn were, as von Pohl at the ADM noted to Tirpitz, "worthless for the purposes of the Imperial Navy".[58]

When war did come in August 1914, German naval forces abroad were rapidly swept from the high seas. Cruiser Squadron Commander Vice-Admiral Graf von Spee, not to be trapped at Kiautschou, departed for the Carolines with armoured cruisers *Scharnhorst* and *Gneisenau* and light cruiser *Nürnberg*, beginning his epic attempt to reach Germany, half a world away. Cruiser-warfare in East Asia was logistically impractical. At forlorn Easter Island he was joined by light cruisers *Dresden*, from the Brazilian coast, and *Leipzig*, from Magdalena Bay on the Mexican west coast. Captain von Müller's *Emden*, which had been detached to wage cruiser-warfare, raised havoc in the Indian Ocean until wrecked by HMAS *Sydney* at the Cocos-Keeling Islands on 9 November. Spee himself scattered Cradock's British squadron off Coronel, Chile, and rounded Cape Horn, but his squadron was caught and destroyed off the Falklands by Sturdee's battle cruisers on 8 December. *Dresden* alone escaped. But with no hope of recoaling, she holed up in the desolate Juan Fernandez Islands off Valparaiso and, discovered by British warships on 14 March 1915, was scuttled by her crew.

The smaller ships in the Pacific likewise suffered a melancholy fate. Yangtze river-gunboats *Otter* and *Vaterland* were interned at Nanking, as was *Tsingtau* at Whampoa. Kiautschou Bay was blockaded by the British and Japanese, and inside the bay the gunboats *Iltis*, *Jaguar*, *Luchs*, and *Tiger*, old steam-sail cruiser *Cormoran*, torpedoboats *S–90* and *Taku*, and disabled old Austrian cruiser *Kaiserin Elisabeth*, were all eventually scuttled. In addition, steam-sail cruiser *Geier* was interned at Honolulu, survey vessel *Planet* was scuttled at Yap in the Carolines, and dispatch vessel *Comet* was captured by an Australian auxiliary off New Guinea.

The German colonial possessions themselves in the Pacific were lost as rapidly. A New Zealand expedition occupied German Samoa without opposition, the Australians took New

Guinea and the Bismarck Archipelago, and the Japanese took over the German island groups in the central Pacific. Kiautschou itself held out against a powerful Japanese invasion force until Governor Meyer-Waldeck was forced to capitulate on 7 November.

Elsewhere Germany's empire was similarly eclipsed. Light cruiser *Karlsruhe* interrupted Allied shipping in the Caribbean until she was destroyed by an internal explosion off Trinidad on 4 November, and the gunboat *Eber* from the West African station proceeded to Bahia, Brazil, where she was interned in September (and burned in 1917). Survey vessel *Möwe* was scuttled at Dar-es-Salaam in East Africa, and the light cruiser *Königsberg*, after a brief attempt at cruiser-warfare, was secreted up the Rufiji estuary where British monitors finally pounded her into wreckage by 11 July 1915. Though Colonel von Lettow-Vorbeck bravely kept resistance alive in German East Africa, the fate of the German colonies was never really in doubt. The defence of a colonial empire depended on sea-power abroad, and this Germany did not have.

Yet Tirpitz's policy of pursuing a battle-fleet strategy was not necessarily detrimental to the colonial interests. As Tirpitz had told the Reichstag in 1899, "Overseas conflicts with European nations possessing greater naval strength will be settled in Europe".[59] But his first concern was always the battle fleet. If he had advocated the acquisition of Kiautschou it was because the German navy required a base in East Asia for its Cruiser Squadron, and not because the bay was intended as a link in a network of bases around the world to support a strategy of cruiser-warfare. The ultimate decision was to be sought elsewhere.

1. Instructions to ambassadors in London and St. Petersburg from Bülow, 19/12/1897; BA, Bülow Nachlass, folder 21.
2. Lamar Cecil, *Albert Ballin* (Princeton, 1967), p.66.
3. In November 1890 there were three steam-sail cruisers in the Cruiser Squadron. A fourth cruiser was on the Australian station and two gunboats were on the East Asiatic station. *Rangliste der Kaiserlich Deutschen Marine* (Berlin annual, 1891). While the Cruiser Squadron was officially renamed the Cruiser Division between 1894 and 23/11/1897, it was generally referred to as the "Cruiser Squadron".
4. Alfred von Tirpitz, *My Memoirs*, 2 vols. (New York, 1919), 1:95. This dependence was vividly demonstrated during the Sino-Japanese war when the supply of coal was cut off entirely for a short time.

5. In 1899 the OKM was abolished as the Kaiser desired to exercise personal command over forces at sea, and the operational planning section went independent as the Admiralstab der Marine (ADM) or Admiralty Staff of the navy. See Walter Hubatsch, *Der Admiralstab und die Obersten Marinebehörden in Deutschland, 1848–1945* (Frankfurt, 1958).
6. See Theodore Ropp's discussion in Edward Meade Earle, ed., *Makers of Modern Strategy* (Princeton, 1952), pp.450ff.
7. See, for example, Admiral von Knorr's memorandum of 28/11/1895 setting forth the OKM views on the future development of the fleet; Hans Hallmann, *Der Weg zum deutschen Schlachtflottenbau* (Stuttgart. 1933), chap. 4. See also Tirpitz's undated memorandum attacking Valois' *Seemacht, Seegeltung, Seeherrschaft* (Berlin, 1899) in BA/MA, N257/44, Tirpitz Nachlass.
8. Specific coal consumption statistics are given in Kapitän zur See Erich Raeder, *Der Kreuzerkrieg in den ausländischen Gewässern*, 2 vols (Berlin, 1922), 1. and Erich Gröner, *Die deutschen Kriegsschiffe, 1815–1936* (Munich/Berlin, 1937).
9. Kaiser's telegram quoted by Chancellor Hohenlohe to Foreign Secretary Marschall, 17/11/1894 *GP* 9, no.2219. The Kaiser's trade statistics were exaggerated, by whatever currency denomination employed. In 1895 the value of German trade was some 48 million marks. John E. Schrecker, *Imperialism and Chinese Nationalism* (Cambridge, 1971), p.23fn.
10. Marschall to Hollmann, 11/3/1895; BA/MA, F2422, RMA, xix. 1.1.1., PG, 60942 (PG numbers refer to material microfilmed by the British Admiralty and shared with the American navy and National Archives); also *GP*, 14, no.3645.
11. Hollmann to Marschall, 17/4/1895; BA/MA, F2422, RMA, xix. 1.1.1., PG, 60942; also *GP*, 14, no.3646. In addition, Hollmann's ideas are presented in a memorandum of 6 April, and Knorr's ideas in a letter dated 25 March; BA/MA, F2422, RMA, xix. 1.1.1., PG, 60942.
12. Knorr to Hoffmann, 26/9/1895; BA/MA, F7562, ADM-B Kreuzergeschwader G. 3a.
13. RMA memorandum on Wei-hai-wei, 25/10/1895; BA/MA, F2422, RMA, xix. 1.1.1., PG, 60942. The British occupied Wei-hai-wei in 1898 only because it was strategically located opposite Port Arthur on the Liaotung peninsula, taken by the Russians shortly before. They never intended to develop it commercially.
14. Schenck to Foreign Office, 29/10/1895; *GP* 14, no.3655.
15. The German concessions, leased 3 and 30 October, are in John Van Antwerp MacMurray, *Treaties and Agreements With and Concerning China*, 1894–1919, 2 vols (New York, London, etc., 1921), 1: 42–50.
16. Marschall to Chancellor Hohenlohe, 6/12/1895; *GP* 14, no.3658.
17. Tirpitz, *Memoirs*, 1, p.92. Tirpitz had apparently already been chosen to succeed Hollmann at the RMA. But Hollmann had just received a vote of confidence in the Reichstag, and Chancellor Hohenlohe hesitated to make the change.
18. Kaiser's marginalia on Heyking to Hohenlohe, 22/8/1896; *GP* 14, no.3664.
19. Tirpitz, *Memoirs*, 1, p.96. Tirpitz to Heyking, from Yokohoma, 28/9/1896; BA/MA, N257/44 Tirpitz Nachlass. Before visiting Kiautschou himself, Tirpitz had dispatched SMS *Iltis* to examine the bay; but on 23 July the little steam-sail gunboat had encountered a sudden typhoon and foundered.
20. Tirpitz to Knorr, 5/9/1896; BA/MA, N257/45 Tirpitz Nachlass; also F2422, RMA, xix. 1.1.1., PG, 60943.
21. Kaiser to Hohenlohe, 27/11/1896; *GP* 14, no.3668.

22. Tirpitz, *Memoirs*, 1, p.97.
23. The plan was approved by the Kaiser on 22/12/1896; BA/MA, F3408, MK, xxii c, PG, 67305.
24. Tirpitz to Knorr, 7/12/1896; BA/MA, F5173, ADM-B, iii. 1. 13. Jonathan Steinberg, in *Yesterday's Deterrent* (London, 1965), p.103fn, quotes the settlement idea as an aggressive one; it would appear, however, that Tirpitz merely mentioned it as a last resort.
25. Foreign Office to RMA, 16/1/1897; BA/MA, F2422, RMA, xix. 1.1.1., PG, 60943.
26. The Kaiser, apparently still unaware of the strategic implications of battleships vis-a-vis cruisers, was only impatient that *some* kind of a fleet should be created; and Tirpitz appeared more dynamic than Hollmann.
27. See Tirpitz, *Memoirs*, 1: 65.
28. The idea that there existed a "Flottenstützpunktpolitik" is a tantalizing but illusory one. Documents in packets such as BA/MA, F5174a, ADM-B, iii. 1–15 (Überseeische Flottenstützpunkte 1898–1915) merely include various political-military reports, and in F 4292 RMA, xiv. 1.1.7. correspondence between colonial and naval officials regarding the navy's lack of interest in the colonies.
29. Hohenlohe to Radolin, ambassador to St.Petersburg, 9/9/1897; *GP* 14, no.3681.
30. Heyking to Foreign Office, 1/10/1897; *GP* 14, no.3684. See also Bülow to Tirpitz, RMA, 10/10/1897; BA/MA, F2422, RMA, xix. 1.1.1. PG 60943.
31. Diederichs to OKM, Wusung, 3/11/1897; BA/MA, F5168, ADM-B, iii. 1. 8.
32. Telegram dated 7/11/1897 in BA/MA, F7562, ADM-B (Kreuzergeschwader), G.iii.b and other sources.
33. See Deputy Foreign Secretary Rotenhan to the Kaiser, 10/11/1897; *GP* 14, no.3693, and ff.
34. Draft of telegram, Tirpitz to Hohenlohe, 10/11/1897; BA/MA, F2422, RMA, xix 1.1.1., PG 60944. Steinberg, *Yesterday's Deterrent* p.155 fn, quotes this to indicate Tirpitz's opposition to Kiautschou. But Tirpitz was very sensitive about his Navy Bill, and probably only objected to seizing Kiautschou at this *particular* time.
35. See the numerous messages in BA/MA, F5168, ADM-B iii.1.8.
36. Diederichs' After-Action Report to the OKM, Kiautschou via Tientsin, 15/11/1897; BA/MA, F5168, ADM-B iii.1.8.
37. Unsigned memorandum of 15/11/1897; *GP* 14, no.3701. The treaty was finally signed on 6 March 1898, and included railroad and mining rights beyond the borders of the leased territory (*Pachtgebiet*) itself.
38. Diederichs' ships now became the First Division of the Cruiser Squadron, and Heinrich's ships became the Second. Prince Heinrich succeeded Diederichs as squadron chief on 2/3/1899.
39. MacMurray, *Treaties and Agreements*, 1:152–53. In addition, France acquired Kwangchow Bay and England acquired Kowloon, while Italy alone failed to gain her demands. The United States insisted on the Open Door while affirming the Monroe Doctrine in the Americas, and then acquired her own empire as a result of the Spanish-American War a few months later.
40. "Die französische Marine", *Nauticus* (Berlin annual, 1899) p.175.
41. Tirpitz, *Memoirs*, 1, p.100.
42. Undated RMA memorandum, presumably January 1898; BA/MA, F2423, RMA, xix 1.1.5., PG, 60949.
43. Bülow to Tirpitz, 15/1/1898; BA/MA, F2423, RMA, xix. 1.1.5., PG, 60949.

44. See, for example, Knorr to the Kaiser, 2/2/1898, BA/MA, F3408, MK, 22c, PG, 67305. This Knorr-Tirpitz argument may reflect the power struggle within the navy which ended with the abolition of the OKM in 1899, and the replacement of it by the more limited ADM.
45. The responsibilities of the governor and the RMA were defined in an AKO (Allerhöchste Kabinetts Ordre) by the Kaiser of 1/3/1898; BA/MA, F2423, RMA, xix 1.1.5., PG, 60949.
46. See in particular Eugen Wolf's articles for the *Berliner Tageblatt* in July and August 1898; BA/MA, F2423, RMA, xix 1.1.4. PG, 60948. Most correspondents and business elements, however, acknowledged the difficulties the navy administrators faced, and commended the progress made.
47. Knorr's memorandum of 13/7/1898; BA/MA, F3419, MK, xxiih PG, 67346. Bülow to Tirpitz, 18/5/1898; BA/MA, F5085, OKM ii Am11a.
48. Flag Lieutenant Hintze's report for Diederichs (Dewey's words in English) to the OKM, Manila, 14/7/1898; BA/MA, F5085, OKM Am.11a.
49. Foreign Secretary Bülow was considering abandoning the Samoan claims for compensation in the Solomon Islands and the mouth of the Volta on the West African coast. Correspondence between Bülow and Bendemann (ADM) and Tirpitz (RMA), 10/10/1899 and 11/10/1899; BA/MA, F5166, ADM-B, iii. 14b. Samoa.
50. Vizeadmiral a.D.Dr von Mantey, *Deutsche Marinegeschichte* (Charlottenburg, 1926), p.198, gives the German contribution as 20 officers, 2 doctors, 487 men and 2 machine guns under Captain Usedom of SMS *Hertha*.
51. Sailing orders, etc., for the squadron are in BA/MA, F4467, RMA China.
52. Müller (MK) to Truppel, 28/12/1910; BA/MA, F3409, MK, xxiic, PG, 67310. For the developing antagonism between Tirpitz and Truppel see the correspondence and Truppel's annual fitness reports by Tirpitz in the Truppel Nachlass, BA/MA, N224/3. See also the reports in BA/MA, F2246 RMA, i.2.1.–20 Nachrichtenbüro PG, 94053.
53. Operations plans in BA/MA, F5170, ADM-B, iii.1.–9b.
54. Messages and reports are to be found in the *Emden's* War Diary; BA/MA, F5122, ADM-B Deutschl. 23b.
55. Vollerthun to the Kaiser, Tsingtau, 14/3/1911; BA/MA, F5122, ADM-B Deutschl. 23b. The Kaiser apparently appreciated Vollerthun's bluntness, for at the end he scribbled an enthusiastic "*Sehr gut*!"
56. Solf to Heeringen, 28/10/1912; and Heeringen's reply, 6/12/1912; BA/MA, F4292, RMA, xiv. 1.1.7.
57. Samoan governor, Dr Schultz-Ewerth, to the RKA, Apia, 9/11/1913; and New Guinea Governor, Hahl, to the RKA, Rabaul, 20/1/1914; BA/MA, F4292, RMA, xiv. 1.1.7.
58. Pohl to Tirpitz, 19/5/1914; BA/MA, F4292, RMA, xiv. 1.1.7.
59. *Stenographische Berichte über die Verhandlungen des Reichstags*, 10. Legislaturperiode, 1. Session 1898–1900, 119. Sitzung, 11/12/1899, p.3295.

# 7

# The German Acquisition of the Caroline Islands, 1898-99

RICHARD G. BROWN

Until the latter half of the nineteenth century the Caroline Islands, like many other far-flung Pacific outposts, were considered exclusively Spanish territory, by no means the object of the imperial designs of European powers. Justifiably so, for Spanish interest in the islands dates back to 1493 when the Papal Bull of that year placed the Carolines in Spain's sphere, giving that country its initial claim in the western Pacific. Moreover, the Magellan voyage of 1521 clearly asserted Spanish hegemony in the Pacific with the discovery of the nearby Ladrones, although it was 1686 before Francisco Lezcano gave the name of Carolina to one of the larger islands in honour of Charles II, and that of Marianas to the Ladrones in honour of the mother of the king.[1] Furthermore, the fact that Spanish blood had been shed in the Ladrones during the Magellan voyage made Spanish claims there a thing of the spirit. Thus for over three centuries Spain claimed jurisdiction in the islands, while taking few overt steps to effect occupation and adminstration there.

With the exception of some missionary and trade activity, the Caroline Islanders were not bothered with European life until the nineteenth century. Even then, the lure of copra and the desire to christianize elicited no more than tacit support from the European capitals. Although trading vessels from many countries visited the Carolines, only a few British and German traders were firmly established in the islands by the middle of the century. American missionary activity dates from 1852 when Congregationalists began the conversion of natives on the islands of Ponape and Kusaie.[2] Inevitably then those countries, other than Spain, with some interests in the islands were England, Germany, and the United States. But, until 1874, no rivalry as such existed between the governments of those countries over the Carolines.

The year 1874, however, saw the first diplomatic crisis between nations over the islands, ominously forecasting greater crises to come. In that year the German vessel *Coervan*, loaded with goods and destined for the Carolines, was ordered by the Spanish consul at Hong Kong to go to Manila for proper authorization since, as he claimed, the Caroline Islands were Spanish territory. Not willing to accept this slap in the face, the German government, in March, 1875, drafted a protest to Spain that "Germany cannot admit the validity of the claims made by the Spanish Consul at Hong Kong ... and that it is hoped the Spanish government will put no obstacle in the way of the direct transit of German ships".[3] The British government, after hearing similar appeals from its merchants in the Pacific, was likewise moved to send notes of protest to Spain rejecting the legitimacy of exclusive Spanish rights in the islands.[4]

Germany, cast in the same role as Great Britain, looked to that country for support in its quest for trading rights in the Carolines, and in April, 1876, an Anglo-German agreement stipulated that the Caroline and Marshall Islands should be considered in Germany's sphere of influence.[5] The question of sovereignty in the islands seemed mute after this. Indeed, the British ambassador to Spain was told by an official of the Spanish government on 13 November 1876 that Spain had never really demanded sovereignty over the Carolines. Accordingly, freedom of traffic was restored in the islands by the Madrid Protocol of March 1877, the signatories being Germany, Spain, and England.[6]

With the advent of Bismarck's conversion to colonialism in 1884, renewed German interest in the islands resulted in the deep involvement of several German trading firms, the most important being the Hamburg firm of Robertson and Hernsheim. This firm had, by 1885, purchased land and established factories there, necessitating its request to Bismarck in January of that year that "the German flag should be hoisted on the East and West Carolines to protect the dominant German interests".[7] Moreover, Germany's recent acquisitions of the Bismarck Archipelago, the Solomons, Marshalls, and a portion of New Guinea proved that Germany stood ready to expand its colonial empire, even if it meant stepping on Spanish colonial feet.

Thus Germany could well claim that no significant Spanish advances had been made in the Carolines since 1875; that

Spain had never taken possession of or occupied the islands, and that it had no merchants, factories or trade there; nor had Spain done anything to entitle it to any extensive jurisdiction.[8] Consequently, Count Eberhard zu Solms-Sonnenwalde, the German ambassador to Madrid, was instructed in the spring of 1885 to find out if Spain could make justifiable claims for the Carolines, and if occupancy by Germany would cause trouble in that country.[9] Meanwhile, Friedrich Richard Krauel, official in charge of Colonial Affairs and one of the most influential voices in the German Foreign Office, succeeded in gaining the outright support of Bismarck. Krauel then took the lead in negotiations with the British government on the question of the islands.[10]

With British acquiescence forthcoming, Solms was instructed on 3 June 1885 to investigate rumours that Spain planned to occupy the Carolines. Properly assessing the Spanish national character, Solms replied that Spain could not make justifiable claims, but that popular sentiment would be unleashed in Spain if Germany occupied the islands. When, on 9 June 1885, Solms revealed that Spain planned to annex the Carolines, the German Foreign Office began contingency planning based on that probability. Spain, however, having anticipated renewed German interest in the islands, had already moved to occupy them. In March the cruiser *Velasco* had been ordered to the island of Yap to collect pertinent data necessary to effect the occupation. This done, the Spanish authorities in the Philippines appointed a Lieutenant Cabriles military governor of the Carolines. The race for the islands was on.[11]

Bismarck, underestimating Spain's reaction of choosing to disregard it, waited until early August to notify Antonio Canovas de Castillo, Spanish prime minister and leader of the ruling Conservative party, of Germany's intentions to occupy the Carolines. Solms, more familiar with the Spanish public than the heady Bismarck, delivered the message on 6 August with misgiving. When the official pronouncement was made on 11 August, the Spanish Conservative party, as well as the Spanish public, was predictably chagrined. During the weeks that followed, the Spanish mood became increasingly hostile, with most Spanish newspapers advocating outright reprisal.[12]

The reaction of the Spanish government was twofold; on the one hand it attempted, through diplomatic channels, to convince Germany of its rights in the islands, while at the same time showing a display of force there.[13] Bismarck, not impressed with either Spanish reaction, was greatly tempered by Kaiser Wilhelm's concern for the fate of King Alfonso's throne. The chancellor would, accordingly, only bluff for so long before reaching an amicable solution. Only when the quarrel reached its peak on 4 September, with the Spanish announcement that the German frigate *Iltis* had hoisted the German flag on Yap, was there a real threat of war. The one stringent demand made by Bismarck, however, was reparations for the destruction of the German embassy by a Spanish mob on the evening of 4 September.[14]

The crisis lasted with some intensity until 21 September, when Bismarck, possibly because the Bulgarian crisis turned his attention to nearer home, agreed to submit the quarrel to Papal arbitration. The Papal decision was signed on 17 December 1885 at Rome by the Marquis de Molins of Spain and Kurd von Schlozer, German ambassador to the Vatican, representing their respective governments. Sovereignty of the Caroline Islands was awarded to Spain, with Germany given virtually the same trading privileges that Spain would enjoy in ownership.[15] Clearly, the long-term victory was Bismarck's however, for he had established the German claim to the islands in the event that Spain should later choose to relinquish them; he established cordial relations with Pope Leo XIII which helped bring about the demise of the troublesome *Kulturkampf*; and by averting war in 1885, Bismarck gained international respect as a man of peace, quite the antithesis of the early period of his rule. Moreover, the Spanish monarchy survived, and German economic activity continued to flourish in the Carolines.

The outbreak of the Spanish-American War in April 1898 once more turned world attention to the Pacific, and Germany was afforded another chance to fulfil its latent desires in that area. The German seizure of Kiautschou in November 1897, had been consummated in the spring of 1898 by a treaty with China, whereby Germany had been able to lease the naval base and a substantial amount of adjacent territory, thus giving her a strategic base on the Pacific and a place from which to effect further expansion. In addition, the first navy bill had been passed in April, marking the beginning of German naval expansion, and this enabled the Kaiser to envision a chain of German islands extending from the Solomons to Kiautschou.

Moreover, a German law, calculated to promote the building of merchant ships, had been passed to reduce freight rates on shipbuilding materials. This law, after one year, was worth fifteen million marks to the shipbuilding industry. The increase in the merchant fleet and the development of a powerful navy were therefore well under way by late 1898, and there can be no doubt that these developments stimulated renewed German desire to acquire additional territory in the Pacific, whether the Philippines, Carolines or Marianas.[16]

Evidence indicated that Germany first considered the acquisition of the Philippines. Having had merchant establishments in the islands for many years, Germany recognized the value of this group to its shipping and the Imperial Navy. The origin of this contention dates back to May 1898, when Prince Henry of Prussia revealed to the kaiser that the Filipinos would welcome German intervention there, as well as the establishment of a German protectorate. Prince Henry, in Hong Kong, had accepted this on the word of a German merchant in Manila. Kaiser Wilhelm II and Foreign Secretary Bernhard von Bülow apparently considered this temptation in earnest, but then vacillated after considering the posture of England and France. Indeed to have secured the blessing of England would have been imperative to Germany had she decided on outright annexation of the Philippines, for she could not have defied both England and the United States on this issue.[17]

After the decision to pursue a neutral policy in the Philippines, and in light of the fact that American and British aims there were at the time unclear, Vice-Admiral Otto von Diederichs was ordered to the Philippines to observe the military situation, watch the mood of the natives, and report any political changes. Accordingly, von Diederichs departed from Nagasaki in early June for the Philippines, where three cruisers awaited his command. In the latter part of June two additional German cruisers arrived in Manila Bay, thereby initiating the uncomfortable relationship between von Diederichs and Admiral George Dewey which was widely publicized and which, to a certain extent, impaired American-German relations. This quarrel was epitomized by furious outbursts from the presses of both countries, and German public sympathy was understandably pro-Spanish during the war. Yet despite German public opinion and the precarious situation in Manila Bay, Bülow's avowed "free hand" policy dictated German restraint during the course of the conflict.[18]

The German Foreign Office set about to demonstrate its neutrality, although neutrality was never officially proclaimed. The American ambassador to Germany, Andrew D. White, was amazed that "they went so far on one occasion as almost to alarm us".[19] This incident occurred when White protested that a Spanish vessel at Hamburg, supposedly loaded with arms to be used against Americans in Cuba, was about to leave the port. The German Foreign Office, therefore, had the vessel overhauled at the mouth of the Elbe and searched to White's satisfaction. Moreover, to demonstrate its acceptance of the American presence in the Philippines, the German Foreign Office recalled four of the five cruisers from Manila Bay in early August, and placed the German nationals and their interests there under the protection of the United States. It then became obvious that German colonial desires were to be predicated on American acquiescence and not on unilateral annexation which would antagonize the United States. Therefore, negotations would have to begin with the United States if Germany were to salvage any territory from the declining Spanish empire. There were, however, some indications that the Foreign Office had second thoughts about this policy, since the United States did not know exactly what it wanted in regard to the Philippines and other Spanish possessions in the Pacific.[20]

The United States was approached in early July on the matter of Spanish possessions in the Pacific. The ambassador in London, Count Paul von Hatzfeldt, and Dr von Holleben, ambassador in Washington, carried the message that Germany could be of practical use to America with regard to territorial expansion if America would practice the cliche "live and let live". The question of the Carolines came up at this time, and the following proposal was made: if Germany were allowed to secure the Caroline Islands, Samoa, and naval stations in the Philippines, Germany would support American occupation of the Philippines. Meanwhile, the American ambassador, Andrew D. White, was approached by Baron Oswald von Richthofen, under-secretary for foreign affairs, with the same message, but White chose to delay the discussion until peace was made between the United States and Spain.[21]

The German Foreign Office, through Ambassador J.M. von Radowitz in Madrid, received word of Queen Maria Christina's decision to accept American peace conditions, and thereby end the war on 8 August 1898. Von Radowitz revealed that the territorial question of the Philippines would be resolved through a Spanish-American Peace Commission, and that uncertainty still existed in Washington over the actual stand that the United States would take in regard to the disposition of the Philippines. He added that he had been informed by the Spanish secretary of state, the Duke of Almodovar, that Spain would keep a strong foothold in the Philippines and protect her sovereignty as much as possible, since "in the future it will be the only territory where Spain can succeed politically and make pertinent connections with other countries".[22]

With prospects of peace ahead, the German Foreign Office turned to Spain with the intention of negotiating, should Spain retain any worthwhile possessions. The under-secretary of state, von Richthofen, instructed Ambassador von Radowitz in Madrid to "keep the matter under surveillance and report such incidents which would clarify any project regarding the sale of the Spanish colonies, be it the Philippine Islands, the Sulu Islands, or the Canary Islands". The idea of having France act as middle party was also mentioned, as that country had initiated the original Spanish peace overtures through Ambassador Jules Cambon in July. There seems, however, to be no additional evidence that this possibility was ever seriously considered by the German Foreign Office.[23]

Meanwhile, Anglo-German negotiations were in progress regarding the Portuguese colonies in Africa. Although the question of Spanish territory was not pursued during the height of these discussions, and was therefore not written into the Final Convention, indications are that Germany assumed England would not abrogate her previous agreements on the Carolines, recent differences between the two countries notwithstanding.[24] That Germany would expend her diplomatic energy in Washington and Madrid, almost to the exclusion of England, suggests, however, that the understanding with London was, at best, precarious.

When news broke of the armistice of 12 August 1898, the German Foreign Office, through von Radowitz, immediately began negotiations with Spain for any colonial cessions which might be forthcoming. It was apparent that Germany still hoped to obtain some tangible benefits in the Philippines, although all hopes of a German protectorate or a neutralized Philippines had been squelched by the stipulation of the protocol. By the terms of the armistice, the United States was to "occupy and hold the city, bay, and harbor of Manila, pending the conclusion of a treaty of peace which shall determine the control, disposition, and government of the Philippines". There remained, however, a chance that Germany could retain, with American consent, a cable or coaling station somewhere in the Philippine Archipelago. But it was to the Carolines that Germany's main attention was fixed at this time.[25]

Von Radowitz confronted the Spanish foreign secretary, the Duke of Almodovar, with the German desire to purchase remnants of the Spanish possessions in the Pacific, whereupon Almodovar suggested that the discussions start with the Caroline Islands. The Spanish foreign secretary then agreed to sell the Caroline Islands of Kusaie, Ponape and Yap to Germany for a sum to be determined later. This met the approval of the Queen, who, nevertheless, expressed concern at American disapproval, and demanded that this provisional arrangement be kept secret and made contingent on the results of the Peace Commission in Paris. The agreement proved to be a good starting point for Germany, especially in view of the fact that it contained the stipulation that Spain would listen first to Germany's bid if other insular possessions were to be relinquished. The premier, Praxedes Mateo Sagasta, the Liberal leader of the Spanish government, approved with the Queen's consent, and on 10 September the agreement was completed.[26]

When the American Peace Commission arrived in Paris to begin peace deliberations, one of its first acts was to flatly reject the Spanish request for the status quo in the Philippines. Somewhat anxious because all the American peace commissioners were avowed imperialists, the German Foreign Office instructed its ambassador to France, Count Georg Herbert Münster, to follow the deliberations carefully, especially those relating to the questions of the Philippines. Münster was explicitly ordered to make both the "Spanish and Americans think we are not interested". This feigned lack of interest was to continue throughout the peace conference, and the German-American informal discussion would be channelled through Peace Commissioner Whitelaw Reid, who would formulate a respectable friendship for Count Münster.[27]

When later the American commissioners demanded the cession of the Philippines and Sulus, Count Münster, in response to the urgent appeal by the Spanish ambassador to France, Leon de Castillo, for German intervention, could only reply that he had no instructions from the Foreign Office which would enable him to make a commitment. In Berlin, Undersecretary von Richthofen was approached by the Spanish ambassador, Mendez de Vigo, with the same plea, to which Richthofen could only dourly reaffirm German neutrality. A telegram from Richthofen to Münster on 2 November 1898 expressed German sympathies for the cause of Spain, but again cautioned Münster not to give the Americans any reason to suspect German interest, and at the same time to have the Spanish understand the German position. This same sense of urgency in the Spanish government over the apparent loss of the Philippine Islands was again relayed to the German Foreign Office on 5 November 1898 when Freiherr von Seefried of the German embassy wired Chancellor Chlodwig zu Hohenlohe-Schillingsfürst that Spain had inquired about the possibility of German and Russian intervention. But intervention was not forthcoming, as the Czar was out of St Petersburg and could not, therefore, consider the request. The Kaiser would only scratch on the margin of the dispatch, "*Das fehlte noch*".[28]

On the night of 8 November 1898, Count Münster called on Whitelaw Reid in Paris, ostensibly to inquire about the reported explosion under the Supreme Court rooms in Washington. Reid, determined to get to the purpose of the visit, turned the conversation to the peace deliberations and explained the progress of the commission, whereupon Münster mildly protested against the American demand for the cession of the Philippines. Reid then explained by use of a map that any division of the Philippines was difficult and unnatural, and that therefore it fell on the United States to take the entire archipelago. Münster, not being thoroughly convinced, was, nevertheless, moved to say, "We certainly don't want them; at least I don't want them and I hope my government does not". On 13 November 1898 Münster again visited Reid and other members of the American Peace Commission where, over dinner, they discussed the upcoming peace contract, with Münster again evincing a great curiosity to know the status of the negotiations. Münster advanced the idea that Spain would not give up the Philippines, and that none of the Spanish commissioners was willing to make a martyr of himself at home for the sake of getting a treaty. Reid then pointed out that if the United States allowed the islands to fall into the hands of England,

Japan, Russia or any other power, this would provoke international difficulties.[29] Later the question of an American cable station on one of the Caroline Islands was discussed, and in this respect, Kusaie seemed attractive to the United States government. A station there would enable the United States to extend the cable service from San Francisco to Manila. Consequently, when the question of Kusaie was brought before the Peace Commission, Germany, through Münster in Paris and the charge d'affaires, Speck von Sternburg, in Washington, lodged a formal protest, contending that American occupation of Kusaie would severely endanger American-German relations as the island was in a German sphere of influence. The German Foreign Office also considered the fact that Kusaie was the centre of American missionary activity in the eastern Carolines and felt that this too was a reason for the sudden American interest in the island.[30]

The question of Kusaie was to prove the greatest obstacle to negotiations regarding the Caroline Islands. In late November 1898, John B. Jackson, secretary of the American embassy, prepared a draft in the presence of the under-secretary, Richthofen, in Berlin which stipulated in part: "Kusaie lies in the midst of a German sphere and would always be a sore spot if it became American. It does not lie in cable route between Honolulu and Guam, and Germany fails to see why the United States wants it. Germany would not in any way oppose the taking by the United States of another of the Ladrones in place of the Carolines".[31] Correspondence between Foreign Secretary Bernhard von Bülow and von Sternburg in Washington, however, did not reflect the optimism expressed by Jackson's draft. Sternburg, through the secretary of state, John Hay, directed the issue to President William McKinley. Accordingly, Sternburg wired to Berlin on 30 November 1898 that the American State Department could not as yet make a commitment on the issue of Kusaie, but that the American president would like to help Germany get a coaling station in the Sulus. Clearly, the American government was not yet convinced of Germany's exclusive right to Kusaie and would not act in any way to intrude on its authorized representatives in Paris.[32]

Meanwhile, in order to maintain its right to the Carolines, even though the question of Kusaie was still unresolved, the German Foreign Office, acting through Münster in Paris, offered to waive its claim to the Sulus for a coaling station on one of them and for American concurrence in her acquisition of the Carolines.[33] While this proposal was being discussed, the Foreign Office pressed the Spanish government for a second provisional agreement which would allow Germany to buy all the Caroline Islands, including the Palau group to the west. Kusaie was to be left out of the discussions until the question was settled at Paris or with the Americans, but Bülow instructed Radowitz to explore the possibilities of Germany also acquiring the Marianas, Fernando Po and a coaling station in the Canary Islands.[34] When the question of Fernando Po and the Canaries came up in Madrid, the secretary of state, the Duke of Almodovar, was willing to discuss it, but Prime Minister Sagasta and the queen would have nothing of it because of possible complications with England. However, they left the avenue open for further discussion and promised to keep it secret.[35]

On 10 December 1898, with the matter of Kusaie still unresolved, the final peace treaty was signed between Spain and the United States. By the terms of the treaty, the United States acquired the Philippines, Puerto Rico and Guam, with Cuba gaining independence. For these cessions, the United States was to pay twenty million dollars within three months after the exchange of ratifications.[36] Perhaps spurred on by this treaty, the German Foreign Office continued to press its demands for the Carolines, Palaus and the Marianas, but the American acquisition of Guam and the Philippines now made it imperative that the Americans concur in any agreement.[37]

Thus it was in mid-December 1898 when the second provisional treaty was taken up with the Spanish by Radowitz in Madrid. Difficulties arose over the price of the islands, whereupon Radowitz suggested to Chancellor Hohenlohe that matters be allowed to remain as they were until the ratification of the peace treaty, when the Cortes could act on both measures simultaneously. Throughout the discussions in December, the queen remained the most reluctant to sign away all the Spanish possessions in the western Pacific, contending that the loss of all the islands would prove embarrassing for her country. Not willing to see the Spanish people humiliated, and in order to impress the army, she demanded that Spain get coaling stations on the islands if they were sold to Germany. After a brief delay, due to the illness of Premier Sagasta, Bülow authorized Radowitz to finalize the provisional agreement, and it was by this secret arrangement that Spain promised to cede to Germany all of the Carolines, Palaus and Marianas, with the exception of Guam, for a price which would be determined later.[38]

The Foreign Office then made a concerted attempt to get American approval for Germany's right to the three island groups to include Kusaie. In late December, Foreign Secretary Bülow spoke to John B. Jackson of the American embassay, and explained the nature of the agreements Germany had reached with Spain, placing frequent stress on Germany's strict observance of neutrality during the Spanish-American War and its refusal to negotiate with Spain for those islands for which the United States made a demand. Germany was willing, said Bülow, to negotiate with the United States for one of the Marshall Islands (Gaspar Rico) in return for Germany's right to a coaling station on one of the Sulus. Similarly, Ambassador von Holleben in Washington carried the same message, but not without drawing a sharp rebuke from the secretary of state, Hay, for Germany's claim to Kusaie.[39] A Holleben telegram to the Foreign Office on 31 December 1898, however, carried a more conciliatory message from the State Department, namely, that the United States would agree to discuss Gaspar Rico in return for one of the Sulus, and would pledge American friendship for Germany.[40]

In early January 1899 Ambassador Andrew D. White conferred with Bülow regarding alleged mistreatment of German nationals in Manila by Filipino insurgents. When the question of the use of German force to quell the disturbance came up, White was adamant in his refusal to grant Germany this privilege. However, when the question of Kusaie was mentioned, he agreed that American retention of that island would lead to embarrassment. Then, using a map, Bülow showed White how Gaspar Rico, which was on a line directly between Hawaii and the Philippines, would be more useful to the United States. On the question of a German coaling station in the Sulus, Bülow reiterated the importance of such a station in relation to Germany's Chinese territory and other Pacific possessions. Ambassador White, always conciliatory toward Germany, concluded that the United States should concede on the point of Kusaie and on granting Germany a coaling station in the Sulus. The same day, Bülow sent Holleben a message expressing gratitude over the new American position on Kusaie, and reaffirming Germany's desire for one of the Sulu Islands.[41]

The new spirit of entente was evident during the week that followed. An example of this new spirit was White's rejection of the question of establishing diplomatic agents in the lesser German capitals for fear of antagonizing the Imperial Government. It was at this time that Wake Island, located north of the Marshall Islands, came up in diplomatic circles. The United States government indicated that Wake Island would be better located for an American cable station than Gaspar Rico of the Marshalls, whereupon Bülow was able to wire Holleben that Germany had no use for the island. He also instructed Holleben to begin negotiations for Palawan or Tawi-Tawi of the Sulu group. Messages from White to the secretary of state, Hay, carried the same requests, as the German Foreign Office felt that the Sulu matter should be resolved before the United States Senate ratified the Peace Treaty of Paris.[42] Holleben, moved to second thoughts, suggested to the Foreign Office that Germany propose to rent, rather than buy, the island because he felt the Senate would never consent to its purchase. He also expressed concern about pushing the Americans too fast on the issue, and cautioned the Foreign Office in this respect.[43]

The brief calm in the German-American exchanges was threatened in mid-January 1899 by an insurrection on the island of Ponape in the eastern Carolines, where, according to Bülow, American missionaries had turned the natives against the German nationals on the island. Bülow, thinking that the United States would send a warship to Ponape to protect its interests there, requested that the Kaiser give him permission to respond in like fashion. This request was denied by the Kaiser, and, but for a brief flurry in the foreign press, the issue did no harm to either country.[44]

During the first week in February 1899, von Radowitz pressed for a final settlement for the Carolines, Palaus and Marianas. The Spanish secretary of state, the Duke of Almodovar, set a price of 25 million pesetas and the right to extended commercial privileges in the islands. Bülow, thinking the price was excessively high, asked Radowitz to obtain German first option rights to Fernando Po also, in the event of Spain's relinquishing the island later. Radowitz received word from Berlin on 4 February 1899, to close the deal. The queen, although ill, gave her consent to the final agreement, and the purchase was finalized on 12 February 1899, with the stipulation that the treaty was not to be revealed until it was formally brought before the Cortes for approval. However, before the Cortes could consider the treaty, the result of the Spanish-American War had its internal effect, and the Sagasta ministry was replaced on 1 March 1899, by the more conservative ministry of Francisco Silvela. Somewhat sceptical of the effect this change could have on the treaty, Radowitz confronted Silvela on the matter and received assurances that the new ministry would agree to the treaty.[45]

Perhaps concerned with the possibility that the treaty would be revealed by the foreign press before the Cortes met, the Official German Telegraph Agency circulated the announcement that the Spanish government had decided to maintain its sovereignty over the Carolines, and was not, therefore, entertaining offers for the purchase of the islands. This was understood to signify that Germany had abandoned the idea of acquiring the Carolines.[46]

The peace treaty was ratified by the Cortes on 11 April 1899, but the Cortes adjourned before considering the Carolines treaty with Germany. When a new session of the Cortes convened 2 June 1899, the Queen's address set the tone: "The Caroline Islands, the Palaus, and the greater part of the Ladrones remained under our dominion, but the late government were of the opinion that it was not expedient for Spain to retain these possessions, and they signed with the German Emperor a convention, whereby they offered to cede him those territories, for which purpose a bill will immediately be submitted to our chambers".[47]

Bülow formally read the text of the treaty to the Reichstag on 5 June 1899. Its main provisions were: Spain was to cede to Germany the Caroline Islands, together with the Palaus and the Marianas, with the exception of Guam, for 25 million pesetas; Spanish trade, agricultural enterprise, and religious orders would be granted the same privileges as Germany; Spain was to have the right to establish coaling depots in the islands and retain these even in time of war; and the agreement was to be subject to the constitutional approval of each country as prescribed by the laws of each.[48]

The debate in the Reichstag during the next two weeks saw vociferous opposition by certain segments of the Social Democratic party and a few Agrarians.[49] Although the discussion in the Cortes was a bit more subdued, it was, nevertheless, bitter. The Cortes approved the treaty on 19 June 1899, while the Reichstag waited until 22 June.[50]

In light of the events of 1885, it cannot be disputed that Germany, after Spain, had a legitimate right to the islands in question. Being caught up in colonial intrigues was an understandable corollary to the *Weltpolitik* pursued by Wilhelm II in the decade of the 1890s, and this quest for colonies was undoubtedly encouraged by the seizure of Kiautschou in 1897 and the beginning of the naval programme in the spring of 1898. Not being subject to the continental prepossessions of Bismarck, Wilhelm II, in searching for his "place in the sun", acquired by the Caroline Islands Treaty over a thousand islands, the value of which was debatable, and the administration of which overextended the empire. For Bülow, the treaty, perhaps, represented his greatest achievement as secretary of state for foreign affairs. That Wilhelm II was elated is an understatement.[51]

During the course of the negotiations, Sternburg and Holleben had the most delicate diplomatic chore in reconciling the American president and State Department to the legitimacy of German's claims in the Pacific. In this respect, the American ambassador, Andrew D. White, played a vital part with his conciliatory gestures to a pro-Spanish German nation during the course of the Spanish-American War. Münster's association with the American peace commissioners cannot be overlooked, nor can one overlook the actual negotiation of Radowitz on the three agreements with Spain. Bülow's conversations with the Spanish ambassador, Mendez de Vigo, provided a direct line of communication from Berlin to Madrid, and may have been the most significant. Although Bülow received the acclaim for "doing what Bismarck could not do", the impulse came from the emperor, Wilhelm II, who was eager to assume for Germany her place among the nations.

But was the German emperor acting in concert with the mood of the nation, as Bülow would lead us to believe. Perhaps the answer lies indeed in the German national character, which the foreign secretary described as "doctrinaire", yet with emotions "capable of endless modulations".[52] Yet, doubtless, domestic unrest—as reflected by certain Social Democrats and Agrarians—made it necessary to divert attention to the Carolines.[53] Nevertheless, the voices of those in Germany who opposed this over-extension of the empire were drowned out by the shouts of the Pan-Germans, who would have become more violently involved with the United States, Spain, or Great Britain. It seems, therefore, that the Carolines treaty afforded an outlet for that emotional response, without bloodshed, and without greatly antagonizing the other powers at the time. Yet, it remains that the German empire had virtually reached its extent in 1899, with the prized possessions having been taken by other powers.

To Bismarck, the role being played by Germany in 1899 would have been reprehensible. That the Carolines would be keenly contested after World War I by Japan, the United States, and Australia, shows the value set on these islands by other powers. The paradox is that Germany's involvement in the Pacific islands proved to be detrimental to its national interest in the final analysis, and the "brief rays" seen by Wilhelm II were at best transitory, as events in the twentieth century would show.

1. Eberhard zu Solms–Sonnenwalde, German ambassador to Madrid to AA, 17/8/1885, no. 6782, University of Michigan Microfilm *German Foreign Ministry Archives, 1867–1920*, vol. 1, frame 51, reel 92, 19/8/1885 to 29/8/1885; John W. Foster, American minister to Spain, to T.F. Bayard, secretary of state, 20/8/1885, no.391, *United States, Department of State, Dispatches From the United States Ministers to Spain, 1792–1906*, microcopy no. 31, roll 105, vol. 114: 18/8/1885 to 31/12/1885 (Washington, 1953).
2. Julius W.Pratt, *Expansionists of 1898* (Baltimore, 1936), p. 302; Edward H. Strobel, secretary of the American legation to Bayard, 22/9/1885, no. 424, *United States, Department of State, Dispatches From the United States Ministers to Spain 1792–1906*, microcopy no. 31, roll 105, vol. 114: 18/8/1885 to 31/12/1885. (Washington, 1953).
3. Foster to Bayard, 20/8/1885, no. 391T1, *US Dispatches From Spain;* Paul von Hatzfeldt, secretary of state for foreign affairs, to HEMA Castro, Minister of state of the king of Spain, cited by the *New York Times*, 14/9/1885, p. 51. Certain German acquisitions in the Pacific could well have been predicted by 1882; See Mr. Sargent to Mr. Frelinghuysen, 12/3/1883, no. 182, *Foreign Relations of the United States 1883* (Washington, 1884), pp.349–55.
4. Foster to Bayard, 20/8/1885, no. 391, *US Dispatches From Spain;* Maximilian von Hagen, *Bismarcks Kolonialpolitik* (Stuttgart, 1921), p. 553.
5. Otto zu Stolberg–Wernigerode, *Germany and the United States During the Era of Bismarck,* trans. Otto E. Lessing (Reading, Pennsylvania, 1937), p. 217; Jeanette Keim, *Forty Years of German–American Political Relations* (Philadelphia, Pa., 1919), pp. 369–71; Otto Hammann, *The World Policy of Germany*, trans. Maude A, Huttman (London, 1927), pp. 82–85.
6. Hagen, *Bismarcks Kolonialpolitik*, p. 554.
7. Foster to Bayard, 20/8/1885, no. 391, *US Dispatches From Spain;* Stolberg–Wernigerode, *Era of Bismarck*, p. 218; *The Holstein Papers*, ed. Norman Rich and M. H. Fisher, 4 vols. (Cambridge, 1957), 2:234.

8. Foster to Bayard, 20/8/1885, no. 391, *US Dispatches From Spain;* The *Times* (London), 25/8/1885, p. 3; *New York Times*, 25/8/1885. The idea that legitimate claims must be preceded by actual occupation was endorsed at the Berlin Conference of 1884–85, which met to adjust colonial claims in Africa. Germany, however, seems to have construed this to apply elsewhere as well hence, its renewed interest in the Carolines in the spring of 1885. For the results of the Berlin Conference see Fred L. Israel ed., *Major Peace Treaties of Modern History, 1648–1967*, (New York, 1967), 2:1081–99.
9. Kuno zu Rantzau to Herbert Bismarck, under secretary of foreign affairs, 24/8/1885, no. 163, *Staatssekretär Graf Herbert von Bismarck, Aus Seiner Politischen Privatkorrespondenz,* ed. Walter Bussman (Göttingen, 1964), p. 290.
10. Friedrich von Holstein, the career bureaucrat so influential in foreign affairs, would thereafter refer to the Caroline Affair as the "Kraueline" Affair, and suggested to Herbert Bismarck that if Germany were to acquire the islands, they should be called the "Krauelines". In his letters, Herbert Bismarck acknowledges the part played by Krauel in the origin of the idea of annexing the islands. See, *Holstein Papers*, 2:237; *Herbert Bismarck Privatkorrespondenz* p. 294.
11. *Holstein Papers*, 2:234; Foster to Bayard, 20/8/1855, no. 391, US Dispatches From Spain.
12. Hagen, *Bismarcks Kolonialpolitik*, p. 255.
13. Ibid.
14. *Holstein Papers*, 2:241–42.
15. Ibid.,p. 250; Solms to AA 24/9/1885, no. 268, Florida State University Microfilm, *German Foreign Ministry Archives, 1867–1920*, vol. 8, reel 128, 24–29/9/1885; Kurd von Schlozer, German ambassador to the Vatican, to AA, 25/9/1885, no. 20, ibid.; same to same, 18/8/1885, no. 85, ibid.
16. Bernhard von Bülow, *Memoirs of Prince Bernhard von Bülow*, 4 vols. trans. F.A. Voight (Boston, 1931), 1:330; Wilhelm II, *The Kaiser's Memoirs*, trans. Thomas R. Ybarra (New York, 1922), p. 7; Malcolm E. Carroll, *Germany and the Great Powers* (New York, 1938),pp.416–17; Mary Evelyn Townsend, *The Rise and Fall of Germany's Colonial Empire, 1884–1918* (New York,. 1930), p. 186.
17. Bülow to Wilhelm II, 14/5/1898, in *GP* 15, no. 4145; Townsend, *Germany's Colonial Empire*, p. 193.
18. An account of the Manila Bay episode is not important here, but good ones are given by: Lester Burrell Shippee, "Germany and the Spanish–American War", *American Historical Review,* 30,754–77; T.A. Bailey, "Dewey and the Germans at Manila Bay", *American Historical Review* 45 (1939): 59–81. For an example of the sentiment of the *New York Times*, see its edition of 14/2/1899, p. 6.
19. Andrew Dickson White, *Autobiography of Andrew Dickson White,* 2 vols. (New York, 1907),2:168–69. For German–American relations at this time see generally: W.R. Braisted, *The United States Navy in the Pacific, 1897–1909*(Austin, Texas, 1958); A Vagts, *Deutschland und die Vereinigten Staaten in der Weltpolitik,* 2 vols. (London/New York, 1935);P.E. Quinn, "The Diplomatic Struggle for the Carolines", *Pacific Historical Review* 14 (1945).
20. Shippee, "Germany and the Spanish–American War", p. 775; Keim, *German–American Relations*, p. 231.
21. Bülow to Dr. von Holleben, ambassador to the United States, 1/7/1898, *GP*, 5:44–45; Oswald von Richthofen, under secretary of foreign affairs, to Count Paul von Hatzfeldt, ambassador to Great Britain, 6/7/1898, tel.no. 606, ibid., pp. 47–49; John B. Jackson, secretary of the embassy,

to John Hay, secretary of state, 28/11/1898, no. 630, *United States, Department of State, Dispatches From the United States Minister to the German States and Germany, 1799–1906*, microcopy no. 44, roll 86, vol. 86: 2/9/98 to 31/12/1898 (Washington, 1953).

22. J.M. von Radowitz, ambassador to Spain, to Chlodwig zu Hohenlohe, chancellor, 8/8/1898, *GP* 15, no. 4167.
23. Richthofen to Radowitz, 12/8/1898, ibid., no. 4168.
24. Arthur James Balfour to Sir Frank Lascelles, ambassador to Germany, 31/8/1898, in *BD* I.
25. Von Derenthall, acting foreign secretary, to Wilhelm II, 12/9/1898, *GP* 15, no. 4172; Alfred L.P. Dennis, *Adventure in American Diplomacy, 1896–1906* (New York, 1928), p. 80.
26. Derenthall to Wilhelm II, 12/9/1898, *GP* 15, no. 4172.
27. Richthofen to Count Georg Herbert Münster, ambassador to France, 22/10/1898, ibid., no. 4173; Dennis, *American Diplomacy, 1896–1906*, p. 81.
28. Richthofen to Münster, 2/11/1898, *GP* 15, no, 4175; Freiherr von Seefrid of the German embassy, to Hohenlohe, 5/11/1898, ibid., no. 4176.
29. H. Wayne Morgan, ed., *Making Peace with Spain: The Diary of Whitelaw Reid,* (Austin, Texas, 1965), pp. 141–42, 148–49; Münster to AA, 16/11/1898, *GP* 15, no. 4177.
30. Richthofen to Münster, 21/11/1898, ibid., no. 4178; Bülow to Speck von Sternburg, charge d'affaires, 26/11/1898, ibid., no. 4180.
31. Jackson to Hay, 28/11/1898, no. 630, US Dispatches From Germany.
32. Sternburg to AA, 30/11/1898, *GP* 15, no. 4181.
33. Richthofen to Münster, 21/11/1898, ibid., no. 4178.
34. Bülow to Radowitz, 3/12/1898, ibid., no. 4183.
35. Radowitz wired the AA on 8/12/1898 that the wires from London to Washington were busy discussing the Carolines and that England's control of Gibraltar would make her very suspicious if Germany obtained a station in the Canaries. Radowitz to AA, 8/12/1898, ibid., no. 4185.
36. William M. Malloy, ed., *Treaties, Conventions, International Acts, Protocols and Agreements, 1776–1909*, (New York, 1910), 2, pp. 1690–96.
37. The United States had been unable to purchase Kusaie from Spain during the negotiations, having offered at one time a million dollars for the island. Whether the secret agreement of 10/9/1898 between Spain and Germany was the greatest factor or not is difficult to determine; however, the Reid diary shows that Count Münster was very active during the discussion regarding Kusaie and persistently objected to the American acquisition of the island.
38. Radowitz to Hohenlohe, 16/12/1898, *GP* 15, no. 4186, Radowitz to AA, 19/12/1898, ibid., no. 4187; Bülow to Radowitz, 20/12/1898, ibid., no. 4188; Radowitz to AA, 21/12/1898, ibid., no. 4189.
39. Jackson to Hay, 29/12/1898, no. 681, US Dispatches From Germany; Bülow to Holleben, 28/12/1898, *GP* 15, no. 4190.
40. Holleben to AA 31/12/1898, ibid., no. 4191.
41. Andrew D. White, US ambassador to Germany, to Hay, 4/1/1899, no. 693, *United States Department of State, Dispatches From the United States Ministers to the German States and Germany, 1799–1906*, microcopy no. 44, roll 87, vol. 68; 2/1/1899 to 31/3/1899 (Washington, 1953): Bülow to Holleben 4/1/1899, *GP* 15, no. 4192.
42. White to Hay, 6/1/1899, US Dispatches From Germany; Bülow to Holleben, 12/1/1899, *GP* 15, no. 4193. White to Hay 11/1/1899, no. 18. From Germany; White to Hay, 12/1/1899, no. 700, US Dispatches From Germany.
43. Holleben to AA, 15/1/1899, *GP* 15, no.4194.
44. Bülow to Wilhelm II, 15/11/1899, ibid., no. 4195.

45. Radowitz to AA, Madrid, 8/2/1899, ibid. no. 4197;Bülow to Radowitz, 4/2/1899, no. 4196; Radowitz to AA, 4/3/1899, ibid., no. 4200.
46. The *Times* (London), 10/2/1899.
47. *Protocols and Agreements, 1776–1909*, 2, p. 1690; The *Times* (London), 3/6/1899.
48. Jackson to Hay, 6/6/1899, no. 892, US Dispatches From Germany; The *Times* (London), 7/6/1899.
49. The debate in the Reichstag was highlighted by the opposition of Bebel and Eugen Richter and will not be discussed here. However, enthusiastic colonial voices were at the same time praising Bülow for doing what Bismarck could not do fourteen year earlier.
50. *The Times* (London), 20/6/1899; Jackson to Hay, 23/6/1899, no. 916, US Dispatches From Germany.
51. On receiving the news of the passing of the Carolines Bill by the Reichstag, Wilhelm II telegraphed Bülow: "I am pleased and delighted at your news of the passing of the bill. I thank God that He has so disposed, and that the acquisition may also be regarded as a justification that does honor to the good ship *Iltis*. Next I thank you most warmly for helping to acquire this pearl for my crown. In order to give special expression to my thanks for this, I am promoting you to the order of Count, since you have enabled me to keep the promise which I made to my Loyal German people on ascending the throne, ever to be an 'Augmenter of the Empire' in Peace. God bless you for it, and our whole fatherland." *Bülow Memoirs*, 1,p, 330.
52. Bülow's characterization of the German people: ibid. p. 331.
53. On this domestic aspect of imperialism, see H.U. Wehler, *Bismarck und der Imperialismus* (Cologne/Berlin, 1969); F.Fisher, *Krieg der Illusionen* (Düsseldorf, 1969); J.C.G. Röhl, *Germany without Bismarck* (London, 1967).

# German Cultural and Political Influence on Japan, 1870-1914

MASAKI MIYAKE

When the Prussian envoy Friedrich zu Eulenburg, who was later to be appointed secretary for home affairs in the cabinet of Bismarck, arrived in Japan on 4 September 1860, he and his followers found a country which was still quite underdeveloped. Japan possessed no vessel comparable to the flagship *Arcona*, the steam corvette of 2,320 tons, in which Eulenburg voyaged from Danzig to Edo (Tokyo).[1] Yet by 1914, Japan was a country equipped with enough military and industrial strength to conquer the heavily armed fortress of the German colonial city Tsingtao in the Shantung peninsula. Even aeroplanes of the Japanese army and navy reconnoitered and bombed the fortress.[2]

Japan's effort to catch up with the highly industrialized Western countries, expressed in the slogan Fukoku Kyohei ("rich country, strong army", or, "enrich the country, strengthen the military"),[3] enabled Japan to take the palm of victory in three successive wars, against China (1894–95), Russia (1904–5) and Germany (1914–18). Germany, like Russia, had been one of those Western powers, which menaced Japan from outside, and compelled Japan to aim at becoming "rich and strong" through Westernization.[4]

Germany deserves special mention in the course of Japan's westernization, or modernization, because it was Germany after 1870, that is, after its victory over France, that offered a "model" for Japan in establishing its modern army and constitution. However, to the intense disappointment of some fervent Germanophile political leaders of Japan like Shuzo Aoki (1844–1914), Germany did not remain merely a harmless and benign instructor for Japan's modernization. Germany suddenly unmasked itself to Japan as an "imperialistic" power, when in 1895, together with Russia and France, it intervened in the terms of the peace treaty between Japan and China, deprived Japan of one of its main spoils of war, the Liaotung Peninsula, and then occupied the Kiautschou Bay in China. In this sense, Germany exerted both a cultural and a political impact upon Japan after 1870.

As regard the cultural impact of the Western countries in the early period of its modernization, Japan experienced vehement personal and factional feuds as to which country of the West should be chosen as the model for the organization of the army as well as for the constitution. The cultural impact of the Western powers was thus transformed within Japan into a highly political issue. Ultimately, the Germanophile faction was victorious. These feuds decided the course of Japan's history.

The Germanophile trend in the foreign policy of Japan, namely, the idea of a German-Japanese alliance, was doomed to disappear because of the German intervention in 1895, at least in the Japanese national psychology as a whole. It seems, however, that the idea of a German-Japanese alliance possessed some possibility of revival, especially when the Germanophile politican Taro Katsura (1847–1913) proposed a visit to Germany in 1912.

These are the problems which will be treated here. In adopting the Prussian Constitution as a model for drafting the Japanese Constitution, Kowashi Inoue (1843–95) played an enormous role as the chief mentor of Hirobumi Ito (1841–1909). Inoue's role will not, however, be treated in depth, because the focus of this study is on Katsura and his circle. Furthermore, only the German impact upon the constitution and army will be considered in any length. Other aspects of the German culture, philosophy, medicine, literature and so forth, are omitted from the scope of this chapter. The impact of the Prussian Constitution will only be treated in so far as it affected Katsura's military reform.

## I

Before the outbreak of the Franco-Prussian War in 1870 and the unification of Germany in 1871, the "image" of Prussia and of Germany in general among the Japanese people was very vague. The Japanese people knew something about Holland, the sole country which was allowed to continue commercial relations with Japan throughout the period of Japan's national isolation (1639–1858). In the later Tokugawa period, Japanese people learned gradually about Russia, England, the United States, and France. About Germany, almost nothing was known until Friedrich zu Eulenburg began negotiations concerning a new treaty between Prussia and Japan on 14 September 1860.

The Tokugawa government had been very reluctant to open Japan to the Western countries, especially at that time, because the statesman Naosuke I'i, who had earlier decided to enter into diplomatic relations with a foreign power (the United States) for the first time in Japanese history, was assassinated by seclusionist zealots on 3 March 1860. Through the mediation of the first American minister in Japan, Townsend Harris, and probably because of the threat posed by the Prussian expeditionary fleet anchoring majestically in the Edo Bay, the Tokugawa government grudgingly decided to open negotiations with Eulenburg. Roju (premier) Nobumasa Ando, lord of Tsushima, ordered two leading officials for foreign affairs (Gaikoku Bungyo), Norimasa Muragaki, lord of Awaji, and Oribe-no-Sho Hori, to conduct the negotiations as the plenipotentiaries for Japan. Hori found in the draft of the treaty proposed by Prussia that not only Prussia, but also all member states of the North German League (Norddeutscher Bund) were enumerated as partner states on the Prussian side. The statesmen of the Tokugawa government who knew nothing about the confederation system, were astonished to hear from Hori of twenty-two states as partners in the coming treaty. They probably thought they were being compelled to open Japan to nearly as many countries as cover the earth. To those officials of the Tokugawa government, the twenty-two states of the North German League comprising Prussia, Hanover, Hesse-Cassel and others, were too much; they wanted to avoid opening Japan to even the single country of Prussia, if possible. Premier Ando therefore ascribed the responsibility of this seeming catastrophe to Hori and denounced him. Hori, who also did not know that these twenty-two states altogether did not cover as much area as France, committed suicide on 5 November 1860. The German political structure before Bismarck's unification brought Hori to his tragic death.[5]

The Prussian-Japanese Treaty of Friendship, Trade and Navigation was signed on 24 January 1861. The relations between Prussia and Japan remained, however, limited until after the Meiji Restoration of 1868. In contrast, the Tokugawa government had invited military instructors from France in 1866, with the aim of creating a modern army in Japan. A French military mission headed by Captain Charles Chanoine then arrived in Japan in the beginning of 1867 and began to instruct the army of the Tokugawa government. Léon Roches, French minister in Japan, also established a French language school headed by Mermet de Cachon in Yokohama in 1865. Both the language school and military instruction were the means by which strong French influence was exerted upon the Japanese army.[6] These were the factors which had inspired Taro Katsura with the desire to study military science in France. However, through a quirk of fate, it was this man who contributed decisively to the introduction of Prussian and German military science into Japan and thus opened a new epoch in German-Japanese cultural contact.

Katsura began his life as a young soldier of the Choshu Clan and had developed the strong wish to study military science in Paris. Before his departure for France, Katsura had studied French at the French language school in Yokohama. For his service in the north of Japan in the war against the league of the clans resisting the new Meiji government in 1868–69, Katsura was awarded a small fief by the Choshu Clan. This he handed over to the clan before leaving his native land, in return for payment of his expenses during his stay in Europe. Katsura's long cherished dream of studying abroad had been postponed by the war in northern Japan which had almost cost him his life. His dream was fulfilled in August 1870 when he left Yokohama for Europe. But when Katsura arrived in London he was hindered from travelling on to Paris by the Franco-Prussian War. Instead, he went to Berlin and studied there at the War Academy until 1873, where his first obligation was to learn the German language.[7]

When Katsura arrived in Berlin in 1870, only three Japanese were there as students: Shuzo Aoki, Susumu Sato and Sankei Hagihara.[8] Aoki was later appointed Japanese minister in Berlin and then foreign minister. Sato was a physician who was later to treat the Russian prince (later Czar Nicholas II) when Nicholas was assulted in the city of Otsu during his visit to Japan. (This affair which occurred in 1891 caused Aoki to resign from his post as foreign minister.) Katsura and Aoki came to be widely recognized as the outstanding Germanophiles in Japanese politics, with the difference that Katsura was more realistic than Aoki, and unlike Aoki, was not moved in his diplomatic decision-making by his affection for Germany.

As Katsura's small stipend had wholly expired in 1873 he was obliged to return home, arriving there in October of that year. In January 1874, he was made a captain in the infantry.[9] He proposed to War Minister (Rikugun-Kyo) Aritomo Yamagata (1838–1922) that the post of military attaché be established. This proposal Yamagata accepted, and the attaché system was started in 1875. Katsura came to Berlin again, this time as the first Japanese military attaché in Germany, and continued to study in Berlin until 1878.

He devoted himself particularly to the study of military institutions and military administration, as well as administration in general. In Berlin Katsura was said to have studied, with the assistance of Aoki, the work by Lorenz von Stein on military administration, and also to have attended Adolf Wagner's lectures at Berlin University.[10]

It was Katsura's ambition to have the Japanese army change from the French to the German system, which he admired and thought better suited to Japan. The years succeeding Prussia's victory over France—years which Katsura experienced on the spot—saw the flowering of German military science. This was represented on the practical side by Paul Bronsart von Schellendorff and Julius von Verdy du Vernois, and on the theoretical side by W. von Blume,[11] Colmar von der Goltz and Jacob Meckel. Thus, Katsura experienced the heyday of the German army as well as of German Military science, and was even said to have been a favourite pupil of Helmuth Karl von Moltke.[12]

After his second home-coming in 1879, Katsura recommended to Yamagata the separation of the General Staff from the War Ministry. Yamagata, who came from the same clan as Katsura and who always favoured Katsura during his career as a soldier, accepted this proposal, and the General Staff was made independent on 3 December 1879.[13] Events during the operations against Takamori Saigo's rebellion in 1878 also influenced this decision. The French way which gave concentrated power to the war minister was thus changed to accord with the German model. The separation of the navy

General Staff from the army General Staff was carried out much later, again on Katsura's advice, on 7 March 1890.[14] Since his second home-coming, Katsura had intended to invite military instructors from Germany. Yamagata, though inclining to Katsura's suggestion, could not decide how to bring this about because Yamagata well knew that almost nobody in the Japanese army understood the German language, in contrast to French, which was in fairly widespread use.[15] Yamagata himself was deeply impressed by the Prussian victory over France. An imperial inspection of the Prussian troops by Wilhelm I at the parade ground of Tempelhof in Berlin, which Yamagata witnessed in 1870, also impressed him.[16]

Though Yamagata favoured the German style of the army organization—especially the German conscription system which he himself enacted at the end of 1872[17], with the aid of Amane Nishi[18]—he did not venture to import the whole German System until 1881. Before the *coup d'état* of 1881, many possibilities were open to Japan other than the Prussian-German way which was later to colour so deeply the national structure of Japan in the constitution, in law and jurisprudence, in philosophy, in medicine, and in the military.

Shigenobu Okuma (1838–1922), a convinced admirer of the British parliamentary system,[19] played an outstanding role as Sangi (councillor or minister) of Sanetomi Sanjo's cabinet.[20] Coming from the Hizen (land of Saga governed by the lord of Nabeschima), Okuma belonged to the numerical minority within the Sanjo cabinet, in which out of sixteen councillors, seven came from Satsuma, six from Choshu, and only three from Hizen.[21]

Each councillor was requested to present drafts of the constitution separately. Okuma's draft was the most radical of all. Actually it was written by Fumio Yano (1850—1931), a pupil of Yukichi Fukuzawa at the Keio Gijuku (Keio University of today), the mentor of Okuma and later minister of Japan in China when Germany captured the Bay of Kiautschou in 1897. A biography of Okuma in English reports as follows:

> We have it from the lips of Yano that he concocted this marvellous doctrine from a recipe taken out of Todd's *Parliamentary Government in England.* He says nothing but the truth; for in some parts of the paper we find out a transcript of the Canadian writer's words. But this document fell on the head of the poor Minister Sanjo like a bomb. Lord Sanjo was so thunder-struck that he showed it to his

> two assistants, Prince Arisugawa and Lord Iwakura. Two points of Okuma's opinion caused greater alarm. One was that a Parliament should be called in less than two years, and the other was that national government should be conducted on the strict line of party politics.[22]

This draft by Okuma aroused the distrust of three powerful councillors, Hirobumi Ito, Kaoru Inoue (1835–1915) and Tomomi Iwakura (1823–83). Okuma seemed to them to be too radical a reformer by their standards. A government scandal concerning Hokkaido which had been exposed by Okuma enhanced their distrust of him even more.

On 11 October 1871 Ito and Tsugumichi Saigo (1843–1902, Satsuma) visited Okuma at midnight and, giving no explanation, demanded Okuma's resignation. As Okuma's biographer insists, his fall had "the effect of changing the whole face of national politics".[23]

This *coup d'état* seems to have tried not only to purge Okuma, but also Fukuzawa and his pupils: Yano, for example, who had penetrated into the government through the mediation of Okuma. Thus, attempts to adopt a constitution moulded on the British model were completely frustrated. Professor Richard Storry summarizes the situation as follows:

> No doubt, if Okuma had been able to prevail, the Constitution would have borne the stamp of his influence, and it might have been a more liberal document than the one, framed in the main by Ito, that was adopted in 1889. It may be that Okuma would have looked to Westminister, rather than to Berlin, for his model. In the event—and not for the last time—it was Germany that exerted a baleful effect upon the course of Japanese history.[24]

In June 1881, one month before the *coup d'état*, Kowashi Inoue had presented to Iwakura, councillor of the cabinet, his draft of the constitution modelled on the Prussian Constitution. Karl Friedrich Hermann Roessler, an adviser to the Japanese government from the University of Rostock, who held this post from 1878 to 1888, was thereby able to influence Inoue decisively.[25]

After the *coup d'état*, Ito, a central figure in the intrigue against Okuma, was ordered by Emperor Meiji to start studying European constitutions immediately. Ito set out for Europe in March 1882. His main aim was to study the Prussian Constitution. In Berlin, he and Aoki, then Japanese minister in

Berlin, who served Ito as interpreter, attended private lectures by Rudolf von Gneist and his pupil, Albert Mosse. In Vienna he heard the private lectures of the aged scholar Lorenz von Stein, as did Munemitsu Mutsu (1844–87).

These moves favoured Katsura decisively in his efforts to remould the Japanese army along German lines. The Japanese government, having purged Okuma and his followers, now consisted mainly of the Sat-Cho faction, and it decided to invite a military instructor from Germany as professor of the Army Staff College (Rikugun Daigakko) in Tokyo, which had been founded in 1882. The French military attaché, Alexandre Bourgouin, protested in vain. Von Moltke, chief of the German General Staff, at Japan's request as conveyed by Minister Aoki, recommended Jacob Meckel (1842–1906) for the post. War Minister von Schellendorff is said to have recommended Captain Colmar von der Goltz, but this recommendation was not accepted.[26]

Meckel arrived in Japan on 18 March 1885. He taught at the Army Staff College and did a brilliant job, staying on in Japan until March 1888. At the same time, Meckel also served as the most important adviser to Katsura in his efforts at military reform based on the Prussian-German model. When Katsura was appointed vice-minister of war under War Minister Iwao Oyama (1842–1916) in 1886, he started to carry out military reform at once. Meckel's advice to Katsura was concentrated in the main on the problem of adjusting the conscription system which Yamagata had ineptly introduced, and of remoulding the military organization in general.[27] Regarding organizational reform, Meckel stressed the necessity of establishing the General Inspectorate as an independent agency. As Professor Samuel P. Huntington points out, one possible weak point which existed in this military structure of authority in Japan was the division of authority among the "Big Three", the minister of war, the chief of the army General Staff, and the inspector general of the military training.[28] Though Meckel's name is not mentioned in Huntington's work, it cannot be denied that Meckel contributed much to Japan's adoption of the German model in general and of the "Big Three" system in particular.

German military institutions lacked effective civilian control, in contrast to the French system.[29] The adoption by Japan of the German example resulted later in the 1930s in the preponderance of the military clique.[30] Japan had originally adopted the French model, not out of any admiration for civilian control, but simply because of the accident of the presence of French military instructors in Japan at the time. The French system did, however, because of its unitary character, have a special appeal to the authoritarian Meiji leaders just after the restoration.[31]

## II

As suggested above, Japanese military officers were at first largely influenced by French military institutions and ideas which they absorbed from the French instructors in Japan, or which they studied on the spot at St Cyr.[32] After the Meiji Restoration of 1868, the Chanoine mission was obliged to return to France. One able instructor Lieutenant Charles-Albert Dubousquet, remained in Japan and wielded some influence on the government and the army there.[33] On 17 May 1872, the second French military mission headed by Lieutenant Colonel Charles-Antoine Marquerie, came to Japan at the invitation of the new Meiji government.[34]

High-ranking generals of the Japanese army such as Goro Miura (Choshu), Koyata Torio (Choshu), Tateki Tani (Tosa) and Sukenori Soga (Fukuoka) were convinced Francophiles as regards the military system and thinking. They opposed Katsura's efforts to reject the French model for the German. Katsura's rapid rise to vice-minister, under Yamagata's sponsorship, aroused the personal animosity of these generals, who were more experienced in commanding field operations than Katsura. One of their tactics was to get control of the so-called "Monday Club" (Getsuyokai). This club was first established as a study group of army officers on 28 March 1881. Katsura belonged to it as well, but the Monday Club gradually became a centre of political agitation against the Yamagata-Katsura group. Goro Miura (1846–1926) and Tateki Tani (1837–1911) resisted Katsura's military reform with particular stubbornness, using this club as their fortress. Not surprisingly, Katsura suddenly withdrew from the Monday Club, together with Gentaro Kodama (1852–1906) and others on 4 April 1888, and then succeeded in dissolving the club in the name of the war minister, Oyama, on 2 February 1889.[35]

The Monday Club affair was to some extent a factional struggle, as Professor Ernst L. Presseisen points out.[36] It may be important to note that whereas this trouble was a dispute on "models" for the modernization of the Japanee army, the conflict itself was more complicated. The political disturbance around Okuma in 1881, which was discussed earlier, was also in some respect a dispute concerning whether Japan should accept the British model or the German for the new constitution of Japan. Similar "model disputes" may be found in modernization periods in many non-Western countries. Such disputes were almost inevitably characterized by violent factional feuds. Through the *coup d'état* of 1881 and through the Monday Club affair, supporters of the British model for the constitution and of the French model for the military system were defeated. The German model could thus be adopted without any further obstacles in either fields. In a sense the Monday Club was a replay of the *coup d'état* of 1881 on a minor scale.

## III

Immediately after its victory over China in 1895, Japan experienced an unexpected shock: the Tripartite Intervention. To cite Professor Toshio Ueda:

> Contrary to the anticipation of the Western powers, the Sino-Japanese War ended in an overwhelming victory for Japan. China recognized the cession of Taiwan, the Pescadores and Liaotung Peninsula to Japan. By this victory Japan took the first step toward a real position among the Western powers. However, the Western powers' uneasiness over the sudden rise of Japan and the Chinese government's entreaty for help found expression in the tripartite intervention of Russia, France and Germany, on 23 April, only six days after the treaty was signed. When Japan yielded and made an unconditional restitution of Liaotung to China, these powers suddenly changed their attitude toward China, and betraying their own territorial ambitions, entered into "a battle for interests and concessions".[37]

Among these tripartite powers, Germany was the most active in its hostile *démarche* against Japan. The German ultimatum of 23 April 1895, which was handed to Foreign Minister Munemitsu Mutsu, by the German Minister Felix von Gutschmid, who was known to harbour strong anti-Japanese feelings, was the most detailed, threatening, and high-handed among the notices of the three powers.[38]

This intervention by Germany was at once a great surprise, disillusionment, and disgrace for the Japanese minister in Germany, Shuzo Aoki, a diplomat whose wife was of the German nobility.[39] Aoki, by far the most fervent Germanophile, had been foreign minister from 24 December 1889 until 29 May 1891, when he had to resign because of the Otsu incident mentioned earlier. After that he was appointed Japanese minister in Germany on 27 January 1892, six years after he had resigned the same office. During the Sino-Japanese War and the ensuing peace negotiations between China and Japan, Aoki had been sending many reports to Mutsu, repeatedly assuring the latter of the friendliness and the full understanding of the German government toward Japan's China policy. Aoki never dreamt that Germany, which was for him Japan's best and most warm-hearted cultural political instructor, should one day suddenly become an "imperialistic" wolf or robber. Actually, Aoki had ignored the warnings of Bismarck to the Iwakura mission (during its visit to Berlin in March 1873) concerning the inadequacy of international law and brutality of *Realpolitik*.[40]

Aoki informed Mutsu from Berlin, on 20 April 1895, of the sudden change of attitude of the German foreign minister, Marschall von Bieberstein, and reported the purport of his conversation with Marschall, adding that the Japanese government had been doing nothing to reward the German friendship toward Japan, in spite of Aoki's repeated warnings from Berlin. Aoki insisted that the Japanese government should have informed the German goverment of the conditions of the peace treaty with China before it was signed. Thus, Aoki's response to the German intervention was to defend and apologize for the German policy and to blame his own government.[41]

In Aoki's report of 20 April, and in his telegram in English of 30 April,[42] we can find not only his tendency to apologize for Germany and condemn Japan, but also his strong personal animosity against Foreign Minister Mutsu, whom Aoki repeatedly denounced later in his autobiography.[43] Aoki made his challenging tone against Mutsu still more forthright in his lengthy report of 27 May 1895, on the origins of the Tripartite Intervention.[44] He pointed out that the true aim of German intervention consisted in separating Russia from France in order to hinder the making of the Franco-Russian Dual Alliance which he believed to be on the eve of being concluded.[45] According to Aoki, Germany intended to win Russian friendship by inspiring the Russian thrust into the Far East through joint intervention against Japan. Aoki insisted that it was necessary for Germany to prevent the Franco-Russian joint interference in Far Eastern affairs without Germany. Aoki thought it highly dangerous for Germany that France alone inspired Russia on this occasion, because a Franco-Russian alliance would then, according to the judgement of Aoki, be established instantly—an alliance which would threaten Germany gravely.

Apart from these general origins of the Tripartite Intervention, there existed, according to Aoki, more immediate origins of the German intervention. These were—

1 actions by the German minister in China, Max von Brandt, which were hostile and disadvantageous to Japan
2 that Japan did not buy war materials from Germany, in contrast to China. China was induced to buy them through Brandt's meditation.
3 that Japan did not care about the vulnerable feelings of the German kaiser.
4 that a newspaper in Tokyo attacked Meckel when he received a decoration from the Japanese government. This incident, highly unpleasant for the German people, was immediately reported to Germany by the German minister in Tokyo.

Aoki concluded that Japan neglected to foster friendship between Germany and Japan. He protested to Mutsu that he was prevented from promoting good feelings toward Japan by an English language telegram that Mutsu sent on 9 October 1894, containing the words: "you [Aoki] will neither act or express your opinions beyond instructions so as not to commit yourself".[46]

When Aoki's extraordinarily provocative report arrived in Tokyo on 2 July 1895, Mutsu was so gravely ill with tuberculosis that he had been temporarily replaced by Kinmochi Saionji (1849–1940).[47] Aoki's challenge understandably irritated Mutsu considerably, and he instantly drafted a sharp reply. This was not sent to Aoki, however Sainoji revised and softened Mutsu's draft and omitted, for example, the following passage:

> Your Excellency [Aoki] seems to consider that the German intervention at this time originated in the errors of the Japanese

> Government. In order to defend Germany eagerly, Your Excellency insists that one of the reasons for the German intervention was that the Japanese Government did not follow your Excellency's advice. I take exception to these démarches by Your Excellency. Besides, Your Excellency had never previously made mention of the "true origins" which Your Excellency enumerated in the last letter for the first time.[48]

Saionji sent a letter to Aoki on 17 August 1895, softer in tone than Mutsu's original, although the essential purport remained the same. Saionji, too, criticized Aoki's *démarches* as well as Aoki's interpretation of the German intervention. So Aoki was rebuked for assuring the Japanese government of the friendly responses of Germany toward Japan's terms of the peace treaty with China. Saionji, like Mutsu, repeated once more, in a quite challenging way, the content of all of Aoki's reports which Aoki had sent to Mutsu from Berlin before the German intervention. Saionji then repudiated all the so-called "immediate origins" which Aoki enumerated, demonstrating that they were all, contrary to Aoki's insistence, wholly unfounded.[49] At any rate in spite of the efforts of this Germanophile diplomat, the nature of power politics forced Japan to revise her attitude towards her former political and military mentor. Ironically, the executor of this re-orientation was the original champion of *Deutschtum* in Japan, Taro Katsura.

## IV

As Prime Minister Katsura concluded the Ango-Japanese Alliance on 30 January 1902. Ironically enough, in the beginning a tripartite pact Berlin-London-Tokyo was proposed to both Great Britain and Japan by the German councillor of the embassay in London, von Eckardstein; but when the negotiation became more concrete, Germany suddenly withdrew from it.[50]

During the process of negotiation between London and Tokyo, there arose in Japan a controversy between the pro-British and pro-Russian groups. Elder statesmen (Genro)[51] like Hirobumi Ito and Kaoru Inoue eagerly defended the idea of an entente with Russia, in order to evade a conflict with that country, which was threatening an invasion of both Manchuria and Korea. Ito visited St Petersburg on 25 November 1901, hoping to realize his idea through his personal prestige and skill, but he failed. Katsura decided to conclude an alliance, not with Russia, but with England. His true intention toward Russia as well as Germany remains, however, unclear even today. Whether and to what extent Katsura saw in those two countries possible future partners of Japan remains enigmatic. It is true, in any case, that Katsura chose England in 1902, despite Ito's objections, though the prime minister was very probably unwilling to continue that alliance with England after Japan's victory over Russia in 1905.

Yosaburo Takekoshi, a liberal historian favoured by Mutsu and Saionji, and member of the Seiyukai party founded by Ito since 1902, has argued that Katsura, having concluded the Third Anglo-Japanese Alliance as prime minister of the second Katsura cabinet on 13 July 1911,[52] changed his mind and came to favour the idea of an alliance with Germany. Takekoshi reports in his biography of Saionji as follows:

> Not knowing that the late Emperor was growing notably weaker, Katsura started for Europe on the 6th of July (1912), accompanied by Wakatsuki Reijiro and Goto Shimpei. His ostensible errand was to meet the Russian authorities in order to lay a basis for the peace of the East, but in reality he cherished an idea of concluding an offensive and defensive alliance with Germany. He intended to have a preparatory negotiation with the German Government, and on his return, overturning the Saionji Government by some means, make the German-Japanese alliance the slogan of the new Katsura Ministry and get the enthusiastic applause of the people. At that time there was not yet an open breach between England and Germany, and from the point of view of England, whose policy then was rather to get closer to Germany in order to preserve peace, the German-Japanese alliance would not necessarily be an anti-English alliance, but, as on the part of Germany theeee anti-English spirit was strong, the German-Japanese alliance would ultimately have become an anti-English alliance. What an irony of fate was it that he who had proclaimed himself the proposer of the Anglo-Japanese alliance and had demanded the applause of the people therefore should have become a schemer for another alliance which would have for its final object opposition to England. Katsura was after all an opportunist, a showman. But when he heard of the serious illness of the Emperor Meiji, he at once turned back and arrived in Japan on the 11th of August.[53]

However, Professor Noritaro Ino points out that Katsura's,

as well as Goto's biographers, insist that Katsura's aim was a Russo-Japanese alliance, and idea inspired by Goto. The latter's biographers maintain that Katsura was converted to this idea in 1912 and visited St Petersburg five years after he had disgraced Ito in Ito's mission to Russian capital.[54]

Be that as it may, it is an historical fact that Katsura called on the Russian prime minister, V. N. Kokovtsev, on 22 July 1912. Katsura's biography reports that he and Kokovtsev exchanged ideas, the Japanese ambassador in Russia,[55] Ichiro Motono, acting as interpreter. They agreed above all on the necessity of Russo-Japanese co-operation in China and on the necessity of a joint occupation of Manchuria and Mongolia.[56]

The Russian ambassador in Japan (1908–16), Nicholas Malevsky Malevich, reported to the Russian foreign minister, Sergei Sasonov, on 7 May 1914, concerning Katsura as follows: "Prince Katsura often repeated to me that the Chinese question had to be decided exclusively by those countries which were the most interested in Chinese matters, namely Russia and Japan. The later Prime Minister forged a stereotyped phrase in order to express these ideas. In his curious German he used to say: when we—Japan and Russia—co-operate in China, no country can come between us".[57]

This report of Malevsky was sent to Sasonov with the aim of informing Sasonov of the policy towards China of the new prime minister of Japan, Shigenobu Okuma,[58] who was appointed to this office on 16 April 1914. According to Malevsky's report, he visited Okuma to celebrate his taking office as prime minister for the second time. Though Okuma expressed on this occasion his friendship for Russia and said that Japan had to follow the example of Peter the Great's emancipation of Russia from feudalism, Okuma wished, contrary to Katsura, to invite France and England to join in the Russo-Japanese consensus. Malevsky paid special attention to this difference between Katsura and Okuma.[59]

While Katsura sojourned in Russia, the Japanese councillor of the embassy in Berlin,[60] Ryotaro Hata, wrote to Katsura on 25 June 1912, to inform Katsura at length how Germany responded to Katsura's planned visit to Germany. Hata asserted to Katsura that German newspapers welcomed Katsura's coming to Germany. According to Hata, German newspapers were seeing in Katsura a pro-German statesman, because Katsura had studied in Germany and because he founded a

German society in Japan and revived and reorganized the German-Japanese Society there. German newspapers were also seeing in Katsura the next prime minister of Japan, reported Hata. Katsura's speeches before his departure, at the German embassy in Tokyo and at Prince Mori's mansion (the Mori family had been the former feudal lords of the Choshu Clan which dispatched Katsura to Berlin in 1870), and their echoes in Japanese newspapers were, according to Hata, all without exception, translated and reported in the German press. On the other hand, German newspapers were afraid lest Katsura's visit to Russia might lead to a division of China by Russia and Japan. Katsura's visit to Russia was looked upon in Germany as aiming at an agreement or alliance between Russia and Japan.[61]

According to Hata, Hannecken of Norddeuscher Lloyd and Bernhard Dernburg,[62] former colonial minister, and others were planning to welcome Katsura's visit to Germany. Hata expressed his hope that Katsura's visit would contribute to tightening German-Japanese friendship, and dared to ask Katsura whether he wished to do something more than merely consolidate friendship between the two countries.[63] Hata seems to have sensed that Katsura harboured some secret intention in connection with his planned visit to Germany. All the plans to welcome Katsura to Germany remained unrealized, however, because the grave illness of Emperor Meiji obliged Katsura to return home. He was never to visit Germany again, for he died the next year.

Although the question of whether Katsura really intended to form a German-Japanese alliance on the occasion of his visit in Germany remains in the realm of conjecture. A new piece of historical evidence has recently come to light which seems to support Takekoshi's assertion and to demonstrate that Katsura really did cherish such an idea. Tsai Chi-t'ao (1890–1949), famous in Japan under his pen-name Tsai T'ien-sh'iu, reveals in his work *Nihon-Ron* [On Japan] the content of a secret conference between Sun Yat-sen (1866–1925) and Katsura during the third Katsura cabinet, in February 1913. The details of this conference were kept secret during Katsura's lifetime. Tsai, Sun's devoted secretary, who had studied in Japan from 1905 through 1909 at Nihon University among others, attended this conference as interpreter with no one else present. In this book, Tsai reveals that Katsura confided to Sun his vision of a

German-Japanese alliance. According to Tsai, Katsura said that he would abandon the Anglo-Japanese Alliance, which he concluded three times as prime minister, because this alliance had become unnecessary both for Japan and England after Japan's victory over Russia in 1905. Katsura's grand vision consisted in challenging the world hegemony of the British Empire through a concert of Japan, China, Turkey, Germany, and Austria, thereby utilizing the coming German-Japanese alliance as the core of this international concert. Tsai reports further that Katsura said that none except the three politicians, Katsura, Sun, and the German kaiser was able to oppose and overthrow the world control of the British Empire. Katsura disclosed that his recent visit to Russia was only a camouflage. To Katsura, a Russo-Japanese alliance was at once impossible to realize and useless, and so he intended to negotiate with the German government in Russia, in order to avoid drawing public attention. Though for a time the dream of a German-Japanese alliance was precluded by the illness and death of Emperor Meiji, Katsura was still willing to try to realize this dream during the period of his own cabinet, Tsai asserts.[64] Katsura's death on 10 October 1913 disappointed Sun gravely, says Tsai. Receiving the news of Katsura's death, Sun is said to have despaired of help from Japan. Katsura, for his part, is reported to have said just before his death that he regretted that he could not help Sun in his efforts to overthrow Yüan Shih-k'ai (1859–1916), and to attain the magnificent scheme of gaining the freedom of the Eastern nations from the yoke of British imperialism.[65]

The German kaiser had been trying to evade the encirclement of the "Entente" powers—that is, France, Russia, England and Japan—by designing a German-American-Chinese entente. These efforts were made intermittently during 1907–8 and 1910–12.[66] Apart from these efforts, the kaiser, who intended to use the "Yellow Peril" theory, was known to be very hostile to Japan.[67] In order to realize Katsura's idea of a German-Japanese alliance, a basic change of the German policy toward Japan was indispensable. For Japan, too, a basic change of her world policy was essential in order to change sides from the "Entente" powers to the "Alliance" powers of Germany, Austria-Hungary and Italy. Could Katsura have attained these premises on both sides, if he had survived after October 1913? Most probably not.[68] Interesting in this context, however, are the German-Japanese secret peace negotiations between the German minister, Helmuth von Lucius and the Japanese minister, Sadatsuchi Uchida, in Stockholm during World War I, an unexplored subject, which leaves many points to be clarified by future studies.[69]

## V

Katsura had to resign, together with this third cabinet, on 20 February 1913. This cabinet, which took office on 21 December 1912, fell when it was confronted with the popular anti-government movement both inside and outside the parliament, a large-scale movement directed at Katsura himself who had organized his third cabinet by utilizing an edict of the young Emperor Mutsuhito (Taisho). After his return from Russia, Katsura replaced Tokudaiji as lord keeper of the privy seal and grand chamberlain on 13 August 1912. In the same year, Katsura became prime minister once again, appealing to the imperial edict as excuse to change his office within so short range of time. This behaviour of Katsura aroused popular hostility against him. Admiral Gonnohyoe Yamamoto (1852–1933), coming from Satsuma, replaced Katsura. The Yamamoto cabinet fell because of the "Siemens Affair"—a scandal of bribery exposed in Berlin by a speech of a delegate of the German Social Democratic party, Karl Liebknecht, in the Reichstag.

Okuma replaced Yamamoto on 16 April 1914. The second Okuma cabinet was able to catch the public eye by Okuma's own popularity and reputation as a militant liberalist in the early Meiji period. In reality, Okuma, who had long been living in retirement from politics and devoting himself to the management of Waseda University which he founded, no longer possessed much political influence. The Okuma cabinet was pulled by strong forces in opposite directions. One magnet which attracted Okuma from within the cabinet was Takaaki Kato (186O–1926), former ambassador in London and now foreign minister and deputy prime minister. The other was Yamagata. Yamagata was at the time the most influential of the four surviving Genro (elder statesmen).[70]

On 7 August 1914 the British ambassador in Japan, William Conyngham Greene, transmitted to Kato the request of the

British foreign minister, Sir Edward Grey, that Japan attack the armed merchant cruisers of Germany in Asian waters.[71] Responding to this request Kato exerted himself to the utmost in persuading his cabinet colleagues that Japan should declare war upon Germany during the cabinet meeting of 7–8 August, which was held from 10:00 P.M. to 2:00 A.M.. Kato insisted that Japan should do so, first because of the friendship with England, and secondly in order to enhance Japan's own prestige by expelling the German bases of operations from Asia.[72]

Yamagata and other Genro were sceptical of Kato's aggessive policy and of the ensuing declaration of war upon Germany made on 23 August 1914.[73] Kato's so-called "Twenty-one Demands" on China of 18 January 1915 irritated Yamagata more. In his "written proposal concerning Japan's policy toward China" (Tai-Shi Seisaku Ikensho), which Yamagata sent to Okuma, Kato, and Reijiro Wakatsuki (1866–1949)—then a young finance minister—in August 1914, Yamagata insisted that Japan should help, not, as Katsura secretly promised, Sun Yat-sen, but the president of the new Chinese Republic, Yüan Shih-k'ai.[74] Kato's Twenty-one Demands drove Yüan, however, into a corner. In his "written proposal of a Russo-Japanese Alliance" (Nichi-Ro Domei Ron), which he handed over to Okuma on 21 February 1915, with the consent of three other Genro, Yamagata insisted that Japan should secure an alliance partner more reliable than England in order to prepare for the coming struggle over China after the end of the world war which would be fought between the "white" and "yellow" races. Yamagata feared gravely that all the countries of Europe which were then absorbed by the war would afterwards throng to China. Japan must secure one very reliable alliance partner among the white powers, Yamagata urged. According to him, the most suitable partner for Japan in this sense was czarist Russia. Though Yamagata did not insist on abandoning the Anglo-Japanese Alliance, he no longer saw England as a staunch partner of Japan.[75]

Kato opposed Yamagata's idea as "diluting the whisky named Anglo-Japanese Alliance with the water of a Russo-Japanese Alliance".[76] Yamagata then compelled Okuma to dismiss the recalcitrant Kato from the cabinet on 4 August 1915. Kikujiro Ishii, then ambassador in Franch, succeeded Kato as foreign minister. Ishii was not weakened by the war, but in the cabinet meeting of 14 February 1916 the Okuma cabinet, including Ishii, decided to follow Yamagata's policy line. The Russo-Japanese alliance became reality with the signing of the Fourth Russo-Japanese Agreement on 3 July 1916. Japan's supply of war materials to Russia contributed much to its realization.[77]

The Russian Revolution of 1917, however, deprived Japan of the ally which seemed in Yamagata's eyes to be Japan's most reliable and powerful partner. The Washington Conference of 1921–22 then officially recognized the demise of the Anglo-Japanese Alliance, which had in any case already become ineffective. Japan's isolation was now evident. Prime Minister Masatake Terauchi (1852–1919), (Choshu),who replaced Okuma on 9 October 1916, is said to have prophesied that in case of "absolute isolation", Japan might be compelled to choose Germany as an ally.[78] Terauchi was reported to have insisted to an interviewer of the *New York Outlook*, Mason, when commenting on the likelihood of a Japanese-German alliance, that such a possibility was highly improbable. Nevertheless, the isolation of Japan, accelerated by Japan's military invasion in Manchuria beginning in 1931, destined her to choose Germany as a partner. More than twenty turbulent and eventful years had passed since 1914 when Japan came to sign the Anti-Comintern Pact with Germany on 25 November 1936, the first realization of a concrete German-Japanese rapprochement which was to be consolidated by the Tripartite Pact between Berlin, Rome, and Tokyo signed on 7 September 1940.[79]

This one aspect of the cultural and political impact of imperial Germany upon Japan has been illuminated by tracing Katsura's career and examining its influences. The difference in philosophies between Western and non-Western countries, a discrepancy of spirit, which agonized many intellectuals of the non Western world, and which in Russia took the form of antagonism between Westerners and Slavophiles,[80] was alien to Katsura. Thus the "identity-crises" did not distress him. Katsura could utilize Western learning as a means of realizing his own political aims. The difference in philosophies between the imperial Germany and the imperial Japan may not have been so great as it seemed to be at first. Some elements common to both enabled Katsura and other Japanese political leaders to understand and absorb the German methods.[81]

Yamagata, who survived World War I, was to be confronted with the world–wide social, political and cultural change which emerged in particular in the form of Wilsonian Democracy and the Russian Revolution. Katsura seems to have had presentiments of the coming change.[82] He recognized the tendency towards parliamentary government and took initiative in founding his own political party—an act which Yamagata never understood. Katsura himself was obliged to retire as the result of the first wave of the "Taisho democracy". Katsura might have dreamt of realizing his pro-German diplomacy with the support of his new party, and one might conjecture that nothing other than this dream made him resort to extraordinary measures to return from the imperial court to the premiership. Be that as it may, Katsura was allowed to live and die in the world of monarchism before World War I. The shift from imperial Germany to the Weimar Republic produced in Germany a new political situation. German-Japanese relations entered into a new, somewhat slumberous stage, until Hitler's rise to power created circumstances in which Japanese-German co-operation could take on a dangerously active form.

1. G. Spieß, *Die Preussische Expedition nach Ostasien während der Jahre 1860–1862* (Leipzig, 1964); *Die preussische Expedition nach Ostasien, nach amtlichen Quellen* (Berlin, 1864); G. Kerst, *Die Anfänge der Erschliessung Japans im Spiegel der zeitgenössischen Publizistik* (Hamburg, 1953); S. Imamiya, *Shoki Nichi-Doku Tsuko-Shi Kenkyu* [Studies on the German-Japanese Transactions in the Earlier Period] (Tokyo, 1971).
2. T. Hora, *Dai-Ichi-Ji Sekai Taisen* [The World War I] (Tokyo, 1971), pp. 92–118.
3. M. B. Jansen, "Modernization and Foreign Policy in Meiji Japan", in *Political Development in Modern Japan*, ed. R. E. Ward (Princeton, 1968), p.155.
4. Professor Cyril E. Black places Japan in his fifth pattern of political modernization, in which "the traditional governments were strong enough to prevent their countries from being overrun by more modern societies ... and also realistic enough in the long run to know that unless they introduced modern reforms they would ultimately succumb to foreign rule". C. E. Black, *The Dynamics of Modernization, a Study in Comparative History* (Princeton, 1966), p. 121. Professor Black seems to overestimate the adaptability of the Tokugawa government to the Western challenge.
5. T. Tanabe, *Baku-Matsu Gaiko Den* [Narratives of Japanese Diplomacy at the Close of the Tokugawa Period] trans. into modern Japanese with comments by S. Sakata (Tokyo, 1966), 1: 164–66.
6. E. L. Presseisen, *Before Aggression, Europeans Prepare the Japanese Army* (Arizona, 1965), pp. 10–11.

7. I. Tokutomi, *Koshaku Katsura Taro Den* [Biography of Prince Taro Katsura] (Tokyo, reprint 1967), 1:310–16.
8. Ibid., p. 315.
9. Ibid., p. 329.
10. Ibid., p. 356.
11. H. Koyama, *Kindai Nihon Gunji-Shi Gaisetsu* [Outline of the Military History of Modern Japan] (Tokyo, 1944), pp. 278–89. Cf. G. Ritter, *Staatskunst und Kriegshandwerk; Das Problem des "Militarismus" in Deutschland* (3rd ed., Munich, 1965), p. 377, fn. 6.
12. Tokutomi, *Katsura*, 1:356.
13. Ibid., pp. 376–79.
14. Ibid., pp. 441–46.
15. S. Shukuri, *Nihon Rikugun-Shi Kenkyu, Meckel Shosa* [Studies in the History of the Japanese Army; Major Meckel] (Tokyo, 1944), p. 110.
16. Ibid.
17. Presseisen, *Aggression*, pp. 30–33.
18. On Nishi, see T. R. H. Havens, *Nishi Amane and Modern Japanese Thought* (Princeton, 1970); and M. Yoshida, "Ichi Keimo Gakusha no Shogai. Mori Ogai Nishi Amane Den o Megutte" [Life of an illuminator: on the Biography of Amane Nishi by Ogai Mori], *Gaikoku Goka Kiyo* [Proceedings of the Branch of Foreign Studies] ed. the Tokyo University, 19, no. 1, 1971.
19. Cf. W. G. Beasley, *The Modern History of Japan* (London, 1963), p. 105.
20. Sanjo's cabinet was not a cabinet in the modern sense of the word, but a *Dajokan* (Executive Council) system. Cf. Beasley, *Japan*, p. 102, and F. Shimomura, *Nihon Zenshi 9, Kindai 2* [A Series of the Whole Japanese History, no. 9, Modern Age, 2] (Tokyo, 1968), p. 4.
21. Shimomura, *Nihon Zenshi 9, Kindai 2*, p. 76.
22. A. Idditti, *The Life of Marquis Shigenobu Okuma, a Maker of New Japan* (Tokyo, 1940), p. 211. On Yano as a political fiction writer, see Y. Okazaki, *Japanese Literature in the Meiji Era*, trans. and adapted by V. H. Viglielmo, (Tokyo, 1969), pp. 136–37.
23. Idditti, *Okuma*, p. 217.
24. R. Storry, *A History of Modern Japan* (Harmondworth, 1963), p. 115.
25. Cf. J. Siemes, *Hermann Roessler and the Making of the Meiji State with his Commentaries on the Meiji constitution* (Tokyo, 1966).
26. G. Kerst, *Jacob Meckel, sein Leben, sein Wirken in Deutschland und Japan* (Göttingen, 1970), p. 33. Cf. M. Miyake, "Meckel ni okeru 19 Seiki Doitsu to Meiji Zenki Nippon no Sesshoku" [Cultural Encounter between Nineteenth Century Germany and Early Meiji Japan Personified by General Jacob Meckel], *Jinbungaku Kenkyujoho* [Bulletin of the Institute of Humanities] pub. the Kanagawa University, 6 (June 1972).
27. Two suggestions Meckel submitted to the Japanese government: "Über die Notwendigkeit des allgemeinen Militärdienstes in Japan", and, "Der organisatorische Aufbau und die Befehlsgliederung der grossen Verbände des japanischen Heeres", are contained in Kerst, *Meckel*, pp. 120–29. Japanese editions are contained in H. Ito, ed., *Hisho Ruisan, 10, Heisei Kankei Shiryo* [Classified Secret Documents of Hirobumi Ito, 10, Source Materials Concerning the Military System] (Tokyo, reprint 1965), pp. 103–4, and 76–83.
28. S. P. Huntington, *The Soldier and the State, the Theory and Politics of Civil-Military Relations* (Toronto, 1957) pp. 132–33.
29. H. Herzfeld, "Militarism in Modern History", in *German History*, ed. H. Kohn (Boston, 1954), p. 109.
30. The so-called "Gunbatsu" (Military Clique) in the 1930s sprang up as an opposition to the Sat-Cho or "Hanbatsu" (Clan Clique) grouping,

represented by Yamagata and Katsura. This may be considered as a sort of egalitarian movement aiming at the modernization of the Japanese army. However, it was soon to result in the dominance of the Military Clique. This movement is said to have had one of its origins in the meeting in Baden-Baden in Germany of the three Japanese generals, Tetsuzan Nagata, Binshiro Kobata and Neiji Okumura on 27 October 1921; Hideki Tojo joined in it on the next day. See M. Takahashi, *Gunbatsu no Keifu* [Genealogy of the Military Clique] (Tokyo, 1969), p. 54. Cf. M. Vié, *Le Japon Contemporain* (Paris, 1971), p. 86.

31. These circumstances are analysed in N. Umetani, *Meiji Zenki Seiji-Shi no Kenkyu, Meiji Gintai no Seiritsu to Meiji Kokka no Kansei* [Studies in Early Meiji Political History, the Making of the Meiji Army and the Establishment of the Meiji State] (Tokyo, 1963), p. 134. It is a noteworthy fact that Soroku Kawakami and Iyozo Tamura, two outstanding generals in the Meiji period, were studying in Germany when Meckel was instructing in Japan. The German military science was thus absorbed into Japan in these days through double channels. Rintaro (Ogai) Mori (1862–1922), a well-known man of letters and high-ranking army surgeon, notes in his diary that he lectured for Tamura on the writings of Clausewitz in Berlin in 1888. See Koyama, *Gaisetsu* p. 288, fn. 2.
32. Chihiro Kosaka and Terutaro Harada studied in St Cyr for six and five years respectively: Kerst, *Meckel*, p. 51, fn. 115.
33. Presseisen, *Aggression*, pp. 34–35; Umetani, *Meiji*, pp. 108–28.
34. Presseisen, *Aggression*, p. 45.
35. Shukuri, *Rikugun-Shi*, pp. 198–205; Tokutomi, *Katsura*, 1 :460–63; Koyama, Gaisetsu, pp. 226–27. After retirement from the army, Tani became, like Miura and Torio, a politician. For an analysis of his political philosophy—a combination of Japanism (Nihon-Shugi) and a sort of liberalism— see J. Banno, *Meiji Kenpo Taisei no Kakuritsu, Fukoku Kyohei to Minryoku Kyuyo* [Establishment of the Meiji Constitutional System 1890–1900] (Tokyo, 1971).
36. Presseisen, *Aggression*, p. 95.
37. T. Ueda, "The latter half of the Meiji Era: the Period between Tripartite Intervention and the Manchurian Problem", in *Japan-American Diplomatic Relations in the Meiji-Taisho Era*, ed. H. Kamikawa, English trans. M. Kimura (Tokyo, 1958), p. 170.
38. *GP*, 7, no. 2252, annexe.
39. Aoki's father was one Miura, a small village doctor, but he was adopted by a Samurai named Aoki, and married a daughter of this family. In Berlin, Aoki divorced his wife and married the daughter of a German noble family. Aoki was said to have spoken only German at home.
40. Jansen, *Modernization*, p. 156; Beasley, *Japan*, p. 114.
41. *Nihon Gaiko Bunsho* [The Diplomatic Documents of the Foreign Ministry of Japan, hereinafter cited as NGB], 28, pt 2, no. 644.
42. Ibid., no. 682.
43. *Aoki Shuzo Jiden* [Autobiography of Shuzo Aoki], ed. with comments by Y. Sakane (Tokyo, 1970), p. 350.
44. NGB, 28, pt 2, no. 840.
45. Aoki seems not to have comprehended that the Russo-French Alliance was already a *fait accompli* by the close of 1893.
46. NGB, 28, pt 2, no. 840.
47. Saionji functioned in place of Mutsu from 5 June 1895, through to 3 April 1896.
48. H. Ito, ed., *Hisho Ruisan, 1, Nisshin Jihen* [Classified Secret Documents of Hirobumi Ito, 1, the Sino-Japanese War] (Tokyo, reprint 1967), p. 590. This volume was first published in Japan in 1932, but its sale was

prohibited by the government especially because it contained among others this original draft of Mutsu, which blamed Aoki vehemently: see book review by M. Fujimura, *Kokusai Seiji, Nihon Gaiko-Shi no Sho-Mondai*, 3 [International Relations: Some Problems of the History of Japan's Foreign Policy, 3) (October 1968).

49. NGB, 28, pt 2, no. 911. Concerning the origins of the Tripartite Intervention, two articles are worth mentioning: J. Nakayama, "Sangoku Kansho to Ei-Doku Kankei" [The Tripartite Intervention and Anglo-German Relations], *Shirin* [Journal of History] 32, no. 1 (January 1948); and T. Sugawara, "Nisshin Senso-ki ni okeru Yoroppa Sho-Rekkyo no Kyokuto Seisaku to Sangoku Kansho" [The Far Eastern Policy of the European Powers during the Sino-Japanese War and the Tripartite Intervention], *Rekishi-Kyoiku* [Journal of History Education] 15, nos 2, 3 (February, March 1967).
50. Kikujiro Ishii, *Diplomatic Commentaries*, ed. of 1931, trans. and ed. W. R. Langdon (Baltimore, 1936), pp. 37–38. Cf. O. Becker, "Baron Kikujiro Ishii, Die Ansichten eines japanischen Staatsmannes über Weltpolitik", *Berliner Monatshefte* (September 1937); and M. Miyake, "Doitsu no Rekishi-Gaku to Kyokuto, 4, Ishii Kikujiro to Otto Becker" [German Historiography and the Far East, 4, Kikujiro Ishii and Otto Becker], *Jinbun Kenkyu*, [Studies in Humanities], pub. the Kanagawa University, no. 43 (November 1969).
51. On the political meaning of Genro, see I. H. Nish, *Alliance in Decline, a Study in Anglo-Japanese Relations 1908–23* (London, 1972), pp. 3–4, and R. F. Hackett, "Political Modernization and the Meiji Genro" in *Polit cat Development in Modern Japan,* ed. R. E. Ward (Princeton, 1968).
52. The Second Anglo-Japanese Alliance was concluded during the first Katsura cabinet on 12 August 1905.
53. Y. Takekoshi, *Prince Saionji*, trans. N. Kozaki, (Kyoto, 1933), pp. 257–58.
54. N. Ino, *Nihon Gaiko Shiso-Shi Ronko, Daini* [Studies on the Intellectual History of Japanese Diplomacy], (Tokyo, 1967), 2:337–38.
55. The Japanese legation in Russia was elevated to embassy status on 1 May 1908.
56. Tokutomi, *Katsura*, 2:574–76.
57. *Die internationalen Beziehungen im Zeitalter des Imperialismus*, Dokumente aus den Archiven der Zarischen und der Provisorischen Regierung, herausgegeben von der Kommission beim Zentralexekutivkomitee der Sowjetregierung unter dem Vorsitz von M. N. Pokrowski. Einzig berechtigte Ausgabe namens der Deutschen Gesellschaft zum Studium Osteuropas herausgegeben von Otto Hoetzsch (hereinafter cited as RD), 1, pt 2, p. 379.
58. The first Okuma cabinet was formed on 30 June 1898, and was replaced by the second Yamagata cabinet on 11 November 1898.
59. RD, 1, pt 2, p. 379.
60. The Japanese legation in Germany was elevated to embassy status on 7 January 1906.
61. Hata's letter to Katsura, cited by Tokutomi, *Katsura*, 2:587–91.
62. Dernburg's letter of welcome to Katsura, dated 15/8/1912, is preserved in the archives of Taro Katsura, National Diet Library in Tokyo.
63. Tokutomi, *Katsura*, 2.
64. Tsai Chi-t'ao, *Nihon-Ron* [On Japan], trans. into Japanese by H. Ichikawa with comments by Y. Takeuchi (Tokyo, 1972), pp. 97–100. This book was first published in Chinese in Shanghai in 1928, and was translated into Japanese in complete form for the first time in 1972. Translations hitherto repeated are defective. After Sun's death in 1925, Tsai became known as a journalist belonging to the right wing of the

Kuomintang (Chinese Nationalist party). Nobutoshi Hagihara, author of an article: "Baba Tatsui, An Early Japanese Liberal", *St Antony's Papers*, no. 14 (Oxford, 1963), pays much attention in his review of this book (*Bungei Shunju*, September 1972, pp. 296–303) to these passages concerning the idea of a German-Japanese alliance and to the fact that Tsai distinguished Katsura from Giichi Tanaka (1863–1929). Both politicians were soldiers originally and are generally looked upon as belonging to the same category of "Hunbatsu" (Clan Clique or Clan Oligarchy) grouping coming from Choshu.

65. Tsai, *Nihon-Ron*, p. 96.
66. On the Kaiser's design for a German-American-Chinese entente, see H. Yoshii, "Nichi-Ro Senso-Go no Doitsu no Kyokuto Seisaku" [German Policy toward the Far East after the Russo-Japanese War], in *20 Seiki Gaiko-Shi no Ichi Kenkyu* [A study in Diplomatic History in the Twentieth Century] (Kyoto, 1964).
67. The Kaiser wrote in his marginal note to the report of the German ambassador in London, Metternich's announcing the coming of the Second Russo-Japanese Agreement (to be signed on 10 July 1910) that in the case of an invasion by the "Yellow Peril", the Slavs would not resist, but would help it: *GP*, 32, no. 11704. On the idea of "Yellow Peril", see H. Gollwitzer, *Die Gelbe Gefahr, Geschichte eines Schlagwortes; Studien zum imperialistischen Denken* (Göttingen, 1962).
68. In the footnote to the report of the German ambassador in Japan, von Rex, of 19/10/1913, which describes the funeral of Katsura, the compilers wrote as follows:

    > Man wird ja nicht annehmen können, dass Fürst Katsura und Graf Aoki bei aller Deutschfreundlichkeit bei dem Ausbruch des Weltkrieges den Dingen, die doch in erster Linie von dem englisch-japanischen Bündnis, in zweiter vielleicht auch von einem gegen Deutschland gerichteten russisch-japanischen Abkommen beherrscht waren, eine andere Wendung zu geben vermocht hätten; immerhin bedeutete der Tod beider Staatsmänner für Deutschland einen besonders herben Verlust. (*GP*, 32, no. 12031).

69. On the German-Japanese secret negotiations in Stockholm, see E. Hölzle, "Deutschland um die Wegscheide des ersten Weltkrieges", in *Geschichtliche Kräfte und Entscheidungen, Festschrift zum fünfundsechzigsten Geburtstage von Otto Becker* (Wiesbaden, 1954); Frank W. Ikle, "Japanese-German Peace Negotiations during World War I", *American Historical Review* 81, no. 1 (October 1965); Fritz Fischer, *Griff nach der Weltmacht, Die Kriegszielpolitik des kaiserlichen Deutschland 1914–1918* (Düsseldorf, 1962), pp. 278–88; Nish, *Alliance*, pp. 178–83; and M. Miyake, "Dai-Ichi-Ji Sekai Taisen ni okeru Nichi-Doku Kankei to Nichi-Ro Kenkei, Nichi-Doku Stockhol, Kosho to Tai-Ro Buki Kyoyo Mondai" [German-Japanese Peace Negotiations in Stockholm, and Russo-Japanese Negotiations for Lend-Lease and Alliance during World War I], *Kokusai Seiji: Heiwa to Senso no Kenkyu, 2* [International Relations: Study on Peace and War, 2] (April 1968).
70. On the antagonism between Yamagata and Kato, see Hackett, *The Meiji Genro*, pp. 90–94, and Hackett, *Yamagata Aritomo in the Rise of Modern Japan* (Cambridge, Mass., 1971), pp. 278–90.
71. Grey's memorandum, which was handed over to Kato, is contained in the English original in NGB (1914), 3, no. 101.
72. M. Ito, *Kato Takaaki*, (Tokyo, 1929), 2:p.78, Grey began to check Kato's move, but in vain.
73. Mitsunojo Funakoshi, who was married to Yamagata's daughter, was obliged to carry this ultimatum, though very grudgingly, to the German

Foreign Office as charge d'affaires *ad interim.* Japan's ultimatum is contained in NGB (1914) 3, no. 306. Cf. M. Funakoshi, *Nichi-Doku Kokko Danzetsu Hi-Shi* [Secret History of the Severance of Diplomatic Relations between Japan and Germany] (Tokyo, 1934), pp. 118–24.

74. A. Oyama, ed., *Yamagata Aritomo Ikensho* [Written Opinions of Aritomo Yamagata] (Tokyo, 1966), pp. 340–45.
75. Ibid., pp. 345–48.
76. Ito, *Kato*, 2:49.
77. K. Kajima, *A Brief Diplomatic History of Modern Japan* (Tokyo, 1965), pp. 47–51, gives a bird's-eye view of the Russo-Japanese Agreements of 30/7/1907 (The First Agreement), 4/7/1910 (The Second Agreement) and 8/7/1912 (The Third Agreement). For detailed studies on the Russo-Japanese Agreements, including the Fourth Agreement, see N. Tanaka, "Nichi-Ro Kyosho-Ron' [A Study of the Russo-Japanese Entente], *Kindai Nihon Gaiko-Shi Kenkyu, Kamikawa Sensei Kanreki Kinen* [Studies in the Diplomatic History of Modern Japan in Celebration of the Sixtieth Brithday of Professor Kamikawa] [Tokyo, 1956; and M. Yoshimura, *Nihon to Roshia* [Japan and Ruaaia] (Tokyo, 1968). The Russian official newspaper *Izvestia* revealed, on 19/12/1917, the secret agreement attached to the Fourth Agreement, with the comments that the supposed enemy of the secret articles 1 and 2 meant the United States. Yoshimura discusses in his book whether the supposed enemy was the United States or Germany: Yoshimura, ibid., pp. 312–15. Concerning the impact on the making of the Fourth Agreement caused by Japan's supplying war materials to Russia see Hora, *Dai-Ichi-Ji Sekai Taisen.*
78. Y. Oka, *Tenkan-Ki no Taisho* [Taisho Period 1912–1925 as a Period of Transition] (Tokyo, 1969), pp. 74–75 fn. 1.
79. Cf. T. Haruki, "The Tripartite Pact and Japanese Foreign Policy" (Ph. D. dissertation, University of Southern California, 1956); and M. Miyake, "Die Achse Berlin-Rom-Tokio im Spiegel der Japanischen Quellen", *Mitteilungen des Österreichischen Staatsarchivs* 21 (1969).
80. On the problem of antagonism between Westerners and Slavophiles as a typical phenomenon in the non-Western countries confronted with the Western cultural impact, see S. Yamamoto, *Bunmei no Kozo to Hendo* [Structure and Change of Civilization] (Tokyo, 1961); and K. Katsuda, *Kakumei to Intelligentsia* [Revolution and Intelligentsia] (Tokyo, 1966).
81. On further German influence upon Japanese local government, see G. O. Totten, "Nihon no Shi-Cho-Son Seido no Tokushitsu to sono Seiritsu" [The Establishment and Character of Japanese Municipal Government], *Toshi Mondai* [Municipal Problems] 44, nos 6–7 (June-July 1953).
82. Katsura's own work, *Shosei-Kun* [Instructions in Worldly Wisdom] (Tokyo, 1912) reveals these presentiments.

# PART 3

# Colonial Rule and Native Response

JOHN E. SCHRECKER

# Kiautschou and the Problems of German Colonialism

## Introduction

From 1898 to 1914 Germany owned the colony of Kiautschou in Chiao-chou Bay in the Chinese province of Shantung.[1] The treaty of 1896 which established Kiautschou also reduced the entire province to a German sphere of influence. The story of the German presence in Shantung is one of considerable interest for the study of German colonialism. It sheds light on the colonial policies of the German navy, which was one of the important sponsors of German imperialism, but which had jurisdiction over only one colony, the leasehold of Kiautschou. In addition, it indicates some of the diffulties Germany faced in its drive for empire in the late nineteenth and early twentieth centuries. Within ten years after the Germans established themselves in Shantung, the sphere of influence in the interior no longer existed. In addition, though the navy had turned Kiautschou into a great commercial centre, and what many considered to be Germany's most successful colony, Germany, itself, received little benefit from the colony.

The German drive for the status of a world power in the 1890s was the immediate cause of the acquisition of the sphere of influence. However, underlying the venture was the rapid expansion of German activity in China in the latter half of the nineteenth century.[2] As the German stake in China grew, the German government began to play an increasingly active role there, both to support existing German endeavours and to stimulate new ones. The acquisition of Kiautschou was the culmination of Berlin's increasing involvement. At the same time, it also fulfilled the long-standing desire of many Germans, particularly commercial groups, for a foothold on the coast which would serve German interests as Hong Kong served British. A sense of rivalry with England permeated every step toward the creation of the leasehold.

By the 1890s Germany had achieved second place behind Britain among the foreign nations which were commercially active in China. The Reich was the second most important source of China's imports. The number of German firms in China was second to England, as was the tonnage of goods carried on German bottoms. With the establishment of the Deutsch-Asiatische Bank in 1890, Germany broke the monopoly which England had held over foreign investment in China. In all these fields Germany, though gaining, still stood a distant second, but this only served to heighten the sense of rivalry with Britain.

The navy was the government department which most consistently advocated establishing a colony in China and was most instrumental in obtaining the sphere of influence. For this reason, it is often assumed that Kiautschou was obtained primarily for military reasons, and operated basically as a naval base. But this was not the case. Certainly, the navy had military aims for Kiautschou, but more important it shared the goals of the German commercial and colonial groups. It did so both because it believed in these goals and because it valued the political support which groups of this type could give to general naval interests.

The ideological and political ties between the navy and commercial groups rested partially on the fact that the liberals who dominated commerce had traditionally supported the fleet because of its original connection with the German movement for unification. In addition, these groups believed that to become a commercial power like Britain a strong navy was essential. Moreover, the navy, lacking the aristocratic background of most Prussian institutions, was controlled by men from the middle class, such as Tirpitz, who frequently reflected commercial attitudes. These ranged from a concern with imperialism to a keen sense of rivalry with Britain. This sympathetic relationship between the navy and the German commercial interests not only laid the basis for the acquisition of a sphere of influence in China, but also for the later efforts of the navy to turn Kiautschou into a model colony and not simply a naval base.

Between 1895 and 1898 there was a debate within the German government and, in particular, between the navy and the Foreign Office, over the sort of colony Germany needed in China. The navy insisted that Germany required a location which could be developed into a major port and which had a hinterland suitable for economic exploitation and political domination. The Foreign Office would have been happiest if Germany had simply established a small naval base or coaling station in China. One reason the Foreign Office opposed the navy was because it was more eager to avoid diplomatic difficulties, particularly with England. Equally important, some members of the Foreign Office, less blinded by the sense of competition with England, recognized the economically irrational element in the navy's plans. Germany was a trading power in China and so was not a nation which would benefit if China were broken up into exclusive spheres of influence.

Significantly, although the naval leaders advocated that Germany's foothold in China should be more than a naval base, they did not want the new possession to be placed, like the other German overseas territories, under the Colonial Section of the Foreign Office. Rather, they wanted the navy to operate the new colony. This was primarily because of the dissatisfaction which German colonial circles felt with the Colonial Section. It had originally been established in lieu of an independent colonial ministry, partly in order to de-emphasize the significance of overseas expansion. As a result, German colonialists considered the Colonial Section to be a symbol of the nation's supposed diffidence toward imperialism. They complained that the Section received little attention from either the Foreign Office or the government as a whole, and that it was chronically short of funds. More important, the commercially orientated colonial groups felt that the men who administered the colonies were conservative bureaucrats who, if they appreciated the importance of overseas possessions at all, understood only their military and political value, and not their economic significance. As a result, it was claimed, such officials overlooked the need for administering the colonies rationally and efficiently, and had no interest in making plans for economic development. While this assessment of the Colonial Section is open to dispute, the navy agreed with it. Therefore, because it hoped for favour with colonial groups, as well as because it genuinely wanted to improve and stimulate German colonialism, the navy was eager to try its own hand at colonial administration.

There were a number of reasons why the navy eventually selected Chiao-chou Bay and Shantung province as the site for

Germany's colonial venture in China. One was the comparative lack of diplomatic difficulties involved in taking the area. Another was the presence of German missionaries in the province. Since 1879 a German Roman Catholic group, the Steyl Mission, had made Shantung a prime area for German missionary activity in China. The chief of the mission, Bishop Johann Anzer, was eager to have the German colony in his province; and Tirpitz's desire to gain political support from the Centre party gave the missionaries considerable leverage with the navy.

But the most important reason for choosing Shantung was because the area seemed to fit the navy's basic desiderata for Germany's colonial venture. The possibilities of Shantung and Chiao-chou Bay were particularly well known in Germany because they had first been spelled out by the famous German geographer, Ferdinand von Richthofen. Shantung, Richthofen pointed out, had a population of thirty million. It was rich in undeveloped mineral wealth, especially coal, and also produced a wide variety of agricultural raw materials. But the province remained comparatively poor, even for China. What Shantung needed, wrote Richthofen, was investment and, in particular, investment in mining and transportation. At the same time, Shantung needed a port which could serve as an outlet for its products. The most logical location for this, Richthofen said, was Chiao-chou Bay which he called, "the largest and best harbor in the whole northern half of China.[3] In fact, he wrote, a railroad from Chiao-chou Bay into the interior would not only become the basis for the economic exploitation of Shantung, but would also be the best terminus for a wider railroad net which would cover all of northern China. In the 1890s the bay was still isolated from international trade, and the site of the future port of Tsingtao was a tiny fishing village.

With the active support of the kaiser, the navy's views prevailed. On 1 November 1897 a band of local people in southwestern Shantung killed two of Anzer's missionaries. This provided Germany with an excuse for action. On 14 November a German squadron occupied Chiao-chou Bay. By March, Germany had forced China to sign a treaty which embodied the navy's goals for Shantung. Section I of the treaty leased Chiao-chou Bay to the Germans for ninety-nine years. They received the sole right to exercise sovereignty in the leasehold, and this made their position analogous to that of the British at Hong Kong. There is no indication that the Germans, either when the treaty was signed or later, ever desired or considered the leased territory to be anything but a German colony. The section further permitted the free passage of German troops within a fifty-kilometre zone around the leased territory.

Section II of the treaty delineated Germany's economic privileges inside the province. The Germans were given a concession to build three railway lines and to operate mines within ten miles on either side of the roadbeds. The projected routes of the railways not only assured that the leasehold would become Shantung's chief commercial outlet, but also traversed almost every coal field Richthofen had mentioned. One line ran westward from Chiao-chou Bay to the provincial capital of Tsinan; another went from the bay to I-chou-fu in the south, and the third closed the triangle around the core of the province, by running from I-chou-fu to Tsinan. The Germans also received the right to extend the first line to the border of Shantung once service to Tsinan was begun. Section III of the treaty granted the Germans further privileges which essentially turned the province into a German sphere of influence. The section said that the Chinese government "binds itself in all cases where foreign assistance, in persons, capital, or material may be needed for any purpose whatever within the province of Shantung to offer the said work or supplying of materials in the first instance"[4] to Germans.

## Kiautschou as a Model Colony

The goals which the Reichsmarineamt established for the new German colony of Kiautschou developed from the same considerations which had originally impelled it to work for a sphere of influence in China rather than a mere naval base.[5] The navy felt that success at Kiautschou would popularize the cause of German colonialism in the homeland. In addition the successful development of the leasehold would vividly indicate the ability of the Reich, and particularly the navy, to match the supposed colonial prowess of Germany's rival, Great Britain. A triumph at Kiautschou would also, of course, garner political support for the navy at home, among the liberal commercial groups it had traditionally cultivated.

For these reasons the navy was not exclusively, nor even primarily, concerned with the military devlopment of the leasehold. Rather, it sought a larger goal, to make Kiautschou into a model colony. This meant that the navy worked to develop the new German acquisition into a place which would reflect the navy's competence in all areas of colonial adminstration, from taxation to education. Most importantly, it sought to turn the leasehold into a great commercial entrepôt which would enhance German trade as well as become the focal point of the economic development of Shantung.

For all these reasons and because developing the new colony required huge amounts of money, Tirpitz, a master propagandist and politician, worked to keep the nation, and especially the Reichstag, informed of the navy's plans and successes at Kiautschou. Between 1898 and 1907, the crucial years which laid the basis for the development of the colony, its budgets totalled 102,337,442 marks, and the actual expenditures, some hidden in the navy budget, were probably higher. The cost of suppressing the great African uprisings of 1904–6 aside, more money went to Kiautschou by 1907 than had ever been spent on any other German colony. This was the case despite the fact that the African colonies were much larger and had been receiving money since the 1880s. Only a small percentage of the money used at Kiautschou was ever raised in the colony itself. By 1913 the government had spent about two hundred million marks on Kiautschou, of which about thirty-six million was raised locally.

Despite its expense, Kiautschou enjoyed unusual favour in the Reichstag during the first decade of its existence. In later years, the huge expenditures came under attack at home, but politicians did not question the fact that the colony itself was being extremely well managed and developed.

The basic administrative structure of Kiautschou was comparatively simple in order to give the local authorities flexibility in dealing with the needs of a developing colony. The chief administrative officer was the governor. He was a naval officer, as were the bulk of the personnel below him. The governor had the right to issue ordinances which took effect immediately. Theoretically, they could be revoked in Berlin, but none ever was. Tirpitz, as naval secretary, was the military and administrative superior of the governor, and was ultimately responsible for the colony. The governor's immediate subordinates were a chief of staff who commanded the military garrison and a civilian commissioner who administered the civilian population. German colonial circles frequently complained that local people did not participate in the administration of colonies, and so the navy made a point of establishing advisory councils of German and Chinese residents to assist the government.

The civilian administration was divided into two separate structures, for Chinese and Westerners. It was also divided geographically into two zones, an urban zone, essentially the city of Tsingtao, where both Chinese and foreigners lived, and a rural zone, the rest of the colony, which was almost exclusively Chinese. The urban zone was tightly administered. However, in the rural zone the government sought to adjust itself to local conditions by coming as close as possible to Chinese models of local government. This meant in practice that except for taxation and the maintenance of law and order, there was not much interference in daily life.

On the whole, the administration served the needs of the colony well. The population of Tsingtao grew from a couple of thousand people in 1898 to 55,700 in 1913. Of these 53,000 were Chinese. The rural zone, which had 80,000 people in 1898, grew to 135,000 by the end of German jurisdiction. No major administrative problems developed and, on the whole, the Chinese population adjusted to German rule smoothly.

The navy established an elaborate system of zoning and real estate taxation at Tsingtao. This was done to maintain control over urban development, to provide a reliable flow of inexpensive building lots, to block speculation, and provide revenue. But as with all elements of the naval administration, the system, almost utopian in its conception, was also meant to embody the image of Kiautschou as a model colony. One feature of the system was strict guidelines and zoning regulations to plan for the physical growth of the city. The rules, which were carefully followed, zoned areas for harbour facilities and storage, others for residence and recreation, and still others for industry. As a result, Tsingtao grew in a very orderly fashion—unusual for the early twentieth century, especially on the crowded China coast.

The essential element of the tax system was a government monopoly over the purchase of land from its Chinese owners. Plots were then auctioned to Chinese and Westerners and careful rules and penalties established to make certain that the land was used for the purposes for which it was bought. In any case, the owners paid a yearly land tax of 6 percent on the current value of the plot. If the owner sold the land, he gave the government 33½ percent of the net profit from the sale. If land remained in the same hands for twenty-five years, a special levy of 33½ percent was to be collected. The chief architect of this system of taxation was Wilhelm Schrameir, a fervent follower of Henry George, who was to become associated with the land reform movement in Germany after he returned home. The rationale for the system, the navy said, was that appreciation in the value of land would "come not through circumstances created by the owner, but rather through the activity of the government or the whole society".[6] As a result of the system, Tsingtao escaped the land speculation which was so rampant in other Chinese ports, and the government also received a modest amount of income.

A significant adjunct to the land system was an extensive and expensive programme of forestation and land reclamation. In 1898 Tsingtao was an area of denuded hills and flat-lands covered with gullies and other marks of erosion. The navy reforested the hills, and elsewhere used planting and land-fill techniques to reverse and eventually erase the marks of erosion. The forestation programme was also extended to the rural zone. The navy was particularly proud of its success in these efforts which were almost unique in the China of the time.

Good social services in such areas as health care and education also figured in the navy's plans for its colony. It should be noted that in these efforts the government received much assistance from the German missionaries who came to Kiautschou. There were three German missionary societies in the colony: two Protestant ones, the Allgemeine evangelisch-protestantische Missionsverein (the so-called Weimar Mission) and the Berliner Gesellschaft zur Beförderung der evangelischen Mission unter den Heiden (the so-called Berlin Missionary Society), and the Roman Catholic Steyl Mission. The German missionaries at Kiautschou devoted much of their work and resources to welfare activities rather than pure evangelism. This partly reflected the general transformation and focus of the missionary movement in China during these years. It was becoming less concerned with amassing converts directly, and more in trying to make Christianity seem relevant to the local scene. This drift away from simple evangelization received a special boost at Kiautschou where the navy actively encouraged the missionaries to become service organizations which would assist the government and private interests in developing the colony. Because of this and its own particularly nationalistic bent, even the Steyl Mission concentrated more on secular activities than was common for Roman Catholic groups.

One of the most pressing needs of the colony in the area of social services was to establish good health conditions. In the early years, the health situation at Tsingtao was very bad. For example, the daily rate of hospitalization for the troops was extremely high at 161.2 per 1,000. For the rest of the population the situation was even worse. The generally poor health conditions along the China coast were made particularly acute by the special difficulties associated with a new town, a rapidly rising population, poor housing, and an unreliable water supply. The navy considered the dismal health to be one of Kiautschou's most serious problems. This was not only because of the intrinsic need for better sanitation, but also because the navy believed that public health provided a particularly significant criterion for assessing the merits of the location chosen for the colony, as well as the skill with which it was being run. The notion of judging the leasehold's administration according to its success in public health was to some extent forced on the navy because the Reichstag showed particular interest in the health conditions at Kiautschou. In response, the navy promised to achieve hygienic standards in the colony which "essentially would not lag behind those of the mother country". In some ways, this was a more utopian conception than the land system.[7]

One thing the navy did to attack the health problem was to promulgate strict hygienic regulations for everything from the handling of food to street cleaning. A special wing of the police force was established to enforce these rules. The government even built and operated the local slaughterhouse, a model of its kind, equipped with all the latest appliances. The navy also undertook an extensive building programme to provide housing for the troops and government officials. At the same time, tracts of land and other inducements were given to private companies to encourage them to build homes for Chinese workers. Rigorous building codes were set up and enforced, together with the town's zoning regulations. With the aid of the missionaries several hospitals and dispensaries were built and both the Chinese and Europeans in the leasehold enjoyed excellent medical facilities. Perhaps the most ambitious undertaking connected to the health problem was the construction of modern water and sewerage systems. The navy built these at considerable expense and by 1907 every section of Tsingtao had safe drinking water piped in.

As a result of the administration's efforts the basic health problems of Kiautschou were solved within ten years. By 1907 the rate of disease among the troops was 36 per 1000, approximately the same as in Germany. Detailed figures are not available for the rest of the population, but its health also improved steadily, though at a lower rate than the troops. By 1907 Tsingtao was reputed to have the best public health record in China. One light-hearted tribute which residents of the coast paid to the salubrious atmosphere there was to flock to the town for the summer. In 1904 there were 500 tourists and the number rose steadily thereafter. One satisfied customer wrote that after the Russo-Japanese War, "gradually the news spread about in the Far Eastern ports that Tsingtao was the healthiest city in Asia and was a delightful summer resort". Eventually, he said, it "became known as the "Brighton" of the Far East".[8]

The navy's desiderata for Kiautschou also included establishing a comprehensive education system for Germans and Chinese. Good facilities for Europeans were considered important not only for the needs of the colony itself, but to serve the requirements of Germans all over East Asia. Such schools would also, of course, make an excellent impression at home. The navy believed that good education facilities for Chinese would help further the development of the colony and control it politically. Moreover, such schools would contribute directly to attaining one of the navy's subsidiary, but often-mentioned goals—to transform Kiautschou into a showplace for German culture.

As in all areas of administration, the navy's educational successes were remarkable. The facilities for Europeans became the best outside the homeland. Not only were there lower schools, but the navy even succeeded in establishing an accredited Reformrealgymnasium which was fully integrated into the German system. When the gymnasium opened in 1902, there was no other school on this level anywhere outside the homeland. The missionaries helped establish a wide variety of schools for Chinese. The most ambitious undertaking was a college called Deutsch-Chinesische Hochschule. It was divided into an upper school and a lower school. The lower school was similar to a gymnasium. The upper school was the college. It had four faculties: law and political economy, natural sciences and engineering, forestry and agriculture, and medicine. The school also boasted libraries, laboratories, a museum, model farm and other facilities.

The fundamental goal of the navy at Kiautschou was, of course, economic growth and, in particular, commercial development. In this field its success was again striking. The navy transformed Tsingtao into a first-class port, and the railway to Tsinan connected the town with the interior. The navy, itself, built and operated the port facilities. The main harbour was a great semi-circular dam three miles long enclosing an area which had been dredged for the largest vessels. The piers built on the dam provided over a mile of modern docking facilities and were directly connected to the railway. There were also several smaller docking areas and an excellent system of lights and navigational aids for the port. The navy also operated a lavish shipyard which both built and overhauled ships. In 1907, the navy could describe what it had accomplished by saying, "Tsingtao now has the safest and easiest facilities for loading and unloading in East Asia ..., even in the older harbours such as Hong Kong and Shanghai, the loading and unloading of large steamships must be done with the aid of lighters. At Tsingtao this can be done directly into the railway".[9] Foreigners were, as usual, equally impressed. As one speaker in London admitted during the height of World War I, the port facilities which the Germans had built at Tsingtao were "the finest in China, not even Dairen excepted".[10]

The navy also developed extensive communications facilities within the leasehold. The government paved the streets in the town and built an extraordinarily comprehensive network of roads into the rural zone. There was a postal system, connected to the Chinese one in the interior. The navy also built and operated a telephone system, laid telegraph cables to Tsingtao and set up a wireless station.

The Schantung Eisenbahn Gesellschaft (or SEG), a private company organized by a syndicate of great German banks in

1898, built the railway from Tsingtao to Tsinan. The line was completed in 1904. Its construction and operation revealed the same thoroughness and care which distinguished all the German undertakings in Shantung. For example, because of Shantung's dense population and poor transportation facilities, the line had many stations. The railroad made a tremendous difference in the ease and cost of transportation along its route. The trip from Tsingtao to Tsinan, which had formerly taken twelve difficult days, was reduced to ten hours. From Tsinan to Shanghai had taken almost a month; now with the railroad and the new maritime connections at Tsingtao the trip took three days. The railroad also stimulated the population along its route to improve their own transportation and communication facilities. There was a striking improvement in the networks of roads surrounding the stations. Some of these were on the outskirts of important towns, but many were in places which had formerly been almost totally isolated.

As the transport facilities at Tsingtao developed, firms involved in commerce and related activities flocked to the town. By 1913 most of the large companies engaged in the China trade, both Chinese and foreign, had offices there. Similarly, numerous modern banks, many Chinese, and at least one from each of the trading powers, established branches at Tsingtao. The port had also become a regular stop for coastal steamers, and its direct trade with Europe was growing.

The navy had clearly succeeded in making Tsingtao into a great commercial colony. By the time Germany lost Kiautschou in 1914, Tsingtao had an import trade of foreign goods worth 26,207,915 taels and of Chinese products worth 11,592,412. Exports were worth 27,330,447 taels. The former fishing village had become the sixth most important port in China. In later years, Tsingtao's commercial growth continued on the foundations which the Germans had laid, and by 1931, the last normal year before World War II, it ranked as the fourth most important port in China, after Shanghai, Tientsin, and Dairen.

During the first decade of Kiautschou's existence, despite the enormous amount of money which the colony consumed, it enjoyed unusual favour in Germany. This support was just the sort of approbation for which Tirpitz had hoped when he put Kiautschou under the navy rather than the Colonial Bureau, and it testified to the navy's success in administering and developing the leasehold.

The most striking manifestation of Kiautschou's unique popularity occurred during the period from 1904 to 1906 when the opposition in the Reichstag to the German colonies reached its peak. This opposition consisted of the usual charges that the German colonial empire was a failure because the Colonial Bureau had administered the colonies poorly, had not tried to develop them economically, and had, therefore, simply wasted tremendous amounts of money. While these charges may not have been totally accurate, what is significant is that many of the Colonial Bureau's vehement critics continued to praise Kiautschou at the same time as they were attacking the other colonies.

In 1905, for example, when the controversy over the colonies was raging, the vote on the Kiautschou budget elicited nothing but a series of speeches praising the leasehold. A highly significant speech was that delivered by the deputy, Eickhoff, on behalf of Eugen Richter's Progressive party, one of the most important parliamentary groups which condemned the other colonies.[11] The speech was applauded from both sides of the house. Eickhoff began by noting the "gratifying development" of Kiautschou, and then said: "Certainly through the years we have granted a large amount of money for Kiautschou but it was used in a rational way."The adjective "rational" was probably the highest compliment a Progressive could pay to any expenditure. Eickhoff continued with a pointed reminder of the differences between the ways the navy and the Foreign Office administered their colonies. "The navy had made a really workmanlike, German job of it. Our party has said this in past years, and our spokesman, Deputy Eugen Richter, therefore, added the suggestion that in the future all colonies should be put under the Naval Ministry. (Very true! *from the Left.*) Gentlemen, I really believe that the Naval Secretary ought to be pleased about this. (*Cheering.*)" Eickhoff then launched into a sympathetic discussion of Kiautschou's problems and progress. At one point he referred to the health situation in the colony, something which had previously bothered the Progressives, by saying, "Gentlemen, I confirm joyfully that the pessimistic conception which I earlier … expressed about the climate of Tsingtao has fortunately not been confirmed by facts. (Hear! Hear! *from the Right.*) The state of health in Tsingtao … has improved from year to year, and the figures from this year's annual memorandum show that one can now say: Tsingtao can be considered completely healthy."

The representative of the Centre party, which had spearheaded the attack on the colonies, devoted his speech to extolling the legal system of Kiautschou. He also discussed the contribution which the navy was making to the entire field of German colonial law through its activities there and urged that it do even more. The Social Democrats generally opposed Kiautschou but, perhaps because they recognized a difference between it and the other colonies, they did not speak at the session at all.

The criticism of the colonies in the Reichstag stimulated the colonial reform movement, which began in late 1906 under the leadership of Bernhard Dernburg. It would be interesting to discover what impact the example of Kiautschou had on Dernburg's plans for the other colonies; for his most famous reforms, which were primarily intended to stimulate economic development, attacked just the kinds of problems which the navy had solved successfully at Kiautschou. Dernburg sought to reform each colony's administration, improve the legal system, better the treatment of the colonial peoples, and bring land speculation under control. His prescriptions for economic progress laid particular stress on the improvement of communications within each colony and the construction of good harbours on the coast.

## The Failure of German Colonialism

The navy succeeded in establishing a model colony at Kiautschou. However, in a broader sense, the colonial venture in Shantung proved to be a failure from Germany's point of view.[12] In the first place, Shantung never became the lucrative field for investment that had been envisioned, nor did Germany gain any political or other special powers there. In fact, within ten years after the Germans arrived, though Kiautschou remained a colony, the German sphere of influence in the rest of the province had disappeared. Secondly, the benefit to Germans from the whole venture was by no means equal to its immense costs.

From 1898 to the Boxer Rebellion of 1900 the Germans had some success in acquiring a position in the interior of Shantung which matched their expectations. The same consortium of banks which had formed the railway company also set up the Schantung Bergbau Gesellschaft (SBG) to exploit the mining concessions along the roadbed of the railway. As the SEG started work on the Tsingtao-Tsinan line, the SBG began mining operations in two locations along the railroad, and surveys on the proposed routes of the other lines. In these early years the Germans also relied upon their general claim to a sphere of influence in Shantung to obtain two additional concessions in the province. A separate company, the Deutsche Gesellschaft für Bergbau und Industrie im Auslande, began negotiations for an exclusive mining concession in five huge zones in Shantung. In addition, the Germans reached a preliminary agreement with the English and Chinese to finance the Shantung portion of the projected railway from Tientsin to the Yangtze River (Tientsin-Pukow line).

These economic undertakings were politically significant because they contributed to the extension of German power in Shantung. The German entrepreneurs strove to remain free of control from the Chinese authorities in Tsinan or Peking and to place their activities under the jurisdiction of the naval authorities at Kiautschou. The naval administration also provided military protection for the railway and the mining operations. German power increased in a similar way when the navy sent troops to protect missionaries far in the interior, and even interfered, on occasion, with internal political matters in Tsinan.

However, after the Boxer Rebellion, Germany's growing role in the interior began to fade, and by 1907 the sphere of influence was a dead letter. This occurred partly because a combination of international and domestic pressures kept the German government from pushing its claims. Equally important, China, increasingly nationalistic after 1900, worked to eradicate every vestige of German influence in the province.

In the years after 1900, the overall international situation directly curtailed German activities in Shantung because the growing diplomatic isolation of the Reich meant that Germany could not afford to antagonize other powers unnecessarily. In particular, as Germany's portentous split with Great Britain widened, the Germans feared that any attempt to exclude other nationals from Shantung would invite retaliation elsewhere in China. Germany had extensive business interests throughout the country, and Berlin became particularly concerned lest a stress on Germany's special position in the poor province of Shantung should lead to the loss of privileges elsewhere, especially in the rich Yangtze valley where England predominated.

Early 1902 marked the first crucial turning-point in the decline of Germany's sphere of interest. First of all, it was in this year that the Foreign Office wrested from the navy control of German affairs in the interior of Shantung. This occurred after a two-year bureaucratic struggle in which the basic issue was what emphasis should be placed on Germany's special role in the province. The victory of the Foreign Office was extremely important in the contraction of role. For the Wilhelmstrasse had been and continued to be far more willing than the navy to subordinate Germany's imperial claims in Shantung to the Reich's broader interests in China and elsewhere.

In a related development, the Anglo-Japanese Alliance of 1902 marked a further decline in the German position. The alliance was not directed against Germany, but rather against Russia. Nevertheless, by underlining the fact that England had selected another country as her main ally in the Far East, the alliance manifested the growing tension between England and the Reich. The year 1902 witnessed a surge of anti-German feeling in Britain, highlighted by a great press campaign against the Reich. The German claims in Shantung provided a readily available target for the British; and the press featured many attacks on Germany's dominance in the province.

In response, the Foreign Office initiated a campaign to convince England, the United States and the other trading powers that Germany had revaluated its special claims to Shantung and did not plan to enforce them. Actually, in 1902 the German government had not fully reconciled itself to giving up the sphere of influence. But pressures continued.

The second and final turning point in the disintegration of the sphere of influence was the Russo-Japanese War of 1904–5. With it, the diplomatic isolation of the Reich reached an even more critical stage, and the German government set about giving up all its claims to special privileges in Shantung. This occurred primarily because the war, by revealing the weakness of Russia, paved the way for the end of the Anglo-Russian rivalry in East Asia. The rivalry had been the main factor in giving the Reich a bargaining position in the Far East and limiting the pressures that England could apply to Germany. In addition, Japan's victory, and her obvious military power, raised the possibility that the Japanese, who had become very important in the economic life of Shantung, would contest the continuation of German dominance.

Another reason why Berlin hesitated to pursue a vigorous policy in Shantung after 1900 was because the support for such a policy within Germany was much reduced. The primary reason for this was the shift of the Centre party into a coalition, with the Progressives and Social Democrats, which opposed an activist policy in the non-Western world. The bloc was particularly hostile to military adventures for colonial purposes. This opposition increased after the great revolts in Germany's African colonies which began in 1903. The Boxer intervention had not been popular in Germany, and by 1905 the new attitudes in the Reichstag severely limited the government's options in Shantung, particularly if the defence of German interests might involve military force.

The culminating factor in the end of the sphere of influence was the development of strong Chinese pressure against it. This was the result of an extremely significant transformation in Chinese attitudes and foreign policy. For it was in these years that an intensely nationalistic approach to imperialism spread to broad segments of the Chinese government and society. This was the era of the great reform movement of the late Ch'ing which, by 1909, had implemented reforms that went far beyond anything advocated before. In foreign policy this nationalist approach resulted in a massive effort to regain Chinese independence and sovereignty wherever and whenever possible. Shantung was a highly visible target. The Chinese government not only undertook diplomatic initiatives and implemented new policies aimed at reducing Germany's role in Shantung, but also carried out institutional reforms in the provincial government at Tsinan for that purpose. In addition, the local élite, the so-called gentry, became active in the efforts to end the sphere of influence, especially in economic matters.

These Chinese efforts, coupled with the foreign and domestic restraints on Berlin, meant that by 1907 the sphere of influence had disintegrated. Kiautschou was still a German colony, but a less independent one than when it began. The demise of the sphere of influence was sometimes marked by agreements, and sometimes simply institutionalized in practice. The chief features of its decline can be summarized as follows:

### 1. The overall claim to a sphere

Germany no longer had any influence over the internal politics of Shantung. In addition, the broad rights, which Germany obtained in Section III of the 1898 treaty, for priority in "foreign assitance, in persons, capital, or material", were a dead letter. In fact, the provincial government, as a matter of principle, did not use Germans as advisers or give them a share of provincial business. As a result, Germany had a smaller role in such matters, especially in military affairs, than it would have had without its original claim to a sphere of influence.

### 2. The original railway and mining concession

The three railway lines specified in the treaty were expected to spread German influence over much of Shantung. This did not occur, and the Germans were only able to exploit a part of the concession, and then only for the most narrowly circumscribed business purposes. Of the three lines, the only one built was the first, from Tsingtao to Tsinan. This line was under extensive Chinese administrative control and protected by Chinese rather than German troops. In addition, China successfully resisted all efforts to use the railway to extend German activities or power within the province. For example, the SEG began to develop large postal and telegraph networks linked to the railroad; by 1907, the Chinese had closed them down.

China's success in limiting the German mining privileges was, if anything, even more impressive than its elimination of the dangers posed by the railway. The threat presented by the SBG was contained in the company's monopoly over some of Shantung's best mining land. To meet this challenge China not only had to limit the scope of the concession, but had to violate its provisions directly. The SBG was not allowed to mine along the routes of the lines which were not built, and it was forced to surrender its monopoly in the zone on either side of the Tsingtao-Tsinan line. The loss of this monopoly was a particularly striking sign of Germany's weakness in Shantung. For, to a considerable extent, the SEG failed financially because of the competition from Chinese mines in the zone—mines which had originally been stimulated by the German railway.

3. Investment privileges

The Germans obtained no concessions beyond those promised before 1900, for the section of the Tientsin-Pukow railway and for the five mining zones of the Deutsche Gesellschaft für Bergbau und Industrie im Auslande (DGBIA). Furthermore, these two concessions were only confirmed after years of negotiation which made clear the impossibility of getting any new opportunities for investment. They were also confirmed in a vastly different form than had originally been agreed upon. The DGBIA concession was reduced in area from 120,000 sq. *li* to a few sites totalling 210 sq. *li*. At the same time, the company did not receive a monopoly over these sites and, like a Chinese company, was completely under Chinese administrative control. The DGBIA never really got its operations going and it closed up in 1909.

The concession for the Tientsin-Pukow railway was delayed for a decade. In addition, when the contract was finally signed, its terms were the most generous ever offered China for a railway loan. The control and operation of the line was not in the hands of the concessionaires, but rather under the Chinese Railway Administration. There was also no provision for the foreign bankers to take over the line if payments were in default; this would have been an unheard of concession in earlier years.[13]

4. Military affairs

Germany lost all military rights in the interior of Shantung, even within the neutral zone. The last German troops in the interior withdrew in 1905 and German forces never again crossed (or even threatened to cross) the borders of the leasehold.

5. Kiautschou

Until 1905 Kiautschou was comparatively independent of the Chinese customs system. After that year, the leasehold was intergrated into the Chinese imperial customs and, in this area, became more like a Chinese treaty port than a fully independent colony like Hong Kong.

Beyond the loss of the sphere of influence, the other, and even more fundamental problem of German colonialism in

Shantung was that Germany got back very little in return for its investment in the province—particularly for the cost of developing Kiautschou. This began to be evident at the end of the colony's first decade, and had no relation to Germany's ultimate loss of the leasehold in 1914.

One reason that the German returns were low was because it was difficult to get modern enterprises going in China. This was particularly true of industrial undertakings, where, among other problems, the German efforts were all too often overcapitalized and complex for the local situation. Because of this, they could not compete successfully with more simple traditional or semi-modern enterprises. And, ultimately, every important German industrial undertaking failed.

In the interior, the most important German enterprise was the SBG. It established large-scale and very modern mines at two places along the railway. By 1911, when the mines were in full operation, the firm employed about 8,000 Chinese workers and 70 German supervisors. In 1913, the company was producing 613,000 tons of coal a year. Still, despite a government subsidy, it never paid dividends or made money, and was liquidated at a loss in 1913. The most important industrial activity at Kiautschou was also a failure. This was the Deutsche-Chinesische Seiden-Industrie-Gesellschaft, a silk-processing company which established a highly modern factory complex at Kiautschou in 1902. The company never returned a profit and went under in 1909. The only German industrial firms which succeeded were small ones, such as a beer company, which catered for a specialized clientele in Tsingtao itself, or elsewhere along the coast.

Even though the naval administration was more concerned with the commercial growth of Kiautschou than with industrial development, it still would have liked to show that the colony could provide a lucrative field for industrial investment. Accordingly, the government tried to attract industrial enterprises to the leasehold. However, because of the difficulties of making a profit, there was little response. For example, the navy wanted a private firm to run the large shipyard at Tsingtao. However, despite considerable efforts, including extensive negotiations with Krupp, it could find no takers. Several other public facilities at Kiautschou were operated by the navy because private entrepreneurs would not undertake the job.

However, it was not only industry which failed to meet expectations. Even more striking was the fact that German returns in the field of commerce itself were disappointing. The SEG was only a moderate financial success. More significant, the German share of business at Kiautschou was not great. At first Germany dominated commerce in the colony. However, since the special advantages which German firms had there could not be institutionalized in the free-trade setting of the China coast, as time passed, the German share of business at Tsingtao approached what it was in other parts of China. This was a smaller proportion than in the 1890s, since Japan had become increasingly important in the China trade, preempting the market for cheap consumer goods which had been Germany's specialty.

In 1907 Japanese goods accounted for between 50 and 55 percent of the imports to Tsingtao, English for between 20 and 25 percent, American for 15 percent and German for something close to, but not equal to the American. Since German goods only accounted for a little over 4 percent of the entire China market, this was a distinct advantage, though hardly a triumph for German trade. However, by 1913, the German share of Tsingtao's trade had declined further to 8 percent, only a little above the German share for China as a whole in that year.

The story was similar for the rest of the commercial picture. The only field in which Germany continued to have a distinct advantage at Tsingtao was in tonnage carried on German bottoms. The reason for this was not, however, particularly attributable to the situation at Tsingtao, but rather to the great strength of the German shipping industry on a world-wide scale. Hapag and Norddeutscher Lloyd had many runs to Tsingtao, but they could have easily sent these ships to Shanghai or other ports if the colony had not existed.

Since the navy was committed to the overall commercial development of Tsingtao, the administration was only moderately disappointed with Germany's small share of the colony's business. Instead, it rejoiced at the growing volume of business, the large number of companies from all nations which came, and the obvious commercial success of the colony. For all this was the ultimate proof that Kiautschou had been rationally and efficiently run, and that the navy and Germany had, indeed, equalled Great Britain as an effective colonial power.

However, many groups in Germany began to wonder if this was enough. Kiautschou never lost its reputation as a model colony, but parliamentary opposition to it developed over the more basic question of whether, in the final analysis, the whole undertaking was worth the cost. A campaign against Kiautschou reached a climax with a broad attack on the leasehold in the Reichstag in 1908. The nature of the opposition is clearly revealed in a speech delivered by Matthias Erzberger, who had, of course, made his reputation in the earlier battle against the colonies.[14] Erzberger gave his speech at budget time in response to the navy's annual "Memorandum Concerning the Development of the Colony of Kiautschou", a beautiful publication complete with text, tables, fine maps and photographs.

Erzberger began by saying that, in the light of the memorandum, he was very impressed by the Colony's progress. "I acknowledge", he said, "that on the basis of all reports, both official and private, which we have received about Kiautschou the money used there has accomplished very much and has been spent very skilfully." Nevertheless, he stressed, "I miss one thing in this very interesting memorandum: everything is enumerated which concerns development and the growth of commerce. But there is one figure which is missing that would seem to concern us Germans quite a bit, namely the 110-million-mark subsidy". Erzberger continued with a jibe at Prussia by noting that although the development of Kiautschou was indeed remarkable, "I believe that if the 110 million had been spent in Germany, one could make the finest garden in the world even out of the Mark of Brandenburg. Very salutary cultural work could also be accomplished at home if 110 million were spent on an area smaller than an ordinary Prussian district, an area only as large as the Free City of Bremen. We must always keep this sum of 110 million marks in mind when we really want to evaluate the accomplishments of the naval administration, which I fully acknowledge."

Even the commercial growth of Tsingtao was, basically, a failure. "As far as the commercial policy of the colony is concerned", Erzberger said, "I don't deny at all that imports and exports have risen sharply in the port, but this has not been to our profit. For all the money we have spent on Kiautschou has been spent entirely and completely for the benefit of the Japanese and the Chinese."

This sort of attack, of course, struck not only at Kiautschou but at the supposed economic value of all imperialism. The navy responded by instituting economy measures at Kiautschou and, in the remaining years, criticism of the cost of the leasehold abated. The amount spent on Kiautschou remained large, and the navy's economies apparently did not set back the development of the colony, for which the groundwork had already been laid. Nevertheless, the whole effort had lost its sheen; no matter how well the navy spent its money to improve Kiautschou the basic question always remained, should the place be developed at all? It may have been for this reason that the 1909 annual memorandum to the Reichstag was the last of these lavish publications which the navy issued. This was a subtle sign of economy, as well as recognition of the fact that there was no point in stressing the wonderful "Development of the Colony of Kiautschou" each year unless it could be shown somehow that Germany was benefiting in an important way. This was hard to demonstrate because it was not true.

This article has not discussed Kiautschou's role as a military base, but a word on the issue is in order. Despite the fact that Tirpitz always emphasized Kiautschou's commercial and colonial function, until 1905–6 there was a steady, though moderate expansion of the colony's military force. The port was a modern naval base and had a German force of 2,300 men stationed there. In addition, the navy built two permanent sets of gun emplacements and a number of smaller batteries. However, after 1906 there was no further increase of troops or armaments. This was partly because of the German desire after the Russo-Japanese War to show that Germany had no military designs on Shantung; but more basically the Germans had come to realize that Kiautschou, far from being a military asset, was really an isolated outpost, hostage to any nation with real strength in East Asia which might decide to move against the colony. The most obvious threat was Japan, with its English alliance, burgeoning commercial interests in Shantung, and growing desire for power in China. This assessment was, of course, accurate and when the outbreak of World War I gave Japan the opportunity to strike, Germany immediately lost all its holdings in Shantung.

1. This article is based on my book, *Imperialism and Chinese Nationalism: Germany in Shantung* (Cambridge, Mass., 1971). I have, therefore, tried to keep footnotes to a minimum. Beyond footnoting direct quotations, I have only cited the sections of the book which provide the basis for a given section of the article; the documentation and further details can be found there. The book is based on German and Chinese archives, though I have tried to take the quotations for this article from published materials.
2. This Introduction is based upon pp. 1–42 of *Imperialism and Chinese Nationalism.*
3. Ferdinand von Richthofen, *China, Ergebnisse eigener Reisen*, 5 vols. (Berlin, 1877–1912), 2: 262.
4. The text of the treaty can be found in John V.A. MacMurray (comp. and ed.), *Treaties and Agreements with and Concerning China, 1894–1919*, 2 vols. (New York, 1921), 1: 112–16.
5. This section is based upon chaps. 3 and 6 of *Imperialism and Chinese Nationalism.*
6. Reichsmarineamt, *Denkschrift betreffend die Entwicklung des Kiautschou–Gebietes* for the year ending October 1898, in *Stenographische Berichte über die Verhandlungen des Reichstages*, vol. 172, doc.79, p. 561.
7. *Denkschrift* for the year ending October 1899, in ibid., vol. 175, doc. 516, p. 2839.
8. Jefferson Jones, *The Fall of Tsingtau* (Boston/New York, 1915), pp. 162–63.
9. *Denkschrift* for the year ending October 1906, in *Stenographische Berichte,* vol. 241, doc. 268, p. 10.
10. William Blane, "Tsingtau", *Transactions of the Japan Society, London,* 13 (1915): 6.
11. *Stenographische Berichte*, vol. 202, pp. 4382 ff. (27/2/1905).
12. This section is based upon chaps. 5 and 6 of *Imperialism and Chinese Nationalism.*
13. It should be noted that in 1913 the Germans received the right to make some railway loans in exchange for officially giving up the railway concessions in the 1898 treaty. Even this, however, was only possible because the Chinese government was in an especially weak condition directly after the revolution of 1911; in any case, none of these loans were made.
14. *Stenographische Berichte*, vol. 231, pp. 417 ff. (21/3/1908).

# 10

PETER J. HEMPENSTALL

# Native Resistance and German Control Policy in the Pacific: the Case of Samoa and Ponape

Native resistance to the imposition of colonial rule has, for some years now, engaged the attention of African historians, and they have played a leading role in correcting the bias of Eurocentric histories of colonialism. They have demonstrated that the process of culture is not simply the story of European initiative and native response, but of a complex pattern of metropolitan conceptions, local initiatives and bargains, and colonial policy as directed on the spot by European administrators.[1] This principle of reciprocity is just as important in the history of Pacific resistance, and the particular events on Samoa and Ponape contribute to a fuller appreciation of the dynamics of early twentieth-century Pacific society and of the reality and meaningfulness of change in the Islanders' past.

Samoa and Ponape afford several convenient bases of comparison. First of all, in terms of open resistance, they presented the greatest threats to German domination of her Pacific empire. While the instances of physical hostility and rebellion in German New Guinea are far more numerous, that colony represents a completely different type of contact situation, involving hundreds of islands, fragmented populations, widely divergent language groups, and different levels of culture. Colonialism in German New Guinea never advanced beyond a crude frontier situation in which survival was the first consideration. Samoa and Ponape were, at least nominally, pacified territories experiencing a more intensive level of contact with the regime. Moreover, they possessed superficially similar cultures and presented similar problems of scale to the German administrations, in that they were dealing with relatively small, homogeneous populations enjoying comparable economic standards and fairly well-developed political systems, and having a long familiarity with European civilization. Their small size and isolation from metropolitan centres meant, too, that the character of their colonial experience bore very much the imprint of their individual chiefs of administration.

But the two islands possessed differences significant enough to offer a good case-study of the dynamics of culture contact under varying conditions of stress. The Islanders' experience of European culture before annexation by the Germans was of a vastly differing quality, and the modes of adaptation achieved during that period conditioned their reaction to German overrule.[2] In addition, official policy to each colony was determined by the role assigned to each within the empire, which had serious implications for the local approach to specific problems of colonial rule. Finally, the quality and quantity of leadership in Samoa varied enormously from that in Ponape, and in the prevailing circumstances this was perhaps the most crucial difference of all.

In both Samoa and Ponape the Germans inherited precarious situations. For more than two decades Europeans and Samoans had been engaged in a constantly fluctuating struggle for the right to control the group's economic and political destiny.[3] The consular representatives of Britain, Germany and the United States competed in attempts to dictate the outcome of Samoan district politics and establish a centralized native government which would ensure a measure of stability and advance their separate interests. Planters and land speculators took advantage of this anarchy to alienate ridiculously large areas of land by trading arms with the Islanders, which in turn helped to perpetuate the conflicts.

For their part, the Samoan district factions encouraged this competition of interests in trying to install their own candidates in power as the paramount chief of the group, the Tafaifa, holder of the four most important district titles. At the same time they would not tolerate European interference in their disputes, above a certain limit. In 1888 Mata'afa, prominent contender for the Tafaifa title, rebelled against the German-protected regime of Malietoa Tamasese, and in an ambush on 18 December his forces defeated a party of German marines sent to disarm them.[4] Again in 1892–93 and in 1898, Mata'afa, urged on by the cartel of chiefs which composed the basis of his power at the sub-district level, refused to admit the pretensions of the Powers to dictate the loyalties of the Samoans, and rose up against their puppet governments in an extended war of resistance which the Europeans never managed to quell. Their tenuous control extended no further than the range of their artillery, and it vanished altogether when the natives withdrew into the bush of the interior.[5]

A three-power commission in 1899 managed to effect a cease-fire and extract from Mata'afa and his main opponent, Tanu, a renunciation of future claims to the paramountcy, and in the same year, after negotiations with Britain, Germany finally acquired Samoa for her colonial sphere. But neither of these events automatically exorcized the instability and confusion of the past, as the new German governor, Wilhelm Solf, realized.

There was a great deal of sympathy for Germany on the part of Mata'afa and his supporters but it was rooted in gratitude for Germany's support in 1898–99 rather than in an inherent predilection for German culture and hegemony. Mata'afa's renunciation of the supreme title could not be taken at its face value; neither his chiefly adherents nor those of Tanu had surrendered their right to choose, more exactly, to create a king of Samoa according to Samoan tradition. There was no prescriptive rule of succession, such as male primogeniture, governing the choice of contenders. The possession of four specific district titles designated the highest-ranking chief in Samoa, and these were conferred by a cartel of chiefs and orators, the latter originally ceremonial officials of the village chiefs who, through their ritual functions and political skills, had acquired a disproportionate degree of influence in the political activities of the districts.[6] It was these "kingmakers", combined into two groups (Tumua and Pule) representing confederations of districts, who mobilized the Samoans into rival warring parties. The majority of this cartel, which supported Mata'afa, now expected Germany to guarantee his party's supremacy in Samoan affairs, and restore the paramountcy to its rightful heir. In other words, Germany was only to function as an agent in reconstituting the traditional political system in favour of one party.

In addition, the Mata'afa party represented the strongest military force in the land in 1900. It was in a perpetual state of mobilization, armed to the teeth with Western firearms, whereas Solf had one small cruiser at his occasional disposal, awe of which the Samoans had long since lost. Finally, Solf was faced with the task of asserting German sovereignty over a

European community predominantly British in its complexion and inclination, and of reconciling international differences decades old.

The security situation which the Germans encountered in Ponape was no less daunting, if the problems were somewhat different. The island had a long history of contact with Western civilization, the first visit being by Ferdinand de Quiros in December 1595. However regular contacts were not made with the natives until the early nineteenth century. By 1850 an average of twenty-nine ships a year were putting in at Ponape, most of them whalers.[7] The American Board of Foreign Mission (Boston Mission) began evangelistic activities in Ponape in 1852, and by then a fair-sized community of beach residents existed, numbering about sixty at its height and consisting of beach-combers, escaped convicts and ships' deserters. While these formed a considerable acculturative influence on the natives, they never possessed the productivity or the power to successfully challenge the domination of tribal chiefs.[8] The commerce of the island remained in chiefly hands, and the European was required to buy protection with a proportion of his earnings. It was probably this independence which acquired for the Ponapeans an early reputation for ferocity and duplicity.

German trading interests had been represented in the Carolines since 1866, and remained dominant even after Bismarck's attempt to annex the group in 1885 failed in the face of Spanish protests. When a Spanish garrison arrived in Ponape in March 1887 to actualize Spain's claim to the Carolines, it was more as a third party stumbling into a situation of endemic hostility between the five major tribes of the island, Sokehs and Not in the north, Madolenihmw, Kiti and Uh in the south. These tribes were named after the exactly demarcated territories which each occupied. Throughout the tribes there existed a theoretically identical series of ranked titleholders in two distinct lines, each line exercising certain privileges and established patterns of behaviour.[9] Outside these two social strata of chiefs, loosely analogous to the European concepts of royalty and nobility, everyone else was a commoner and bound to a particular chief within the tribe by ties of obedience, tributary labour and war service. A strictly authoritarian relationship governed social behaviour at all levels of society. Failure to observe proper etiquette, to respond to a call for service, invited punishment by one's chief, which could take the form of confiscation of land, stripping of titles, and banishment. Commoners had virtually no legal right of land tenure, holding property at the will, ultimately, of the high chief of the tribe.

Ponapean political life centred round the pursuit of enhanced status, the capture of titles, and personal prestige competition. Within the tribe the major cause of conflict was an inherent contradiction between the rules of succession to titles by matrilineal seniority and the principles of personal performance (enterprise, industry, exploits, etc.) incorporated into the system. Between the tribes most disputes resulted from the desire for territorial gains and tribal prestige.

Largely ignorant of the social dynamics, and indifferent to traditional independence, the Spaniards immediately assumed the role of colonial masters, making demands which quickly brought them into conflict with the Islanders. At the same time they introduced a new element of rivalry in the form of Roman Catholic friars, and the confessional rivalry with the Protestant mission soon became the aegis under which the tribal conflicts continued.

A decade of military clashes followed in which the Spanish were more often than not defeated. By 1899 Spain had lost all credibility with the Ponapeans as a superior power and, in a fit of exhaustion hastened by the Spanish–American War, the Spanish sold the Carolines to Germany.

Unfortunately this did not alter the circumstances prevailing on Ponape. The Germans inherited a virtual frontier situation with a population unmastered by its previous colonial rulers. The natives' experience of colonialism only reinforced their independence and sense of superiority, while it in no way diminished the hostility between the tribes, deftly disguised as religious disagreement. Like Samoa, Ponape was an armed camp, while the incoming administration of Deputy Governor Albert Hahl had virtually no military apparatus with which to assert its nominal overlordship.

A variety of factors conditioned the response of Solf and Hahl to the state of affairs in their respective colonies. In Samoa the long apprenticeship under three-power administration had made it comparatively easy to isolate the particular problem, namely, the centralized paramount chieftaincy and the power of the Tumua and Pule at the local level.[10] Solf's impotence in the face of Mata'afa's military power prevented his laying overt siege to these interest groups, but it was his ultimate goal to destroy their influence on Samoan politics.

The lack of military support for Solf in 1900 was largely a function of the metropolitan conception of Samoa. Berlin regarded the new colony as a windfall—a ready-made, productive, going concern, and because of the political sophistication of the islanders it did not envisage any great problems.[11] It was probably on this account that Solf was accorded a free hand to determine "the most judicious method of solving the issue of native administration".[12]

This was a vital concession, for Solf brought to Samoa a philosophy of native control which clashed at several points with prevailing assumptions of the need to militarize colonies and govern with the mailed fist. Solf refused to consider the native as a *quantité négligeable*, a person without rights or a commodity to be exploited for the sake of colonial profits. He possessed a natural respect for the intrinsic values of exotic cultures and a readiness to treat the Samoans on their own terms, even if this sympathy was based on the customary Eurocentric condescension of his age. From the outset, Solf realized that the Samoans could not be bullied into subjection, but must be won over to the colonial relationship. He was increasingly convinced that tact and discreet handling of their disputes would achieve this.[13]

Hahl was of a slightly different disposition with regard to the Ponapeans. He saw them as a people embittered by contact with the worst elements of Western civilization, proud and independent. This was also the conception held by the Colonial Department, and it had an immense effect on the lines of policy over the next seven years, though not as much as Berlin's reluctance to become too expensively involved in a very insignificant corner of the empire. Its agents on Ponape, in theory at least, did not enjoy the same freedom of action as did Solf in Samoa, the limits of their initiatives being clearly set down.

These were, in short, to take no action which might unsettle the natives and make a military expedition necessary. Ponape was not worth a war, and Berlin was prepared to sacrifice economic development for the sake of communal peace.[14] Hahl set himself the ultimate tasks of breaking down the "feudal" structure and controlling the predatory activities of the clans, but he envisaged these reforms in terms of years hence, after the natives had become accustomed to German suzerainty.[15] In the beginning he concentrated on winning the trust of the people and upholding the local configuration of chiefly power. Hahl did take positive steps to reconcile clan differences in the tribe of Uh, sending off a number of ringleaders to Rabaul, and he managed to negotiate a voluntary surrender of certain jurisdictional rights from the assembled chiefs. But in general he was reluctant to impose any direct administrative control on the tribes at the local level, preferring to cultivate friendly relations with the missions and using them as an extension of the administrative apparatus.[16]

Above all, Hahl and his immediate successor in 1902, Heinrich Berg, made no colonial demands on the population, eschewing the imposition of any personal taxes or compulsory labour on public works. The maintenance of peace depended wholly on the moral authority of the regime, and they were aware of it.[17]

This policy of negative control contrasted sharply with Solf's approach in Samoa. He had been forced to compromise with the Mata'afan party in 1900, acknowledging Mata'afa as paramount chief (though not as supreme sovereign), and his band of chiefs and orators as the ascendant Samoan power (Malo). But he had also set up a paid native bureaucracy at the district level, owing its loyalty only to the kaiser, with a view to undermining the influence of the old-style Malo.[18] As Solf's patriarchal administration gained authority with the Islanders he was able to carry off the disarmament of the population by profferring financial compensation, and so further reduced the possibility of an armed uprising. His first open confrontation with the Malo came in 1904 when they petitioned for a more explicit acknowledgement of their control over the indigenous polity.[19] Solf was able to divert this pressure, and by 1905, in the wake of the Tumua and Pule's tactical mistake in the Oloa movement, he had achieved one of his aims in peacefully abolishing the two bodies.

By 1907–8 the prospects for lasting peace and progressive economic development seemed assured, at least in Samoa. Solf had achieved an unprecedented degree of rapport with the native community at large, based on a fuller understanding of the nature of the system of conflict and choice which defined the range of action open to the Samoans. Solf's refusal to force the Samoans to work on European plantations and his initial defence of their land against pressure from the large plantation companies can be seen as deliberate policy to keep the Samoans isolated and protected from the consequences of culture contact. His victory over the Malo suggests that he had already gained control of the indigenous structure. By constructing a new native assembly and administration in 1905 out of chiefs drawn from districts which did not traditionally hold power,[20] Solf created a front against the old élites with a vested interest in maintaining their positions and dependent on Solf for them.

Finally, Samoa seemed in a sound economic position by 1907–8. The colony was virtually self-supporting, the labour problem for the plantations was being comprehensively tackled by the importation of Chinese coolies, new export crops were making headway on world markets, and the Samoans were being drawn some way into the process of development by means of a head tax and regulated plantings of coconuts.

The German administration in Ponape did not enjoy a similar state of affairs. The previous seven years had been a period of temporization with the native community, while economic development had suffered a grievous set-back from a remarkably destructive typhoon in April 1905. Neither Hahl nor Berg, who died in 1907, had taken positive steps to deal with the causes of conflict within and between the tribes, the competition for enhancement of status, and the pursuit of territorial power. Virtually the only initiatives taken with regard to control policy were the partial disarmament of the people, a fortuitous success which Berg brought off by exchanging, after the typhoon, much-needed foodstuffs for arms and ammunition, and by the control of American whalers which had been running guns to the natives. Nevertheless the uneasy calm which prevailed on Ponape was being interpreted as a sign of progress.[21]

Despite appearances, neither the Samoans nor the Ponapeans were mere sounding boards for administrative policies in these years. The initial passivity of the Samoans was due to the fact that German annexation brought with it a return to peace and a certain order desired by the natives after two decades of strife. But the community's leaders had also concluded that nothing was to be gained by resistance, assuming that they would now be granted the power for which they had so long struggled. As they became gradually conscious of Solf's real intentions, the chiefs who composed the Malo began a campaign of political intimidation to try and regain the initiative. Lauaki, orator chief of Savai'i and nominal spokesman for the Pule, tried to undermine the authority of Solf by ridicule;[22] hence, too, the petition of 1904. The failure of these gambits is directly related to the emergence of the Lafoga Oloa movement—a complex phenomenon with a number of political foci.

In 1904 the world market price of copra slumped dramatically, disconcerting the Samoans, who were dependent on the sale of copra to obtain their trade goods. In addition, Solf's administration was undergoing a concerted attack from a clique of disaffected German settlers, and rumours were circulating among the natives that Solf was in disgrace and was about to be recalled.[23] The Malo, in response to the uncertainty pervading the island community, seized on an idea mooted by an American-educated half-caste to form a copra-producing and copra-marketing company run by Samoans themselves. It was an opportunity to acquire the economic power which, from their observations of European commercial enterprise and colonial practice, the élites conceived as the prerequisite for political power. While it was designed to discomfort Solf and force him to concede the Malo its traditional claims, the co-operative, or Oloa, was also an attempt to adapt the growing Samoan copra industry (especially in the light of the harvest from the compulsory growing of coconuts) to the new demands made on island life by dependence on a world market. It indicated a certain, if imperfect understanding of the crude mechanisms of market exchanges. The Malo ordered all Samoan males to contribute four to eight marks which would provide the capital necessary to begin the company and also give them a financial lever against the German administration.[24]

Solf was determined to put a stop to the Oloa, as it presented a challenge to the white traders, the primary *raison d'être* of colonization; but he also recognized it as a bid by the corporation of chiefs and speakers to arrest the decline of their power.[25] In speech after speech he tried to point out, with some reason, the weaknesses of the idea and the lack of experience Samoans had in such enterprises, and he forbade native officials of the administration to pay what amounted to direct taxes to the Malo. Solf even attempted to recruit Lauaki to work against the scheme.[26]

Solf did manage to slow the movement, but when he left

Samoa for a holiday in New Zealand at the end of 1904 this was construed as confirmation of his recall and the Oloa sprang up again, soon developing an overtly hostile attitude to the regime. Solf's deputy, Erich Schultz, promptly imprisoned two of the ringleaders at Vaimea, but in a gesture of independence and an attempt to reinforce a sense of solidarity a number of the Malo chiefs broke in and freed the prisoners.[27]

However the unity of the movement was already severely strained, for members of the non-Mata'afan party were reluctant to sponsor a scheme which would only further entrench their enemies in power. The Vaimea incident only increased this stress. Solf's return in 1905 hastened the disintegration of the Oloa, while the Malo's indiscretion at Vaimea afforded him the necessary excuse to insist on its dissolution.

The inherent instability of Samoan district politics contributed to the failure of the co-operative,[28] but so also did the inability of its leaders to mobilize the masses behind the scheme for any length of time. They remained tied to their traditional economic organizations and descent groups at the local level, while Solf consciously encouraged this through his appointed district government. Solf's one error of judgement was to allow Lauaki to remain in Samoa. Lauaki had consistently championed the conservative cause against Solf's political reforms and he was seriously implicated in the events following Solf's departure in 1904. He had deftly retraced his steps when retribution appeared, working against the Oloa in his own district,[29] and this about-face further confused the Samoan camp. It was a victory for Lauaki in persuading Solf that he did not deserve deportation.

While the Ponapeans exhibited a greater measure of passivity during this period, it did not mean that they had implicitly acknowledged the hegemony of Germany. In fact, the natives had been so far largely unaffected by the administration, and in effect tolerated the Germans because no demands had been made on them. There had been several clashes within the tribes in which Hahl and Berg had mediated, and the Roman Catholic mission gave some cause for concern by its desire to expand into Protestant strongholds. In 1905–6 the attention of the Islanders was devoted mainly to the problem of recovery from the effects of the typhoon. But by 1907 the small colony of Europeans was "living on a powder keg".[30] The official policy of non-action only encouraged the continuation of local social and political conflicts, while deteriorating relations within the white community were tending to weaken the moral authority of the regime.

The course of culture contact had always been affected by relations within as well as between cultural groups; differences within the white community of Samoa had a particularly long history. The growth of a Pan-German planting class essentially opposed to Solf's policy goals, methods, and philosophy was a fairly typical development of the German colonial empire. The size of white settler communities, their ability to organize metropolitan support for their sectional interests against those of the administration, generally determined the degree, if not the kind of exploitation of the resources of a colony. In Samoa, Solf was faced with a clique of ex-officer planters with small capital, who had been lured to the island by one Richard Deeken, himself an officer of the reserve, who had painted an exaggerated picture of the prospects for cocoa culture in the group.[31] With the help of his influential contacts in the Zentrumspartei at home, Deeken sought to have Solf removed and his place taken by a military regime which would govern the colony solely for the benefit of German settlers. In this contest Solf managed to retain the upper hand because of the support of the largest plantation company and the non-German population, and because his non-militant policies were repeatedly vindicated on the occasions of unrest.

The discontented of both racial groups constantly used each other for their own ends: it is likely that Deeken encouraged the rumours of Solf's disgrace in 1904 and the idea of a native co-operative;[32] it is certain that the Malo, on its own initiative, was endorsing Deeken's activities in order to discomfort Solf and dispose him in favour of its demands.[33] The Malo also tried to use Deeken's expertise in the Oloa by making him the prospective manager, which was more than a purely business manoeuvre. If Deeken proved more powerful and Solf was disgraced as rumoured, it obviously made sense to support the former and commit him to the future of the scheme.

The trading and planting establishment in Ponape was much smaller, consisting almost entirely of employees of the Jaluit-Gesellschaft, which possessed the monopoly of commerce and plantation agriculture in the Carolines.

In Ponape, the mission societies probably exercised most influence on relations between both racial communities. In a situation where the regime left control at the local level mainly to the missions, its primary concern for law and order clashed with the competitive proselytism of the different confessions. Moreover, religious jealousy had the effect of reinforcing tribal particularism which, in turn, was actively encouraged by the more astute indigenous leaders in order to ensure their positions within the traditional power structure.

Berg was the first to suffer from this conflict, and his commitment to the status quo above all else meant that the interests of administration and mission were never successfully harmonized.[34]

Solf never experienced the same degree of difficulty in Samoa. A similar state of rivalry existed between the Roman Catholic and Protestant missions, but the governor possessed a great deal more manoeuvreability in his relations with them, while the Samoans had attained a stable level of adaptation through their long history of contact.

In so far as one can speak of turning points in the state of relations between the Germans and the natives, the year 1908 best represents that point. In April 1908, after a year without firm official supervision, Ponape received its third administrator, Georg Fritz. He brought with him a programme of social reform and economic development devised by himself and Hahl. Freehold land tenure was to be granted to the present occupants of property held in fief to tribal chiefs, in return for which the emancipated tenant must work fifteen days a year on government projects. Half of the accumulated wage would go to the chiefs as recompense for their lost prerogatives over land, and the other half would fall to the budget.[35]

These plans owed less to the policy of the new colonial secretary, Dernburg, or to Hahl's need to justify his government of the Carolines from New Guinea, than to the conviction of Fritz and Hahl that a continuing policy of non-action in Ponape would only lead to unrest.[36] The simultaneous revival of a violent personal feud between two Kiti chiefs, Nanpei and Joukiti, indicated that this was so. But the announcement of the reforms, as well as Fritz's uncertain handling of the Nanpei-Joukiti affair only resulted in further disquiet. The effect of the reforms was to release land ownership from direct connection with the old feudal structure of society,[37] and this not only undermined the sense of clan solidarity, but also aroused resentment from tribal chiefs by removing Ponape's most important resource from their control.

However the reforms in themselves were not the cause of the eventual rebellion against Germany, for they were accepted voluntarily by most tribes. Basically, Fritz misread the state of affairs in Ponape, and completely misunderstood the importance of traditional tribal rivalry in his analysis of the discontent, preferring to see its origins in mission activity. The dispute between Nanpei and Joukiti was an episode in the struggle for the high-chieftaincy of Kiti. Joukiti represented the logical candidate in terms of hereditary succession. Nanpei's claim was based on his exceptional position as a wealthy, independent, acculturated chief, Protestant leader, and enterprising trader.

In July 1908 Nanpei orchestrated a raid on Joukiti's land and harassed natives working on the government roadworks. His aim was, first, to provoke Joukiti to revenge for the raid, and then to implicate him as the culprit in the threat to the labourers.[38] Joukiti would then appear to the new administrator as a major troublemaker and be removed, leaving the high-chieftaincy in Nanpei's grasp.

However, Joukiti possessed clan connections with the northern tribes of Sokehs and Not, and the Roman Catholic mission, with its base in these tribes, feared an outbreak of civil war and a return to the anarchy of the Spanish period.[39] Unfortunately the mission's pressure on Fritz to settle the affair was construed by the latter as an attempt to recruit the regime as an ally for the Catholics in a religious war against the Protestants of the south. Relations between Fritz and the Catholic mission deteriorated drastically and Fritz henceforth was wont to attribute all unrest to Catholic machinations.[40]

This was the first mistake, also made by Fritz's successor Karl Boeder, who arrived in Ponape in December 1909. Boeder made a more fundamental error in dismissing the Ponapeans' sense of independence and racial pride which, hitherto, had not been modified by the experience of German administration.

Fritz had made the inauguration of the social reforms conditional on the consent of each tribe. Sokehs alone stood firm against them. The tribe regarded the reforms with suspicion as the inspiration of Nanpei, who stood to gain most from the redistribution of land because of his considerable inherited estate. The Sokehs chiefs feared that he wished to stake a claim to the overlordship of all Ponape, and Nanpei himself had spread the rumour that he had formed an alliance with the Germans to develop the island's economic resources.[41]

Boeder, however, was rather contemptuous of Fritz's "leniency", and in February 1910 simply forced the reforms on the chiefs of Sokehs. This invoked their wrath. Not only had Boeder broken Fritz's promise but he seemed deliberately to be supporting the pretensions of Nanpei and the Kiti tribe. Despite this duress the initiative remained mostly with Sokehs, for Boeder was intimidated into employing the actual leader of the tribe, Jomatau, as overseer on the roadworks. The progress of these projects was still entirely dependent on the co-operation of the tribe, and in August, when there were no ships in Ponape to maintain communications with the outside world, the chiefs of Sokehs made use of their advantage to demand an increase in their day-wage.[42]

The responsibility for subsequent events lies largely at Boeder's feet. In contravention of the principles laid down by the Colonial Office, he deliberately quickened the tempo of change without having at his disposal the military support which Hahl and Fritz had come to regard as a prerequisite for order.[43] He seemed to spurn evidence that plots against the white colony were circulating in Sokehs in June, and even after this was proved he neglected to use the visit of the East Asian Cruiser Squadron in July to make an example of the leading dissidents, specifically Jomatau. All this only diminished the deterrent effect of his authority. Then on 17 October 1910, Boeder had a Sokehs labourer thrashed for insubordination, despite warnings that such action would not be tolerated by the Islanders. Thrashing was a form of punishment unknown to the Ponapeans, and more than anything else outraged the dignity and independence of the tribe in its enemies' eyes as well as its own.[44] It finally released the emotional energy sufficient to spark off a rebellion.

Samoa did not suffer from the same lack of continuity in leadership, nor was the colonial relationship as suddenly imposed as in Ponape. The change in 1908 came with the increasing senility of Mata'afa and the consequent revival of interest in the question of succession to his position as paramount chief. This was the situation which Solf, from the beginning, had regarded as critical for the success of his control policy. He had succeeded in abolishing the Malo without provoking any rebellion, and he considered the elimination of the paramount chieftaincy—the focus of most Samoan conflicts—as the next step in reducing the Samoans to docile subjects. However the removal of the Tumua and Pule did not erase the old district jealousies, nor had the traditional élites been cowed by Solf's success. Lauaki in particular, who as the leading exponent of the skills and power of the orator chiefs had most to lose, intensely resented Solf's programme of political transformation, and was determined to reassert the rights of the Tumua and Pule as "kingmakers" of Samoa. Moreover, his long-term ambition was to have his candidate, Malietoa Tanu, succeed to Mata'afa, thus ensuring his own position at the apex of Samoan politics.

In this sense the movement, *o le mau*, which began under Lauaki's auspices in August 1908, was simply an extension of the old divisions in local society. With Solf once more absent from Samoa on leave, Lauaki began propaganda throughout the districts for the Tumua and Pule and the succession question. His plan was to organize a mass demonstration of natives to greet Solf on his return, and after the welcoming ceremonies, to present Solf with a list of petitions or *maus*, urging, among others, that several chiefs from the old maximal lineages be appointed as salaried officials, that the Tumua and Pule be restored, that the Islanders be supplied with records of government revenue and expenditure, and that the head tax be eased.[45] The variety of these requests was deliberately designed to gather behind Lauaki as large a cross-section of Samoan society as possible. At the same time the last two *maus* represented a confused, ill-defined groping towards a share in the new dimension of political and administrative life which the Germans had introduced into Samoa.

At this stage no intention of armed rebellion existed. The whole scheme was a traditionally Samoan act of political intimidation which presupposed reciprocity from Solf. But in November, on the eve of Solf's return, his deputy Schultz was made aware of these activities, and he issued orders to Lauaki and his followers not to come to Apia to meet the governor.[46] Schultz's refusal to allow Lauaki to present his *maus* was probably the turning point in the movement, at which time it became an open, if not very aggressive act of defiance. Lauaki obeyed Schultz's order, but continued his campaign to create a united front of Samoans against the regime.

By the time of Solf's arrival on 22 November, Lauaki was in a formidable position, having mobilized the politically important districts, Saleaula and Safotulafai in Savai'i, Leulumoega and Lufilufi in Upolu, which represented the corpus of chiefs in the Pule and Tumua. The movement took on rebellious overtones when Lauaki began ridiculing Solf, and made secret overtures to the American administration on Tutuila in an effort to gain its support.[47] In the absence of any military power on which to fall back, Solf responded by trying to wean away the Tumua chiefs of Upolu, who were naturally suspicious of political initiatives which did not originate in their own districts. He succeeded in persuading them that Lauaki's plans did not include them in the final victory—which was not altogether devoid of truth.[48]

When Lauaki became aware of the sudden hostility of the Tumua he lodged himself in Vaiusu, Upolu, with a thousand of his adherents, and prepared to make war on the Tumua. In a desperate bid to avert a collision, Solf personally confronted Lauaki in Vaiusu to dissuade him from violence. The meeting, however, was an object lesson in the political skills which had preserved Lauaki throughout the German period. In the presence of his followers Lauaki disclaimed responsibility for the unrest, and designated Mata'afa as its inspiration. The moral onus was now squarely on Solf's shoulders: he could not take Lauaki from his supporters to examine him, nor could he abandon Mata'afa as appointed high chief if he wished to avoid civil war. All he could do was to pardon Lauaki on condition that he returned to Savai'i and ceased his activities. Lauaki did return, but his incitement went on unabated.[49]

Under increasing pressure from the chiefs of Upolu to allow them to begin hostilities, and from the white community for a more positive policy of protection Solf finally telegraphed on 13 February for a detachment of warships.[50] Until they arrived Solf concentrated on restraining the Upolu chiefs from taking action on their own initiative, and on calming the Europeans. At last, on 22 March, with cruisers from the East Asian squadron at his disposal, Solf issued an ultimatum to Lauaki to surrender himself by the end of the month for deportation, or risk the consequences.[51] The demand was rejected at first, but after judicious persuasion from the missions Lauaki and nine accomplices gave themselves up on 1 April, and were deported to Saipan, in the Marianas.

Unlike Ponape, Lauaki's *o le mau* cannot be regarded unequivocally as a colonial "rebellion" in the sense of a militant rejection of external hegemony and occupation by another race.[52] It at least began with the premise of German rule and was designed initially to modify that rule. There is no evidence of a pre-existing plan to get rid of all the whites. At any time before the arrival of the navy the Europeans as a community were powerless to defend themselves against a concerted attack by Samoans, but Lauaki made no attempt to capitalize on the fact. At no point did he unconditionally renounce Germany's hegemony. At Vaiusu his followers had prepared a timetable for war, and one of the contingencies in this case was the murder of Solf, but the question of revolt was conditional on Solf's response, and the belief that he had capitulated to Lauaki at Vaiusu was what probably prevented the outbreak of violence.[53]

Lauaki failed to achieve a united front against the colonial regime and this jeopardized the movement from the outset. He tried to mobilize the community by using the traditional élite status of the orator chiefs as kingmakers and high priests of the political citadel, by appealing to the old ways and corporate political issues and to the desire to command the resources of the island group. But Solf had deliberately undermined the status of the old cartels among the population at large, and given power to new and lesser chiefs who had failed to secure it under the old law. Their collaboration with the regime, in moving among the people, mediating between the hostile parties, and supplying Solf with complete details of Lauaki's activities, was invaluable in defusing the situation. The missions, too, had a tranquillizing effect at the critical stage in late March when their representatives secured the peaceful surrender of Lauaki and his accomplices.

Although the forward-looking aspects of the movement, Lauaki's *maus* concerning control of the administrative apparatus, were still prominent towards the end of the crisis, it would be exaggerated to interpret *o le mau* as progressive. Lauaki's goals remained predominantly traditionalist, and his methods reflected this. His appeal, first to American and later to British support,[54] was a very traditional strategy which had been employed for more than two decades. In not appreciating the nature and consequences of the new configuration of power in Samoa it had little to offer.

The rebellion of the Sokehs tribe on Ponape was also an act in defence of traditionalism. Jomatau, effectual high chief of the tribe and inspiration of the revolt, was a self-styled defender of the old Ponapean ways, the *Lamalam en Ponape*. He had little difficulty in marshalling the stratified classes of Sokehs behind him, appealing to the old fears of domination by the southern tribes and the loss of independence and self-respect which the Germans had inflicted. Sokehs had led the original revolt against the Spanish in 1887 and had never been suppressed by a European power; moreover most of the arms and ammunition still held by the natives was centred in Sokehs. It was natural that the tribes-people were confident that the Germans could be thrust from the island as had been the Spanish.[55]

Boeder and his three assistants had been deliberately attacked and murdered on 18 October, the day after the thrashing. Quick action by the local doctor, Girschner, in summoning the remaining tribes to help the Europeans, and arming the white residents, transformed the small, compact colony into a fortress. But Sokehs seemed reluctant to press home its advantage once the first passion had subsided. The rebels confined themselves to nocturnal sniping and foraging raids, and proceeded to dig themselves in on the inaccessible peaks of their island, clear a line of fire and fatalistically wait for the inevitable German invasion.[56]

They had to wait a long time. Because of Ponape's isolation between visits by the Norddeutscher Lloyd postal steamer, the newdid not reach New Guinea until the end of November, and Berlin till 26 December. A detachment of cruisers was immediately dispatched from China, and by 10 January the *Emden*, *Leipzig*, *Nürnberg*, and *Cormoran* were anchored off Ponape with 300 German marines on board. Though there were several precedents on which to base an expedition against a relatively developed Pacific island society, the ensuing campaign was noticeable more for the erratic use of strategy and the mistakes of the inexperienced German forces.

On 13 January the rebels were driven from the heights of Sokehs by an assault which took even the Germans by surprise. It was the inspiration of Dr Kersting, the newly-arrived administrator of the group, who persuaded a senior naval officer to mount an immediate frontal attack rather than prepare for a war of attrition. Even then the accompanying force of Melanesian police bore the brunt of the fighting. A blockade of the little island of Sokehs proved ludicrously unsuccessful, and almost the entire tribe escaped to the mainland by night. A week later, on 26 January, the rebel band escaped, without a loss, from a four-hour battle at an old Spanish fortress in the interior, and continued easily to elude the German troops.[57]

Kersting finally adopted a strategy he had learnt in Africa. The "loyal" tribes-people were recruited as informants and threatened with the devastation of their localities if they did not co-operate; in a variation of a scorched earth policy, Kersting had all the indigenous crops harvested and stored in order to deny them to the rebels; small detachments of marines were stationed at various points on the island to constantly search for and harass the enemy.[58] Nevertheless the Germans were still surprised when fragmented groups of Sokehs began to surrender in quick succession, culminating in the surrender of Jomatau on 14 February, barely a month after the beginning of the campaign. After a hastily convened war trial, fifteen of the ringleaders were executed and the rest of the tribe banished to one of the underpopulated atolls of the Palau Group.[59]

Unlike *o le mau* in Samoa, the Sokehs revolt was from the start a regional phenomenon and an outright rejection of German supremacy. The natives followed an improperly understood idea of freedom which they associated with the past. This is not to say that the "loyal" tribes were more progressive, or willing allies of Germany. They were more successful in coming to terms with the new order, but in the light of their successful challenge to the Spanish and of their discontent at the introduction of the German reforms, the tribes of Madolenihmw, Kiti, Uh, and Not were at least potential rebels. They remained faithful to Kersting throughout the military operations, but it seems likely that their leaders were waiting to see which side proved the more powerful. The quick suppression of the revolt more than anything deterred them from making common cause with Sokehs, although it is true that there was no precedent for an island-wide mobilization of resistance against an external enemy. In the circumstances of minimal communication between tribes, the forces for integration were not strong, particularly as, in this case, mutual suspicion formed part of the motivation for the uprising.

Official handling of the rebellion also differed vastly from that in Samoa. It was the logical consequence of the assumption which had ruled in the Colonial Office, and on the spot, since Ponape had become a German colony. This was that if once the Islanders rose against the administration, only a massive military commitment and full-scale amphibious operation could hope to restore Germany's authority.[60] This was probably why no efforts were made to negotiate a surrender, except by Girschner on his own initiative in the immediate aftermath of the events of 18 October.[61] The campaign was more than a punitive expedition; it was a positive act of policy designed to establish once and for all Germany's rule over the Carolines.

It was Girschner, too, who took the gamble of calling the remaining tribes to the defence of the colony, deliberately exploiting the political dichotomy of the island. By resorting to the principle of divide and rule, as in Samoa, Girschner managed to contain the rebellion geographically, which was an important factor in the success of the subsequent operations. However at a later stage Kersting did not have a body of committed collaborators on which to rely, as did Solf in Samoa. His method lay in intimidating the other tribes into supporting the administration by the overwhelming effect of German military power. Without the latter it seems certain that a durable measure of peace would never have been restored in Ponape.

The relatively quick dissipation of physical resistance indicates that there was insufficient commitment to the ideals of the revolt to maintain effective opposition. The original uprising was primarily an explosion of frustration engineered by a few, and the bonds of tribal solidarity counted for more than a sustained dedication to the *Lamalam en Ponape*. Perhaps prolonged contact with Western civilization had diminished their will to suffer the privations of an extended jungle war.[62] It is certain that the long period of waiting before the arrival of the German forces had weakened the resolve of the tribe, and the weight of the German response discouraged them.

As in Samoa, the missions took an active part in helping the expedition to its conclusion. The Roman Catholic Capuchin Mission in particular, in view of its past conflict with the regime, was impelled to prove its loyalty and forestall any moves trying to associate its activities with the cause of the rebellion. The insurrection at least destroyed the myth that religious sectarianism was the cause of all unrest on Ponape. The reputedly Roman Catholic tribe of Sokehs was still one-third heathen in October 1910, and the Roman Catholic tribes of Not and Auak were among the first to hasten to the defence of the colony.

Some tentative generalizations emerge from this analysis which may help in working towards an eventual theory of Pacific resistance. They cannot be considered as relevant or complete for all cases of culture contact in Pacific societies. First of all, reaction to German colonialism was conditioned by the experience of Western civilization prior to annexation. The degree of accommodation or rejection of European preconceptions of superiority largely determined the attitude of the natives to the new administrations, and thus the manner in which they handled subsequent conflicts of interest.

It follows that the native interpretation of what the regime was setting out to do was at least as important as the regime's preconceptions concerning native relations, and the leaders of the native community consciously weighed the question whether they stood to gain most from resistance or collaboration. The degree of communication between the two cultures thus helped shape the continuing relationship. Both the metropolitan government and its representative on the spot played vital roles in accomplishing this, the former through its conception of the colony and the freedom of action it granted to its local officials, the latter in the qualities of leadership he exhibited.

The differential rate at which colonization proceeded, in the sense of the economic, social and political pressures imposed on a subject people by reason of the colonial relationship, seems to have influenced the level of acceptance of the Germans by the islanders. The Samoans were, as a people, only peripherally affected by the demands of German rule. Solf would not force them to provide plantation labour for the white man, nor allow their land to be alienated by planters and speculators. The head tax which they were required to pay was familiar to them as a form of revenue from their substantial mission contributions. The Ponapeans, on the other hand, were required to surrender their previously total control of relations with outsiders and accept a fundamental transformation of the system of land tenure and tributary associations.

The above equation is, however, susceptible to certain qualifications: Ponape, for example, was not subject to many of the pressures which caused friction in other colonies—labour recruitment, the acquisition of large areas of native land, a sizeable and vocal white settler community. Perhaps the ultimate link lies in the Islanders' conception of the Germans as a ruling race: in both colonies, the administrations acted initially as though the natives had nothing to lose by their presence, and it was gradual disillusion with the goals and methods of the regime which provoked hostility.

The course of culture contact was affected by relations within as well as between cultural groups, and divisions in local society particularly influenced the causes and consequences of resistance movements. Opposition to the Germans was often an extension to and a manipulation of traditional feuds and political rivalries, and this severely compromised the possibilities of mobilizing entire island populations. It also gave the administrations an effective lever against the rebels, and they deliberately encouraged pre-existing conflicts as a means of defeating the dissidents.

Similarly, relations within the white community were turned to their own advantage by the Islanders, both in pursuing traditional goals (e.g., the Nanpei-Joukiti affair, Lauaki 1909), as well as in attempts to modify the direction of old policies in line with the demands of the new situation (e.g., Oloa). Factions in island politics adopted Western economic and political mechanisms for these same ends, and their initial failure was due less to indigenous incapacity than the destructive opposition of colonialist regimes.

This article has not attempted to examine intensively the role played by mission societies in the process of culture contact, but several important features do emerge in the present context. Competitive religious teachings became reinforcing sanctions for local social and political dichotomies, but as an ally and yet an alien authority, the missionary was an important intermediary in the resolution of conflict between the natives and the colonail administrations. In the absence of independent native churches, the ultimate loyalty of the missions lay with the colonial regimes, and the European missionary basically supported the regime's primary instincts of law and order and native discipline.

The comparatively early surrender of resistance by Pacific rebels did not denote a fundamental element of defeatism in their personalities. It rather testified to an acknowledgement that they had chosen the wrong strategy in trying to achieve their ends, and subsequent resistance movements regarded these early rebels not as failures but as pioneers. The campaigns of the German period cannot be regarded as proto-nationalist revolts; they were primarily élitist movements which succeeded in mobilizing only small sections of the population, already susceptible to integration through traditional bonds of authority and solidarity. What they illustrate most clearly is the degree of reciprocity involved in the interaction, albeit hostile, of distinct cultures.

1. J. Iliffe, *Tanganyika under German Rule, 1905–1912* (Cambridge, 1969), p. 6. To this study of the Maji Maji rebellion must be added H. Stoecker (Hrsg.), *Kamerun unter deutschen Kolonialherrschaft*, 2 vols. (Berlin, 1960); T.O. Ranger, *Revolt in Southern Rhodesia, 1896–1897* (London, 1967); S. Marks, *Reluctant Rebellion: The 1906–1908 Disturbances in Natal* (Oxford, 1970).
2. C.W. Newbury, "Resistance and Adaptation to Colonial Rule in some Pacific Island Societies",(Paper presented to Institute of Commonwealth Studies, Postgraduate Seminar, University of London, 2 March 1972), p. 5.
3. For detailed studies of Samoan political and social history in the nineteenth century see, K. Schmack, *J.C. Godeffroy: Kaufleute zu Hamburg* (Hamburg, 1938); P.M. Kennedy, "The partition of the Samoan Islands, 1898–1899", D. Phil. thesis, (Oxford, 1970); R.P. Gilson, *Samoa 1830 to 1900: The Politics of a Multi–Cultural Community* (Melbourne, 1970).
4. For first–hand accounts see, Private papers of Herrn von Wolffersdorf, Ms.: "Elf Jahre in Samoa und andere Aufzeichnungen" (1895),(BA, Anhang zu Solf Nachlass, vol. 161.); Commander SMS *Adler* to Admiralität, 4/1/1889, in BA/MA 5078, with enclosures.
5. BA/MA7577 Vol. 1, Commander SMS *Bussard* to Admiralität, 11/9/1894; and BA/MA7577, vol. 1, Commander Scheder's plan for pacification and disarmanent of Samoa, 30/10/1894.
6. E. Schultz, *Die wichtigsten Grundsätze des samoanischen Familien– und Erbrechts* (Apia, 1905), pp. 7–10.
7. S. Riesenberg, *The Native Polity of Ponape* (Washington, 1968), p. 4.
8. A. Tetens, *Among the savages of the South Seas: Memoirs of Micronesia, 1862–1868*, trans. from the German by F.M. Spoehr, (London, 1958), p. 96. Manuscript in the Staatsarchiv, Hamburg: see also D. Shineberg, ed., *The Trading Voyages of Andrew Cheyne 1841–1844* (Canberra, 1971), Introduction, pp. 10–15.
9. For a description of Ponapean social structure, see A. Hahl, "Rechtsgewohnheiten und Sitten der Eingeborenen auf Ponape", *Ethnologisches Notizblatt 1900;* and Riesenberg, *Native Polity Ponape*.
10. Solf to KA, 4/9/1900, Solf papers, BA 20.
11. J.A. Moses, "The Solf regime in Western Samoa 1900–1914", *The New Zealand Journal of History* 6, no. 1 (1972): 55.
12. Rose to Solf, 31/5/1900, in RKA. 3059.
13. See Solf's "Decennial Program of colonial development", dispatched in stages to the Reichskolonialamt in 1906–7 in Solf papers, BA 27; and RKA. 2953. Also Solf's correspondence with Professor Passarge, Oct. 1906, in Solf papers, BA 28; and E. von Vietsch, *Wilhelm Solf, Botschafter zwischen den Zeiten* (Tübingen, 1961), p. 65.
14. KA. to Berg, 26/2/1902, in RKA. 2999; Hahl to Irmer, 10/6/1900, in RKA. 3000.

15. Hahl to KA, 2/12/1899, in RKA. 2999; Hahl to Irmer, 10/6/1900, in RKA. 3000.
16. Spanische Missions Chronik (freie Übersetzung), in KAP, file 58.
17. Berg to KA, 11/10/1902, in RKA. 3002.
18. Solf to KA, 9/4/1900, in Solf papers, BA 20: Anlage 2 zu Bericht Nr. 410; Solf's address to chiefs 14/8/1900, in *Samoanisches Gouvernementsblatt,* vol. 3, no. 4, 5/9/1900.
19. Solf to KA, 11/6/1904, in RKA. 2950; Tumua and Pule to Solf, 8/6/1904, in R.K.A. 2950.
20. See Solf's speech of 14/8/1905 to the assembled chiefs in Mulinuu in *Samoanische Zeitung*, 19/8/1905.
21. Commander SMS *Condor* to Admiralität, 5/12/1907, in BA/MA 5121, vol. 2.
22. Memorandum of conference between Solf and Mata'afa, 27/11/1903, in A.L. Braisby, "A documentary record and history of the Lauati Rebellion in Western Samoa 1909", 3 vols (unpublished, Comp. from original Native Office documents.) NZ National Archives, Wellington, 1, pp. 21–22.
23. Report of SMS *Condor*, Apia 23/9/1904, in BA/MA 630.
24. Schultz to KA, 18/2/1905, in RKA. 3063.
25. Solf to KA, 4/8/1905, in Solf papers, BA 26.
26. Solf to Malo, 12/11/1904, and Solf to Lauaki, 25/12/1904, in Braisby, "Documentary Record", pp. 42, 49.
27. Statement by Moefaauo, 29/7/1905, enclosed in Solf to KA, 4/8/1905; Solf papers, BA 26.
28. Gilson, *Samoa*, p. 62. The Malo itself was not a united party government but only a loose structure of convenient alliances.
29. Schultz to KA, 11/3/1905, in RKA. 3063.
30. R. Deeken, *Die Karolinen*, (Berlin, n.d.), p. 107.
31. R. Deeken, *Manuia Samoa. Samoanische Skizzen und Beobachtungen* (Oldenburg, 1901).
32. Solf to KA, 11/6/1904, in Solf papers, BA 25.
33. Deeken to Solf, 31/5/1904, in RKA. 2950.
34. For instance, he clashed with the Roman Catholic mission several times over expansion into Protestant areas and the conversion of natives bound by feudal ties to Protestant chiefs. Spanische Missions Chronik, KAP 58, pp. 73b; Deutsche Missions Chronik 1906–7, KAP 59, pp. 24–34; Berg to KA, 9/5/1905, in RKA. 3006.
35. Fritz to Hahl, 26/8/1908, in RKA. 3005; see also G. Fritz, *Ad majorem Dei Gloriam: die Vorgeschichte des Aufstandes von 1910/11* in Ponape (Leipzig, 1912), p. 41.
36. Hahl to RKA. 30/9/1908, in RKA. 3005; Fritz to Hahl, 21/7/1908 RKA. 3005.
37. Riesenberg, *Native Polity Ponape*, pp. 29–30.
38. Fritz to Hahl, 21/7/1908, in RKA. 3005; *Liebenzeller Missionsbote* no. 1, Jan. 1909, pp. 4–5.
39. P. Kilian OPM to Zentrumsfraktion, 2/11/1911, in KAP 75.
40. Fritz to Hahl, 26/8/1908, in RKA. 3005; Kapuziner Mission to Fritz, 12/8/1908, in KAP 69. Fritz's 1912 publication, *Ad majorem Dei gloriam*, is a polemical denunciation of the activities of the Capuchin Mission in Ponape.
41. Deutsche Missions Chronik 1908, KAP 59; pp. 47–48.
42. Boeder to Hahl, 19/9/1910, in RKA. 3006.
43. Hahl to RKA. 30/9/1908, in RKA. 3005; Fritz to Hahl, 7/1/1909, in RKA. 3006.

44. Nanpei to Mr. Antonio, Saipan 11/12/1910, in RKA. 2589; Girschner to RKA. 20/11/1910, in RKA. 3009; Riesenberg, *Native Polity Ponape*, p. 54.
45. Schultz to RKA. 21/11/1908, and Pule and Aiga to Solf, 18/1/1909, in Solf papers, BA 30; Anlagen zum Lauaki Bericht.
46. Proclamation of Schultz to various district officials, 10/11/1908, in Braisby, "Documentary Record", 2: 177.
47. Statement of chief Mauga of Tutuila concerning conversation with Jiga Pisa, 30/1/1909, in Solf papers, BA 30; Anlagen zum Lauaki Bericht.
48. Solf to RKA. 10/5/1909, in R.K.A. 3069.
49. Solf to RKA. 10/5/1909, and Solf to Schnee, 3/6/1909, in Solf papers, BA 131; *Samoanische Zeitung*, 6/2/1909.
50. Solf to RKA. 13/2/1909, in R.K.A. 3069.
51. Proclamation by Solf, 22/3/1909, in Braisby, "Documentary Record", 2: 107.
52. See R.I. Rotberg and A. Mazrui, eds., *Protest and Power in Black Africa* (New York, 1970), 17, for definitions of resistance and rebellion in the context of African colonialism. They are not readily applicable to the Pacific case.
53. Taumei to Solf, 28/1/1909, in Solf papers, BA 30: Anlagen zum Lauaki Bericht; also Solf to Schnee, 3/6/1909.
54. In a final, desperate bid to save the situation, the Lauaki party on 27 March appealed to the British vice–consul in Apia to call in the "three powers" to the protection of Samoa. Pule and Aiga to Trood, 27/3/1909, in Solf papers, BA 30: Anlagen zum Lauaki Bericht.
55. MS: P. Hambruch, "Die Ursachen des Aufstandes der Jokaschleute", 27/11/1910, in KAP 75. Hambruch, a German anthropologist, was an eyewitness of the rebellion in its early stages.
56. Girschner to RKA., 20/11/1910, in RKA. 3009; "Tagebuchblätter von P. Ignatius, Ponape", in *Aus den Missionen...der Kapuziner: Jahresbericht* 1911, pp. 17–28.
57. Jahn to Bezirksamtmann, 16/5/1911, in RKA. 3010; Commander SMS *Emden* to Chef des Admiralstabes, 18/2/1911, in BA/MA 3438; *Amtsblatt für das Schutzgebiet Deutsch Neu–Guinea*, Simpsonhafen, 15/2/1911, pp. 19–20, and 1/3/1911, pp. 27–28.
58. Kersting to Gouverneur, Rabaul 10/6/1911, in RKA. 3010; Kersting to Vollerthun, Ponape 11/1/1911, in RKA. 3009.
59. Gerichtsprotokoll: Verfahren gegen die Mörder von Boeder..., Ponape 22–23/2/1911, in RKA. 3010.
60. KA to Berg, 26/2/1902, in RKA. 3001; Hahl to Fritz, 28/8/1908, in RKA. 3005; Oswald to RKA., 29/12/1910, in RKA. 3009.
61. Girschner to RKA. 20/11/1910, in RKA. 3009.
62. Kersting to Gouverneur, Rabaul 10/6/1911, in RKA. 3010.

11

JOHN A. MOSES

# The Coolie Labour Question and German Colonial Policy in Samoa, 1900-14

As the unrestricted influx of coolies desired by most of the planters as well as the Chinese governments during the period would have had long-term deleterious effects upon the Samoan people, the problem of supplying Chinese coolie labour, essential for the European plantations on that part of Samoa under German rule, became one of most critical importance for the colony.

The availability of German Colonial Office records now enables a revelation of the German understanding of the problem, the word "German" covering both the planter attitude as well as that of the government. Although the latter was concerned to a degree for plantation interests, it is by no means true that the colony was administered solely on their behalf. The documents show that the policy makers were guided by rather more than purely economic aims. Indeed, they had determined that Samoa was to be administered primarily for the Samoans, not the planters and traders—a decision which the succeeding military administration from New Zealand had to confront afresh when they inherited the problems of governing Samoa after the outbreak of war.[1]

## I

German plantation enterprise in the Pacific had by the second half of the nineteenth century become very extensive; by 1880 the original Godeffroy firm which had in 1878 become the Deutsche Handels und Plantagen-Gesellschaft (DHPG) owned four plantations on Upolu and one on Savai'i with a total area

Reprinted with permission of the editors of the *Journal of pacific History*, 1973 issue.

of 4,933 acres—the largest single complex of tropical agriculture in any of the German colonies. In addition the firm had acquired some 93,000 acres of uncultivated land.[2]

The growth of German plantation activity brought with it the demand for an increasing number of labourers. But already by 1867 it had become apparent that the indigenous population could not supply this demand. The Germans considered the Samoans to be naturally indolent and unreliable, and in addition they were frequently involved in violent clan disputes. In short, their unpredictability ruled them out as a source of labour. A solution to the problem was found then in recruiting labourers from the other islands which the Godeffroy ships had originally visited for barter purposes. The statistics supplied by the imperial Germal consul in Apia, Dr O. W. Stuebel, to Bismarck in 1886 show the origins of the labourers recruited to that year.[3] When Germany assumed sovereignty over the Bismarck Archipelago in 1885 a ban was imposed on the emigration of labour. But as the DHPG would not have survived the drying up of this source of workers, and as the New Guinea Company (NGC) and the DHPG were financially linked, making the NGC willing to see the emigration ban waived in favour of the DHPG, the company was after 1886 privileged to continue recruiting there.[4] However, the DHPG needed government intervention to maintain its barely adequate labour supply, and that from an area which could ill afford the loss.[5] So the Melanesians who actually went to Samoa represented virtually the maximum available. The chronic shortage of labour threatened the DHPG plantations from the beginning with economic crisis. Indeed, in 1885 Consul Stuebel predicted, "The most difficult question is the labour question. One will ... have to get used to the idea of acquiring Chinese workers. Indigenous labour will only be of subsidiary usefulness."[6] Stuebel went on to point out that the long-standing interests of the DHPG were being threatened by the scarcity of labour, and that a way would have to be found urgently to ensure the supply of workers to the newly acquired German territories in the Pacific. And developments since then had shown that the Melanesian labourers were hardly numerous enough to maintain even the one German firm in Samoa. The early prediction by Stuebel that sooner or later Chinese labour would have to be sought became only too true after 1900 when German enterprise in Samoa was intensified.

When German rule over Samoa was proclaimed on 1 March 1900 an era of new German commercial activity began there, some of it certainly stimulated by such colonial enthusiasts as Richard Deeken, a Prussian officer of the reserve, who had toured the Pacific in 1901 and spent a short time in Samoa. The book which he published on return to Germany (*Manuia Samoa*) had a remarkable impact on public opinion. Its message was simple and direct: "Samoa is without question at this time the best colonial enterprise. Let us therefore exploit it and not wait until the competition of foreign enterpreneurs has destroyed the present favourable prospects."[7] Deeken's formula for rapid and profitable exploitation of Samoa's agricultural potential was to plant cocoa on a large scale. He noted that the world market at the time was exceedingly favourable for this commodity.[8] Further, he observed that if Samoa was to become a world supplier of cocoa, labour would have to be imported from East Asia.[9] At that time the most promising source was China. Deeken wrote then concerning the prospect of a Chinese immigration to Samoa:

> In Samoa people fear that the Chinese will create a serious competition for merchants through establishing their own businesses and would afterwards remain in Samoa. Of course, they can be stopped legally from starting businesses but if they later contribute to the economic development of Samoa as independent, industrious farmers they can only be welcome to us. Naturally, they must always be watched carefully by the authorities so that they do not get the upper hand.[10]

By July 1902 the impact of Deeken's propaganda in Germany about Samoa was having marked effect upon the colony. At that time the acting governor, Schnee, felt constrained to communicate to the Colonial Department in Berlin:

> Almost with every steamer now a number of settlers from Germany arrive in Samoa intending to establish cocoa plantations... As far as one can see the settlers for the greater part have been caused to emigrate to Samoa by the exaggeratedly favourable representations of lieutenant Deeken through his lectures and his book *Manuia Samoa*. It would be advisable to refute Deeken's representations in a suitable way.[11]

Steps were indeed taken in Berlin to disseminate more realistic information about the prospects for new settlers in Samoa[12], but these could not stem the wave of enthusiasm which is reflected in the rise in the number of plantation, commercial, and trading enterprises from 42 in 1900 to 124 in 1903.[13]

Among these was the Deutsche Samoa-Gesellschaft (DSG) which dispatched the redoubtable Lt Deeken to Samoa to take up cocoa planting operations at Lotopa, Upolu, on 2,000 acres[14] purchased from an earlier German settler, Kunst.[15] On his arrival on 28 August 1902 Deeken announced his intention to import 400 coolies from China.[16] At that point he had not imagined what difficulties were yet to be overcome. The governor, Wilhelm Solf, had indeed earlier given his word that he would do all in his power to solve the labour difficulty, and on the eve of his departure on leave for Germany at the end of 1901 had declared his intention to study the availability of labour in East Asia on his return journey.[17]

It is clear that plantation interest groups in Germany were behind Solf's visit to the Far East in the autumn of 1902 when he interviewed the *Vizekönig* (viceroy) in Canton, and gained his approval in principle of the recruitment of coolies to work in Samoa.[18] While on leave in Berlin in 1902 Solf had been importuned by the DSG to take some positive steps to meet the labour difficulty in Samoa, and indeed the new company reminded Solf of his earlier promise to try to find some solution.[19] The problem for the DSG was that while it wished to develop cocoa planting in Samoa it was not prepared to assume the task of recruiting labour from China, and had hoped that the firm of Zuckschwerdt and Voigt in Apia would act as recruiting agents.[20] When the latter declined this function because of the scale of financial outlay involved, the DSG, having already purchased 2,000 acres, was forced to take the initiative in the question of labour recruitment. This was to prove the beginning of an administrative and diplomatic problem of unforeseen dimensions.

In urging Solf to facilitate coolie recruitment in China for the new Samoan plantation, the DSG went so far as to request the exclusive right to import coolies for a period of fifteen years. To this Solf was decidedly cool, and pointed out that the importation of Chinese coolies to Samoa was illegal.[21] However, so strong was the planter lobby in Berlin that Solf was finally persuaded to amend the law prohibiting Chinese immigration, but only to the extent that a limited number of coolies might be imported for a stipulated period, and then only if circumstances from time to time would justify this.[22]

The dilemma which was to hamper the Samoan administration for the remainder of the German period had already been recognized by Solf. He had no desire to run the colony merely for the benefit of the planters. On the other hand the governor was subject to pressures from Berlin, where the *raison d'être* for colonies was to afford German investment an opportunity for handsome profits. Solf's "policy of diagonals"—trying to strike a balance between opposing forces—is clearly illustrated in the coolie problem.[23]

Government support for the plans of the DSG was much less than the firm expected. It was agreed that 300–400 coolies could be engaged in Swatow; the firm itself required only 100 and the remainder would be allocated under government supervision to other planters. A recruiting agent began activities in Swatow on 13 February 1903. After initial difficulties with the Chinese authorities, a transport with 289 coolies arrived in Apia on 28 March 1903.[24]

The coolies had been induced to sign on for three years at a wage of M 10 per month plus keep, free medical supplies, and a paid return fare to China. Other stipulations in the contract presented to the coolies in Apia included a working day of ten hours for six days a week, and holidays on "major Chinese holidays". The employer was obliged to supply "sufficient" food, lodging, and medical supplies, and in cases of refusal to work, he was empowered to withhold wages for the time lost. The same applied in cases of sickness, "if due to the worker's own fault". In the event of disputes between employer and employee the help of an appointed government official would be invoked, who could decide each individual case.[25] The looseness of this contract contained the seeds of much future discord, and indeed the muddled manner in which the whole transport was initiated and executed was an omen of worse to come. The entire venture which was supported by the government only with reservation was regarded at first as a tentative experiment, and the organization of subsequent transports failed to improve greatly upon this.[26]

It was never really grasped by anyone concerned that the only reliable source of labour was China. Instead, planters perennially complaining about the expense and trouble of the Chinese transports continued to hope for other sources of allegedly cheaper labour from such places as New Guinea and Java, not appreciating that neither of these areas had a surplus of labour. In a sense both the governor and planter interests were to blame for the future confusion: the governor, since he refused to regard the Chinese transports as a permanent necessity, and the planters, since they unrealistically hoped for better replacements elsewhere, and were niggardly and harsh in their treatment of coolies.

On this last point the editor of the *Samoanische Zeitung* made a prophetic pronouncement a few days after the arrival of the first transport: "We would like to advise the gentlemen planters, now that the labour question has apparently been solved through the introduction of Chinese by the DSG, to treat their workers decently—something which a few of the gentlemen appear not to understand."[27]

## II

By June 1904 it had become apparent that with the advent of about 300 coolies the year before, the labour question was still a long way from being solved. On 18 June, 1904 an open letter to the governor appeared in the *Samoanische Zeitung* in German and English: "The undersigned settlers of all callings lay before your Excellency the humble request that the Government may take in hand the importation of Chinese this year and that the speedy execution of this work—an urgent necessity for the prosperous further development of our Colony—may receive your favourable consideration. Apia, May 16 1904."[28] One hundred and five signatures were appended; that of Deeken was not among them. As a result the governor constituted a committee (the Chinese Committee) of six leading planters and business people to discuss the issue. It was then agreed that the government would initiate recruitment of 300–400 coolies through the mediation of the imperial German consul in Swatow.[29]

The method Solf chose to organize the second transport was to invite the Safata-Samoa-Gesellschaft (SSG) to recruit the required number of coolies through the immigration agent in Swatow, while the government dispatched a so-called Chinese commissioner, a police officer named Fries, to accompany the transport to Apia.[30] By February 1905 the SSG was successful in recruiting 523 coolies in Swatow, who finally arrived ashore in Apia on 30 May 1905.[31]

As with the first transport, the government supervised the distribution of coolies to the various planters who applied for them. The DSG, which had been responsible for launching the enterprise of Chinese transports in the first place, was in bad odour with the governor because of the machinations of its manager in Samoa, Lt Deeken. It is therefore not surprising that Solf had passed over this firm and empowered its rival, the SSG, to execute the second transport. However, the howl of complaint sent up by the DSG, together with the expressed wishes of the other planters, finally moved the chief justice, Erich Schultz, who was at the time acting governor, to take over the entire future organization of coolie transport on behalf of the government.[32] To initiate the third transport in 1906 he sent Commissioner Fries to China, with full powers to engage any immigration firm he might choose.[33]

This time 564 coolies were finally recruited, and these arrived on 22 July. Fries reported that future recruitment would be far more difficult since coolies could earn much better wages elsewhere, such as in South Africa (M 60), than the M 12 now being offered in Samoa. Also rail construction projects in China itself attracted numerous labourers, and even these earned more than was offered in Samoa. Fries considered that since the awakening of China as a result of the Russo-Japanese War, wages had risen sharply. Further, Chinese agents in China claimed that in the past no letters or transfers of money to relatives came from the coolies in Samoa, and this also tended to make it an unpopular place for emigration. In Fries's view the planters themselves, by guaranteeing increased wages during the period of contract, by good treatment, and by enabling the coolies to write and send money home, could do a great deal to improve the prospects of future recruitment.[34] This is the first firm indication of real difficulties to come, but the planters could not imagine the extent these would take.

The beginning of complications which led to far-ranging political manoeuvring at the highest level between Germany and China came early in 1907. The German minister in Peking forwarded to the chancellor extracts from the Chinese press which accused the Germans in Samoa of breach of contract towards the coolies: they were forced to work eleven and a half instead of ten hours; their wages had been reduced from the agreed $7 (Mexican) to $4.80 a month; the food was unfit for human consumption, and sick coolies were seriously neglected.

Further, German officials were extremely partial in the exercise of justice. Coolies who complained received ten stripes with the rattan or were fined M 10 or imprisoned seven days.[35] These accusations in the press came at a time when Chinese students in England, France, Belgium, and Germany were beginning to agitate about ill-treatment of coolies in Samoa.[36] It was also a time when there was a general upsurge of concern in official Chinese circles for the plight of overseas Chinese, brought about by the coincidence of reports from many parts of the world where coolies were employed (e.g., Mexico, the Panama Canal, South Africa and the East Indies).[37] The German consul in Shanghai, von Buri, reported that now the Chinese for the first time wanted to protect their nationals abroad, and that this could lead to a possible ban on emigration altogether.[38] In the case of Samoa, the Chinese press was demanding the installation of a Chinese consul.[39]

The response in Berlin is reflected in a letter from the newly appointed colonial secretary, Dernburg, to Governors Hahl in New Guinea and Solf in Samoa, in which he referred to difficulties in recruiting coolies caused by Chinese officials imposing new conditions. As far as Samoa was concerned, the bad press had given rise to the wish to send out an official to make a study of the situation before further recruitment could be considered. Dernburg noted, "In view of the importance which an adequate supply of labour for the plantations and phosphate enterprises in the South Seas has for economic and national reasons it is intended to take preparatory steps towards the conclusion of a treaty with China for the granting of coolie transports to German protectorates." The model was to be the convention between Britain and China of 18 May 1904.[40] Dernburg's intention remained but an optimistic hope, because the conclusion of such a treaty to ensure a regular supply of coolies to the South Seas was not in China's interests; she hoped in the event to extract from Germany far more favourable conditions than the latter was prepared to grant.

In the meantime the Samoan planters' demand for coolies was growing, and on 22 November 1907 Commissioner Fries was dispatched once more to Swatow, this time armed with a letter signed by 360 Chinese denying the false reports circulated in China by a few bad and lazy workers.[41] Fries's intention had been to get his new contingent back to Samoa before the end of April 1908 in order to relieve the second transport, but he found the local authorities unco-operative and so diplomatic negotiations had to be begun at the highest level.[42] Indeed, the provincial authorities of Canton and Foochow had banned recruitment for Samoa, and this necessitated the German minister's intervening with the Waiwupu, the imperial Chinese Foreign Office.

In his interview the German diplomat, Count Rex, persuaded the Waiwupu in Peking to instruct the Cantonese officials to negotiate ways and means of promoting coolie transport to Samoa, and this resulted in more co-operation with Fries in Swatow. However, the Waiwupu had for the first time indicated to Rex that the Chinese government really wanted the coolies to be treated as completely free immigrants, with the right to settle in Samoa at the expiration of their contracts. The German minister evaded the issue by stating that he was not empowered at this stage to negotiate it, but simply wanted a new transport to go on the previous conditions, and if the Chinese government had new conditions to impose they ought to be formally presented.[43]

However, shortly after the arrival of Fries, the provincial governments of Kwantung and Fukien had sent a special commissioner of their own to Samoa—one Lin Shu Fen, alias Thomas Ling—to report on conditions there. But his report did not return to China in time to have any direct influence on the 1908 transport which Fries was trying to organize. This was effected largely by conceding to a number of conditions mainly directed at improving the health and welfare of the next group of coolies, in addition to an emigration tax of $3.00 per head to be paid by the agents.[44] So on 9 June 1908 the fourth transport arrived in Apia.

The German consul in Swatow, von Borch, informed the chancellor that this transport, in contrast to those of 1903, 1905 and 1906, had encountered more difficulties, and had required urgent diplomatic representations in Peking, Canton, and Swatow in order to be launched. This, he predicted, was only a foretaste of what to expect in future. The Chinese, now that they had fully realized Germany's dependence on their available work force, could be expected to exploit the advantage to the full, especially at provincial level, so long as no international convention existed delimiting their powers. Therefore such a convention as the British had achieved to recruit coolies for Transvaal in 1904 was an urgent necessity.[45]

Accompanying the 1908 transport of 341 workers were a high Chinese official named Lin Jun Chao and two secretaries. Lin's commission was separate from that of Thomas Ling, but the purpose was essentially the same. The separate reports of the two Chinese observers were very concerned about the treatment of coolies, not only at the hands of their masters, but also by the officials of the German government. There were alleged examples of cutting wages and otherwise breaching contracts, as well as over-much flogging. As a result of this the German minister in Peking urged that it would be in Germany's own interests to concede to the demands of the Chinese. He reported, "The economic future of our South Seas possession depends, as is well known, basically on the unhindered flow of the Chinese work force. Also, further negotiations with the Chinese government for a coolie-transport treaty will be favourably influenced only by granting the widest possible guarantee for good treatment of the Chinese workers."[46] Rex also noted that the Waiwupu desired a consulate in Apia, and the abolition of regulations forbidding the descendants of the old established Chinese firms from continuing their trade and prohibiting them from taking other Chinese into their service.[47] The pattern of demanding equality before the law was clearly emerging. The Chinese lever for gaining concessions was to exercise stricter control over coolie recruitment. This became evident with the next German attempt in 1909.

In February 1909 the Chinese Committee in Samoa had resolved to send a senior government official to China to prepare the ground for the 1909 transport, and Dr Erich Schultz, the chief justice, departed on 8 April 1909. He had a threefold brief: to study the emigration situation, to arrange a new transport, and to participate in the negotiations for a convention with China to regulate coolie immigration to Samoa and New Guinea.[48]

Schultz found the Chinese in Canton very difficult. They alleged many instances of ill-treatment of Chinese in Samoa. These Schultz tried to explain, and gave assurances of future improvements. After futile attempts in Hong Kong and Kwangchauwan, Schultz succeeded finally in arranging the transport of 600 coolies from Swatow. But at this point the Waiwupu intervened to veto the embarkation. Count Rex in Peking then had to go cap-in-hand to the Waiwupu, which only granted permission after extracting new conditions, the chief of which were a nine-hour day for the coolies, and the requirement of strict adherence to the contract article 11, which the Chinese interpreted as allowing their new consul the right to arbitrate in disputes between coolies and their employers.[49]

The 1909 transport of 535 contract labourers arrived in Apia on 28 November. And now begins a serious confrontation between the Chinese government and the German Colonial Administration. The first Chinese consul arrived in mid-December 1909, and was formally accredited on 23 March 1910.[50] This man was none other than Lin Jun Chao, who had earlier reported so unfavourably to Peking about conditions for coolies in Samoa. He now assumed the role of champion of his oppressed countrymen with the particular aim of establishing their equality before the law.

German regulations such as the provision for flogging of offenders, and the ordinance of June 1910, which in practice denied the right of appeal to coolies in litigations, understandably irritated the new consul, and he was not slow to present the governor with a list of conditions which he considered discriminatory.[51] At the same time Lin's grievances were made known in the Chinese press, which urged the prohibition of coolie transports if the governor of Samoa refused to abolish the oppressive conditions.[52] On the diplomatic level this was taken very seriously—the areas of friction between China and Germany in the Far East and South Seas were growing. Public opinion in China was rising against coolie emigration and Germany, and since almost half of Canton's foreign trade was in German hands, a mistake which offended the coolies from southern China would have wide repercussions. As a result the authorities in Apia were warned not to antagonize the Chinese further.[53] The consequence of German dilatoriness in amending their ordinances was shown at the end of 1910, when an approach made to recruit 500 coolies in Swatow was rejected officially on the grounds that the German ordinances in Samoa kept the Chinese on the level of Islanders.[54]

In Samoa the German authorities were well aware of the Chinese demands, but felt they could not relax their ordinances which limited the rights of coolies. It was reasoned that this would have disastrous results for the Samoan population. Rear-Admiral Guehler of the South Seas Cruiser Squadron, in his military-political report of 7 September 1910, commented that a policy which placed the interest of the white settlers over that of the natives would lead to bankruptcy and pauperization of the Samoans. Guehler praised Solf's aims: "The native policy hitherto pursued emerges from a penetrating judgment of the Samoan national character; it protects the Samoan way of life (*Wesen*) and individuality not only for its own sake but in recognition of the far-reaching significance for the welfare of the country and all of its inhabitants."[55] On the other hand it was recognized that to abolish the ordinances and allow free Chinese settlement would solve the labour problem and stimulate the economy; all of which would have accrued to the benefit of the white settlers.

The dilemma of German Samoan policy is revealed in the coolie problem; the planters were faced with economic ruin in 1910 when the transport failed to materialize. It is this hard economic fact which caused them as a body to appeal to the Colonial Office to initiate a new transport under the old conditions. Since Lin Jun Chao had become consul the planters were under the constant threat of having future transports stopped because he insisted upon new conditions which were uneconomical for them.[56] Lin's agitation was certainly having an effect; the Chinese grievances had been re-presented to Berlin in a memorandum of 23 December 1910. It was asserted that the Chinese coolies were treated as members of a primitive tribe, and that therefore a number of intolerable legal disabilities were imposed upon them—for example, they were refused the right of appeal in the frequent litigations, and the punishment inflicted on Chinese offenders, as well as the offences, was repugnant to German law. Further, in introducing an ordinance on 18 June 1910, which empowered the governor to alter the specific times of work, the Germans were guilty of breach of the labour contract signed in Swatow in 1909.[57]

This memorandum was followed up by a direct complaint by the Chinese minister in Berlin, Yin-ch'ang, to the German foreign secretary, Kiderlen-Waechter, on 22 January 1911, in which the basis of the problem was seen as the inferior legal status of the coolies created by the government ordinances in Samoa. These ordinances were irreconcilable with the principles of international law. In particular the ordinance of 25 April, which stated that the coolies had the same status as natives "insofar as is not otherwise stated in this ordinance", was attacked.

The Chinese minister drew specific attention to the section

which dealt with the misdemeanours of coolies—such as laziness, absconding, "disobedience, insulting behaviour or threatening the employer or overseer". For these offences a contract labourer could be imprisoned for up to three months, or fined up to M 30, or flogged with up to twenty stripes, or have his leave cancelled for up to three months. On the other hand an employer who infringed the regulations of this ordinance, or was guilty of inflicting grievous bodily harm on a Chinese, would only be punished with a fine up to M 500, or with imprisonment up to one month. In exposing this dual standard of justice the Chinese minister drew attention to §224 of the *Reichsstrafgesetzbuch*, according to which the infliction of grievous bodily harm was punishable by imprisonment with hard labour for up to five years, or imprisonment for not less than one year. Clearly the particularly hard provisions for Chinese labourers on the one hand, and the relatively light punishment of Germans for offences against Chinese, represented an inconsistency in the application of the juridical principles operating in imperial German law.

The Chinese minister emphasized that he considered the conditions in Samoa for Chinese contract labour to be "slavelike" in their relationship to the planters, and that had the workers known of the existence of the 1905 ordinance they would never have signed a contract. The diplomat then pointed out that these circumstances represented a serious affront to Chinese prestige, and he entreated the German government to rectify the situation by placing the labourers on the same legal footing as Europeans in Samoa.[58]

Solf had arrived in Berlin on leave at the end of 1910, and he took advantage of the opportunity to discuss the question of coolie transports with the Chinese minister. The latter, however, reiterated the point that the legal disabilities imposed by German law on the coolies were an affront to Chinese national feeling and should be abolished. If this was not done there would be no future transports. Solf for his part recognized the Chinese point of view, and tried to impress on the minister that German law did not discriminate against Chinese as such, but that with contract labourers in very large numbers in Samoa there was a special situation which required exceptional legislation. Nevertheless, he promised to have the offensive regulations amended, while at the same time pointing out that the failure to get a transport in 1910 was very damaging to the colony, and he would be grateful if the minister would cable Peking to grant permission for coolies to be recruited.[59] This request by Solf did not, however, have the desired effect. The Chinese waited for concrete results.

## III

By May 1911 the existence of a labour crisis in Samoa was recognized in Berlin. The colonial secretary, von Lindequist, recommended conceding to the Chinese demands for legal equality with Europeans so that coolie recruitment could continue, and thus save the plantations from economic ruin.[60]

Solf was decidedly unhappy with this prospect, since he rightly regarded the Chinese demand for legal equality with Europeans as the first step in securing the right of free immigration and settlement in Samoa. Solf predicted that in the event of legal equality, Chinese would leave the planters and set up their own businesses, and this would benefit neither Europeans nor Samoans. Indeed, he wrote, "as far as the Samoans are concerned it is as though I am being asked to sign their death warrant."[61]

The Berlin officials were less sentimental. They saw that there would be no solution as long as the coolies were not placed on the same legal footing as Europeans. The alternatives were clear: either Chinese demands were met, or the planters dependent upon coolies faced the prospect of total ruin. A new ordinance which it was hoped would overcome Chinese objections was drafted. It provided that the German civil law code (*bürgerliches Recht*) could be applied to the coolies. However, this did not automatically concede the right of free immigration—a sphere covered by public law (*öffentliches Recht*). In practice the coolies would be accorded the same rights and be subject to the same penal provisions as Europeans. Flogging, for example, would be discontinued, but the immigration restriction would remain. Solf agreed, then, to the envisaged amendments.

In Apia the acting governor, Schultz, after consultation with the Planters' Association and with the government council, preferred not to apply full civil law provisions to coolies, and favoured the retention of some special control over them. He wished to re-formulate the key paragraph of the ordinance to read, "The Chinese contract labourers have the same status and enjoy the same privileges as the subjects of other nations, *in so far as is not otherwise stated in the ordinance.*"[62] By this device he hoped to place the coolies on a level between Europeans and Islanders, and allow for occasions when the strict application of German law to coolies would render their control on plantations more difficult than it already was. The Chinese consul in Apia, Lin Jun Chao, had made no secret of the fact that this aim was to secure the right of free immigration and settlement in Samoa. And Schultz warned that once such concessions were made, the results for Samoa would be disastrous. The only "small settler" would be Chinese. European storekeepers would be driven out, and a situation resembling that in Tahiti would emerge. In that event Europeans would be limited to running a few wholesale businesses, and even these in time would be taken over by the Chinese. Such a situation, he felt, was to be avoided at all costs, and understandably the planters and business community agreed with Schultz's assessment. The new ordinance which applied only civil law to the Chinese was as far as officials in Apia in 1911 were prepared to go.

Solf, in Berlin, had already acquiesced in this, but again rightly predicted that the Chinese would not let the matter rest until they gained the right of free settlement.[63] Solf and Schultz could see the apparent justice of the Chinese demands, but they were more worried about the effects of that justice on the prime object of their concern, the Samoan people. Also Solf regarded the Chinese pressure on Germany over coolie transports as an expression of a general Chinese attempt to win prestige at the expense of the Western powers. Solf felt he had to exercise all the influence at his command to prevent Samoa from becoming an object of Chinese experiments in the realm of power politics.[64]

Berlin was well apprised of the reservations of both Solf and his deputy. Nevertheless, in October 1911 instructions were given that the new ordinance be promulgated *without* the amendments suggested by Schultz. It was reasoned in Berlin that the Chinese would not have accepted it. Any restricting conditions would have frustrated the organization of a new transport.[65] Indeed, the approval for the 1911 transport was the direct Chinese response to Germany's promise to grant coolies the legal status of Europeans.[66]

The decree empowering the governor in Apia to publish the

new ordinance was issued on 16 October 1911. The permission to begin recruiting arrived in Swatow just as the revolution in China broke out. The foreign consuls had taken the precaution of requesting warships to protect their interests, Germany was represented by SMS *Jaguar*, and her captain reported on 16 November 1911 that their presence in Swatow would have the desired effect on the organization of the coolie transports.[67]

This transport duly arrived in Apia on 28 December 1911 with 551 men. The new ordinance was promulgated on 6 January 1912. Schultz explained the delay as being caused by the Chinese consul's list of new conditions which he proposed on 23 December 1911, after having seen the contents of the new ordinance.[68] Schultz reported in January 1912 that he understood the new ordinance to be the German *quid pro quo* for the Chinese government's agreement to permit the 1911 transport to be recruited. He therefore refused to discuss the conditions of the new ordinance with Lin Jun Chao, who immediately began to find fault with details of its provisions.

Lin had been reconfirmed in his office by the regime which emerged after the revolution, and the former pattern of forwarding memoranda complaining about the discriminatory treatment of contract labourers both by the planters and by the German colonial government was resumed. The planters had considered Lin to be their sworn enemy, and had appealed to the government to have him removed.[69] But in addition to this members of the Planters' Association had, in November 1911, at a time when they were extremely pessimistic about their future, appealed to the Reichstag to intervene to guarantee an uninterrupted supply of labourers. They put forward a persuasive case to show that there was a surplus of labour in New Guinea, and that a regular steamer service should be established to ensure a reliable transport of men and goods. At the time it was estimated that Samoan planters needed over 600 extra men. However, at its conclusion the petition urged the government to give in to Chinese demands for the right of free settlement in Samoa if this would mean the ready supply of labour,[70] indicating that the Samoan planters did not expect the government to accede to their requests for Melanesian labourers.

It is abundantly clear that, with few exceptions, the planters had very little concern for the welfare of the Samoan people. The chairman of the Planters' Association in Apia, E. Langen, was convinced that the Samoan race was already showing signs of dying out because of its own lethargy and intermarriage with other races. For this reason, argued Langen, the government's policy of reserving 25,000 hectares of land for the future Samoan population was based on an illusion, and to limit European plantation enterprise because there could be in 100 years a Samoan population of 100,000 was virtually criminal. By 1912 Langen judged that the Samoans had almost reached the limit of their productive capacity. There was no prospect of their being able to raise their exports or increase their native products. What was needed was the introduction of new energetic blood. Langen's model was the Dutch colony of Java, whose prosperity was at once due to the efficiency and submissiveness of the Javanese. It would be of great advantage, argued Langen, to acquire some of these to solve Samoa's labour problem. However, he recognized that this was unlikely and preferred to envisage the free settlement of Chinese. In this event the Samoan population would in time come to resemble that of Hawaii; experience showed there was nothing to fear from lifting the ban on free Chinese immigration. A mixed Chinese-Polynesian race would emerge with possibly favourable characteristics.[71]

Langen continued to cultivate these ideas and publish them with the intention of refuting the views upon which Dr Solf had based his "native policy", the essence of which was the restriction on land sales to non-Samoans and a ban on Chinese immigration. For Langen the first priority of the German government must be the economic development of the colony, and therefore the administration must select a suitable non-white race to provide the most efficient labour force; if Javanese were not available then Chinese must be accepted.[72] It is a matter of considerable significance for Samoa that the German colonial government in Apia, and indeed the Colonial Office, at no time considered giving in to the wishes of the planters or the Chinese government to lift the ban on Chinese immigration.

Sino-German correspondence after 1911 on this issue shows how concerned the Germans were with avoiding at all costs conceding to the central Chinese demand for the right of free settlement. Because of this problem the chief aim of German colonial policy had been to conclude a convention to regulate the recruitment of contract labour from China to Samoa. However, until the revolution of 1911 the Chinese had successfully evaded German diplomatic feelers in this direction. Instead the Chinese officials preferred to deal with German requests for coolies on an *ad hoc* basis, whereby they increased the number of demands upon the Germans with each additional request. By 1912 the Germans had come to realize that so many concessions had already been made to get the previous six transports launched that they had gradually forfeited all ground for diplomatic manoeuvre to achieve a convention which would ensure a regular supply of coolies, and at the same time protect the Samoans and German enterprise from the inevitable results of wholesale Chinese immigration and settlement.[73]

The advent of the sixth transport at the end of 1911 with 551 men was only a palliative. It soon became an urgent necessity to negotiate yet another transport without delay. However, when in 1912 the German consul in Swatow requested permission from the provincial Chinese government for the recruitment of 700 more workers, he received two reports originating from the Chinese consul in Apia which described the ordinance of 6 January 1912 as a breach of the workers' contract and demanded the lifting of the ban on Chinese settlement in Samoa. Further, several examples of maltreatment of coolies were cited. The Chinese authorities were therefore understandably reluctant to allow the Germans to begin recruitment. The German consul in Canton could only report that if these charges could not be satisfactorily refuted and the Chinese demands fulfilled, then the supply of labour would be cut off.[74]

Lin Jun Chao in Apia was insistent that his countrymen were being exploited, and that therefore no permission for coolie recruitment should be given.[75] It was then Consul Roessler's task to explain to the Chinese military governor of Kwangtung province that most of Lin's complaints were groundless; that the ordinance in no way violated their contract, nor was their food inadequate; and that the alleged limitation of the coolies' right of appeal in litigations rested on a false understanding by the consul of German regulations. Finally, the chief grievance of the consul was the ban on Chinese settlement in Samoa. The German consul pointed out to the Chinese governor that the ban was only limited to Samoa because it was such a small country; in the other German possessions in the South Seas Chinese settlers were welcome. It was simply economic necessity which compelled the German government to adopt this policy, not hostility towards the Chinese people.[76]

In October 1912 it was reported that many coolies in Swatow were in fact desirous of going to work in Samoa, and that also the Chinese bureaucracy would be glad of the opportunity to collect the immigration fees normally payable on the sailing of such a transport. But because of Lin Jun Chao's reports senior Chinese officials would not allow recruitment. Consul Borch in Swatow noted therefore that the Chinese ban would be lifted if Lin's proposals were met to some degree. These included an improvement of food supply, approximately 100 per cent increase in wages, the waiving of court costs to coolies whenever they were the accused or the plaintiff, as well as the granting of permission to acquire land after expiration of contract, and to pursue a trade.[77]

Attempts by Consul Roessler in Canton to reach some compromise with the governor of Kwangtung, especially with regard to the right of settlement, proved quite fruitless.[78] Indeed Lin's complaint had been forwarded to the Chinese minister in Berlin, who delivered a sharp verbal note to the German Foreign Office, observing that the concessions made by Germany in placing the Chinese under European jurisdiction (ordinance of 6 January 1912) had not in reality altered conditions for the coolies, who were still being exploited as before.[79]

## IV

In 1911, while Solf was on leave in Berlin, the post of colonial secretary became vacant, and Solf, the governor of Germany's smallest colony, suddenly found himself promoted to head of the Colonial Office. From this position he urged the most rapid conclusion of a convention with China.[80] However, at this stage both the possibility and the usefulness of a convention to regulate contract labour between China and Samoa were extremely doubtful; there were no advantages left to be gained by confirming through treaty those conditions which the Chinese were sure to demand. Circumstances in China, as well as the ill-treatment meted out by German planters to their coolies, had combined to destroy the basis upon which a mutually acceptable convention could be settled.

With this in mind Schultz, by this time governor, recommended conceding to the new Chinese demands regarding higher wages, more food, and the waiving of court costs in individual cases. He also suggested a device for giving the appearance of allowing right of settlement. This involved raising a landing tax of M 1,000 if the permission to grant the right of settlement had to be given, or in case the Chinese demanded it at the next transport. Schultz was, however, first in favour of offering German New Guinea as a place for Chinese settlement rather than Samoa.[81]

On receipt of these proposals, Solf wired Apia to determine the attitude of the planters and the government council there to the new Chinese demands. The central question was, of course, to what extent the Chinese should be allowed the right to settle in Samoa. The existing regulations did indeed allow some room for manoeuvre. For example, while ordinances controlling the purchase of land in Samoa by non-Samoans virtually prohibited any further sale to new settlers, the governor was empowered to grant the *right of domicile* in Samoa to expiree Chinese contract labourers who wished to apply to remain in some occupation, such as that of tailor, fitter, saddler or gardener (ordinance of 7 March 1903). On the other hand there was no possibility of Chinese actually buying land or becoming traders (*Händler*). This, however, could be allowed in New Guinea. Solf had urged the Foreign Office to make all this clear to the German minister in Peking, who should exert all possible effort to get another transport of coolies to go to Samoa. Only this would preserve German enterprise there from catastrophe.[82] If there were no chance of a convention, then the German minister in Peking should at least try to secure a permit either for a definite period of time, or for a maximum number of coolies (about 3,000) who could be distributed over several transports. By this means, having to make valuable concessions on every occasion without any permanent advantage accruing from them would be avoided.[83]

In a verbal note on 18 January 1913 to the Chinese legation in Berlin the German Foreign Office made a determined effort to answer all previous Chinese grievances, giving assurances that reported instances of maltreatment of coolies would be investigated and righted, and also pointing out the special conditions prevailing in Samoa which allowed only a limited number of expiree workers to remain and pursue some occupation. The possibility of settlement in New Guinea was offered as a more practical alternative; the unrestricted settlement of Chinese in

Samoa on the other hand would soon lead to overpopulation and the pauperization of the Samoan people. The German Foreign Office then offered increased wages, food rations, and gardening plots for the coolies, as well as improved rights vis-à-vis the planters. In view of these concessions the Foreign Office expressed the hope that in future the Chinese government would not place any more obstacles in the way of coolie recruitment for Samoa, especially in view of the fact that compared to the large number of coolies allowed to work in British and Dutch colonies the Germans required so few.[84]

The response of the Peking government to these requests was surprisingly accommodating; the governor in Canton had been instructed to allow recruitment on the basis of a monthly wage of M 20.[85] The Samoan planters agreed to this condition. They also agreed, if it were demanded, that they would concede to the settlement of expirees in Samoa, but only as tradesmen, with the governor's permission, and after such expirees had paid the prescribed immigration tax.[86]

The explanation for this sudden change of attitude by the Chinese government was supplied by the German minister in Peking, von Haxthausen. For six months, tedious negotiations had been conducted to arrange a coolie transport. The stumbling block had always been the demand by the provincial government in Canton for the absolute right of settlement for expirees in Samoa, made as a kind of blackmail to wring further concessions from the Germans. Von Haxthausen pointed out to the Peking government that it was improper for the provincial government in Canton to insist on demands which required a change in German law; such questions could only be negotiated directly between Peking and Berlin, and would require a convention which Germany was always ready to discuss.

The Chinese foreign minister had repeatedly assured von Haxthausen that he would try to persuade Canton to allow the transport to depart under the new contract offered by the Germans. However, because of the apparent inability of the central government to exert effective control over the south Chinese province, and because southern Chinese feeling was extremely hostile to coolie transportation, the German wishes could not be fulfilled. German diplomacy was then faced with the task of pursuading the Peking government to more energetic action against Canton. A memorandum of 20

January 1913 from von Haxthausen to the central government pointed out that the Samoan planters had conceded to the chief Cantonese demand for an increased wage, and that therefore Germany might now expect all obstacles to be removed and the transport to go under the previous conditions; that if on the other hand China still refused to grant the necessary permission, Germany would be forced to consider this an unfriendly act. The memorandum therefore urged Peking to issue the necessary instructions, while pointing out Germany's readiness to conclude a treaty which would regularize the legal status of the contract labourers once and for all.[87]

The idea of exerting pressure on China for this end had also been put forward by Governor Schultz, who suggested that the granting of full diplomatic recognition to the revolutionary Chinese government be conditional on the latter's co-operation in the coolie transport question.[88] Other factors of a more immediate urgency led the Chinese government to change its mind. The southern province was suffering from overpopulation and lack of work as an aftermath of the revolution.[89] Consul von Borch reported a great rush of men dislocated by the revolution who were being exploited by the coolie brokers. There were riots and much adverse publicity in the Chinese press, which depicted coolie recruitment as slave trading. The consul agreed that the conditions were those of trading in human cargo, and that Germany's prestige must suffer if a proper convention could not be signed between China and Germany to regulate recruitment through a permanent organization.[90]

On 3 March 1913 the military governor in Canton informed the German consul that recruitment could begin. A contract was agreed upon on 19 March which conceded the demands for higher wages and increased rations only; the German minister in Peking promised to instruct the governor in Samoa to allow Chinese to *lease* land and to pursue a variety of trades. The Chinese authorities then responded by promising that all future German demands for coolies could be met without special permission provided that the Samoan planters adhered strictly to the provisions of the contract and treated the coolies well.[91]

A diplomatic situation had thus been achieved which satisfied both parties. The Chinese central government was apparently glad to have done with the protracted negotiations.

The Germans were relieved, too, that their future coolie supplies were to be assured. Everything now depended on whether the planters' treatment of their workers in Samoa could avoid giving rise to complaint from the zealous Lin Jun Chao. It is not surprising that the Germans in Samoa had been agitating to have Lin replaced.[92]

There was no difficulty in recruiting; indeed there were greater numbers seeking work than could be either employed in Samoa or accommodated on the ship. Nearly 1,500 had been signed on, but only 1,039 could sail from Swatow on 25 April 1913.

The new Chinese minister to Berlin arrived in May 1913, and the signal was given for negotiations for a convention to begin again after the interruption of the revolution.[93] Both the official German view and that of the planters in Apia was that the basis for any future convention ought to be the contract of the March 1913 transport. However, some planters were willing to grant concessions to Chinese demands for settlement on expiration of contract if other sources of labour (e.g., Java, New Guinea or the Solomons) proved inaccessible. Governor Schultz, on the other hand, insisted that no further concessions be made, arguing that even if an immigration tax was imposed of M 800 or M 1,000, the influx of Chinese would be great enough to displace the white settlers, and in time would lead to the demoralization and absorption of the Samoan population, and that if negotiations for a convention collapsed, private initiative should be relied on and hope placed in Java.[94]

A convention such as that between China and Great Britain of May 1904 was, of course, never brought to fruition. The advent of war led to the expulsion of the Germans from Samoa, and the new colonial masters from New Zealand gradually returned most of the 2,184 Chinese workers to China.[95] Despite all the difficulties of the past eleven years the Germans had been employing Chinese contract labour with relatively great commerical success. It is clear, however, that this would have been even greater had the government allowed a free enterprise economy to function in Samoa. The evidence is that the chief consideration in preventing this was the government's concern for the effect of uncontrolled Chinese immigration on the future of the Samoan population. Had Solf and Schultz been less sensitive to the cultural aspirations of this Polynesian *Herrenvolk*, as one German naval officer described them,[96] the present ethnic composition and social-political structure of Western Samoa would be markedly different.

1. Peter O'Connor, "The Problem of Indentured Labour in Samoa under the Military Administration", *Political Science* 20 (1968): 22.
2. Erika Suchan–Galow, *Die deutsche Wirtschaftstätigkeit in der Südsee vor der ersten Besitzergreifung 1884* (Hamburg, 1940), p. 39
Statistics for DHPG land under cultivation (in acres); 1879–4337; 1880–4933; 1881–5550; 1882–6020; 1883–6237; 1884–6569; 1885–7110; 1886–7285; 1887–7579; 1888–7938; 1889–7952; 1890–8005; see STAH, Bilanzen Figures for 1888 from the brochure by Th. Weber, *Ländereien und Plantagen der Deutschen Handels–und Plantagen–Gesellschaft der Südsee–Inseln zu Hamburg in Samoa* (Hamburg, 1888); for 1889/90 see "Bericht der Direktion......" 1890 in STAH, DHPG Archiv. (These details were kindly supplied by Mr. S. G. Firth, Oxford University, from his doctoral research on the subject "German Recruitment and Employment of Labour in the Western Pacific before the First World War".)
3. Origins of Labourers Recruited

| Year | Total Numbers | Kingsmill Gilbert Islands | Carolines | New Hebrides | Solomons | New Britain New Ireland |
|---|---|---|---|---|---|---|
| 1867 | 81 | 81 | — | — | — | — |
| 1868 | 115 | 115 | — | — | — | — |
| 1869 | 40 | 40 | — | — | — | — |
| 1870 | 69 | 69 | — | — | — | — |
| 1871 | 48 | 48 | — | — | — | — |
| 1872 | 15 | — | 15 | — | — | — |
| 1873 | 438 | 358 | 80 | — | — | — |
| 1874 | 140 | 140 | — | — | — | — |
| 1875 | 280 | 280 | — | — | — | — |
| 1876 | 101 | 101 | — | — | — | — |
| 1877 | 251 | 251 | — | — | — | — |
| 1878 | 272 | 189 | — | 83 | — | — |
| 1879 | 718 | 115 | — | 570 | — | 33 |
| 1880 | 535 | 300 | — | — | 226 | 9 |
| 1881 | 378 | — | — | 179 | 199 | — |
| 1882 | 264 | 8 | — | 153 | — | 103 |
| 1883 | 355 | 2 | — | 29 | 37 | 287 |
| 1884 | 245 | 29 | — | — | — | 216 |
| mid-1885 | 512 | 124 | — | 187 | 156 | 45 |

Source: Stuebel to Bismarck, Apia, 27 Jan. 1886, Potsdam, Deutsches Zentralarchiv, Auswärtiges Amt Kolonialabteilung—Arbeiterfrage, vol. 2316. The documents of the imperical German Foreign Office (AA), Foreign Office—Colonial Dept (AAKA), and of the Colonial Office (RKA), which was constituted separately in 1907, are organized under subject headings and numbered in volumes which usually correspond to a year's transactions. Hereinafter referred to as AA for the period to 1890, AAKA 1890–1907, and RKA thereafter, with the relevant vol. no.
4. Recruitment of DHPG in German New Guinea: 1887, 261 workers; 1888, 115; 1889, 3; 1890, 351; 1891, 54; 1892, 1893, ?(Maximum number, 250 recruitees granted); 1894, ? (DHPG applied for 350.)—New Guinea Company (NGC) to Colonial Dept, Berlin, June 1903, AAKA 2319, 1889, 1900, 1901, 1902—total of only was recruited, although the DHPG had permission to recruit 1,360 workers; 1903—permission for 450, but due to the sickness of the recruiting vessel's captain only 93

workers were recruited. Hahl to Colonial Dept, 1/10/1903, AAKA 2320. Total recruitment in the Bismarck Archipelago and the German Solomons from 1887 to 1913 was 5,285.—Hahl to Colonial Office (CO), 16/11/1913, RKA 2313.

5. In negotiation with the government early in 1885 the NGC was at first in favour of a complete prohibition on the emigration of labour from its territory. However, an exception was soon made in view of the needs of the DHPG. See NGC Comité to Bismarck, 25/3/1885, AA 2800 and NGC Comité to Bismarck, 8/4/1885. AA 2801. In its final form the original German ban of Aug. 1885 which forbade the export of labour was amended to read "except for German plantations" and then only from "Those parts of the New Britain Archipelago where it [had] previously occurred". See *Amtliche Bekanntmachung*, Matupi, in Oertzen to Bismarck 20/3/1886. AA 2298. (Details supplied by S.G. Firth—see fn. 2). See also NGC to Colonial Dept., Berlin, 23/1/1903, AAKA 2319; NGC to Colonial Dept., Berlin, 6/4/1904, AAKA 2320; Petition of the Planters Association in the Bismarck Archipelago to Governor Hahl asking him to speak in their favour in Berlin, 20/3/1906, AAKA 2321.
6. Stuebel to FO, Apia, 23/3/1885, AA 2316.
7. Richard Deeken, *Manuia Samoa! Samoanische Reiseskizzen und Beobachtungen* (Berlin, 1902), p. viii.
8. Ibid., p. 209.
9. Ibid., p. 184
10. Ibid., p. 185.
11. Schnee to Colonial Dept, Apia, 28/7/1902, AAKA Ansiedlungen in Samoa, 2269; cf.*SZ*, Apia, 15/2/1902 and 21/6/1902.
12. A brochure was prepared by Solf giving general information on Samoan climate, commercial and agricultural conditions. See AAKA 2260.
13. *Jahresberichte* (Annual Reports), AAKA, Jahresberichte, 6521, 6522.
14. *SZ*, 13/9/1902.
15. *SZ*, 18/1/1902.
16. *SZ*, 13/9/1902.
17. *SZ*, 21/12/1901 and 15/2/1902.
18. Cf. Wandres to Colonial Dept., Apia, 20/5/1903, AAKA 2319. Also Götz to von Bülow, Peking 5/4/1903, ibid.
19. DSG to Colonial Dept., Berlin, 3/7/1902, ibid.
20. Ibid.
21. Cf. *Samoanisches Gouvernementsblatt* 3, no. 63.
22. Solf to DSG, Berlin, 14/7/1902, AAKA 2319.
23. Solf to colonial sec., 12/1/1908 (no. 09174, 13/1/1908) *Nachtrag zu dem Decennial–Programm. Decennial–Programm*, 2/46, Wellington, New Zealand National Archives, GCA 2/46.
24. *SZ*, 9/5/1903. In this article the German mark will be abbreviated to M, as in M 400.
25. *SZ*, 9/5/1903. The government in Apia stipulated the exact quantities of daily rations, as well as dates of Chinese holidays and pay days, etc. However, these were to become the subject of much dispute between coolies and their employers as the latter not infrequently altered these stipulations on occasion to suit themselves.
26. NGC to Colonial Dept, Berlin, 6/4/1904, AAKA, 2320.
27. *SZ*, 2/5/1903.
28. *SZ*, 18/6/1904.
29. *SZ*, 9/7/1904.
30. Cf. Schultz to consul in Swatow, Anlage zum Bericht no. 1/05; Solf to Colonial Dept, 9/5/1905, AAKA 2321.

31. Cf. *SZ*, 18/2/1905 and 17/6/1905.
32. *SZ*, 10/2/1906; Schultz to Solf, 11/2/1906, AAKA 2321.
33. Ibid.
34. *SZ*, 28/7/1906. In May 1906 Schultz had asked the Colonial Dept to make possible, free of charge, remittances by Chinese coolies to China, as this would improve the reputation of Samoa and be welcomed by the coolies. Schultz to Colonial Dept, Apia, 5/5/1906, AAKA 2322.
35. *SZ*, 15/6/1907; Kaiserliche Botschaft to chancellor, Peking, 8/4/1907, AAKA 2323. The punishment was not for complaining but for absconding. As the coolies had to get permission from the planter or overseer to leave the plantation, and as it might be denied to them if their reason for asking was to issue a complaint to the Chinese commissioner, they usually went without permission and were then punished for absconding.
36. *SZ*, 15/6/1907.
37. Buri to von Bülow, Shanghai, 3/4/1907, AAKA 2323.
38. Ibid.
39. *SZ*, 15/6/1907.
40. Dernburg to Solf and Hahl, Berlin, 8/7/1907, RKA 2323. The Convention referred to is that between Great Britain and China respecting the employment of Chinese labour in British colonies and protectorates, signed at London, 13/5/1904.
41. *SZ*, 23/1/1907.
42. Walter to Rex, Swatow, 22/1/1908, RKA 2323.
43. Rex to von Bülow, Peking, 19/3/1908, ibid.
44. Roessler to Rex, Canton, 3/4/1908, ibid.
45. Borch to von Bülow, Swatow, 16/5/1908, ibid.
46. Rex to von Bülow, Peking, 12/1/1909. RKA 2324. The German ordinance of 25/4/1905 provided for flogging of coolies with the rattan up to twenty stripes. However, there is much evidence that planters themselves flogged coolies for insubordination, etc. See Trood (British consul) to colonial sec. in Hong Kong, 13/6/1906, British Consular Service Documents, Wellington, NZ National Archives, 5/19. Also, when the Chinese sent commissioners to inspect conditions in Samoa, the acting governor, Erich Schultz, admonished the planters in a circular letter not to take it upon themselves to punish coolies, Apia, 1/7/1908, RKA 2324. See also Roessler to Bethmann Hollweg, Canton, 16/11/1910, RKA 2325: "The uneducated German has frequently a quite definite feeling of racial superiority and mastery towards the members of coloured nations ...If the government of Samoa sets store by ensuring recruitment of Chinese labourers effective measures in this direction have to be taken."
47. Rex to von Bülow, Peking, 12/1/1909, RKA 2324. The legal status of Chinese in Samoa was spelled out in the ordinance of 7/3/1903 which banned Chinese immigration, as well as the right to purchase land and to enter commerce. This did not apply to previously established residents. Also, the governor was empowered to allow the leasing of land to Chinese and their practising a trade.
48. Schultz to CO Apia, 4/1/1910, RKA 2325.
49. Rex to Bethmann Hollweg, Peking, 26/8/1909, RKA 2324. German officials disputed the Chinese Consul's right of arbitration. They knew that the paragraph was ambiguously phrased, but stressed that it meant only a right to advise and arbitrate among coolies, but no legal jurisdiction.
50. *SZ*, 26/3/1910.
51. Rex to Bethmann Hollweg, Peking, 3/9/1910, RKA 2325; *SGB* 3, 18/6/1910, no. 294.

52. *Gildenzeitung*, 16/9/1910, rka 2325.
53. Roessler to Bethmann Hollweg, Canton, 28/9/1910, ibid.
54. Roessler to Bethmann Hollweg, Canton, 16/11/1910, ibid.
55. Guehler to HM the Kaiser, 7/9/1910, ibid.
56. Planter's Association to CO, 10/1/1911, RKA 2326.
57. Chinese legation to CO, Berlin, 23/12/1910, RKA 5588; cf. *SGB* 3, no. 95. especially §1. With the consent of the Chinese consul the governor had changed the working time from nine hours daily with two free Sundays a month to ten hours daily work and all Sundays free, so that workers of different transports had the same working time. But officials insisted on the nine–hour working day and claimed that the German governor was guilty of unilaterally altering the contract.
58. Yin–Ch'ang to Kiderlen–Waechter, Berlin, 22/1/1911, RKA 5588.
59. Solf to CO, Berlin, 28/1/1911, ibid.
60. Lindequist to FO, Berlin, 31/5/1911, ibid.
61. Solf to Schnee (private), Berlin, 28/5/1911, ibid., 2326. Cf. also Solf to Schnee, 28/5/1911, Koblenz, Bundesarchiv, Nachlass Solf, vol. 131, pp. 106–7: "I am not blind to the fact that for political reasons the lesser interests should be sacrificed to the greater; but I am the representative of the lesser interests....My position with regard to the small settlers stems not from antipathy towards them but from profound sympathy for people who are the victims of their own false convictions. They will not be helped by granting the Chinese equality before the law. And for the Samoans it is as though I am expected to sign their death warrant."
62. Schultz to CO, Apia, 22/7/1911, RKA 2326.
63. Cf. John E. Schrecker, *Imperialism and Chinese Nationalism* (Cambridge, Mass., 1971), 253,f.
64. Solf to Lindequist, Dorf Kreuth, 26/8/1911, RKA 2326.
65. Cf. Conze to Schultz, Berlin, 10/10/1911, RKA 5588.
66. Liang Cheng to Kiderlen–Waechter, Berlin, 20/9/1911, RKA 2326.
67. Vanselow to Commander Imperial Cruiser Squadron, Swatow, 16/11/1911, RKA 2327.
68. Buri to Bethmann Hollweg, Shanghai, 21/2/1912, ibid.,cf. Schultz to CO Apia, Jan. 1912, ibid.
69. Planters' Association to Schultz, Tuvao, 19/6/1911, RKA 2326.
70. Schultz to CO, Apia, 17/11/1911, RKA 2327.
71. E. Langen, "Deutsch–Samoa", in *Jahrbuch über die deutschen Kolonien* 5 (1912): 212–20.
72. Cf.E. Langen, "Wie wandelt sich Samoa und seine Bevölkerung?" in *Jahrbuch über die deutschen Kolonien 6* (1913): 120–30. The Samoan population was counted every five years. On 1/10/1911 there were 33,554 Samoans living in German Samoa, 76 more than on 1/10/1906. Cases of death had been quite numerous in 1911 because of an epidemic of measles. *Die deutschen Schutzgebiete in Afrika und der Südsee. 1911/12.* Amtliche Jahresberichte, pub. Reichskolonialamt (Berlin 1913), Stat. pt, 51.
73. Cf. Roessler to Bethmann Hollweg, Canton, 7/11/1912, RKA 2328.
74. Roessler to Bethmann Hollweg, Canton, 24/10/1912, ibid.
75. Cf. Ho Jow to German Consul von Borch, Swatow, 14/10/1912, ibid.
76. Roessler to military governor of Kwantung province, Canton, 24/10/1912, ibid.
77. Von Borch to Bethmann Hollweg, Swatow, 17/10/1912, ibid.
78. Roessler to Bethmann Hollweg, Canton, 7/11/1912. ibid.
79. Chinese legation to FO, Berlin, 9/11/1912, ibid.
80. Solf to FO, Berlin, 9/11/1912, ibid.

81. Schultz to CO, Hamburg, 11/11/1912, ibid.
82. Solf to FO, Berlin, 25/11/1912, RKA 2327.
83. Solf to FO, Berlin, 23/12/1912, RKA 2328.
84. FO to Chinese legation, Berlin, 18/1/1913, ibid.
85. Von Körner to colonial sec., Berlin, 28/1/1913, ibid.
86. Schlettwein to CO, Apia, 24/1/1913, ibid.
87. Haxthausen Memorandum to Waichiaopu, Peking, 20/1/1913, ibid.
88. Schultz to CO, Berlin, 10/2/1913, ibid.
89. Roessler to Bethmann Hollweg, Canton, 1/2/1913, RKA 2340.
90. Von Borch to Bethmann Hollweg, Swatow, 30/4/1913, RKA 2328.
91. Roessler to Bethmann Hollweg, Canton, 26/3/1913, RKA 2340. Cf. Roessler to Chinese FO, Canton, 15/3/1913, ibid.
92. Roessler to Bethmann Hollweg, 26/3/1913. ibid.
93. FO to CO, Berlin, 9/5/1913, ibid.
94. Schultz to CO, Apia, 12/1/1914, ibid.
95. Logan to Liverpool, 12/11/1915, G 2999/15, and Logan to Liverpool, 2/10/1918, G 2884/18; see Mary Boyd, "The Military Administration of Western Samoa, 1914–1919", in *The New Zealand Journal of History 2* (1968): 154–5 Cf. O'Connor, "The Problem of Indentured Labour", where the coolie problem as dealt with by the New Zealand administration is examined.
96. Admiral Guehler. See fn. 56.

# 12

**PETER G. SACK**

# Law, Politics and Native "Crimes" in German New Guinea

This paper is concerned with European attitudes towards native "crimes" in German New Guinea, and with possible changes in these attitudes from the beginning of European settlement in the 1870s to the end of German rule in 1914. Although the relevant colonial laws will be examined, greater emphasis will be placed on the actions of the colonial administration. The position of native "crimes" between colonial law and colonial politics is the paper's main theme. Since research into the history of New Guinea is still in its infancy, it would be premature to try to develop this theme in a systematic fashion. Instead this paper merely contains a few somewhat impressionistic variations. The aim is to portray colonial practice rather than to analyse it.

## I

Native "crimes" have been punished by Europeans since they began to explore the area which was to become German New Guinea. Yet their visits had made little impact when the first settlements were founded in 1875, more than 300 years later. But then native "crimes" quickly turned into a very real problem. British and German warships started showing their flags, though most of their commanders hesitated to take military action. Instead they demonstrated naval strength to force the "chiefs" into paying compensation for "crimes" committed against Europeans. The settlers were more prone to use violence: "one of them shot a Native the other day because he had stolen a piece of tobacco from *another* trader some time before . . . ."[1] Under these circumstances it is surprising that not more Europeans were killed. The numbers increased, but on the whole the natives still preferred merely to burn down the houses of unpopular individuals. Nevertheless, the Europeans lived in constant fear, and regarded the killings which did occur not as individual "crimes" but as signals for general "uprisings" against the beginnings of European rule. They felt they had either to fight or to "withdraw from these islands altogether at once".[2] Since they were not prepared to withdraw, they began to carry out large-scale punitive expeditions, firmly convinced of their "beneficial effects". The Methodist missionary G. Brown, the reluctant leader of the first of them, was afterwards sure that the natives "respect us now as they never did before ... ", and that "we occupy a better position with them than we have ever done".[3]

The British authorities gradually took a more active interest in affairs in New Guinea. From 1881 onwards Deputy Commissioner H.H. Romilly made occasional visits to the islands, but this was, in Sir Arthur Gordon's words, not more than "an ambulatory mission of inspection of British Beachcombers".[4] It was only in 1883, when the "labour trade" reached the area and large numbers of ships began to recruit natives to work on the plantations in Samoa, Fiji, and Queensland, that Romilly was sent there on a more permanent basis. Not long afterwards his German counterpart the imperial commissioner, G. von Oertzen, appeared on the scene. Both Romilly and Oertzen had no independent means of enforcing law and order; they still had to rely on the assistance of visiting warships; and their respective legal authority was far from clear or extensive.

At the end of 1884 two warships hoisted the German flag at different points along the northeastern coast of New Guinea and in the Bismarck Archipelago. They had not been instructed, however, to annex this area for Germany; they merely proclaimed that the property of German nationals living there (especially land they had acquired) was being placed under the protection of the Reich. The settlers were not unaware of this situation. The planter R. Parkinson, for instance, commented that "the taking into possession of individual small areas of land in New Britain by the German Government will contribute little or nothing to the opening up of this island". To achieve this " it is ... necessary to declare the whole island to be a colony of the Reich".[5] B. Danks of the Methodist Mission saw matters less clearly. He understood from his conversation with German naval officers "that Germany had annexed the country in order to protect its commercial interests", but he also knew "that there was no intention to constitute a government there and then" and "that for the time being (only) certain restrictions would be laid upon the natives and some jurisdiction over the whites would be established".[6] Nevertheless he began to write embarrassing letters to the German imperial commissioner, asking him to intervene, claiming that since "the annexation of these islands by Germany I have endeavoured to make the natives understand that the laws of Germany would protect them as well as the whites".[7]

It is not clear when German New Guinea was annexed; it is not even certain that its entire area was ever brought under full German sovereignty. But these are legal niceties which have little practical significance. Politically the area was undoubtedly in the process of becoming a German colony. Early in 1885 the British and German governments agreed on a division of eastern New Guinea, and Britain accepted the German claim to the Bismarck Archipelago. On this basis the Neuguinea Compagnie was granted an Imperial Charter on 17 May 1885.[8] The charter gave it authority to administer the German part of New Guinea (Kaiser Wilhelmsland) and the archipelago under the supervision of the Reich, which remained responsible for the legislation as well as the administration of justice. The first group of company employees arrived in New Guinea in November 1885. By the middle of 1886 the administrator, G. von Schleinitz, the imperial judge, G. Schmiele, and J. Weisser, the company's manager for the Bismarck Archipelago, were well on their way to take over from the imperial commissioner, Oertzen.

The initial step towards setting up a system of colonial law for German New Guinea was an Imperial Ordinance of 5 June 1886.[9] Its provisions regarding native "crimes", however, were purely negative: natives were not subject to any colonial jurisdiction until this was specifically directed. Nevertheless native "crimes" were not left unpunished by the colonial authorities. The imperial judge, Schmiele, in particular, was determined to establish the rule of law without delay; or as the settlers saw it, he seemed to have written *fiat justitia et pereat mundus* on his flag and would have brought all trading to a complete standstill, had he but had the means of enforcing his decisions. Fortunately, from the settlers' point of view, he had no police force but depended entirely on the German navy which turned down most of his requests for assistance.[10] The settlers continued to administer their own "justice"; they even invited the imperial judge to be present when corporal punishment was carried out on one of the natives they had "sentenced".[11]

Weisser, his administrative counterpart, followed a different course. He explained a prepared statement to the natives living near his station; this statement was then signed by their leaders. According to this remarkable document,[12] the natives declared that they would bring all disputes they could not peacefully settle before him and that they would accept his decision as final. They also declared that they would cease to murder, burn, and steal, and abandon all other similar barbaric customs; that they would prevent all crimes of this kind whenever possible, and do all they could to bring a person committing them before him for punishment. Even the Neuguinea Compagnie's board of directors was not naive enough to believe that the problem of native "crimes" could be solved by merely getting its new subjects to sign such a document.

## II

In its first annual report the company announced that laws regulating the punishment of native crimes had been drafted, believing that the approval of the German government, needed to give them effect, would be a mere formality. It was more concerned with the problem of providing the practical means for enforcing judicial decisions and carrying out police measures, especially against natives living outside the sphere of actual government control. The company's stations and ships had been supplied with arms for their defence, but the number of employees was not sufficient to protect the stations from any serious attack, let alone to punish the attackers. A native attack, the company claimed, would be one of the cases covered by the German government's general promise of protection — but so far no specific arrangements had been made; only warships, which were usually unable to give adequate protection, had visited the colony for short periods. Thus, the company claimed, it had no choice but to form its own police force, provided the necessary soldiers could be recruited from among the local natives.

The company was mainly interested in establishing criminal jurisdiction over its native and imported coloured labourers, and felt the major problem lay in working out a suitable system of penalties.[13] On instructions from the board of directors, Administrator Schleinitz appointed a commission chaired by Schmiele, to look into this question. The aim was to find a solution which took the low level of cultural development of Melanesians, Malays and Chinese into account ("who are from early childhood used to corporal and other severe punishment") and which avoided cruelty, but also the necessity of setting up an expensive prison system.[14]

The outcome was predictable: the area for which fines were regarded as an adequate punishment was expanded — compared with German law — , the prison terms envisaged by the German criminal code were drastically reduced, and the gap was filled by using the death penalty more freely as well as by adding corporal punishment — as a criminal punishment, not merely as a disciplinary measure — to the metropolitan law. However, Schmiele had gone too far for Schleinitz's taste: he had reduced the maximum prison sentence to a mere month (compensating for loss of time by intensive whipping — up to 200 strokes) and had made the death penalty mandatory for a large number of offences. Schleinitz increased the maximum prison sentence to six months (reducing at the same time the weekly whipping rations) and made the death penalty in most cases optional.

Schleinitz had also prepared a penal ordinance for natives outside European employ. Although much shorter ( a mere 16 instead of almost 200 sections) it tells a great deal more about official European attitudes towards native "crimes" at that time. It shows first of all that Schleinitz had, for the time being, no intention of interfering in internal native disputes (unless they occurred between natives permanently employed by Europeans). He had made provisions only to protect the life, health, and property of Europeans (and natives permanently employed by them). But Schleinitz's draft also dealt with the problem of general native "uprisings".

If preparations for an attack on a station were discovered, its manager was to arrest the ringleaders and to take certain temporary measures to protect the station's safety: he could occupy hostile villages and take hostages, or forbid hostile tribes to enter the station area. He had to report as soon as possible to the administrator who would then give the necessary orders. It remained in particular the latter's prerogative to declare war on a hostile tribe, to have prisoners or hostages brought as forced labourers to other stations, and to order a hostile tribe (or certain of its members) to pay fines of shell-money, pigs or crops.

In case of open hostilities, the station manager was free to take any steps necessary to protect the station. On the other hand he had to prevent atrocities and to avoid unnecessary harshness so as not to preclude the re-establishing of peaceful relations. Again he had to report to the administrator as soon as possible.

Intentional killings of individual Europeans (or their coloured labourers) or serious forms of assault usually carried the death penalty. The draft also stipulated a limited collective responsibility of native groups for these offences. If an individual offender could not be arrested but it was known that he belonged to a particular group, the station manager could take hostages, explaining that they would be released if the offender was handed over within a certain time. What happened if this was not done depended primarily on whether the village or tribe was able to hand him over, and also on the amount of general hostility shown. If an intensely hostile group refused to hand over one of its members, the station manager was to destroy its garden and canoes. If it was either impossible to hand over the offender or if there was no intense general hostility, he could order the group to pay a fine or refrain from any punitive measures. It was again the prerogative of the administrator to decide whether any of the hostages were to be punished.

The provisions for minor assaults and thefts are interesting in two respects: firstly, because the station manager was not allowed to take any action against the offender's group, and secondly, because they illustrate the extraordinary jumps in the range of penalties. Whereas serious assault usually carried the death penalty, the maximum penalty for minor assault or theft was a mere two weeks' imprisonment with hard labour — although corporal punishment and/or a reduction in food rations could be used as a supplementary punishment. The basic penalties for damage to property were the same, but in addition the offender was obliged to repair the damage, if this was possible, or to pay a fine. If he did not fulfil this obligation, corresponding damage could be inflicted on his house or garden. Moreover, special provisions were made if an individual offender could not be detected, or if an entire group was responsible for the damage. In both cases the group was held collectively liable, and the property of all its members subject to counter-damage.

The company's board of directors passed Schleinitz's two drafts and explanations on to the Foreign Office, adding its own comments and a detailed list of proposed minor changes. The directors began by setting out why regulations of the proposed kind were required: the mere fact that Europeans acquired land from natives, traded with them, and employed them as labourers, created relations between the races which, even in a young colony like New Guinea, had to be governed by rules of law. It was necessary for humanitarian reasons, as well as in the interest of public peace and the safety of the small white population, to replace arbitrary actions by individual Europeans with objective standards of justice, since it was impossible to establish government control over the native population or to maintain discipline among the coloured labourers without using some force. Further, the existing legislation did not draw a line between the legal and the illegal use of force by Europeans against natives, so that employees of the company using force in exercise of their duties were open to criminal charges, whereas the natives against whom the force was used remained outside the sanctions and restrictions of colonial law.

Turning to the contents of the proposed penal ordinance for coloured labourers, the directors agreed with Schleinitz that it would, in principle, have to follow the German legislation, although one might doubt whether the coloured labourers would understand the concepts of the German Criminal Code or whether they would ever accept them. However, it was at present impossible to ascertain what their ideas were and how far they were capable of changing them, especially since the labourers in question belonged to very different tribes and races. Thus there was no alternative but to define the criminal offences according to European views, no matter how wide the gap between the different cultures.

The directors were more concerned that the suggested system of penalties might give the ordinance the appearance of cruelty. Still, they defended most of the proposals, though rather meekly, and were obviously pleased that the German government would have to make the final decision. About the draft penal ordinance for natives not employed by Europeans, the directors had little to say. They merely stressed that so far only limited contacts between Europeans and natives had been established, so that the provisions had to be very general and flexible.[15]

The Foreign Office strongly questioned the advisability of enacting such extensive legislation to maintain order among New Guinea's coloured population. But since the company, despite similar hints in the past, persisted in its preference for a legalistic approach to colonization, and since it was most sensitive to any orders by the government, it did not think the proposals could be rejected outright. Instead it appointed a commission to discuss the matter further. On one point only did the Foreign Office take a strong stand: the proposed corporal punishment was not to be included in any criminal legislation.

When the commission had completed its discussions little else of the Neuguinea Compagnie's proposals was left.[16] The commission began by excluding the instructions to company officials in case of native "uprisings": leaving the doubtful practicability of such general instructions out of account, it was at least undesirable to incorporate them in legislation dealing with the criminal jurisdiction over natives. The commission saw also no reason to have separate legislation for natives within and outside European employ. The company's main justification had been the assumption that the coloured labourers would include large numbers of Asians who required treatment differing from that of Melanesians. Since the company, according to its annual report, no longer intended to import Asian labourers, this justification had disappeared, so that the rest of the penal ordinance for natives outside European employ could also be eliminated.

The commission further found that large parts of the remaining draft were materially unsuitable. A good deal more experience was needed before a detailed criminal law for the natives of German New Guinea would become possible and desirable. All that was known about their customs justified the conclusion that they were people of a very low culture whose notions of law were completely undeveloped. For a long time to come they would have to be educated rather than punished, although criminal punishment would — in a very few cases — be unavoidable.

The commission suggested transferring the criminal jurisdiction over natives for a transitional period of ten years to the Neuguinea Compagnie as the administrative authority. The company, however, was not to be free to enact its proposed ordinances; instead the chancellor of the Reich, in exercise of its general right of supervision, was to instruct it on the rules to be followed.

The proposed brief instructions were based on the view that the official exercising criminal jurisdiction over natives had to be given as much discretion as possible. A few vital limitations to protect accused natives were stipulated. The official could only punish a native whose behaviour constituted a serious offence under German law — unless his authority had been extended by specific legislation — but he was not bound to prosecute any "crime". No specific penalty was prescribed for any type of offence. But the official could only choose between certain types of penalties: fines, forced labour, imprisonment, and the death penalty. In case of the death penalty the limitations were more specific. It could only be pronounced in certain cases where the death of another person had been caused. Moreover, no official could pronounce it on his own, but only together with two European assessors, who could outvote him. Further, it had to be confirmed by the administrator, who also had full discretion to alter or quash any other punishment.

The commission's suggestions were accepted. On 7 July 1888 the emperor signed an ordinance transferring the jurisdiction over natives until the end of 1897 to the Neuguinea Compagnie.[17] Three days later the chancellor issued his instructions. The company, however, was not satisfied with simply adopting them, but decided to redraft and expand them. The main aim was to restrict the discretion of individual officials, mostly in the interest of accused natives. An upper limit for imprisonment (five years), for forced labour (one year), and for fines (300 marks) was stipulated. On the other hand, revolt, serious assault, rape, and robbery carried a minimum penalty of six months' imprisonment. Of all procedural provisions section 19 had probably the most significant consequences. According to the instructions the presence of assessors was required only if the death penalty was to be pronounced, whereas they had now to be present whenever the court dealt with an offence which could carry the death penalty, or which carried a minimum prison sentence of six months, so that the court had to consist of three Europeans in almost all cases where court action was likely to be taken — even if the accused was in the end only fined. It was this section more than anything else which caused H. Schnee, one of Schmiele's successors, to complain that the ordinance contained "well intentioned but completely impractical provisions".

Before blaming the Neuguinea Compagnie exclusively for these impracticable provisions — as Schnee did, giving a highly misleading account of their history[18] — it must, however, be remembered that the company's original draft for a penal ordinance for natives outside European employ did not contain any provision of this kind. The company, had, in fact, received a great deal more than it had bargained for. Leaving the coloured labourers out of account (for whom section 19 and other procedural rules provided few practical difficulties), the company had merely asked that rather modest and realistic provisions be made for general native "uprisings" or for cases in which natives killed or assaulted individual Europeans, or stole or damaged their property. Instead, it had received almost unlimited jurisdiction over all non-Europeans, including all internal native disputes.

## III

The new draft was approved, signed on 21 October 1888, and on 1 January 1889 the Penal Ordinance for Natives became effective.[19] In 1893 the Neuguinea Compagnie published a summary of the activities of the station court regarding native "crimes" in the Bismarck Archipelago between 1887 [*sic*] and 1892. No figures were given for the number of cases in which action had been taken between 1887 and 1890. The summary merely stated that five matters — all murders of non-natives — had not been completed. In 1891 the station court dealt with twenty-one criminal matters, but in thirteen of them — mostly thefts of crops and attacks on native women — it decided that court action would be unsuitable; instead administrative measures were taken. Only six cases were finalized by court decision. Two cases of arson and murder remained uncompleted.

The report does not indicate what kind of natives were involved in these cases. It is quite possible that the court had not dealt with one truly internal native dispute — the thefts of crops could have been from European plantations and the attacks on native women by coloured plantation labourers. At least, it does not suggest that the natives had begun to bring their disputes before the station court, or that the judge had attempted to go out into the villages. The main emphasis was still on "crimes" against Europeans, especially killings. Even in this context the report does not sound too optimistic. The earlier killings of European traders on outlying stations remained unresolved. The company justified this by pointing out that it would have been "inopportune" to arrest the suspects. In one case only was there still some hope of arresting the main culprit; in the others it was unlikely that those responsible would ever be called to account.[20] The report did not mention that in the fifth case of murder (that of a Filipino overseer in the Gazelle Peninsula in 1890) the native Toruruk had been sentenced to death by Schmiele. But although this case ended in formal court proceedings, they were only the last and possibly the least important steps in a series of political and military operations.

When Toruruk had been executed and the natives had paid substantial fines of shell-money, the Europeans thought that the punitive measures taken had been sufficient to prevent further unrest, at least in the Gazelle:

> So far such extensive expeditions have been usually carried out by imperial warships, which gave the natives the impression that the whites were not able to protect themselves. This assumption has now been destroyed .... The quick and decisive actions taken by the settlers will have a lasting effect on their personal safety and the safety of their property.[21]

Two years later the settlers in the Gazelle were confronted with the most determined challenge to European rule in the history of German New Guinea: a war involving almost the entire population of the Blanche Bay hinterland. It lasted for almost six months, until the heavy artillery of the navy shelled the natives into submission.

This time the company felt that a change in policy was needed.

> The unrest among natives of Blanche Bay has shown that, in the interest of humanity and justice as well as an undisturbed development of European enterprise in the area, it will be hardly sufficient in the future to leave the natives to themselves as long as they remain peaceful but to put them down as soon as they open hostilities. It will prove necessary to enter into closer contacts with these tribes by gaining confidants among them who can maintain order in their districts, thus preparing the ground for an indirect rule of these tribes by the administration. In this way lasting peace and fruitful relations can be established with these industrious and diligent tribes of agriculturalists.[22]

Yet the company was not anxious to put this policy into practice, although tensions in the Blanche Bay area continued and fighting broke out on the north coast of the Gazelle in 1895. This was not because it did not really believe that a change in policy was required, but because it was trying to persuade the Reich to take over the full responsibility — and the expense — of administering German New Guinea. The company was not prepared to spend money on pursuing an active native policy, but it was only too pleased when the new imperial judge, Albert Hahl, showed a keen interest in native administration. It watched his endeavours, full of admiration and praise, as long as they did not involve the company in any extra expenditure.

Hahl arrived in the Bismarck Archipelago on 14 January 1896. As imperial judge he had jurisdiction over all non-natives living in the area. The Neuguinea Compagnie had also put the imperial judges in charge of the station courts exercising its jurisdiction over natives. This decision had been made shortly after the 1888 Penal Ordinance. More important was a recent decision to make the imperial judge (in place of the company's station manager) responsible for the administration of the Bismarck Archipelago.

When Hahl discovered that his responsibilities towards the Europeans, despite his impressive list of functions, kept him busy only for a few days before the arrival of the two-monthly steamer from Germany, he decided to concentrate his energies on the native population.[23] His discussions with the leaders of the European community were hardly encouraging. They could merely offer a simple recipe for the colony's economic progress: more and more natives had to be talked into working for Europeans and into spending more and more of their income on European goods. But many of them had doubts as to whether this would be possible. The pessimists believed the Stone Age inhabitants of New Guinea were too weak a race to survive the unavoidable clash with modern Western civilization. According to the optimists the culture gap could be gradually closed, provided this was left exclusively to the missions. Any attempt on the part of the administration to speed up the process by establishing law and order among the native population was not only bound to fail but would seriously undermine the safety of the Europeans. Hahl was advised to buy himself a nice library, to enjoy his stay as much as possible, and not to interfere.[24]

Hahl was not the person to accept such advice. Although neither an idealist nor a colonial theorist, he believed experience in other parts of the world had shown that a colony would develop only if its native population was properly administered and if it could be convinced that the development was in its own interest. To find out whether this view held good for New Guinea, Hahl wanted "to hear the other side". He began to learn the local language, to talk to the natives, and to explore the northeastern Gazelle Peninsula on horseback and foot. Within three months he could follow simple conversations, and had acquired a general idea of the size of the native districts and the relations between them.[25]

Hahl's first aim was to persuade the natives to renounce blood feud and self-help as illegal and, instead, come to him with their disputes and worries.[26] He quickly found that this could only be the result of a well-established native administration rather than the first step towards it, or at least, that it was impossible to achieve this aim in isolation. As soon as the administration went beyond punitive expeditions to protect the life and the property of Europeans there was no stopping: the land problems had to be solved, native officials had to be appointed, the development of semi-feudal relations between the planters and traders and their native neighbours had to be prevented, the influence of the missions had to be restricted, native cash cropping had to be encouraged. All this meant more staff, more money, more roads, more vessels. Besides, it was impossible to limit the expansion of native administration geographically. It was not sufficient to stop the natives living under government control from using violence against Europeans or amongst themselves; they had also to be protected from raids by their uncontrolled enemies, and they had to be stopped from attacking them, so that punitive expeditions, at least along the fringes of government control, would be a necessary evil until *Pax Germanica* had been established in the entire colony.

Hahl's experiences in 1896 were to shape the official policy in New Guinea for at least twenty years. They did not cause him to formulate an administrative programme as a result of conscious political choices. He was convinced that the task of any administrator was to develop the area for which he was responsible, and from this axiom everything seemed to follow almost automatically. There was hardly a question of priorities, let alone alternatives; it was simply a matter of making the best use of inadequate resources in order to do what was necessary. His attitude towards the native population of New Guinea was not based on a particular theory or ideology but was, to him, purely pragmatic. He would do his best to develop the native people and with their help, New Guinea. If unfortunately this proved impossible, however, there were always enough Malays, Chinese, Japanese or even Indians to do the job. This is not to say that he did not care about the natives of New Guinea. He was clearly not a person who would have felt duty-bound to protect and advance the native races — as an abstraction (though possibly despising all its individual members). On the other hand, he was not a ruthlessly efficient administrator either. Hahl was by no means free of the racial prejudices of his time, but he liked people, even if they were black or brown or yellow.

Native "crimes" against Europeans were understandably still uppermost in Hahl's mind. He felt that mistrust of Europeans was one of the natives' most conspicuous characteristics. He also saw that the behaviour of the Europeans, whose mere presence threatened the traditional order, had much to do with this antagonism, but felt that it was deeply rooted in the traditional order itself.

> The custom of pay-back as a binding obligation of the clan combined with the complete lack of any state control had to lead to an unequalled harshness in any dealings with the outside. The mighty warrior ruled his surroundings and tried to enrich himself. To rob someone else's property was an honourable deed. This explains to a large extent why attacts on remote trading stations and small boats and ships are again and again attempted and carried out.[27]

Typically Hahl was not interested in establishing who was responsible for past attacks; instead he wanted to discover the motives behind them in order to limit and prevent "those regrettable occurrences" in the future. He concluded that the attitude of the natives had to be changed gradually to achieve this aim, but that "this work of patience" did not fulfil the needs of the day.

> Although it seemed indispensable to investigate acts of violence and to call the culprits to account, deterrence alone could never bring about any changes. The only chance was to expend the area of public order as much as possible by establishing permanent government stations as visible manifestations of protection for both sides. At the same time a carefully maintained system of native administration had to be developed based on their own co-operation.[28]

Native violence against Europeans was for Hahl not a problem which could be solved by criminal punishment, but an educational and administrative problem. He did not even believe that colonial courts could make a major contribution to the "advancement" of the native population in this field. Criminal jurisdiction over natives was not yet seen as part of the administration of justice. It had to meet the needs of the day, but was not to interfere with the progress of the overall education and administrative programme which had to change conditions until an administration of justice in native matters became possible.

Hahl's attitude toward internal native disputes was more complex. For most Europeans it was neither necessary nor desirable that the administration should get involved. Hahl's clerk, Steusloff, was one of them. When Hahl put him in command of an armed expedition which was to stop the fighting between the people of Paparatava and Tamanairiki and those of Vundadidir, Steusloff assured Brother Mueller of the Sacred Heart Mission that neither the Neuguinea Compagnie nor the Reich were anxious to get mixed up in native quarrels. The savages were quite welcome to kill each other as long as they did not touch any European. "What strange pinciples and what a lack of Christian morals", Mueller commented.[29]

Hahl's reasons for interfering in the fight were different: it threatened public order in the newly pacified hinterland of Herbertshöhe.[30] Since his actions were based on administrative necessities and not on moral principles, Hahl was also not interested in *punishing* "crimes" natives committed against other natives. It was the mission's job to teach the natives the Ten Commandments before it could become his job to punish them for breaking their secular counterparts. Although it was Hahl's aim to establish and maintain public order by eliminating the use of violence (rather than upholding Christian morality by punishing offenders), his exercise of jurisdiction in internal native matters had a much stronger and more immediate educational impact than the punishment of "crimes" natives committed against Europeans.

Hahl did not intend to make the settling of native disputes the prerogative of the colonial administration. It was initially the most important function of the headmen, luluai or kukurai, he appointed (or whose election he confirmed) to settle all minor disputes peacefully by using their own discretion. Only if this proved impossible or if the matter was of major importance was the headman required to inform Hahl — in urgent cases immediately, otherwise when he held court in the area.

It appears that almost all of Hahl's decisions were compromises rather than the result of applying any firm rules. The most important ones, however, were at the same time amendments to the traditional law. Hahl's role was in a way rather that of a social engineer than a judge. He was not concerned with creating enforceable laws by setting precedents, but with changing the norms of native social behaviour. He neither intended to protect the traditional order nor to stamp it out. He did not apply traditional law without modifying it, and was also against a strict imposition of Western law. Yet Hahl was not an unprincipled opportunist looking for the way where he would meet the least opposition. He compromised because he believed that good things take time. He did not shrink back from a vigorous use of pruning-hooks, but he knew that colonization — or development, as he saw it — was a slow process of osmosis.

## IV

When the Reich took over on 1 April 1899, the 1888 Penal Ordinance remained unchanged, though experience had shown that many of its detailed provisions were unsuitable and that probably some of its basic principles were also inadequate. This legally unsatisfactory state of affairs neither worried Hahl nor the German government. But some of the new administration officers had different ideas and legalistic scruples. They detested, in particular, the idea of treating smelly cannibal chiefs, open to bribery and fond of misusing their powers, as an integral part of the imperial German administration. Hahl left no doubt that he would not tolerate these views. On 2 November 1903 he issued an official warning: he had noticed that the role of the native chiefs had been mistaken and that they had been slighted. Instead of involving them in the exercise of administrative and judicial functions, their activities had been regarded as undesirable. In their place the administration had used large numbers of police boys to transmit orders to natives "certainly with detrimental effects".[31] On the other hand, in a decree on 20 November 1903 he assured his officials that the limits of their "jurisdiction" were not as narrow as they thought. According to section 2 of the Penal Ordinance the station courts could punish only those natives whose acts constituted a serious offence under German law. This did not mean, however, that natives were not accountable for other actions which appeared to require punishment. The right and duty to take any measures directed at the maintenance of public order followed from the general police power which had been transferred to the district officers. Yet in this context, too, Hahl added a reminder: in native matters "decisions should generally be left to the chiefs appointed by the administration".[32]

Hahl gave his European officials much less freedom of action. Although the decree at first glance implied that natives were accountable for all actions which appeared to require punishment (whether or not they constituted a serious offence under German law), its specific provisions show that Hahl had merely minor offences of individual natives in mind. Moreover, he stipulated that punitive actions by the administration in cases not covered by section 2 of this Penal Ordinance were still governed by its procedural principles. This could have meant that from now on any punitive measures in exercise of the administration's general police powers had to take the form of court actions against individual offenders — and thus in particular the end of punitive expeditions — but these possible consequences were, at this stage, neither recognized nor intended.

When Hahl issued this decree the limits of the general police power towards non-natives had not been defined either. This changed on 14 July 1905 when an Imperial Ordinance regarding the Rights of Coercion and Punishment of the Administrations in the Colonies of Africa and the Pacific was enacted.[33] It was not until 16 January 1908 that Hahl drew the consequences for the native administration in New Guinea.

> Since the Imperial Ordinance ... has come into force, it is only legitimate [for the administration] to use penal coercion ... [in police matters] in accordance with this Ordinance (sections 9 to 22). The administrative penal procedures which have been laid down in the decree of 20 November 1903 appear thus superseded and the decree is herewith repealed. On the other hand ... [the district officers as chairmen of the station courts] are empowered to adopt the formal [judicial] procedures in accordance with the Penal Ordinance of 21 October 1888 in all cases of punishable behaviour in which it appears necessary to take action in order to maintain public peace and safety.

The long interval between the 1905 Imperial Ordinance and Hahl's decree of 16 January 1908 indicates that he not merely intended to bring the colonial law in German New Guinea up to date, but rather felt that the time was now ripe for a change, that the policies he had adopted more than ten years earlier had partly fulfilled their purpose, and that it was possible to begin replacing the mixture of punitive expeditions and education with a system of colonial justice.

The decree disturbed the district officer in Friedrich Wilhelmshafen, who felt that such changes might be feasible in the Bismarck Archipelago but not in Kaiser Wilhelmsland, where the native population had "by no means been brought completely under the jurisdiction of the station courts". The District Office would have considerable difficulties if the previous informal method of dealing with native "crimes" (administratively) was now abolished — the result, he thought, of the 1908 decree. Punitive measures by the administration were still necessary when entire villages had to be called to account; either because it was impossible to ascertain the guilty individuals, or because they were not handed over, or because all inhabitants of a settlement were more or less involved in a criminal action and it was impossible to determine the extent of the responsibility of the various individuals. Formal procedures before the station court, the district officer claimed, would in all these cases result in acquittals, if the judge took his duties seriously and considered nothing but the evidence available against each individual accused — and if the serious communication problems could be overcome. These cases should therefore not be left to courts, they still had to be dealt with by the administration, which needed a considerable amount of discretion, so that it could take action against entire villages, and use measures other than those envisaged in the Imperial Ordinance of 1905. He rounded off his practical arguments with a legal point: "the instruction that any criminal infringements of public peace and safety can be punished by the station courts appears to me to contradict section 2 of the 1888 Penal Ordinance which is still in force".[34]

In his reply Hahl tried to dispose of the legal point by arguing that the limitation of the station courts' jurisdiction to serious offences under German law in section 2 of the 1888 Ordinance did not preclude the use of its procedural provisions as a *basis* (Hahl's emphasis) for dealing with cases where the administration had to take action outside this jurisdiction in order to maintain public peace and safety. Beyond that Hahl could only admit that he was aware of the difficulties the introduction of the new order would cause, and promise that the district officer would be covered by his decree if he had to depart from the procedures laid down in the 1888 Ordinance. Hahl was, at this stage not interested in pursuing the matter, because the Colonial Office was preparing a draft for a new native penal code for all German colonies. He assured the district officer that he had passed on his memorandum to Berlin to be considered in the discussions of this draft.[35]

The basis for a reform and unification of the law for the native population in the German colonies was laid with the Imperial Ordinance regarding the Organization of the Administration and Native Jurisdiction in the Colonies of Africa and the Pacific of 3 June 1908.[36] Despite its imposing title it merely comprised four short sections — the last two confirming or repealing previous legislation. The result of the first two was also very simple: section 1 authorized the chancellor of the Reich for the time being to enact regulations regarding the administration, the law, and the courts for the natives in the

German colonies — in so far as matters were not already covered by statutes of the Reich or by imperial ordinance; section 2 empowered the chancellor to transfer his authority to the governors of the various colonies.

In the case of criminal jurisdiction over the natives of German New Guinea, the chancellor himself exercised his authority. His Ordinance of 28 October 1908[37] was even shorter than that of the emperor. Instead of embarking on a general reform, it merely repealed section 2 of the 1888 Penal Ordinance, which had bound the station courts to the criminal laws of Germany.

This removed not only the basis for the legal objections against Hahl's decree of 16 January 1908, but superseded the entire decree by going a step further in the same direction. Hahl circulated the new ordinance, which had become effective on 1 January 1909, and formally withdrew his decree. This did not help the district officer in Friedrich Wilhelmshafen in his practical difficulties. He found some consolation, however, in a decree of the Colonial Office accompanying the new ordinance — excerpts of which Hahl also circulated.

The decree first of all stated that it had been the aim of the ordinance to bring the legal situation in New Guinea in line with that existing in the African colonies since 1896, where the officials had not only discretion in deciding whether or not to prosecute a native "crime", but could also decide whether or not the behaviour of a native constituted an offence which was open to prosecution. This was not quite what the district officer wanted. Instead of being concerned with expanding the jurisdiction of the station court, he was interested in limiting it — or at least in preventing formal court procedures from becoming the only legitimate way of dealing with native "crimes".

The next step was more promising. The Colonial Office pointed out that, contrary to the view underlying Hahl's decree of 16 January 1908, the 1905 Imperial Police Ordinance did not necessarily apply to the relations between the police and natives. Hahl had overlooked that the ordinance — with its limits as well as powers — only applied to natives if specifically directed by the governor of the colony. Consequently the district officer was not — at least by law (though possibly by way of an internal administrative instruction) — bound (or covered) by its provisions when dealing with natives. On the other hand, the right of the administration to use force against natives in order to maintain public peace and safety followed from general legal considerations, so that it was to this extent unnecessary to declare that the Imperial Ordinance of 15 July 1905 was applicable to them. Formal punishment, however, could, as long as this had not been done, only be based on the Penal Ordinance of 1888.

The main importance of the Colonial Office's explanations, however, lay in the final comment: "(M)easures of the kind the district officer has in mind, for instance actions against entire villages in case of breaches of the public peace, have nothing to do with either criminal punishments or police actions in the ordinary sense. They must be characterised as military actions whose admissibility is governed exclusively by political or similar considerations as in the case of war."

This spelled out a third aspect of native "crimes", which had already been clearly recognized by Schleinitz in his 1887 draft, but which had not been expressly mentioned for the last twenty years. There were three ways of looking at native "crimes": they could be regarded as criminal offences by individuals against individuals, they could be regarded as breaches of the public peace, and they could be regarded as acts of war. Depending on the view taken by the colonial authority, native "crimes" had to be answered in different ways: by judicial, administrative, or military action — each of these approaches being governed by a different set of rules and considerations. The main problem was that the same native "crime" could be treated as an individual offence, as a breach of the public peace, or as an act of war, depending on the circumstances in which it occurred, the general policies of the colonial authorities, and the personality of the officials dealing with it, as well as the "tribal" and individual characteristics of their native "opponents".

The annual report for 1901–2 suggests, for instance, that the murder of Mrs Wolff, a few miles inland of Herbertshöhe, was initially treated as an individual crime committed by four natives, and that the judicial approach only developed into a punitive expedition when "the murderers' clan resisted arrest". The annual report for 1902–3 gives quite a different impression:

> The fights with the mountain tribes around the Varzin ended in June. The Paparatawa tribe, which was largely responsible for the

> unrest, was limited to half its original area. The remainder was taken into possession for the government. The establishing of a police post at Toma (Paparatawa) secures peace for the expanding plantation as well as among the quarrelsome natives themselves. The suppression of the Varzin tribes, especially the inclusion of the Tamanairiki districts into the sphere of orderly administration, completes the establishment of government control over the ... [entire Tolai population]. The Taulil who live between the Varzin and the Baining Mountains and have suffered until now heavily at the hands of both sides [the Tolai and Baining]) ... were the main beneficiaries of the establishing of public peace ...

The confiscation of half of the Paparatawa's land was not a punishment for the murder of Mrs Wolff; but part of a complex set of political arrangements aimed at pacifying the inland Tolai and opening the way to the Taulil. The murder, which the settlers had again regarded as a signal for a general "uprising" of the Tolai, was for Hahl a signal to bring the inland Tolai under full and permanent government control. Hahl was not merely concerned with the murder as an individual crime but with the total network of relations between the Tolai, their native neighbours, the European settlers and the administration.

The 1904 "uprising" in Friedrich Wilhelmshafen, on the other hand, was, on the part of the natives involved, clearly intended as a war. Yet District Officer Stuckhardt, in full control of the situation, approached it in an almost exclusively judicial way, questioning witnesses, singling out and arresting ringleaders, confiscating weapons, and demanding fines in the form of pigs and food — although they were, at the same time, to serve as peace offerings. The affair would probably have ended in prison sentences for the ringleaders, had the settlers not sent a petition to the governor asking him to intervene. Hahl being away in Micronesia, Acting Governor Knake decided to respond; but only the information that the coloured plantation labourers had also been involved in the conspiracy made him take additional action: he proclaimed martial law. Instead of embarking upon military operations, however, a court martial was constituted. It sentenced to death, six of the ring leaders, who were publicly executed on the spot; ten others were sentenced to terms of imprisonment to be served in Herbertshöhe. Leaving out of account subsequent punitive expeditions against the Bilibili who had escaped from "colonial justice" into the bush, this was still very much a judicial reaction to a military challenge.

Eight years later, when the Madang natives — with the exception of the Bilibili — allegedly were about to "rise" again, the emphasis on a judicial approach was even stronger. Having temporarily removed the "guilty villages" to their trade friends across the Astrolabe Bay, District Officer Scholz tried his best to bring the affair within the framework of the 1888 Penal Ordinance. Finally he decided that court action could not, for several reasons, do justice to the case. Firstly, he believed that even the most extensive investigations could not determine the extent of the responsibility of the various individuals involved. Secondly, none of the applicable provisions provided adequate punishment for them. A punishment for revolt in accordance with section 15 of the 1888 Penal Ordinance and section 115 of the German Criminal Code was impossible because the plot had been discovered before it had reached the stage of a punishable attempt. Section 49a of the German Criminal Code, which made the mere planning of a serious crime an offence, was inappropriate because it did not consider the danger to the public "which manifests itself in a conspiracy of the black race against the white". To get around this difficulty it was necessary to treat the planned revolt as analogous to treason, the preparation of which carried under German law life imprisonment as the maximum penalty. This view would have been justified and the penalty adequate, but according to section 9 of the Penal Ordinance the limit for prison sentences for natives was five years — which was too low. To arrive at a higher penalty martial law had to be declared, but, in contrast to Knake in 1904, Scholz doubted whether even this would help, since the "crimes" had been committed before the state of war had been proclaimed.[38] Instead he opted for an administrative approach. As a result the ringleaders and their families were banished for life to the Gazelle Peninsula and the temporary banishment of the "guilty villages" was confirmed.

To decide whether native crimes should be answered with judicial, administrative, or military measures was difficult not only when they were directed against Europeans. In 1911 Hahl could finally afford to establish a permanent government station in the Admiralty Islands, where colonial administration had so far consisted exclusively of punitive expeditions, although few Europeans believed any longer in their long-term beneficial effects. District officer Zwanzger became almost immediately involved in the constant fights between the coastal and bush "tribes". He chose a judicial approach and arrested six of the bush people who had broken the peace he had arranged, sentenced them in the station court, and locked them up until they could be sent to prison in Rabaul. They escaped. Only two of the minor culprits could be recaptured, and the whole island lived in fear of their leader, the notorious Kabu.[39] When the government vessel finally delivered the two remaining prisoners and Zwanzger's report in Rabaul, Hahl instructed him to base his actions in future "(much) more or (even) exclusively on political or similar considerations".[40]

The Admiralties had to go through the same stages in the process of colonization as, for instance, the Gazelle Peninsula. This is not to say that history had to repeat itself over and over again in exactly the same way — not even within the framework of the same policy: mistakes could be avoided, methods could be modified, the process could be speeded up, the administration of justice in native matters, however, was, even in the Gazelle in 1914, still a political goal rather than an established means for dealing with native "crimes".

## V

During the first years of European settlement, the settlers' attitudes towards native "crimes" were dominated by their fears of a native revolt against the beginnings of white rule. Their prime aim was not to mete out just punishment but to get the natives to accept this rule, and they felt that by "teaching them a few lessons" this aim could be easily achieved.

Initially the Neuguinea Compagnie was in its own way equally optimistic. It was convinced that all problems could be overcome if only white domination were coupled with the rule of law. It realized that the "culture gap" would not disappear overnight, but was more concerned with finding a way of bridging it as humanely and cheaply as possible. When it became apparent that the company's optimism in this as well as in other fields was unjustified, it reduced its administrative activities to almost nil — mainly for financial reasons — and left New Guinea with an ambitious but incomplete facade of colonial law which had little practical significance.

After about ten years of colonial government and twenty years of European settlement, Albert Hahl made a fresh start. He believed that the problem of native "crime" could be solved neither by punitive expeditions nor by judicial decisions, but had to be treated as an educational problem within the framework of a general native policy which gave the native population an important role in the development of the colony.

These ideas were not new, but Hahl, first as imperial judge and later as governor, demonstrated that they could also be put into practice. At the end of German rule this educational and administrative programme was fairly advanced in some parts of New Guinea, but in others it had not even begun. Still, after about ten years, Hahl felt that an increasing emphasis could and should be placed on a judicial approach to native "crimes". On the other hand the settlers' fear of a native revolt continued. We know now that this fear is a necessary ingredient of the relationship between all colonial masters and their "subject races". We also know that the idea of colonial justice is an illusion or an alibi. But who can or really wants to learn from history?

1. G. Brown, "Letter Books" (unpublished, Mitchell Library, Sydney), letter to Chapman of 24/2/1878.
2. W. Powell, *Wanderings in A Wild Country* (London, 1883), p. 125.
3. Brown, "Letter Books", letter to Weber of 6/7/1878.
4. H.H. Romilly, *Letters from the Western Pacific and Mashonaland* (London, 1893), p. 148.
5. R. Parkinson, *Im Bismarckarchipel* (Leipzig, 1887), p. 68.
6. W. Deane, ed., *In Wild New Britain: The Story of Benjamin Danks, Pioneer Missionary, from his Diary* (Sydney, 1933), p. 279.
7. B. Danks, "Letter Books" (unpublished, Mitchell Library, Sydney). The quoted letter is not dated, it was probably written during the last days of May, 1886.
8. DKG, vol. 1, pp. 434–36.
9. DKG, vol. 1, pp. 442–43.
10. E. Hernsheim, "Memoirs" (Staatsarchiv, Hamburg), p. 144.
11. O. Schellong, *Alte Dokumente aus der Südsee* (Königsberg, 1934), p. 150.
12. NKWL, 1887, p. 189.
13. The following account is based on files RKA 4781–82, microfilms of which are held by the National Library in Canberra.
14. Report by Schleinitz of 27/8/1887.
15. NGC to AA, 28/1/1888.
16. Report of 29/6/1888.
17. DKG, vol. 2, p. 365.
18. H. Schnee, *Als letzter Gouverneur in Deutsch–Ostafrika* (Heidelberg, 1964), pp. 16–17.

19. DKG, vol. 1, pp. 555–62.
20. NKWL, 1893, pp. 26–27 (no author).
21. *Monatshefte zu Ehren unserer Lieben Frau vom h.h. Herzen Jesu* (Monatshefte, 1890), pp. 134–45 (no author).
22. NKWL, 1894, p. 19 (no author).
23. A. Hahl, *Gouverneursjahre in Neuguinea* (Berlin, 1937), p. 23.
24. Ibid., p. 20.
25. Ibid., p. 21.
26. Ibid., pp. 24–25.
27. Ibid., p. 48.
28. Ibid., p. 49.
29. F. Mueller, *Monatshefte*, 1897, p. 37.
30. Hahl, *Gouverneursjahre,* pp. 30–31.
31. In so far as no other reference is given, the unpublished source material used in this section is contained in the file on native affairs of the District Office in Friedrich Wilhelmshafen (Australian Archives Office, Canberra, CAO, AA) (Archives Accession) 1963/83, box 212, item 4.
32. CAO, AA 1963/83, box 212, item 5, decree of 20/11/1903.
33. DKG, vol. 9, pp. 169–76.
34. CAO, AA 1963/83, box 212, item 5, memorandum of 30/1/1908.
35. CAO, AA 1963/83, box 212, item 5, letter of 19/2/1908.
36. DKG, vol. 12, p. 201.
37. DKG, vol. 12, p. 468.
38. ARM, Barmen, E No. 942 2/12 12.
39. *Amtsblatt,* 1912, pp. 98–100.
40. Kaiserliches Gouvernement, *Briefjournal* 1912, No. 882, CAO, AA 1963/83, G. 30.

13

INGRID MOSES

# The Extension of Colonial Rule in Kaiser Wilhelmsland

For thirty years, from 1885–1914, Germany enjoyed the status of a colonial power in the South Seas. German New Guinea, her first acquisition in the Pacific area, included north-east New Guinea, the Bismarck Archipelago and the Solomon Islands (called the Old Protectorate), and from 1899 on the Micronesian islands. In 1906 the Marshall Islands, which had previously been administered separately, became administrative districts of German New Guinea. The Old Protectorate was administered for fourteen years by the Neuguinea Compagnie (New Guinea Company) which by charters of 17 May 1885 and 13 December 1886 had been granted sovereign rights and duties in that territory.[1] Kaiser Wilhelmsland, the northeastern part of the island of New Guinea (on which this paper will concentrate) was an untouched country at the time of annexation. It lay off the blackbirders' route, and while traders had strong footholds in the Bismarck Archipelago the only white person who had actually lived in Kaiser Wilhelmsland was the Russian scientist-cum-explorer Mikloucho-Maclay.[2] At the end of 1885 the first ship bringing German officials landed in Kaiser Wilhelmsland, soon followed by missionaries of three mission societies.[3]

This study attempts to describe the means by which a very few people established and maintained power and authority over an extensive country and its inhabitants. Only two groups of people will be considered here, government (administrative), and commercial staff of the New Guinea Company. Missionaries, who together with their dependents and auxiliary staff were numerically the largest group, merit a separate survey (see Klaus-J. Bade, in this symposium, "Colonial Missions and Imperialism: the Background to the Fiasco of the Rhenish Mission in New Guinea"). The source material on which this study is based includes official government publications,

Colonial Department and Colonial Office records, station and court files, as well as colonial newspapers and travel literature.

New Guinea is a large island of rugged terrain, high mountain ranges, and fast-flowing rivers. The population, Melanesians on the offshore islands and coastal fringe of the mainland, and Papuan further inland, is divided into numerous small tribes living in isolated communities based on kinship and language, some being as small as a few dozen people.[4] The tribes, which were contacted first after the establishment of the Protectorate, showed no developed political system and their members little differentiation and specialization in their social roles. Although headmen or chiefs were found in some communities, their position did not seem to be hereditary and was ascribed to their age, skills and other recognized achievements.[5] Small protective "village unions" based on either blood relationship or communal living were observed, and considered to be an intermediate stage between family and district confederation; peace was kept within these unions, attacks from the outside were jointly resisted, while feasts and secret cults were celebrated together.[6] During initiation ceremonies public peace might prevail in an area allowing otherwise hostile villages to participate in the feasts.[7] Also, extensive trade relations existed between the island and coastal people and coastal and inland population.

## I

The New Guinea Company, as agent of the German state and commercial enterprise, could expect then to encounter little concerted organized resistance. For exploitative purposes the company found itself indeed in a fortunate position. With no kings, no rulers or even paramount chiefs or powerful headmen, the legitimacy of their invasion was never questioned or challenged by the natives. As the communities were so isolated through language barriers and warfaring, and as the tribes did not recognize any authority or law beyond their own, it was of no consequence to them whether or not the German Reich had claimed the whole of northeastern New Guinea. They were affected only by measures which interferred with their customs or curtailed their rights.

The legitimacy of this superimposed white government was,

of course, recognized by all the Europeans living in its territory. Although the New Guinea Company had ideas of developing Kaiser Wilhelmsland into a settlers' colony, the harsh climate, the terrain, and lack of cash crops and trading goods soon ruled this out.[8] In fact never more than 300 Europeans lived in Kaiser Wilhelmsland.[9] Perhaps for these reasons the staff which Berlin kept sending out found it hard to adjust to the situation in a colonial environment where the mass of the people were subjects but not ruled, nor had they rights or positive duties, while the ruling élite which included all white persons assumed virtually sovereign powers on their outposts as representatives of European and, in particular, German culture and civilization.

The New Guinea Company, in its dual role, tried to discharge its duties economically by appointing officials and creating positions which served the company as well as the territorial administration. The supreme official in the Protectorate received the title of Landeshauptmann; administrative functions such as handling of police and registry office, as well as tax and customs matters, were delegated to the station superintendents, who were also responsible for the commercial management of the stations, and for their white staff. Passing of legislation remained the privilege of the imperial chancellor, and administration of justice to the white population was the preserve of imperial judges, one of whom resided in the Bismarck Archipelago and one in Kaiser Wilhelmsland.[10]

After two German warships had raised the German flag on several places in 1884, the imperial commissioner in the new Protectorate published in the *Sydney Morning Herald* a decree of the imperial chancellor to the effect that new purchases of land without the administration's consent were invalid; that trading in weapons, ammunition, and alcoholic beverages was prohibited, and that recruitment of workers from the German Protectorate for foreign plantations was also prohibited.[11] With the establishment of stations a semblance of a colonial government, at least, became necessary. As the country had been annexed for purely commercial reasons, it was urgent that the economic role of the natives be defined and regulated. The function of the colonial administration was to establish and maintain a control and monopoly of force in its territory, and thereby render possible and facilitate its economic exploitation.[12] This involved setting down rules for the acquisition of land, delegating authoritative powers to the station managers in their dealings with the coloured labourers, and controlling the "free natives" to an extent, so that they would not impede the exploitation of the country.[13] A directive concerning the procedure in acquisition of land by the New Guinea Company was issued by its board of directors in Berlin on 10 August 1887. The status of coloured workers and their recruitment and transport to the stations was subsequently regulated. The station manager was empowered to discipline his labourers, and the coloured workers, as well as the free natives, fell under his jurisdiction for criminal offences.[14]

The sanctions which could be employed against the free native were limited, as the central administration or stations had hardly any means of acquainting him with German law, or inducing or compelling him to accept it and then enforce it. By the end of 1890 no verdict in a criminal matter against a native had been passed by a station court, and it was admitted that actions which were repugnant to German law could hardly be brought before a regular court, as the culprit would escape the enforcement of justice.[15] Instead, swift retaliatory actions were employed to impress the natives, discourage further violence, and accustom him to seek regular administration of justice in preference to traditional means of revenge. Whereas the government could afford to ignore raids, practices like headhunting and cannibalism, and other violent crimes in areas not yet contacted by Europeans, its "prestige" and claim to authority forced it to act when offences were committed against white staff, coloured labourers (as they were in a state of dependence on the Europeans), or against or by a village to which the administration had indicated or proved its supremacy. There were several courses of action possible. If a culprit was known but could not be arrested his village could be held responsible and be forced to supply hostages. Pigs or other property traditionally given in compensation for damage done could be demanded. The village or villages could be forcefully subdued. This was usually carried out when offences had been committed communally and the villages showed general hostility. The Landeshauptmann would send his police troops, reinforced by some of the white staff, to try to negotiate with the village, and, if negotiations failed, would burn the village and destroy canoes and fruit trees. As the Landeshauptmann had an extremely restricted budget and very limited police forces at his disposal, the station managers often did not wait for the central administration to act, but organized retaliatory raids with the coloured labourers on their own responsibility. These could degenerate into a general raping and looting expedition. Von Kotze, nephew of Bismarck and short-term employee of the company, described one such raid undertaken from Kelana station: the natives had become hostile after a series of infringements and had attacked the labourers and after a while had even shot at the white staff. Some of the workers had been wounded and a strike was threatening. Von Kotze reports, "We decided to make a punitive expedition, partly to kill the hostile kanakas, partly to kill time."[16] This was carried out with disastrous results: while the village men were out on a raid the workers rushed into the village, raping and plundering, and could not be restrained; the village was then set on fire, and a feast held with the stolen food; on the way back to the station the workers were ambushed by the returning villagers and some workers were killed; with the timely arrival of a steamer soon after they returned to Finschhafen.

Every white man in the colony was in an extremely exposed position, with powers over human beings which far exceeded anything previously customary. And the further he was stationed away from the seat of government the more strongly developed was the rule of force governing the relations between white and black.[17] With no colonial experience to draw from, a slender budget, and complete lack of insight into colonial conditions and administration, the company had no guide as to the selection of its overseas staff. Officials were recruited for a period of three years, with the option of renewal. Men from various kinds of professions applied for the positions, among them a sizeable group of young noblemen, officers of the reserve, and discharged officers who transplanted the rigidity of German society into the young New Guinea colonial society.[18] All these men arrived in the country, many without any knowledge which could be of use to the colony, high-spirited and adventurous. They kept the judicial and bureaucratic wheels turning with pointless paper work and numerous court cases for charges such as libel, slander, and defamation.[19] The large turnover of personnel, many of whom preferred breaking their contract rather than seeing it out, is another indication of the general lack of meaningful purpose which would unite the white personnel in their common task of developing the country.[20]

Social Darwinism in various forms was the prevailing ideology among the commercial staff — often modified by the belief in the civilizing mission of the white race. Count Pfeil, for example, very strongly argued that the only valid justification for the primitive races' existence lay in their auxiliary function as suppliers of land and labour to the superior race who spared them extinction and endeavoured to raise them to a higher cultural level by acquainting them with the goods, ideals, and achievements of European civilization.[21] Whereas those who were inspired by the idea of spreading *Deutschtum* to the farthest corner of the earth realized the moral obligation of white domination to the subjugated peoples, others discredited this as humanitarian sentimentality. All protective measures for natives were, in the final analysis, reducible to the economic motive and goal: the labour "material" had to be preserved for future exploitation.[22]

Whereas responsible officials tried to gain the natives' trust, co-operation, and even friendship by learning the vernacular, getting acquainted with local customs, and respecting these in their dealings with the native population, others found it impossible to communicate with them at all. Contempt for as well as fear of the numerically superior masses, indifference to their culture, or hatred of them, as well as personality problems, which were accentuated by the isolation of a station, by the pressure and stress of their position, and by the trying climate, led these men to abuse their privileges in a ruthless and sometimes savage way. It was realized that the authority of the administration was largely determined by the authority which the individual official commanded. As it was difficult to establish and maintain a position of dominance without resorting to some force, and because many officials, fearing uprisings and guided by the social attitudes of a *Herrenvolk*, demanded strictest adherence to a set of behavioural patterns which they had introduced to maintain and increase the social distance between master and labour force, the administration tolerated occasional overstepping of the authority delegated to them. Relatively numerous cases of manslaughter and serious maltreatment of workers came to the notice of the administration and court; but for the reasons mentioned, the accused often escaped with a mere reprimand, fine, or transfer to another post.

## II

As the New Guinea Company was primarily a commercial enterprise, economic considerations determined its policy decisions. It had been decided to concentrate its commercial activities on mainland New Guinea where there were no competitors. The explorer Finsch, who through land purchases on behalf of the company executed during several journeys along the coasts of Kaiser Wilhelmsland and in the archipelago in 1884 and 1885, had been instrumental in the annexation of New Guinea, reported favourably about the coast of Kaiser Wilhelmsland.[23] His advice was heeded and the first settlement founded on 6 November 1885 in Finschhafen on the Huon Peninsula. When the landing party arrived in the harbour they were awaited by a brig with building material and supplies on board which had been anchored in the harbour for eighteen days, the crew having enjoyed friendly relations with the indigenous population. The organ of the New Guinea Company, *Nachrichten für und über Kaiser Wilhelmsland und den Bismarck Archipel* was happy to report that the natives were amiable and eager to sell land. It stated, "With loud shouts of joy they received our hint that we intended to stay here and build a house, and willingly sold us the island which we had chosen for our settlement."[24] However, in contrast to this idyll of harmony, the missionary Flierl reports that Yabim people tell the tale of the white man who had laid an axe into their house, telling them to go by using the Yabim word for "gone", this being the only way he could make himself understood.[25] More land was purchased soon after on the mainland for experimental plantations and gardens. Formalities, for example, bill of sale, were used perfunctorily. Of course the natives did not understand the legal consequences of these transactions, in fact they often did not even realize that a transaction had taken place, but believed that they were leasing some land or receiving the trade goods in return for ethnologica.[26] This was caused not only by the lack of proper communication, but more so by the entirely different notion of land usage and ownership in native society. Land was owned communally by a tribe, clan or lineage, but every family cultivated a piece of the jointly cleared land and the fruits grown there belonged to them. Also, fruit trees which had been planted by individuals became their property. As no one individual was owner in the European legal sense of any particular plot of land, no one person could sell it, as indeed there was no concept for sale of land at all. In German law the concept of "unclaimed land" provided the New Guinea Company with the justification for claiming any land which showed no visible signs of ownership or cultivation. This could be appropriated without further formality. However, in reality there was scarcely any unclaimed area in the coastal districts. Although the bush might not be used at a given time it still represented part of a tribe's territory where they could shift their fields, where they dared to go without arms, and where sacred trees and rocks might be. The company regulations, of course, obliged the buyer to establish ownership of the land in question, but there was so little communication possible that nearly all bills of sale would have been regarded as null and void. Yet the Finschhafen natives did not raise any stronger objections to the increasing expansion than to throw a spear at a Malayan worker.

At this point the question arises: why did the Finschhafen natives, for example, tolerate this expansion when they felt uncomfortable and resentful of the presence of the white invaders? On the Huon Peninsula no legend existed which predicted and prepared for the coming of the white man; indeed, again and again it is reported that the natives lacked all understanding for the reasons for the white men's prolonged presence in their country. They themselves would only venture to other tribal territories to raid or to wage war, to go on trade journeys to tribal friends or kinsmen, or to shift their site to a new location if it was attacked too often or proved unsuitable in any other way. So one explanation within their own framework of experience was that the white men had nothing to eat in their own country and had come here instead. Yet they obviously were very rich, and had an abundance of goods and unlimited supplies coming to them. The old influential man, Makiri, of the Yabim tribe near Finschhafen, for example, was convinced for a long time that the Germans would one day return to their homeland — he had seen too many officials come and go. In fact his people had already deliberated as to who was to have which trade goods and which house to live in.[27] Three years after first contact the company medical officer reported that "actually we appear to him [the native] with our civilized superstructure as nearly supernatural beings, a fact which gives more cause for fear than for trust."[28]

This fear was nourished by the white people's immunity to local magic and evil forces.[29] Whereas the native would not normally venture beyond the tribal boundaries, the official was eager to explore the villages around the station, and contact foreign, possibly hostile villages. He was immune, of course, because of the different and obviously superior protection he had from his gods. But subjectively he was superior because he was a member of the white race and regarded these people as noble savages, harmless children of nature, or spiteful and murderous savages who would cringe when confronted with a stern, self-assured eye and Germanic manly virtues.[30] Also, he knew that he was supported and protected by a highly organized and complex country, whereas the native could only draw on his fellow primitives for help. The status of these white men was accepted as one of command, as they were seen daily to command the imported coloured labourers. This facilitated their acceptance of his authority, as indeed they were used to listening to, though not necessarily obeying, the man of authority. The obvious superiority of the fire arms was easily recognized, as was the excellence of iron tools, chemical dyes, matches, in fact all the implements these invaders had brought with them. As they themselves were initially objects of curiosity, and their field produce and ornamented implements were in high demand, they found it very easy to obtain, by means of barter, tools, tobacco and other trade goods. It was lamented that "not the savage but the white shows economic needs and ... documents himself in a certain sense as the economically weaker party".[31] Their own needs were easily satisfied, and so they used the iron tools to strengthen their trading position with other villages; iron implements were later found in villages which had no previous contact with white people. The new tools facilitated cultivation and other tasks without changing the method of production or the product itself, and so required no adjustment.[32]

When the Finschhafen natives realized that the white people were not visiting their shores temporarily (indeed they had sent for their families) but were actually expanding the station, they sold more land and shifted their plantations further inland where their women were no longer under the eyes of the foreign workers and in danger of being molested by them, and where through physical distance causes for conflicts were minimized.[33]

Only a few months after Finschhafen, the Hatzfeldhafen station was founded. It had an unhappy and short history of frequent hostile encounters with the surrounding natives — a history which culminated in the murder of seventeen people in 1891, among them three whites. The culprits were punished and the station subsequently abandoned. The hostilities there arose mainly from the encroachment on native rights by company labourers, fast expansion, the natives' greed for the trade goods, and their general warlike characteristics.[34] Konstantinhafen was founded as a main station in 1886, Stephansort in 1888, Friedrich Wilhelmshafen (Madang) in 1891 — to be the central station of Kaiser Wilhelmsland after an outbreak of fever had killed more than a dozen officials in Finschhafen and Seleo in 1894. Several plantation stations were also set up in these years: Butaueng, Kelana, Erima, Yomba and Maraga.[35] The expansion was carried out by officials who, together with labourers and sufficient supplies, would set out to the new location, buy land if nothing had been acquired previously, and then proceed to clear sites for buildings and plantations. All stations have a history of native resistance to this expansion; although the white people often were welcomed because of their trade goods, conflicts inevitably arose with the increasing need for more land. Even with the most careful investigation and surveying, disputes over the validity of the purchase and boundaries would arise.[36] Also, the influx of foreign workers created problems when they stole field fruits and interfered with local women. For a few years all economic activity in Kaiser Wilhelmsland was concentrated on Astrolabe Bay, and relations were described as generally good. It was felt that the population here had been treated rather fairly, and although violence erupted at times, this was due to the practice of individual planters, and rectified with their removal. More resistance was, however, expected with further advancement.[37] The aim of the administration was to extend the area of influence gradually, and eventually to control all villages within the colonial territory and integrate them in the colonial economy. From the stations the New Guinea Company pushed further inland; the first Landeshauptmann, in particular, was very interested in explorations, and he himself, together with scientific expeditions sponsored by the company and other organizations, advanced into the hinterland as well as navigating the big rivers. Contact with the native population was mostly fleeting; where resistance to their presence was shown, the expeditions would retreat. Although the existence of white persons in the country was known to some inland tribes, the impact which the white men made was not less great.[38]

The company shared the prevalent view that the white man was morally justified in demanding physical work from the native for the benefits of the civilization he was enjoying.[39] But no free natives were forcibly induced to work on the plantations. Indeed the New Guinea Company lacked all means to establish and sustain a system of forced labour. The Astrolabe Bay people were generally unwilling, too proud and too self-sufficient to work as contract labourers. The Finschhafen natives had worked playfully on occasions; they were held back by sentiments such as: our work will contribute to strengthening the whites' position, so we had better abstain from it (Makiri).[40] Yet a well-liked station manager was able to recruit sixteen Yabim men in 1888 to work on plantations further away; they performed well and were satisfied with the pay and conditions and were expected to encourage other young men.[41] With the extension of plantations and increasing difficulties in recruiting overseas, the labour question became one of prime importance. Whereas some held that New Guinea could not do without Asian workers, others pointed out that the Papuans had to be educated to work regularly.[42] Attempts at recruiting continued, and had varying success. From one such trip in the Huon Gulf it was reported that the young Kai men (mountain people) were eager to join, but were forcibly restricted by the old men who claimed that traditionally they were not allowed to go down to the sea. Other villages assured the recruiter of their general willingness, but explained that they were involved in warfare and could not very well spare their young men. And the inhabitants of Village Island refused recruitment for fear of being eaten.[43]

On the whole the enterprises of the New Guinea Company in Kaiser Wilhelmsland were not very successful during their first years of existence. They suffered from mismanagement and lack of direction, stations were established, abandoned, and re-opened, crops were introduced and then relinquished. The administrative obligations were a burden and not approached in any systematic way. Here, too, frequent changes in the organization and lack of finance and policy prevented steady development. After years of negotiations the Reich finally agreed in 1898 to relieve the New Guinea Company of all sovereign duties for the Protectorate as from 1 April 1899. A governor was appointed, and district officers were put in charge of the administration districts. Kaiser Wilhelmsland became the western administration and jurisdiction district, Friedrich Wilhelmshafen the seat of its district officer and judge. The New Guinea Company was amply compensated in cash, land, and mineral rights for past expenditure, and the property and buildings taken over by the Reich.[44]

## III

The administrative apparatus set up now very clearly distinguished between administrative and commercial interests. It remained one of the functions of colonial government to ensure that conditions favourable to economic growth and activity prevailed or were created in the country. Yet through the separation of administrative and commercial agencies a wider and more detached perspective evolved which included the whole of the country. No dramatic changes took place in the government, no long-term programme for the development of country and integration of the natives into colonial society was followed. But pragmatically and empirically, with more funds, and directed by a governor who was sympathetic towards the native population and aware of the conflicts which the "clash of cultures" and the dominance of the white race would bring, the administration was able to clarify the land situation, continue in the exploration of the country, involve the native population to an increasing degree in the economy as consumers and labourers, organize the pacified villages into administrative units, and delegate responsibility for public work to them.

The Colonial Department[45] had been aware for years that the land appropriations were causing unrest among the population and that most of the land deals were of rather questionable legality.[46] Registrations in the land registers were now checked, as was the validity of all purchases, and surveying was intensified. The company was considerably entagonized by the legalistic approach to this by the imperial officials who were not, so it was claimed, taking into consideration the circumstances which prevailed in an undeveloped country.[47] However, although the Colonial Department noted that there were legal faults in most contracts, it was nevertheless agreed that the company had to be allowed to claim the 50,000 hectares granted in the treaty with the Reich.[48] The pressure on the indigenous people to sell land did not decrease, despite the administration's monopoly of granting and selling landrights, and strict rules for acquisitions. On the contrary, the concerted efforts of the government, commercial interests, and missions in pacifying the warring tribes and opening up the country, increased the demand for land in the pacified areas. On 1 January 1904 the New Guinea Company, still the only commercial enterprise operating in Kaiser Wilhelmsland (apart from mission plantations) had 1,312.5 hectares under cultivation, one year later 3,537 hectares of the 22,086 hectares it held. On 1 January 1913 six enterprises had 6,990 under cultivation and owned 72,000 hectares.[49] The rate of plantation extension now was determined wholly by the availability of labour.

The attitude towards recruitment in Kaiser Wilhelmsland was somewhat ambiguous. Although it was desirable for financial reasons (lower costs, greater resistance to the climate), the New Guinea Company feared that the workers, who in their tribal surroundings were too isolated to organize rebellions, might unite on the plantations and rise up against the rule of the white employers and government.[50] Imported labour was safer in this respect, since because imported workers were strangers and much resentment was focused on them, they had to rely on the white government and employer for protection. Yet the labour situation demanded that the untapped labour reservoirs on mainland New Guinea be used, and it was found that more and more young men were willing to sign up for periods of time. The trend had already been noticeable at the end of the company's rule; indeed, even the Astrolabe natives finally agreed to work on the stations, help with loading and unloading of steamers, and engage in works such as road construction.[51] For years the main contingent of workers came from the Huon Peninsula, but after the establishment of Eitape government station in 1906 this fairly densely populated area provided labourers as well. The station officials there very strongly favoured recruitment as one means of providing the native people with education to enable them to work and with an opportunity to earn cash.[52] The increase from this area, as well as the beginning of successful recruitment in Morobe district (established on 1 April 1910), compensated for the decreasing recruitment figures in the Huon Gulf, where the population had been working for twenty years and where stations and mission needed the available local labour.[53] In 1912 935 workers were recruited in Friedrich Wilhelmshafen district, 851 in Eitape and 227 in Morobe district.[54]

The government tried to curb excesses and ensure the voluntariness of recruits by introducing new legislation (the decree of 4 March 1909) regarding the employment of workers and the procedure in recruitment. Disciplinary power (*Disziplinarerlaubnis*) had been granted to employers and certain lay brothers of the Roman Catholic Mission by the ordinances of 20 June 1900 and 22 January 1907. The permit holders were, in fact, performing a state office in that they carried out judicial functions in addition to their disciplinary authority as employers. Because of this power the government was strict in enforcing the prescribed rules and limitations, and withdrew the permit from those who abused it.[55] Indeed, the protective legislation by the government, and favourable rulings for natives in court and other disputes, roused the indignation of the planters in the Bismarck Archipelago, for whom the labour problem was not one of how to edcate the natives to work or how to preserve their vitality and increase their future desire and capacity for work, but one of short-term solutions for the immediate labour shortage.[56]

The long-term programme of educating the native population to a "higher cultural level" was attempted by persuading the natives to take up systematic work (though never by forced labour on plantations), through teaching of new skills (preparation of gutta) and insistence on more economic activity by enlarging native coconut plantations. Whereas contract labourers had always been medically cared for, and while the missionaries had cared for the population in their districts, the state of health of the general population had been rather neglected. In 1910 attempts were renewed in Friedrich Wilhelmshafen district to extend health services to include free natives, to train them to build their houses more solidly, and keep the villages clean. They were also induced to bury their dead outside the villages.[57] Increasingly natives submitted to the judicial authority of the government. In the first years of colonial rule missionaries had succeeded in gaining recognition as mediators in conflicts, and instead of taking the law into their own hands the natives would bring their disputes before them; also, individual company officials, who commanded the authority and respect of the native population in their district, convinced the people of the advantages of peaceful settlement by a third uninvolved party.[58] With the extension of pacified and controlled areas the authority of the government started to replace that of the individual, and more cases were brought before the court. The statistics of court sessions thus do not indicate an increase in crime but rather the consolidation of German government.[59]

In order to disseminate information, publicize and enforce the new laws of the government, an indigenous administrative "staff" of intermediaries between government and the mass of the people was necessary. Already in 1892 Rose, then imperial commissioner for the Protectorate, had suggested uniting villages into administrative units, appointing spokesmen and seeking their co-operation in matters such as land purchases, establishment of reserves, and settling of disputes. The security of the New Guinea Company stations would then be guaranteed by orderly, regulated relationships between native and white inhabitants, and not through fear of firearms.[60] The first step in delegating some judicial and administrative functions to native representatives was not undertaken in Kaiser Wilhelmsland until 1905, when government control seemed sufficient in the neighbourhood of Friedrich Wilhelmshafen to warrant the appointment of village chiefs as agents of the government.[61] Following the pattern on the Gazelle Peninsula where the first chief (luluai) had been installed in 1897, these chiefs were given authority to ajudicate in small matters (claims up to the value of twenty-five marks). They were obliged to implement the policies of the government and to fulfil certain administrative and police functions — in particular to supervise building and maintenance of roads in their district.[62] It was planned to unite villages of similar language and of possible relationship by blood and trade ties, into larger units, and to appoint as chiefs men who commanded some authority within the traditional social structure, or where there were chiefs, to confirm these in their position by bestowing upon them the insignia of office — cap and rod. A village or village union thus included in the "organization" was called upon to perform for two months of the year forced labour for the government on public projects, mainly on works such as road construction and filling in of swamps. Some of the villages to be organized resisted, passively but tenaciously, the inclusion into communities, and had to have a chief each; others refused to do their share of public work and had to be compelled by force.[63] Nevertheless, the organization was extended gradually and the influence of the government strengthened in these areas. In Eitape district the station officials succeeded in pacifying some of the warlike tribes through continuous intervention and punishment of breaches of public peace, and persuaded them to build the station, bridges and roads.[64] Governor Hahl saw this as proof that after initial resistance had been overcome the natives were quite willing to be included in the organization, as they quickly learnt to appreciate public peace and the freedom of movement this entailed.[65] Soon chiefs were appointed in Eitape district whose influence gained more recognition of station orders and helped reduce the feuds between villages. Public peace was generally maintained, and disputes, once they arose, brought to the attention of the station officials for settlement.[66] Similarly successful was the third station, Morobe, where the area of control was steadily extended through frequent expeditions and public works which were performed voluntarily.[67]

In 1910 Kaiser Wilhelmsland followed the Bismarck Archipelago by substituting payment of tax for forced labour in those communities which had opportunity to earn cash; thirty-six communities were taxed as from 1 April 1911.[68] The adult male population had to pay this headtax of five marks once a year; whoever worked for ten months of a year for a non-native or was employed by a native paying trade licence tax, was exempted. The money was collected by the luluais who were permitted to keep 10 percent of the village total for themselves. Taxation was seen as having a threefold benefit: it was educational by fighting the natural native tendency to indolence; it provided officials with increased contact with the native population, thus increasing mutual understanding; and the financial proceeds were considerable.[69] The introduction of taxes, unlike that of forced labour, found no opposition; indeed the men seemed to prefer to earn money and pay off their obligations rather than perform forced labour. The Malayan assistants of the Guttapercha und Kautschuk Expedition des kolonial-wirtschaftlichen Komitees who were to instruct the population on how to extract gutta percha found willing students once these realized that it would earn them cash, and thus provide an alternative to forced labour.[70]

The geographical extension of government influence was largely determined by finances and means of communication. European settlement had mainly followed the coastline and was thus very dispersed, requiring great expenditure for transport and public administration.[71] From the time of the company administration this had been an impediment to the process of pacification and in bringing the country under control. In 1897 the commander of the surveying ship *Möwe* wrote to his admiral that the power of the administration which relied on company ships reached at that time no further than rowing boats could take the Landeshauptmann![72] With the new imperial government the situation improved, though never to the full satisfaction of the officials. Governor and district officer frequently travelled along the coasts visiting untouched areas and strengthening the position of the administration by appointing chiefs. In uncontrolled villages young men were encouraged to accompany the district officer back to Friedrich Wilhelmshafen in order to learn the language (Pidgin) and to familiarize themselves with the administration; on their return to their home villages they would be installed as luluai or tultul, assistant to the chief, and usually versed in Pidgin. Also, German public interest in New Guinea had increased, and expeditions financed by various organizations explored the country; the Sepik and Ramu were navigated further, the Huon Peninsula and the border areas to Dutch and British New Guinea were explored. The government stations Eitape and notably Morobe carried out expeditions into their hinterland. Anthropological, botanical, and economic research expeditions increased the knowledge of the country and its potential. Whereas the expeditions generally were careful to avoid encounters with the native population, gold-diggers and bird-of-paradise-hunters who penetrated farthest into the inland, disturbed the population by their presence. When several hunters one after the other had been murdered by natives, hunting was restricted, and in 1914 no permits at all were issued.[73]

Governor Hahl regretted that the government had not been everywhere in the forefront in contacting new tribes, as this might have saved the life of many an adventurous white man.

But violent conflicts were seen as a natural phenomenon in the contact situation.[74] The means of punishment and subjugation were essentially the same as the company had employed but they were used more purposefully. It was no longer a matter of merely "teaching the natives a lesson", but of conscious and continuous display of power to impress the population and suppress or nip in the bud any resistance. The company had frequently requested ships of war to "show the flag" or shell some villages or punish a village, as the number of police troops (about two dozen native police) was inadequate for these tasks. Indeed the company regarded it as the duty of the imperial government to provide for protection against hostile attacks by natives.[75] But when the ships were engaged elsewhere, insurrections and crimes could not be punished, and the natives were openly contemptuous of the administration's power. Some tribes were proud and defiant and could not be persuaded peacefully to accept German dominance; so the superiority of the German government, and its power to inflict punishment upon them, had to be demonstrated again and again. It was reported that the island natives near Friedrich Wilhelmshafen, for example, acted arrogantly and with impunity towards the individual white man. They would disregard the power supporting all white men in the colony, and so limited was this power in fact that they could order unwanted visitors off their islands or refuse their landing on it. In these cases the temporarily defenceless white man would have to retreat.[76] So war-ships remained an invaluable aid to the government in demonstrating to the native population the superiority and the support of the Reich. It had been realized that "occasional punishment of native excesses proves to be useless, even harmful, as the natives invariably tend to take revenge on the next to come. The employment of military force is only effective if a permanent government post follows up the advantage gained by acts of intimidation and suppresses warfare among the natives, gradually reconciles them with each other and guarantees by its presence alone safety of life and property".[77] With increased police personnel (every government station had fifty to sixty men under a white police officer) and troops from war ships available, it became possible to keep up the pressure on resisting villages, harass them continually, and follow them into swamps and the bush where they had believed themselves to be unassailable. But as the troops could be employed only at one trouble spot at a time, and there were many flash points in the whole of the Protectorate, pacification was comparatively slow. The tribes of the Finisterre Mountains, who only forty miles away from the seat of the district office dared continually to raid the coastal population of the Rai Coast, were finally subjected to a series of punitive expeditions, as the government felt that it could not tolerate this defiance any longer without losing prestige and credibility among the raided villages.[78] Similarly, the warlike tribes in the Markham area continued to attack, and nearly annihilated, the coastal population. Lack of troops here again had delayed government interference, but when a bird-of-paradise-hunter was murdered the opportunity was taken, a punitive expedition set out, and in the course of a pitched battle between the Lae Wombas and the government police force, forty of the enemy were killed.[79] The Hatzfeldhafen villages, which from the beginning had resisted domination and continued their hostilities, were subdued by frequent relentless engagements. These punitive actions by the government to suppress unrest were not only seen as the appropriate means for pacifying hostile native villages, but were also essential to protect the coastal populations who, through pacification and recruitment, had become weakened and defenceless; their protection then had become the obligation of the government, because the pacified tribes now relied on the authorities to avenge and redress wrongs perpetrated on them.[80]

Punishment by the government did not occur automatically, however. Particularly in the latter days of German rule, peaceful and forceful attempts of pacification were undertaken side by side. The murder of a gold-digger in the then unorganized hinterland of Morobe remained unpunished because the natives had only reacted in their traditional way against violations of their customs. Retaliatory action by the station would have created hostile feelings and prejudiced future relationships.[81] Hansa Bay was to be pacified in 1912, and an expeditionary force was stationed there for a few months to punish several murders and establish contact and eventually peaceful relations with the headhunting and warfaring tribes. The population had also been greatly troubled by bird-of-paradise-hunters; the people were mistrustful and hostile. Captain Prey, the leader of the expedition suggested that they either had very bad consciences or very bad experiences.[82] This latter view was emphatically shared by Professor Neuhauss who had in Germany become an authority on New Guinea.[83] Prey went to Hansa Bay "to fulfil his cultural task". He said that meaningless demonstrations of superior means of power and the winning of cheap war-laurels were not to be the purposes and aims of the troops. Rather the advantages of a higher civilization and the benefit of peaceful conditions were to be brought home clearly to the savage tribes.[84] In the Potsdamhafen area frequent unrest caused the government to intervene and punish the murderers. But expeditions against the hostile tribes were not undertaken; instead, efforts were to be concentrated on bringing the villages into the organization.[85]

Hostilities between tribes and towards individual whites (taking the form of unrest) threatened the authority of the government if they remained unpunished, but they did not basically endanger the foundation of colonial government. When, however, villages and tribes united to concerted action in order to overthrow the government and kill all the white persons, the superstructure of white government and society was threatened because of the precarious nature of the government's power basis and lack of legitimacy. Consequently the white population reacted strongly in the face of such danger and demanded severe punishment for rebels. Such uprisings were planned twice by the island natives near Friedrich Wilhelmshafen, in 1904 and again in 1912, involving mostly the same villages. Neither attempt was successful; the natives were thwarted by betrayals from their own ranks before blood was shed. Increasing land purchases, general resentment against the white dominance, as well as racial hatred, were given as reasons for the planned uprisings.[86] The plans had been worked out in detail, prepared well ahead, and were considered "a credit to the organisational talents" of the natives.[87] It was the deep-seated and widespread resentment against those who had pushed them off their land, restricted their freedom, destroyed their traditional way of life, imposed their moral values on them, and treated them as inferiors, which made those proud people revolt. They were going to kill the white population with their own native arms — spears — the effectiveness of which had been scorned so often by the white men. But not all of their own people shared the confidence that the yoke of the colonial masters could be thrown off, and so the villages not only lost their leaders by execution and deportation (1904), but their land as well (1912), which was conveniently confiscated.[88]

## IV

When during the first few weeks of World War I Germany lost her colonies in the Pacific the colonial government in New Guinea had just started a renewed concerted effort to consolidate its power. With a budget of 7 million marks the governor had hoped finally to open up the interior of New Guinea and to encompass the areas of the Waria, Sepik, Ramu and Markham rivers into an orderly administration and economy by establishing more outposts there. From three points this advance had already begun, Morobe station was moving into the valley of the Waria, the Neuendettelsau mission had advanced into the Markham valley and the station Angorum on the middle Sepik (founded in 1913) into the lower Sepik Area.[89] The "organization" extended from the British border to Hansa Bay on the coastline and included also the immediate hinterland of government, mission and commercial stations.

The native population in Kaiser Wilhelmsland had on the whole reached an accommodation with the government which had imposed itself on them. The native people had in the beginning accepted it as transitory, but then it had consolidated its position by force and inflicted changes upon them which were alien to their society and culture. Yet whereas the punitive expeditions, the time-lag between crime and punishment, the practice of applying group responsibility for offences, and the destruction of property may be repugnant to modern administrators of foreign territories, these were in fact compatible with native customs. Even defeat could be acknowledged, as had been done with regard to tribal enemies. Submission to the new legal and moral order had to be enforced, but when feuding, raiding, warfare, headhunting, and cannibalism were successfully prohibited, the result was a new freedom of movement which was generally appreciated. The young men, in particular, made use of the opportunity to see new places and meet new people by joining the labour force or entering government service. Resentment arose when the government destroyed trade monopolies by handing out trade goods and opening the way to the sea to tribes previously barred, and also when it made the dominance of one group over another impossible. But the loss of one group was the gain of another, and that tribe which benefited from government intervention was more inclined to support the power of a universal authority which the Reich through its personnel on the spot represented. In fact the natives were not slow in utilizing the administration for their own ends; for example, they tried to participate in punitive expeditions to raid their traditional enemies, and abduct women.[90] This lack of traditional unity and of leaders, and the hostility and mistrust among the many tribes, had facilitated the establishment and maintenance of a colonial government even in the face of sporadic resistance. But the continuing unrest in those areas assumed to be pacified served as a reminder to the German population that colonial government might well be transitory, just as the indigenous population of the first point of contact, Finschhafen, had believed it to be.

1. A. Hahl, "Geschichte und Entwicklung von Neuguinea", in A. Haenicke, ed., *Das Buch der deutschen Kolonien* (Leipzig, 1937), pp. 191–92.
2. Sept. 1871–Dec. 1872, June 1876–Nov. 1877, and March 1877. See D. Fischer, *Unter Südseeinsulanern. Das Leben des Forschers Mikloucho Maclay* (Leipzig, 1955).
3. Neuendettelsauer Mission, Rheinische Missionsgesellschaft and Mission vom Göttlichen Wort.
4. All anthropological material is generalized and should be understood as such.
5. H. Zöller, *Deutsch–Neuguinea und meine Ersteigung des Finisterre–Gebirges* (Stuttgart, 1891), pp. 13, 62–63. Later on chiefs were encountered in the northern area. See *Nachrichten über Kaiser–Wilhelmsland und den Bismarck Archipel,* Publ. NGC, Berlin, 14 (1898): 48.
6. M. Krieger, *Neu Guinea* (Berlin, 1899), pp. 191–93.
7. *NKWL* 5 (1889): 37–40.
8. E. Tappenbeck, *Deutsch–Neuguinea* (Berlin, 1901), p. 30.
9. H. Schnee, ed., *DKL* (Leipzig, 1920), 2, p. 158.
10. A. Danckelmann, "Das Schutzgebiet der Neuguinea Gompagnie", in *Deutsche Kolonialausstellung. Deutschland und seine Kolonien im Jahre 1896*, p. 183.
11. *NKWL* 1, no. 4 (1885): 1.
12. H.M. Johnson, *Sociology. A Systematic Introduction*, 3d ed. (London, 1963), p. 313.
13. Those natives who were not employed as contract labourers were called "free natives."
14. "Anweisung betreffend das Verfahren bei dem Grunderwerb der Neu Guinea Kompagnie", *NKWL* 3 (1887): 123–28; "Verordnung des Landeshauptmanns, betreffend die Anwerbung und Ausführung von Eingeborenen des Schutzgebiets der Neu Guinea Compagnie als Arbeiter. Vom 15. August 1888", *NKWL* 4 (1888): 121 ff.; "Verordnung des Landeshauptmanns betreffend die Arbeiter–Depots im Schutzgebiet der Neu Guinea Compagnie. Vom 16. August, 1888", *NKWL* 4 (1888): 140 ff.; "Strafverordnung der Neuguinea–Kompagnie für die Eingeborenen, vom 21. Oktober 1888"; "Verordnung über die Erhaltung der Disziplin unter den farbigen Arbeitern, vom 22. Oktober 1888", *DKB. Amtsblatt für die Schutzgebiete des Deutschen Reiches*, pub. Kolonial–Abteilung des Auswärtigen Amtes, 1 (1890): 177.

15. *NKWL* 7 (1891): 18.
16. St. von Kotze, *Aus Papuas Kulturmorgen. Südsee–Erinnerungen* (Berlin, 1905), p. 67.
17. A. Hahl, *Gouverneursjahre in Neuguinea* (Berlin, 1937), p. 19.
18. *NKWL* published regularly a list of new employees and their previous professions. For the atmosphere among the white population see O. Schellong, *Alte Dokumente aus der Südsee* (Königsberg, 1934), pp. 31 ff, 139ff; see also Kotze, *Aus Papuas Kulturmorgen*, pp. 22 ff.
19. Ibid., p. 76, and Schellong, *Alte Dokumente*, pp. 31 ff., 139 ff.; court files of Bezirksgericht Friedrich Wilhelmshafen, Stephansort, Finschhafen, CAO, AA (Archives Accession) 1963/83 Box 210, Box 214 and Box 215; von Hansemann to Landeshauptmann, 2/7/1896, in RKA 2142.
20. H. Blum, *Neu–Guinea und der Bismarckarchipel, Eine wirtschaftliche Studie* (Berlin, 1900), p. 52.
21. J. Graf Pfeil, *Studien und Beobachtungen aus der Südsee* (Brunswick, 1899), pp. 245–47.
22. In particular, churchmen and Social Democrats in Germany were believed to be more influenced by ideals than economic considerations. See F. Fabri, *Bedarf Deutschland der Kolonien?* (Gotha, 1879); See also Kotze, *Aus Papuas Kulturmorgen,* p. 194. For the economic motive see O. Dempwolff, "Die Erziehung der Papua zu Arbeitern", in G.Meinecke, ed., *Koloniales Jahrbuch*, 11 (1898): 1–14; an appeal for cooperation in preserving the health of coloured labourers, by government medical officers, *Amtsblatt 1* [1909]: 150.
23. *NKWL* 1, no. 2 (1885): 3–8; *NKWL* 1, no. 3 (1885): 2–6 and *NKWL* 1, no. 4 (1885): 3–19.
24. *NKWL* 2 (1886): 9.
25. J. Flierl, *Forty Years in New Guinea*, Memoirs of Senior Missionary J. Flierl, Pub. by the Board of Foreign Missions of the Evangelical Lutheran Synod of Iowa and Other States (1927), p. 114.
26. Ibid., Also Aktennotiz 10/11/1900, in RKA 2988.
27. Zöller, *Deutsch–Neuguinea*, p. 14; Pfeil, *Beobachtungen*, p. 239.
28. Schellong, *Alte Dokumente*, p. 194.
29. O. Mannoni, *Prospero and Caliban. The Psychology of Colonization* (London, 1956), pp. 18–19.
30. E. Helfferich, "Kolonialpolitik", *Dietrich Reimer's Mitteilungen* 6 nos. 2–3 (October, 1913): 64–66.
31. Dempwolff, "Die Erziehung der Papua zu Arbeitern", pp. 9–10.
32. Pfeil, writing mainly about the native population of the Bismarck Archipelago, believed that they would gladly forego all these implements if they could "get rid again of the hated white man". *Beobachtungen*, p. 157. Schellong noticed quick saturation of the market. *Alte Dokumente*, p. 100.
33. Zöller, *Deutsch–Neuguinea,* pp. 12, 296; Schellong, *Alte Dokumente*, pp. 102–3.
34. Rose to Caprivi, 27/7/1891, in RKA 2980.
35. Blum, *Neu–Guinea*, p. 49.
36. Rose to Caprivi, 27/11/1891, Anlage 9/9/1891, in RKA 2980.
37. Ibid.
38. Knappe to Bismarck, 3/9/1886, in RKA 2977. Knappe, German consul in Brisbane, reported, for example, about an expedition on the Sepik. The natives there believed them to be children of the sun and were highly excited. See also expedition reports in *NKWL*.
39. Dempwolff, "Die Erziehung der Papua zu Arbeitern", p. 14; "Denkschrift der Unternehmer des Bismarck Archipels, Sept. 1913", in RKA 2313.

40. *NKWL* 4 (1888): 234.
41. *NKWL* 5 (1889): 34.
42. Rose to Caprivi, 1/7/1890, in RKA 2300; Möllendorff to KA, 29/9/1890, in RKA 2300; Dempwolff, "Die Erziehung der Papua zu Arbeitern."
43. *NKWL* 7 (1891): 83–84.
44. *NKWL* 14 (1898): 2–8.
45. The Colonial Department was part of the Foreign Office. In 1907, a separate Colonial Office (Reichskolonialamt) was created.
46. Rose to Caprivi, 9/11/1892, in RKA 2982.
47. NGC to KA, 5/4/1901, in RKA 2278.
48. KA Aktennotiz, 10/1/1901, in RKA 2988.
49. *Jahresbericht über die Entwickelung der deutschen Schutzgebiete in Afrika und der Südsee im Jahre 1903–4* (Berlin, 1905), stat. pt., Anlage E. 3, p. 341; *Jahresbericht 1904–5*, p. 72; *Die deutschen Schutzgebiete in Afrika und der Südsee im Jahre 1912–13*. Amtliche Jahresberichte, p. 186. By the end of 1902 the NGC had selected 50,000 hectares. NGC to Rose, 24/12/1902, in RKA 2280.
50. NGC to KA, 3/12/1904, in RKA 2308; W. Wendland, *Im Wunderland der Papuas* (Berlin, 1939) p. 120.
51. *Jahresbericht 1899–1900*, p. 202.
52. Stellvertr. Gouverneur to RKA., 7/8/1907, in RKA 2310.
53. Klink to Hahl, 4/8/1910, in RKA 2312.
54. *Jahresbericht 1912–13*, stat. pt. p. 81.
55. CAO, AA (Archives Accession) 1963/83, Box 213, Box 215; NGC to KA, 4/9/1900 in RKA 2307.
56. *Denkschrift [des Pflanzervereins] des Bismarckarchipels über die Arbeiterverhältnisse im Schutzgebiet Deutsch–Neuguinea* (Sept 1913), unbound, located at Hamburger Weltwirtschaftsarchiv.
57. *Jahresbericht 1910–11*, p. 159.
58. Rose to Caprivi, 9/11/1892, in RKA 2982.
59. *Jahresbericht 1909–10*, p. 166.
60. Rose to Caprivi, 9/11/1892, in RKA 2982.
61, *Jahresbericht 1904–5*, p. 70.
62. *Jahresbericht 1899–1900*, p. 185.
63. *Jahresbericht 1908–9*, p. 8
64. *Jahresbericht 1906–7*, p. 4.
65. Hahl to Kommandant SMS *Condor*, 11/10/ 1908, in RKA 2993.
66. *Jahresbericht 1907–8*, p. 6; *Jahresbericht 1909–10*, p. 66.
67. *Jahresbericht 1910–11*, p. 155.
68. *Amtsblatt* 3 (1911): 18.
69. B. von König, "Die Eingeborenen–Besteuerung in unseren Kolonien", in *Verhandlungen des deutschen Kolonial–Kongresses 1910* (Berlin, 1910), pp. 424–25.
70. *Jahresbericht 1908–9*, p. 8.
71. *Jahresbericht 1912–13*, p. 170.
72. Kommandant "Möwe" to Komm. Admiral, 20/5/1897, in RKA 2986. The acting Landeshauptmann complained to the board of directors of the NGC that no war ship had been in the territory for 1½ years. Rüdiger to NGC, 9/6/1895, in RKA 2984.
73. *DKB*, 25 no. 1 (1914): 37.
74. Hahl to RKA., 21/10/1912, in RKA 2995.
75. NGC to KA. 22/12/1891, in RKA 2980.
76. Kommandant "Möwe" to Komm. Admiral, 20/5/1897, in RKA 2986.
77. *Jahresbericht 1902–3*, pp. 94–95.
78. *DKB*, 22, no. 1 (1914): 53–54.

79. Berghausen to stellvertr. Gouverneur, 8/2/1911, in RKA 2994.
80. Hahl to RKA., 27/10/1911, in RKA 2994.
81. Klink to Gouverneur, 8/3/1911, in RKA 2994.
82. Prey, Lagebericht, 14/9/1912, in RKA 2995.
83. R. Neuhauss, *Unsere Kolonie Deutsch–Neuguinea* (Weimar, 1914), pp. 9295.
84. P. Ebert, *Südsee–Erinnerungen* (leipzig, 1924), p. 188.
85. Oswald to RKA., 31/5/1910, Anlage, Bericht Scholz, 20/3/1910, in RKA 2994. 86. Scholz to Hahl, 3/9/1912, in RKA. 295.
87. Kommandant *Condor* to HM the Kaiser, 28/9/1912, in RKA 2995.
88. Hahl to KA, 21/10/1904, in RKA 2991; *Jahresbericht 1912–13*, p. 171.
89. Hahl, *Gouverneursjahre*, pp. 249–50.
90. *DKB* 20, no. 2 (1909): 759; Hahl to RKA., 15/11/1910, in RKA 2994; Full to Hahl, 7/1/1909, in RKA., 2993; Berghausen to Hahl, 8/2/1911, in RKA 2994; Scholz to Hahl, 24/7/1912, in RKA 2995.

# 14

KLAUS-J. BADE

# Colonial Missions and Imperialism: The Background to the Fiasco of the Rhenish Mission in New Guinea

The problem of a "national" colonial mission activity posed itself for the German missionary societies only in the three decades from the mid-1880s until World War I. A critical analysis of the problem of colonial missions can neither be understood under the head of "mission history" nor under that of "colonial history". One is rather forced to analyse the interdependence, consensus and collision of missionary and commercial, as well as political, interests. The task of the first section of this investigation is to show that there already existed in Germany in the middle of the 1880s a definite programme for colonial missions. In the following case-study the reasons for the failure of this programme when put into practice in the German colonial mission in New Guinea will be examined. The subjects are the prehistory and history of the work of the Rhenish Mission in Kaiser Wilhelmsland, the German-occupied part of New Guinea. The significance of the Rhenish Mission and the key position held by its chief official—between mission, colonial enterprise and colonial politics—appear to justify this approach.

## The Rhenish Mission and its Director, Friedrich Fabri

The Rhenish Mission based in Barmen was one of the largest and most important of the German evangelical mission societies. Shortly before the beginning of German colonial expansion this society, which was also represented in the emigrants' mission in North and South America by several auxiliary organizations, had 1,172 members, including overseas personnel as well as the families of missionaries. The mission congregations abroad in Africa, the Dutch East Indies,

Reprinted with permission of the editors of the *Australian Journal of Politics and History* (vol. 21, no. 2, 1975).

and China encompassed the stately figure of approximately 26,000 members, growing to about 230,000 by 1914, and to more than 300,00 by 1920.[1] The Rhenish Mission had not only quite early gathered relevant experience by working in overseas regions under the control of other colonial powers,[2] but was also the first society which *nolens volens*—as a result of the occupation of the mission's sphere of operation in Southwest Africa by the Reich—carried on German colonial mission in the proper sense. That the mission had a particularly national concept of its task is understandable in the light of the fact that at its head from 1857 to 1884 stood a man in whose ideas the three spheres of interest of importance here—missions, colonial economy, and colonial policy—overlapped and dovetailed to a degree which scarcely anyone else represented at that time.

The Rhenish Mission and the personality of its head, Friedrich Fabri (1824–91) are of equal significance.[3] By the end of his almost twenty-five years in office he was becoming the most important proponent of the idea of colonial mission in Germany. In his last decade, which he himself in an understatement described as the "colonial-political episode" of his life,[4] Fabri was far in advance of other expansionists in the missionary camp such as A. Merensky and C.G. Büttner, not only in publicist activity, but also as an agitator and organizer. His pamphlet *Bedarf Deutschland der Kolonien?*[5] published in 1879, made, besides those of Wilhelm Hübbe-Schleiden[6] and Ernst von Weber, a decisive contribution to the opening of an agitated and long-lasting discussion on overseas expansion within the German public. With this publication Fabri broke into the field of journalism advocating expansion. In an equally active and successful way he functioned as an organizer of the German colonial movement. The German Colonial Society named him with certain justification the "father of the German colonial movement".[7] In each of the executive committees of the most important interest groups and propaganda organizations of the German colonial movement his word carried weight: Fabri was confidant of the Centralverein für Handelsgeographie und Förderung deutscher Interessen im Ausland (founded in 1878 and dominated by the export industry), and he was founder and chairman of the powerful Westdeutscher Verein für Colonisation und Export (formed in 1880 and representing the export-orientated interests of industrial and commercial capital in Rhineland and Westphalia). In addition, he was not only vice-president and later member of the board of directors of the Deutscher Kolonialverein (German Colonial Association, founded in Frankfurt in 1882) but also "honorary member" in the executive committee of the parallel organization, Gesellschaft für deutsche Kolonisation (Society for German Colonization, founded by Peters in Berlin in 1884). Later he became a member of the executive committee of the nationwide Deutsche Kolonialgesellschaft (German Colonial Society) which was formed in 1887 as the result of a fusion of the two rival interest groups. Finally, as foundation member of the Allgemeiner Deutscher Verband, the predecessor of the Pan-German League, he was an active participant in the ideological as well as the organizational transformation of the colonial into the pan-German movement. While Fabri, in the five years from 1880 on, was publicly propagating the idea that overseas expansion was a socio-economic question of vital importance to the nation,[8] he was equally indefatigably working behind the scenes to raise capital investment for concrete overseas projects, some of which he had helped to plan.

All this agitation for expansion, the activity at the head of powerful expansionist pressure groups, and discreet endeavours to stimulate interest in investment, gained for Fabri a wide range of confidential contacts to leading bank, industrial and commercial circles such as Adolph von Hansemann, Gustav Mevissen, Eugen Langen and Adolph Woermann, as well as to politicians such as the Free Conservative, Hohenlohe-Langenburg, and the National Liberals, Miquel and Bennigsen, who were themselves active in the organization of expansionist interests. The mission chairman also had good contacts to the Auswärtiges Amt in the person of Heinrich von Kusserow (Geheimer Legationsrat), to the minister of culture and education, Gustav von Gossler, and finally even to Bismarck himself. Fabri's exuberant expansionist propaganda, and the detailed memoranda to the Auswärtiges Amt which urged colonial ambitions either latently or openly, were a nuisance and an embarrassment to the chancellor at the beginning of the 1880s.[9] However, when the Reich adopted an active colonial policy the ideas of the by then retired mission inspector were received by Bismarck with growing interest, particularly because Fabri warned against colonial illusions at a time when "colonial fever" was rife. He had drafted a concrete programme of "colonial tasks"[10] which received much attention in the Auswärtiges Amt[11] and made often penetrating public and confidential commentaries on the practice of German colonial policy. A change in Bismarck's attitude to Fabri was noted to the extent that the chancellor at the end of the 1880s repeatedly ordered Fabri to write critical papers, at times extensive memoranda, on the development of German colonial policy, and finally took up personal contact with him.[12] In this way Fabri, because of his equally marked missionary, economic, and political interests, and his decade-long experience as head of the mission, was virtually predestined to become the spokesman of the colonial mission concept. Moreover, his wide-ranging contacts enabled him to assume the function of mediator between mission societies, the imperial government, and commercial interests.

## The Genesis of the Early Imperialistic Programme of Colonial Mission

Fabri propagated from the end of the 1870s an "energetic and intelligent campaign for a real colonial policy",[13] chiefly because of socio-economic considerations caused by his experience of the "Great Depression" (Rosenberg). But there existed right from the beginning an indirect missionary interest in overseas expansion. And decisive for Fabri were the experiences of his society chiefly in their Southwest African field—a veritable crisis zone. The history of the early Rhenish Mission in Southwest Africa is an illuminating example of the way in which missionary, commercial, and political interests followed upon each other to become intertwined.

The indirect commercial involvement of the Rhenish Mission on the mission field which was opened in the mid-1840s, and the problematic relationship between missionary activity and commerce in their mutual interest, was caused primarily by the initiative of its chief inspector. At first the missionaries in Southwest Africa carried on a limited barter with the natives in order to cover their own needs in foodstuff. However, after 1863 a regular missionary commerce developed. Christian tradesmen sent to the main station, Otjimbingue, were soon making a profitable business with their products for which the native population had a demand. The most flourishing trade in a crisis area which was repeatedly the scene of warlike disturbances was that in small arms. By the end of the 1860s the complaints in Barmen about the "misuse" of Christian tradesmen were increasing.[14] The separation of both the organization and the personnel engaged in the mission on one side, and commerce on the other, was being considered. Fabri then succeeded in getting through his plan—suggested years before—based on the model of the Basel Mission which set up a special missionary commercial company.[15] When the Wuppertaler Aktien-Gesellschaft für Handel in den Arbeitsgebieten der Rheinischen Mission, succinctly and aptly named Missionary Trading Company (Missions-Handelsgesellschaft, MHG), was formed in 1869, the mission officially disassociated itself from any more responsibility for the business practice of the trading company. At the same time it avoided the risks of investment, which were an intolerable drain on mission funds, while remaining a participant in the profits.[16] In contrast to the Basel Mission which itself had acquired a significant number of shares in its associated commercial enterprise,[17] the Rhenish Mission contributed no investment capital. Nevertheless this apparent non-material participation was for the MHG as valuable as cash in hand. This was because the contribution of the Rhenish Mission had, as the later head of the mission, Kriele, emphasized, "immediately provided for the company a considerable circle of clients and had prepared and was extending the base upon which the company could expand". That it was here less a separation than a well-thought-out division of missionary and commercial interests was evident in the fact that not only did the mission share in the profits, but also its director was a permanent member of the board of directors of the MHG.[18]

In Fabri's eyes the interests of the mission and trading company were seriously hampered and endangered by the friction and conflicts of rival tribes. This strengthened him in the conviction that "peace, law and order"[19] on the mission field were indispensable preconditions for the success of the mission work, as well as for the progress of the trade for which the mission had paved the way and provided the clients. And such guarantee appeared to him to be only possible in the form of the effective political control of a European power over Southwest Africa. As early as 1868–69 he had tried in vain to interest Prussia, or the North German Confederation, and then Britain, in establishing a presence in Southwest Africa, even if only in the form of a naval base.[20] The British moves at Walfish Bay in 1876 did not bring the expected guarantees of peace, but rather hampered the influence of the mission and the interests of the MHG.[21] In the spring of 1880 a new conflict loomed. In the event of war the fate of the entire missionary endeavour, hitherto in which almost three million marks in contribution had been invested, as well as the existence of the MHG, could be at stake. The MHG, which had been progressing well up to the mid-1870s was working by the end of the decade with a total capital of over seven hundred thousand marks. Of this, approximately half a million marks were invested in the Southwest African mission field.[22] Several serious miscalculations had at the end of that period forced the MHG to the brink of ruin. There was, however, still a chance of rescuing the severely afflicted firm. But a war would have administered the death blow to the tottering enterprise. Again, Fabri had as little success in Capetown with his renewed requests for protection as he had in Berlin or London.[23] The expected war broke out, severely damaged the mission, and sealed the fate of the MHG.

The coincidence of an unexpectedly strong response to his colonial brochure in the years 1879–80 with these serious disappointments finally caused Fabri to promote for the remainder of his life the organization of expansionist interests, and to place himself at the head of this activity. The events in Southwest Africa had appeared to produce the proof of his conviction that without guarantees of political security overseas, neither mission nor commerce could flourish. These ideas precipitated in the first five years of the 1880s that programme of colonial mission which Fabri outlined in a paper, "The Importance of Ordered Conditions for the Development of Missions",[24] of March 1884 to the Bremen Mission Conference. In the following year he expanded the paper by dealing with critical economic aspects in his much discussed series of articles on Germany's "colonial tasks".[25] These led to a remarkable shift in balance: already in 1860 in a promemoria to the Dutch colonial minister on the conditions of the Rhenish Mission in Borneo, Fabri had cautiously hinted "that missions in heathen lands would always promote the aims of the government".[26] In 1879 he emphasized considerably more strongly in his first colonial publication the "cultural significance" of missions and their "usefulness for commercial enterprises or colonial annexations coming afterwards".[27] In 1884 Fabri was speaking tentatively of the interdependence of missionary, commercial and political interests, but by 1885 quite openly. The programme of colonial mission which he presented in 1884–85, and strove to realize within the limits of his possibilities through semi-official channels, centred on the following basic ideas: missions by virtue of their "cultural ground work" overseas paved the way for commerce, which followed on their tracks. Then the "pioneering service" performed by the missionaries and traders legitimized colonial occupation by the nation to which both belonged. The colonial government, for its part, brought about "ordered political conditions" which were needed by mission and commerce for greater and more permanent development.

Since the end of the 1870s there had been much propaganda for the idea of export via colonial expansion, which to Fabri meant the promotion of exports through extending overseas markets for manufactured goods. This required that the indigenous population in the less-developed overseas territories (from the point of view of markets) would "develop more sophisticated needs" through consumption stimuli.[28] On the other hand, however, he already urged an intensification of imports of raw material from overseas, primarily in the interest of the German consumer goods industry. But systematic exploitation of overseas resources would not be achieved by merely "robbing" the riches of nature, but rather by means of an organized plantation production. The success of this, Fabri thought, would be determined by an adequate application of the three factors of "intelligence, capital and labour."[29] Because of the considerable and not wholly calculable risks involved in pioneer investment overseas, Fabri understood by "capital" exclusively that from large industrial and bank interests, which would add its support to the mobile commercial capital overseas. By the blanket concept "intelligence", he understood detailed project studies, expert know-how on the spot, and good management. Both capital and "intelligence" had to be provided by Europeans. The indigenous were to provide the wage-labour on the plantations.[30] Here Fabri's argument reached an impasse, because he contemptuously summed up the indigenous collectively as more or less slack, careless, and lethargic.[31] The way out of this dilemma was indicated by the postulate under the heading of "national educational work"—that is the elevation of the subject peoples to a higher cultural level. All this meant nothing more than the demand for "educating the natives to work" in the service of obtaining German import requirements in raw materials. Fabri himself made no secret of the fact that the actual motive, in spite of all the veiled humanitarian arguments, was economic: "We require in the first place economic advantages from our overseas possessions", he soberly affirmed. "What is first necessary for this is the education of the natives to work".[32] This "education to work" for the raw material needs of German industry was partly to be carried out with the aid of that consumption stimulation which also was to increase export market possibilities. Obviously the "large scale cultivation of valuable products" would not be possible if the indigenous population "was not first stimulated by increased needs to cultivate them".[33] On the other hand, Fabri also considered from the beginning the possibility and necessity of extra-economic compulsion. He was realistic enough not to deceive himself that the "subjugated peoples" in the occupied areas would not show much interest in a "cultural education" to contract labour on the plantations of the "ruling nation". So, concluded Fabri, "the education of the negro (as of the South Seas Islanders and New Guineans) to work" would not function without "slight" compulsion, but of course "a compulsion humanely supervised and introduced with good sense".[34]

Further, it was not only the export trade for which the mission was to prepare. Fabri was also able to identify an important preliminary economic function of colonial missions for the creation of conditions and bases for the organized production of raw material. As early as 1879 he had indicated "mission enterprises with a practical-pedagogic character, i.e., also providing training for work which would above all be valuable here: secondly, and together with them, capital and staff for plantations and larger trading enterprises".[35] In 1885 Fabri made this aspect the core of his suggestions for an "education of the natives to work". Three groups representing the European *Kulturvolk* had to fulfil this "colonial task" overseas: planters and traders should carry out the external education, controlled as far as possible by imperial officials. The missionaries were to assume suitable mediating functions, but chiefly to guarantee the ready acceptance and inner stabilization of the imposed educative process. Fabri knew that by making the missionaries responsible for the inner "restructuring" of the indigenous peoples he had given them the most difficult and, in the final analysis, decisive function in the "cultural education" in the interests of the colonial economy. This was because he was convinced that without systematic application of influence on "the mentality, intelligence, and moral and religious conceptions of uncivilized, still barbaric peoples" the training for work would be "only temporarily effective and could not achieve sufficient success". For the fulfilment of this "task" only missionaries seemed suitable because they, in contrast to employees of trading firms and respresentatives of the administration, by virtue of their method of work, gained a close relationship of trust with the indigenous, and besides, remained as a rule considerably longer, if not for life, in the country.[36]

Fabri considered this "education to work" a long-term programme, the realisation of which he wanted kept within humane limits, because overhasty action and pressure would only provoke resistance. He believed that in German protectorates those "atrocities of the worst kind" in which colonial history abounded could be avoided. The "economic wisdom" of the colonial entrepreneur would prevent such "foolish stupidity". "As strong as the desire often may have been to consider other peoples, particularly those on a lower level, as objects of exploitation, the consequences have always turned to the disadvantage of the initiator. Everyone knows that it is not very clever to saw through the branch on which one is sitting in order to collect its fruit". In this economic lesson of colonial history lay, in Fabri's view, "a providential compulsion which of itself reined and moderated the lust for profit".[37]

It is not surprising then, that such utterances from the mouth of a well-known man experienced in mission affairs, and for decades a mission leader, aroused considerable attention in commercial and political circles to which, of course, Fabri's ideas were directly addressed. The response to Fabri's feelers is part of the background history of the Rhenish Mission in New Guinea.

## The Background History of the Rhenish New Guinea Mission

Even Fabri's first public suggestion that missions had a "usefulness" for commercial and political overseas interests did not go unnoticed. At the very latest, in June 1880, von Kusserow had put out confidential feelers to determine whether and to what extent the Rhenish Mission could be co-opted in the early New Guinea plans of his brother-in-law, Hansemann. Hansemann tried to find out discreetly from Kusserow whether Fabri "would be able to provide the missionaries who were considered to be absolutely necessary for the acquisition of the island". As Fabri noted with pleasure, the director of one of the leading German banks who, since the previous year had been increasingly urging overseas expansion, was quickly convinced "that German missionary work was a virtually indispensable factor for the cultural national enterprise in question". Fabri replied to Hansemann's question via Kusserow with a "delighted yes", and proposed, in view of his society's deficit, that the financing of the New Guinea mission, which was requested for the most profane motives, be done via the planned company. While Kusserow was trying to co-opt Fabri's mission society for Hansemann's New Guinea plans, the head of the Barmen mission was trying to interest the director of the Diskonto-Gesellschaft in a Southwest African mining enterprise. In this way he wanted to secure a business partner for the shaken MHG, who would help to maintain peace and order in the land.[38] There can only be conjecture concerning Hansemann's reaction, since there are no relevant records. That he was not prepared to proceed without political guarantees from the Auswärtiges Amt for his investment capital is obvious from his New Guinea plans of the same year. Bismarck's attitude to Fabri's memoranda showed that the imperial government was not yet prepared to involve itself in Southwest Africa.[39] The Diskonto-Gesellschaft held back, and Fabri's hope for a business connection between the MHG and a mining company was in vain.

Likewise in 1880 Hansemann had to postpone his New Guinea plans because Kusserow was unable to persuade the chancellor not to file all suggestions "ad acto Samoa" even if they contained only a latent colonial expansionist character.[40] Four years later Kusserow, as champion of the Diskonto-Gesellschaft, achieved a breakthrough in the Auswärtiges Amt. His brother-in-law and Bismarck's banker, Bleichröder, came to an arrangement with a New Guinea consortium which, a little later, Adolph Woermann as representative of Hanseatic capital also joined, as well as other significant representatives of banking capital, and exponents of industrial capital. The charter which Kusserow had drafted was granted in March 188 5 and published on 17 May 1885.[41] Immediately, all the South Seas lobbies involved with the Diskonto-Gesellschaft displayed renewed active interest in missions. And because these groups were not concerned with a "protectorate" to be administered by a chartered company, they were able to avail themselves of the mediation of the Auswärtiges Amt.

It was not only the Neuguinea Compagnie (NGC) which showed a lively interest in Fabri's programme of "education for work" with the help of the missions. The Deutsch-Ostafrikanische Gesellschaft (DOAG), at that time still directed by Carl Peters, offered a prize for the best answer to the very clear question "How best to train the negro for plantation work?" The judges who formed a three-man panel with the task of evaluating the manuscripts of forty authors were Professor Dr Schweinfurth, Gerhard Rohlf and Friedrich Fabri.[42] There was even commercial and political interest displayed for mission work in the Cameroons, which had not yet been occupied by a German mission. Already in September 1884, when he spoke in Hamburg for the first time with Woermann about the recent proclamation of a protectorate over the Cameroons, the shipping entrepreneur, merchant, and owner of West African plantations expressed himself, "emphatically: without German missions we will not make progress in the cultivation of those coastal lands". Woermann, who did not even regard it as necessary to pretend religious motives in discussions with Fabri, and indeed on the contrary emphasized that he was "personally non-church" requested Fabri "urgently to work for the start of a mission in the Cameroons". From West Africa the senior reporter of the *Kölnische Zeitung*, Hugo Zöller, wrote: "what we need most in our possessions here is a German mission". The new governor of the Cameroons, Baron Julius Soden, personally sought out Fabri for this very purpose, and urged him once more in a letter before departing not to forget his request.[43] Fabri was more than prepared to carry out these wishes which had also been expressed by others interested. On 2 June 1885, after a series of confidential preliminary talks, he approached the Prussian minister for education and religion, as a responsible official, with a memorandum intended for Bismarck. In this he elaborated mainly economic arguments for the establishment of German colonial missions and now assumed on behalf of the missions total responsibility for the "education task":

> Only missionaries ... are capable of effecting a gradual regeneration of a barbarian people, to educate them to work—the basis of all cultural development. Without this education of the natives to work the richest possessions in tropical areas are fairly worthless ... Only by such means do uncultivated countries gradually achieve a rising export as well as import capacity.[44]

Fabri informed Bismarck that he had already approached Inspector Zahn of the North German Mission Society, the official secretary of the Bremen Continental Mission Conference, to hold an extraordinary conference of the German mission societies in the autumn of 1885 at which "the attitude of the mission to the German colonial movement" was to be clarified in principle.[45] The chancellor then informed himself in detail about the nature of the Bremen institution which Fabri had founded in 1866, and about the programme of the projected extraordinary conference. Ludwig Raschdau, as representative of the Auswärtiges Amt, was dispatched to Bremen. All German mission societies invited sent delegates to the conference in Bremen, which was held 27–29 October in the house of the West African merchant, Fritz Vietor, who had contact with the Bremen North German Missionary Society and the Rhenish Mission.[46] Fabri had succeeded in bringing together in Bremen under his chairmanship the most outstanding representatives of the evangelical German missions, including the two well-known mission experts, Warneck and Grundemann.[47] This extraordinary Bremen Mission Conference marked an important turning point in the history of the German evangelical missions in the last third of the nineteenth century.

The change was essentially a result of the increased value placed on mission work after Germany's entry into active colonial politics. In 1879 Fabri had held up the "cultural pioneering" function of missions for overseas trade and colonial expansion, not least with the intention of overcoming the widespread lack of public interest in mission activity, and to advertise the mission under the national banner.[48] By this Fabri had gone a step too far in the eyes of important missionary circles. The press discussion which was unleashed by his first colonial article had provoked the most influential journal in evangelical mission circles, G. Warneck's *Allgemeine Missions-*

*Zeitschrift*, to raise a critical voice.[49] But Fabri's expectation—that the desired beginning of German overseas politics would earn the mission long-denied recognition, even among those groups of the public who were indifferent to its religious task—was confirmed.[50] This also overcame the reservations of sceptics such as Warneck towards any coupling of mission and colonial policy. In 1884 his *Allgemeine Missions-Zeitschrift* celebrated Fabri's "highly significant essay", even made indirect propaganda for the German Colonial Association, and felt justified in recommending it "even to Christian minded people" because of the "supreme importance of the colonial question for the future of our nation".[51] In 1886 Warneck had to admit that only the "great colonial movement" had made the "missions acceptable". He believed now he could see that "the German colonial movement was a divine command to intensify our missionary efforts". He knew as well as Fabri that "public opinion" had not developed such a surprising interest in mission work from religious motives, but rather because it was expected that the "civilizing influence of missions would advance colonial political plans". At base public opinion tolerated the mission's "pietistic activity" only in so far as it was prepared "to co-operate with the aims of its new friends". Yet even Warneck now called in full awareness upon the "old mission guard" to work in the service of "their new friends". "The German colonial movement even though its motives and goals are not those of the Kingdom of Heaven, is a great divine missionary cause, and if God in heaven provides an opportunity then his servants on earth have to take up the work".[52] Such allegedly divinely willed "opportunities" were given to the mission societies at the extraordinary Bremen Mission Conference in October 1885.

In a heated debate on the problem of "education to work", the Basel delegation, in particular, protested against Fabri's allowance for the "necessity of a certain compulsion to work", and warned against entrusting such education to the questionable responsibility of private interests. The conference declared itself against an intermingling of mission and colonial policy because of differences in motives and goals and in the interest of both sides. Nevertheless, they were prepared to "offer their voluntary service to the colonial power in terms of their expert knowledge and moral influence, for the protection they received". In their declaration, the "sacred duty"

(Warneck) to preach the gospel was linked with their "national duty" (Kriele) to co-operate with the colonial power.[53] The Bremen delegates whose societies were mostly working in foreign colonial territories were actually acting in their own interests when they diplomatically recalled then that the missions had an "international character".[54] On the final day of deliberations Raschdau read a letter from the German consul in the Bismarck Archipelago in which a request was made for the "rapid entry of the mission into New Guinea" and urged the Rhenish Mission to begin immediately there. The Bremen delegates likewise voted for the Barmen Society which had already in 1880 been confidentially approached in this matter, and which was already working in the neighbouring islands of the Dutch East Indies.[55]

As late as 11 August 1885 the general assembly of the Rhenish Mission was still unable to reach an agreement on the pros and cons of mission work in the new colonial territories. The decision was postponed with the intention of waiting on a "sign from heaven". The request of the Auswärtiges Amt communicated by Raschdau, and the declaration of the Bremen delegates, were taken to be such. Already on 9 November the Barmen deputation agreed with his view that there was a "special task for the Rhenish Mission" in the Diskonto-Gesellschaft sphere of interest. The next general meeting on 12 May 1886 agreed unanimously with the views of the Barmen deputation which Fabri had energetically supported.[56] So the "sense of colonial duty" replaced the international character of missions which had been emphasized hardly six months previously in Bremen. For now, as the evangelical German mission societies proclaimed in an appeal for funds in March 1886, signed by Warneck, "the work of spreading the Christian faith has become for us a matter of patriotic honour and national duty as well".[57]

## The Mission and its "New Friends"

With its promise to missionize in New Guinea there began a chain of disappointments for the Rhenish Mission which remained unbroken until World War I. At the start there were tedious negotiations with the NGC; the interest of the NGC in the mission had remarkably declined since the Bremen conference, and the company displayed a marked reserve. The

NGC apparently observed, with as much suspicion as the Hanseatic West Africa Syndicate with the DOAG, the penetrating first criticism of practices of exploitation overseas, which had started with the gradual decline of enthusiasm for the establishment of colonies and the beginning of sobering assessment of possibilities. This early protest movement had two directions of attack: against the trade in alcoholic spirits, and against the methods of labour recruitment in the new German protectorates which were mostly known only by rumour. In both cases the participation of evangelical mission circles in this first stirring of opposition aroused considerable scepticism among commercial interests towards the originally much desired mission work.

The North German, the Basel, and then the Rhenish Mission protested in memoranda to Bismarck against the increasing import of spirits into the protectorates. The Bremen Mission Conference directed a petition to the chancellor, and a public declaration to our entire German nation".[58] The alleged "new friends" of the mission, who saw their profits threatened, struck back immediately: on 9 November 1885 Adolph Woermann, the largest German exporter of spirits, called in his capacity as chairman of the Hanseatic West Africa Syndicate a meeting of the Association of German West African Merchants, a group which had been formed as a result of Bismarck's urging. Woermann's interest in evangelical mission work had noticeably declined. Scarcely more than a week after the Bremen Mission Conference, where his request for setting up a Cameroon mission had been considered, Woermann suddenly reported to the syndicate that Roman Catholic missionaries in various African colonies had proved themselves "more useful cultural elements than the Protestant Germans" who had ventured to tell him how to run his business. Those members of the syndicate present unanimously voted for a motion of protest against the Bremen petition.[59] Governor von Soden, who had likewise approached Fabri about a Cameroon mission, now denounced to Bismarck the "missionary and pharisaic logic".[60] The chancellor, who was pressing for a rapid beginning of mission work because he was interested in having the English Baptist Mission in the Cameroons replaced by Germans, saw himself forced to mediate and to re-establish a semblance of harmony between the confronting groups.[61]

Of course the NGC was not involved in this criticism of

overseas trade in spirits because in the German South Seas territories the import of spirits had been prohibited since 1885.[62] Nevertheless, the "movement against this trade in spirits" (Fabri), predominantly from mission circles, was a highly unpleasant object lesson. It demonstrated what a negative effect public criticism of the exploitative practices in the German protectorates could have, particularly if it was coming from mission societies which had recently gained much public attention.

The NGC had sufficient cause to be on guard because the second object of the early criticism—the method of recruiting labour—could become unpleasant for them. The Congo conference had stimulated a debate on emancipation; this caused a public discussion of "education to work", which problem then was placed on the agenda of the "General German Congress for Promoting Overseas Interests".[63] In the light of this the criticisms of the opposition were most inopportune. The main point of this criticism was directed against the indisputable fact that in this discussion on education the dividing line between "education to work" and forced labour was fluid. This caused a Frankfurt women's organization to send a petition with thousands of signatures to the Reichstag in the winter of 1885 requesting "energetic intervention against the evil efforts to introduce or continue slavery in German East Africa".[64] Fabri, who felt himself personally reproached by the "few thousand women and girls", hastened to the aid of the attacked DOAG. He sought to play down these serious allegations against the DOAG by pointing to the supposedly unmitigated and continuing cruelty of the East African slave trade. Fabri even constructed, with the aid of this sinister image of the alleged "misery of the slave trade" in East Africa,[65] an ideology of colonial justification in favour of the DOAG: "The actual situation is thus quite the reverse from that imagined by the Frankfurt ladies. The German acquisitions in East Africa confront our nation and her representatives with a great humanitarian task, the suppression of the slave trade".[66]

The NGC, as much as the DOAG, was exposed to this criticism of the methods of compelling natives to work which were still being discussed, and which were to some extent being put into practice. The NGC, having been disillusioned in its expectation of profit through land speculation,[67] and trying to regain its investment capital, now set out to get plantation production going as quickly and profitably as possible. For the immediate future this could not be done by employing native help, but only foreign labour. Such imported labour, in contrast to the indigenous, could not just down tools and go back to their villages if they were badly treated. If they wanted to see their homeland again in the foreseeable future, which was mostly possible only on European-owned ships, they were bound to fulfil their labour contract. The latter could, in practice, result in a type of legalised or disguised forced labour. For a long time labourers had even been forcibly recruited, in fact rounded up. The supervision of labour recruitment in the German South Seas by the consulate in Apia was admittedly directed against the long-established practice of "kidnapping" labourers, but did not change the situation of the imported labourers.[68]

The news, that already in 1886 the importation of foreign workers to New Guinea had begun, reached the public with unexpected rapidity, and led almost immediately to an extremely embarrassing situation for the NGC. At the end of April 1886 the Reichstag deputy, Charles Grad (Protest party for Alsace), armed with knowledge "from a well informed source", ventured to make the shocking assertion at the general meeting of the Colonial Society "that slavery was being practised on the German plantations of New Guinea". By this he meant "the employment of labourers against their will, that is, under compulsion". Hammacher, shareholder of the NGC and well known to Fabri, indignantly felt that he had to repudiate this most emphatically. The National Liberal mine owner and colonial financier tried as hard as he could to calm down the stir which Grad's provocative remark had caused, and angrily asserted he knew nothing of "this nonsense", but was nevertheless unable to deny that the "actual situation often takes on the form of involuntary labour".[69] Fabri, who at this early stage still maintained good faith in the NGC, tried to help Hammacher out of his embarrassment, but got himself more and more involved in revealing contradictions.[70] He employed even here, as a diverting manoeuvre, that anti-slavery argument which early became a favourite instrument in the arsenal of colonial apologetic defence weapons. However, the all too obvious attempt to gloss over Grad's criticism and Hammacher's tactical mistakes, with his only remotely objective contribution to the discussion, did not pay off. With delicate irony Grad picked up Fabri's irrelevant explanations about the difference between slavery and slave trade in Africa, and even "gladly" allowed that the NGC itself was perhaps not practising "slavery", but unimpressed, repeated that in any case it was happening in its territory, and backed this up with the astonishing information: "it has been confirmed to me by the well-known explorer, Baron von Miclucho-Maclay, that on German plantations in New Guinea labourers are employed by force".[71] The name of the Russian explorer-traveller, who was regarded in colonial circles as anti-German and had since 1871 often visited New Guinea and protested against the German occupation in the mid-1880s, left Hammacher and Fabri with nothing to say.[72] Grad's additional information that Miclucho-Maclay was preparing "his reports" in Petersburg about these abuses, and had already informed the British government in dispatches, had an alarming effect. The long-standing vice-president of the Colonial Association, Miquel, a confidant of Fabri and close to Hansemann's Diskonto-Gesellschaft, recognised how negative this discussion was becoming for the NGC, and intervened abruptly. The "question of the permissible limit of forced labour", Miquel declared—and conceded therewith that he too did not consider forced labour overseas non-permissible—was not under debate here. Conveniently the standing orders of the agenda brought the embarrassing discussion to a sudden end.[73]

The NGC had been warned. The spectacular incident showed that critical observers in the territory of the chartered company could be a considerable risk for its reputation with the public. Apart from the recognition that "education to work" was disputed in mission circles,[74] there was the fact that the chief exponent of this programme in the mission camp, Friedrich Fabri, was no longer head of the Rhenish Mission after 1884. However, the NGC was all the more concerned to get the Rhenish Mission committed to co-operation in "education to work", and, moreover, to make suitable arrangements which would neutralise the mission's potential as a disturbing factor. Both these things delayed by nearly two years the beginning of mission work originally requested for 1885. The NGC had, for the time being, refused the entry of the missionaries (who had been prepared to go from the start), the excuse being that the company wanted to see that the agents in New Guinea had carried out certain "instructions concerning their reception".[75] Only after they themselves had a "firm footing in the country" should the mission follow.[76] Thus right from the beginning Fabri's programme was reversed. After tedious negotiations for a proper contract between commercial interests and the mission society,[77] the NGC finally presented its conditions on 25 November 1887.[78] The mission society was neither free to choose its field of work nor to make decisions on the position or transfer of stations, but had to submit its plans to the Landeshauptmann for approval. Only in their function as "spiritual and religious educators" were the missionaries responsible to the mission administration; for the rest they were obliged to bow to the laws and regulations of the local authorities in the same way as other settlers. The expenses for the maintenance of the missionaries and their stations had to be borne by the Barmen people themselves. They were allowed only a few material concessions.[79] The NGC officials were instructed to do all in their power to assist the work of the missionaries. In return the missionaries were obliged "without reward to support the administration as interpreters and mediators in disputes etc." and, in particular, to endeavour "to instruct the natives in all manner of useful knowledge and arts and to accustom them to regular work". The Rhenish Mission knew only too well what kind of "knowledge and arts" were intended. They accepted the unmistakable requirement "that our missionaries should accustom the natives to work and instruct them in agriculture" with certain "reservations", particularly because the Basel Mission in the Cameroons had from the very beginning strictly refused to have anything to do with the controversial "education of the negro to plantation work".[81] However, such reservations did not prevent the Barmen deputation from accepting the NGC conditions on 29 November 1887, only four days after their arrival.[82]

## The Rhenish Mission in New Guinea

The expectations which the NGC had placed in the attempt to build up a productive system of exploitation with the help of the mission could not be fulfilled in New Guinea. Of the three basic requirements for success which Fabri had named, intelligence, capital, and labour, the NGC had only one: capital. Its hasty procedure, which was the result of an impatient interest in profits, was witness of a serious lack of just that "economic wisdom" which in Fabri's judgement was the prerequisite for a profitable organization of the colonial economy—a lack which was accentuated by the company's inexperience in handling the natives. However, in his assessment of the category "work" Fabri, who considered the New Guineans to be lazy and lethargic, erred greatly. He knew New Guinea just as little as the NGC which—contrariwise, and just as falsely—expected that considerable numbers of natives would even voluntarily report for work. In fact they showed little interest in plantation work, and instead cultivated their own gardens, the products of which were adequate to meet most of their needs. The expectation of creating a wide colonial market with the help of consumer stimuli proved to be just as illusory as the associated hope of being able to entice the indigenous to regular work in plantation producation by "accustoming them to more sophisticated needs". The opposite was the case. As soon as they had satisfied their needs in interesting imported articles, these objects depreciated in value in the barter trade. Only a small number of indigenous—in comparison to the quantity of imported foreign labour—could be recruited for work, and then mostly through the mediation of missionaries.[83] Apart from increasing the number of foreign labourers who came from the Bismarck Archipelago, and then from Java, Sumatra, and Singapore, a situation regarded by the mission sceptically since they were mostly non-Christian,[84] there remained only the avenue of forced labour.[85] The third long-term possibility, namely the auxiliary function of the mission in "education to work", was unintentionally blocked by the NGC itself. The mistrust of the natives which was aroused and strengthened by the measures of the administration was an extraordinary hindrance to mission work.

Only at the beginning of 1887 were the first pair of Rhenish missionaries in New Guinea allowed to take up their duties. At first they concentrated their attention on the neighbourhood of the NGC station at Hatzfeldhafen on Franklin Bay.[86] This area was comparatively densely populated, especially towards the west. On one stretch within fifteen hours march along the coast there were about twenty-five villages spread out. The missionaries noticed the most friendly welcome they received came from the remoter villages, whereas in the immediate neighbourhood of Hatzfeldhafen there already existed a tense relationship between the indigenous people and Europeans which the missionaries, too, came to experience.[87] They had just received permission from the NGC to set up their first station in the neighbourhood of Hatzfeldhafen near the large village of Tugumor when colonial atrocities also began in this area. The NGC had been trying to create for itself the respect it considered necessary by inflicting punishments, which were in the eyes of the indigenous as draconic as humiliating, for trivial crimes—mostly petty "thefts"—committed in ignorance of the European legal norms.[88] Outraged at the imprisonment of one of their tribe, the incensed natives attacked a plantation, killed a Malayan worker, and wounded several others. As reprisal and deterrent a punitive expedition was carried out against the "insurgent villages", whereby the armed strength of the European Kulturvolk was ostentatiously demonstrated. "Such an act, said the gentlemen of Hatzfeldhafen, could not be allowed to remain unrevenged", reported the Rhenish mission inspector, von Rohden, bitterly in 1888,

> and so they sallied forth in war-like procession, shot into the houses, set fire to the village, then a second and third, in the conviction that thereby they had taught the black people respect, and that no one would ever again venture an attack. But these wild people are not so easily intimidated. Their hostility towards the whites increased all the more. There was no more chance of peaceful intercourse; even the missionaries were barred entry to the villages.[89]

And so it remained. The Rhenish Mission had to withdraw, and began to set up a few stations in the small area around Nobonob, renamed Hansemannberg in Astrolabe Bay which extends to the north of Dampier Island.[90] The initially more friendly behaviour of the natives here towards the whites was, ironically, due to the lasting influence of Miclucho-Maclay, who had lived among them for a few years, gained their trust, and had left them as a friend.[91] However, the NGC and the Astrolabe Company took care that that trust which he had painstakingly built up was soon transformed into mistrust.[92]

In the same year as Rohden complained about the NGC, Fabri, too, raised his voice in criticism of the company. However, in contrast to Rohden, he did not attack the mistakes of the NGC *coram publico*, but discreetly made his criticism in a memorandum to Gossler which was passed on to Bismarck. As the most serious "mistake" of the NGC, he criticised the attempt to impose abruptly an administrative system orientated to European norms on a population which was split up into innumerable tribes with different languages and customs and, in contrast to the population of the African protectorate, which was not used to communicate with "whites". "What a missionary and what a trader actually want, will after a period of mistrust be grasped by the native", wrote Fabri.

> What these German officials want who have suddenly appeared in his country must be incomprehensible to him. He can only gain the impression, "they want to rule over us", and naturally he resists this if not compelled by force. Also, up to the present there is no German in the country who has been able really to make himself understood to even a small section of the population. It is no wonder that the New Guinean, frightened by a few signs and incomprehensible words of a perhaps highly well-intentioned official who lacks all understanding for the mentality, customs and usages of the people, takes up an attitude of resistance, and, as has happened, opposes and attacks the settlement. Who is in this case at fault?

The NGC had not yet learned to wait. Economic gains in New Guinea could only be expected to come in decades. The period had to be employed to advance the population gradually to the point "where they can understand and bear a European system of administration". An attempt to accelerate this process in the hope of quick profits must result in force replacing peaceful communication. "This oversight of NGC will, as we must fear, result in much sacrifice in money, time and human life", warned Fabri with accurate foresight. The NGC had to entrust the task of leading the indigenous population "quite gradually into the paths of civilization", not to inexperienced officials but rather to the "pioneer work of the missions".[93]

The NGC was, of course, unwilling to wait for the long-term success of missionary pioneer work. The relationship between the company and the natives, who at first had welcomed its employees jubilantly because they believed them to be superhuman beings, as they had thought of Miclucho-Maclay before,[94] deteriorated rapidly. The results were friction and bloody disputes which further intensified the mutual distrust. The mission manoeuvred between both sides. Understandably the tension had immediate repercussions on their work, especially because in 1892 the NGC transferred its administrative headquarters from the "fever-hole", Finschhafen, to Friedrich-

Wilhelmshafen on Astrolabe Bay in the immediate neighbourhood of the Rhenish Mission station.[95] The mission, which more and more frequently had to act as "mediator in disputes", was able only with great effort and for short periods to win the trust of the natives. It was not surprising that the mission was having little effect on the objects of its work in the light of that virtually classical situation of the colonial mission: a minority of the same "ruling nation" was preaching peace and neighbourly love while the majority was resorting to the means of repression in order to create the ordered political conditions which Fabri, too, had requested in the interest of the mission. A report of the Rhenish Mission in 1903, five years after the Reich had assumed direct responsibility in place of the NGC, commented, "Our missionaries there are acting as advocates of the natives against many an unscrupulous European. How often did they avoid bloodbaths by their mediation, how often were they able to resist injustice and partial treatment". In New Guinea the "preservation of the people has to be credited mainly to the missions".[96]

The subjects of "disputes" were mainly land and legal questions. The indigenous felt themselves not only intolerably restricted by the NGC in their rights to use the land, but also limited in their other free rights. As a result they regarded the imposition of foreign legal norms as a burdensome negative catalogue of crippling prohibitions, the purpose and legitimacy of which they were neither able to understand nor to accept. In addition there was friction between the imported labour and the indigenous.[97] And in their efforts of mediation in such disputes, even if they were sincerely trying to act as "advocates of the natives", the missionaries were still functioning as agents of the colonial power, a fact of which they were less aware than the natives themselves, who soon came to regard the missionaries as "the whites" and behaved accordingly.

In 1893 smallpox was introduced via the coolies whom the NGC had brought in.[98] The result was a devastating epidemic, which severely decimated the number of painstakingly and expensively recruited NGC labourers. For this reason the NGC planned the installation of a quarantine station on Oertzen Island, situated about one hour's journey from Siar Island. This island belonged to the inhabitants of Siar where the Rhenish Mission maintained a station. The use of Oertzen Island was a question of basic existence for the Siar people because of the fruit trees which they had planted there, the surrounding oyster beds, and the fishing. They pleaded strenuously with missionary Bergmann to help them to get their island back, which had been suddenly occupied by the NGC. His mediation attempts failed. The NGC would not give in. As Bergmann saw that the Siar people were prepared to fight to the death for their island, he requested the administration to interrupt work on the already-begun construction for one day so that he could gather his belongings without becoming involved in the fight which was undoubtedly coming. Even this was rejected. The over-zealous Landeshauptmann wanted to have the quarantine station ready for the arrival of the next postal steamer. His counter-proposal was characteristic of that ignorant intransigence and shortsightedness which contributed essentially to the fiasco of the NGC: he offered the missionary ten police troopers for his personal protection, and advised him to remain on Siar because his relationship with the natives would "only become stronger" when the "catastrophe" had passed. In reply to the missionary's objection that the reprisals of the NGC against the Siar people after their expected attack would possibly render further mission work impossible, the Landeshauptmann had to agree that then "nothing more could be done on Siar" because "everything would be shot and destroyed". He had nothing to offer the missionary but police protection and early information before the bombardment. The same evening the missionary announced his departure to the natives of Siar, who were determined to resist to the limit. Then suddenly they gave up their intended but quite hopeless resistance, and explained this helplessly impotent turn in events with the following significant words: "No, we do not wish to fight. You should stay with us because if you go away then it is not only we who will fall but also the other islands in the neighbourhood". This explanation could have provided the missionary with some food for thought. But he did not understand it.[99] Missionary Bergmann saw, just as little as the Barmen deputation and Warneck's *Allgemeine Missions-Zeitschrift*,[100] that the Siar people were not seeking to hold him back there as proclaimer of the stubbornly resisted gospel nor as a trusted friend, but more as the final salvation from the feared and powerful NGC. The Siar people kept their missionary, the NGC their island.

The supposed relationship of trust between the indigenous

population and the Rhenish missionary was soon to be revealed for what it was. Already in May 1891 two missionaries, together with a NGC official and fifteen indigenous helpers, were murdered as they were making a renewed attempt to set up a mission station in the neighbourhood of Hatzfeldhafen. In reply, the NGC in exercising "stern justice" executed eighteen New Guineans.[111] In July 1904, one decade after the assumed proof of trust of the Siar inhabitants, the natives conspired to begin a struggle of resistance. An uprising of the Siar, Ragetta and Bilibili people was nipped in the bud only because the carefully-planned operation was betrayed by one of their number at the last minute when they were actually preparing the attack. The missionaries received the news in dismayed shock that the long-prepared and detailed "murder plan" had been worked out in the main by those villages with which they had been in constant touch for fifteen years and was directed "against all whites", including the missionaries.[102] A siege situation was declared in this area where two of the four stations of the Rhenish Mission (Siar and Ragetta) were situated, and the mission station on Siar closed down. Those natives who were suspected of having been the ringleaders were taken prisoner, and nine of them were court-martialled and shot. Deportation of the Siar and Ragetta inhabitants to the Bismarck Archipelago, which was being considered, became superfluous because the entire adult population fled in fear of reprisals. The natives of Bilibili, who had likewise fled, and whom the administration had at first planned to declare "free game" (*vogelfrei*), could see from the enormous cloud of smoke over their island in Astrolabe Bay that their village had been burnt out. When the Siar and Ragetta natives were finally requested to return from their hide-outs they were threatened that if they ever again started something "against the whites", then it would be "their end". The Barmen people fulfilled the request of the Siar tribe to reopen the mission station because the natives did not want to return without a missionary. But the mission was now, of course, wary of again making a hasty interpretation of this as a proof of trust and a sign of their influence. On the contrary, the missionaries regarded the natives with scepticism and mistrust.[103]

The year 1912, in which the Barmen Society celebrated the twenty-fifth anniversary of the New Guinea Mission, saw the uncovering of a new conspiracy of the natives which was again directed against the life of all white people, including the missionaries. The results of this for mission work on Siar and Ragetta were devastating. The inhabitants of the six most committed islands and villages, including Siar and Ragetta, were deported. By this measure, as was recorded with some bitterness in Barmen, "the mission work was robbed of its object".[104] Until the end of the German colonial rule in New Guinea the inhabitants of the villages lying within the operation fields of both these mission stations were not allowed to return home. The Australians, after they had occupied the country in 1914, later recalled the expellees.[105]

As well as the extraordinary difficulties which had to be met by the missionaries that arose from the tensions, friction, and bloody conflict between the colonial administration, imported labour, and indigenous, there was the dangerous climate which contributed decisively to making the "dark island" of New Guinea into the "Death Land" of the Rhenish Mission.[106] A few missionaries narrowly escaped death by leaving the area, sometimes only after a short sojourn, with severely broken health. Those who remained in the country were often unable to work for months on end because of severe illnesses. For this reason the Rhenish New Guinea Mission suffered from the lack of continuity of personnel, a factor so essential in missionary work. This was all the more marked because the indigenous here were by no means accustomed to contact with Europeans, and were so fragmented in small language groups that at times even neighbouring villages could not understand each other.[107]

Finally, the natives quickly saw the connection between the "Jehova talk"[108] and the foreign norms of social behaviour forced upon them by the administration, and therefore held all the more stubbornly to their "heathen beliefs and superstitions". This provided the only spiritual support against the new socio-cultural norms which to them were an incomprehensible and therefore oppressive burden of prohibitions and threats of punishment.[109] Most of the adult Siar people who spurned the sermons of the missionaries strengthened each other in the feeling "that it made them sick to hear always about Jesus". Those who came to services but who strictly rejected baptism explained their attitude, which was incomprehensible in the eyes of the missionary, with the revealing statement, "We do not want to let ourselves be bound by God".[110] So, motivated by sober practical considerations they showed in the form of their church-going and school attendance just sufficient co-operation as was necessary in their view to keep the missionary on the spot. Although he, too, was considered a burdensome interloper, he was esteemed as a mediator between them and the colonial regime.[111] However, whereas these indigenous people by refusing baptism were seeking quite consciously to offer a passive resistance to the colonial regime, others did in fact accept baptism precisely because they misunderstood the punitive expeditions as "divine judgment" on their disobedience towards the missionaries,[112] Both these reactions had, as one missionary recognised, their basis in the wide-spread belief of the indigenous people "that our sermons and the government regulations were the same and therefore whenever they failed to follow what we said they could expect difficulties or punishment from the authorities in power".[113] Both interest and disinterest in the "God talk" from the "heavenly village"[114] were often equally profane, and therefore in the eyes of the missionary falsely motivated.

All of this cut away the ground from beneath Fabri's programme of colonial mission. At first missionary work made no progress whatever, then later only tentatively, and achieved even in the third decade scarcely more than a depressing alternation of short-term successes and serious set-backs. As "statistics" for 1896, mission Inspector Kriele could only note: "Three (at the moment only two) stations, no Christians; but ten graves in eight years".[115] The move to accustom natives to Christianity through long years of communication by putting them in boarding schools from their early youth to detach them from the influence of their village cults had just as little durable success as the attempt to make a contribution to "education to work" through missionary plantations, the profits of which were to finance these training homes.[116] After sixteen years of effort they succeeded in baptizing only one permanently employed house boy.[117] When in the year 1906 after nineteen years of work on the Ragetta station there was a larger baptismal celebration with twenty candidates, the Rhenish Mission had buried the same number of mission personnel—ten missionaries, five missionary wives and five missionary children.[118] Even the small but dearly purchased successes were only of short duration: in 1906 there were four stations of the Rhenish Mission, where in all twenty-four natives were baptized and fifty-one catechumens were enrolled, but in the next year on Siar and Ragetta alone, twenty-seven baptized had to be expelled from the "congregation", who then in 1912, in place of the Christmas festival, demonstratively celebrated their traditional secret rites.[119] Only with the end of German colonial rule did the Rhenish Mission achieve the greater successes which it had long striven for in vain. At the beginning of World War I it was able to count, after twenty-seven years of sacrifical work, just ninety-six, in part highly uncertain, parish members in New Guinea. At the end of the war there were in its area 600 baptized New Guineans.[120] But this success, too, had its reason, as the missionaries suspected, partially in the above-mentioned, quite profane motivation of the natives, who quickly realized that the end of German colonial rule had not brought them their longed-for freedom, but rather only a change in colonial masters.[121]

There was not much time left for the Rhenish Mission to secure and increase these surprising successes, because they took place against the background of World War I, in the wake of which first Germany lost New Guinea, and then the Rhenish Mission its mission field. In 1920 the Rhenish Mission encompassed in New Guinea 1,264 members.[122]In 1921 the Barmen Society received notification from the Australian government that it had to hand over its mission territory to the United Evangelical Lutheran Church of Australia. Attempts at mediation by Australian Lutherans were in vain. The Australian government remained firm.[123]

The national *leitmotiv* of the colonial missionary concept turned against its very advocates: in November 1911 the Rhenish Mission had invited the president of the German Colonial Society, Duke Johann Albrecht of Mecklenburg, to the Barmen mission house. In this speech of welcome Inspector Kriele emphasized the role of missions as "promoters of colonial interests" and called to mind the significance of the deceased mission head, Fabri, for the beginning of German colonial propaganda, and pleaded for an intensification of the "team work between missions and colonial policy". By way of reply the president of the DKG admonished those present members of the mission seminary to grasp missionary work in specific nationalistic terms: "I am confident that the younger generation will never forget that they are Germans, German men and German Christians, and so the obligation rests upon them to function as German missionaries in the awareness that God the Master has placed them there as Germans".[124] Those evangelical societies active in the South Seas—in the first instance the Rhenish Mission—besought the chancellor seven years later to insist on the return of the German South Seas territories at the coming peace negotiations. Their fear "that an abandonment of German territorial claims in the South Seas might threaten and endanger the future of our missionary work", was only the consequence of their concept of colonial missions.[125] In vain did the Barmen Society protest in 1921 against the decision of the Australian government. Its late appeal to the idea of the "supra-national character of missions"[126] must have sounded a little less than convincing. The concept of colonial mission had finally lost for its champions in New Guinea the object of their work.

1. *BRM*,41 (1884): p. 24; *JbRM*,55 (1884): p. 53; 85 (1914): p. 177; 91 (1920): p. 83 cf. L. V. Rohden, *Geschichte der Rheinischen Missions–Gesellschaft* (Barmen, 1888), pp. 399–404; E. Kriele, *Geschichte der Rheinischen Mission* (Barmen, 1928), pp. 142 ff., 272ff.
2. cf. *BRM*, 44 (1887): pp. 228–36.
3. See my dissertation now published as *Friedrich Fabri und der Imperialismus in der Bismarckzeit* (Zürich, Freiburg i Br., 1975). From an analysis of the socio–economic motivation behind the organization and propaganda of expansionist interests this work offers a contribution to the critical discussion of the expansionist policy of early German imperialism which has been re–opened by H.U. Wehler, *Bismarck und der Imperialismus* (Cologne, Berlin, 1969).
4. Fabri, *Wie weiterßirchenpolitische Betrachtungen zum Ende des Kulturkampfes* (Gotha, 1887), p. 4.
5. Fabri, *Bedarf Deutschland der Kolonien? Eine politisch–ökonomische Betrachtung*, 3d.ed. (Gotha, 1884).
6. I am working on a critical study of this important and hitherto neglected publicist of German expansion.
7. *DKZ* NF 4 (1891): p. 143.
8. Fabri, *Kolonien*, p. 78.
9. Aktennotiz, 13 May 1880, RKA. 2098. p. 10; 23 May 1884, RKA. 1896; p. 32.
10. Fabri, "Koloniale Aufgaben", *Kölnische Zeitung*, 13–16 July 1885. I am quoting from the expanded version, *DKZ* 2 (1885): pp. 536–51.
11. RKA 6893, p. 107.
12. I am preparing an edition of these memoranda of Fabri to Bismarck, together with the accompanying correspondence.
13. Fabri, *Kolonien*, p. 26.
14. Fabri to Stanley, September 1868, ARM CB(Copierbuch)F, p.1; Rohden, *Geschichte der Rheinischen Missions–Gesellschaft*, p. 235.cf. J. Spiecker, *Die Rheinische Mission im Hereroland* (Barmen, 1907), pp. 3–20; H. Driessler, *Die Rheinische Mission in Südwestafrika* (Gütersloh, 1932), pp. 3–53; H. Vedder, *Das alte Südwestafrika* (Berlin, 1934), pp. 219, 228 ff.;J.E.

Esterhuyse, *South West Africa* (Cape Town, 1968), pp. 8 ff.; W.R. Schmidt, *Mission, Kirche und Reich Gottes bei F. Fabri* (Stuttgart, 1965) p. 44.

15. ARM *QS* [*Quartalschreiben*] 33, April 1869. p. 3; *PB* (*Protokollbuch der Deputation*) 1861–72, p. 295. cf. Rohden, *Geschichte der Rheinischen Missions–Gesellschaft*, p. 96, pp. 372 ff; on the Basler Missions–Handels–Gesellschaft AG, founded in 1859 see: G.A. Wanner, *Die Basler Handels–Gesellschaft AG 12859–12959* (Basel, 1959).
16. ARM *QS* 33,p. 3; *BRM* 27 (1870); pp. 324 ff., 327. cf. Kriele, *Geschichte der Rheinischen Mission* p. 225; H. Loth, *Die christliche Mission in Südwestafrika* (Berlin, 1963), pp. 31 ff.
17. W. Schlatter, *Geschichte der Basler Mission 128125–129125*, vol. 1 (Basel, 1916), pp. 389 ff.
18. Kriele, *Geschichte der Rheinischen Mission*, p. 225.
19. ARM *QS* 33, p. 4.
20. Fabri to Stanley, September 1868, ARM CB F, pp. 1–5; to Wilhelm I, September 1868, ibid., pp. 6 f; to Bundeskanzleramt, September 1868, ibid., pp. 7 ff; to Abeken, 3 November 1869, ibid., pp. 61 ff; to Bernstorff, 9 December 1869. ARM M. Fabri (file letters to and from Dr. Fabri). pp. 20 ff. cf. Vedder, *Das alte Südwestafrika*, pp. 462, 466 ff; Driessler, *Die Rheinische Mission in Südwestafrika*, p. 126; H. Drechsler, *Südwestafrika unter deutscher Kolonialherrschaft* (Berlin, 1966), p. 25.
21. Fabri to AA, 3 June 1880, ARM CB G, p. 347.
22. Fabri to AA, 14 October 1880, ibid., pp. 389 ff.; 28 August 1881, ARM CB H p. 51.
23. The most important of Fabri's memoranda are in RKA 2098; copies in ARM CB G and CB H. cf. Fabri, "Englands Lage in Südafrika", *Kölnische Zeitung* 25–28 January 1881; Loth, *Die christliche Mission in Südwestafrika*, pp. 140 ff; Drechsler, *Südwestafrika unter deutscher Kolonialherrschaft*, pp. 27 ff; S. Neill, *Colonialism and Christian Missions* (London, 1966), pp. 390 ff.
24. *AMZ* 11 (1884): 314 ff.
25. See footnote 10.
26. Promemoria Fabri, November 1860. ARM CB E, quoted by Th. Sundermeier, *Mission, Bekenntnis und Kirche* (Wuppertal, 1962), p. 58.
27. Fabri, *Kolonien*, p.95.
28. Fabri, *Koloniale Aufgaben*, p. 544.
29. Ibid., pp. 538, 540, cf. Fabri, *Fünf Jahre deutscher Kolonial–Politik, Rück– und Ausblick* (Gotha, 1889), p. 12.
30. Fabri, *Koloniale Aufgaben*, pp. 539 ff., 551.
31. Fabri, *Kolonien*, p. 37.
32. Fabri, *Koloniale Aufgaben*, pp. 541 ff.
33. Fabri, *Kolonien,* p. 94.
34. Fabri, *Koloniale Aufgaben*, pp. 541 ff.
35. Fabri, *Kolonien*, p. 94.
36. Fabri, *Koloniale Aufgaben*, pp. 542,545–48. cf. Neill, *Colonialism and Christian Missions,* p. 392.
37. Fabri, *Koloniale Aufgaben*, p. 542; *DKZ* 3 (1886); p. 316.
38. Fabri to Kusserow, 30 June 1880, ARM CB G, pp. 363–66.
39. Fabri to Pilgram, 18 July 1882, ARM M Fabri, p. 80.
40. On Hansemann's early New Guinea plans see Wehler, *Bismarck und der Imperialismus*, pp. 223 ff.
41. Ibid., pp. 396 ff.
42. *Kolonial–Politische Correspondenz.* Organ der Gesellschaft für deutsche Kolonisation und der Deutsch–Ostafrikanischen Gesellschaft 1 (1885), no. 9, p. 1; *AMZ* 13 (1886): p. 6.
43. Fabri to Gossler. 2 June 1885, RKA 6893. pp. 86 ff.
44. Ibid.; cf. Aktennotiz 15 June 1885, RKA 6893, p. 85.

45. See footnote 43.
46. RKA. 6893, pp. 110 f., 113, 118–20, 125, 132 f., 141, 144 f; *BRM* 42 (1885): p. 356; *AMZ* 12 (1885): pp. 345 ff. The Neuendettelsau Mission was not yet represented in Bremen. On the history of the Neuendettelsau New Guinea mission which had a completely different development from the Barmen Society's, see the detailed books by G. Pilhofer, *Die Geschichte der Neuendettelsauer Mission in Neuguinea*, 3 vols. (Neuendettelsau, 1961–63).
47. *AMZ* 12 (1885): pp. 545 f. 550; Kriele, *Geschichte der Rheinischen Mission*, p. 238. The Basel Mission was regarded in mission circles as a German society and was therefore also represented in Bremen, RKA 6893, pp. 118–20; *AMZ* 12 (1885): p. 556.
48. Fabri, *Kolonien*, pp. 94 ff.
49. *AMZ* 6 (1879): p. 237.
50. See footnote 43. cf. *BRM* 44 (1887): pp. 232 ff.
51. *AMZ* 11 (1884): pp. 182, 344.
52. Ibid., 13 (1886): pp. 3 ff., 37 f., 213 ff.
53. Ibid., 12 (1885): pp. 552, 561; Kriele, *Geschichte der Rheinischen Mission*, p. 300.
54. Ibid., 12 (1885): p. 551; *BRM* 42 (1885): p. 361.
55. *BRM* 43 (1886): pp. 100 ff. cf. Rohden, *Geschichte der Rheinischen Missions–Gesellschaft*, p. 509.
56. *BRM* 42 (1885): p. 360; 43 (1886): pp. 101 f., 164, 167; *JbRM* 57 (1886): p. 6, *AMZ* 23 (1896): p. 358; *MB* 62 (1887): p. 8; Kriele, *Geschichte der Rheinischen Mission*, p. 301.
57. *BRM* 43 (1886): pp. 103–105.
58. *AMZ* 12 (1885): pp. 290–99; *DKZ* 2 (1885): p. 543; *BRM* pp. 357–59. cf. *AMZ* 12 (1885): pp. 547–50; *MB* 60 (1885): pp. 46, 95.
59. Report about the meeting of the syndicate for West Africa to Bismarck, 9 November 1885, RKA 6894, pp. 44–47, . Besides Gaiser from Hamburg, only the Bremen West African trader Vietor was missing. He did not trade in spirits and later disassociated himself from the resolution. Ibid., p. 72.
60. Soden to Bismarck, 16 July 1886. RKA 6830, p. 30.
61. A.A. (Ausfertigung. Berchem) to Basel Mission, 12 June 1886, printed in Schlatter, *Geschichte der Basler Mission 1815–1915*, 3 (Basel, 1916): p. 219.
62. *DKZ* 2 (1885): p. 410; 3 (1886): p. 310; *BRM* 44 (1887):p. 235; *KM*, 18 (1886): p. 36.
63. *ADK* (Report of the negotiations of the Allgemeiner Deutscher Kongress zur Förderung überseeischer Interessen, Berlin. 13–16 September 1886), pp.9–12, 45 ff. In the resolution from the section for German missions presented to the congress and unanimously accepted it said, "It is to be expected from the German missions in German overseas territories that their activity is a national one as well . . .as one including education to work". Ibid., p. 87.
64. Fabri, *Deutsch–Ostafrika. Eine colonialpolitische Skizze* (Cologne, 1886), p. 29.
65. In reality the export structure in the later German East Africa had changed some considerable time before German occupation from traffic in human beings to trade in goods. See: H. Loth, *Griff nach Ostafrika* (Berlin, 1968), p. 39: H. Loth, *Kolonialismus and "Humanitätsintervention"* (Berlin, 1966). p. 74 c.f. P. E. Schramm, *Deutschland und Übersee* (Brunswick, 1950), pp. 324 f. Schamm relies still on the apologetic Wissmann literature.
66. Fabri, *Ostafrika*, p. 29.

67. S.G. Firth, "The New Guinea Company, 1885–99: A Case of Unprofitable Imperialiam", *Historical Studies* 15, no. 59 (October 1972) c.f. P. Biskup, "Foreign Coloured Labour in German New Guinea: A Study in Economic Development", *JPH* 5 (1970): 87 ff.
68. In an attempt to recruit workers on the Solomon Islands the NGC in 1886 received from a chief the following laconic reply: "Suppose you catch him he will come". O. Schellong. *Alte Dokumente aus der Südsee* (Königsberg, 1934), p. 90.
69. *DKZ* 3 (1886): 313 ff.
70. Fabri, *Koloniale Aufgaben*, p. 550.
71. *DKZ* 3 (886): 314 ff.
72. *Deutsches Kolonial–Lexikon*, 2 (Berlin, 1920), pp. 555 ff.
73. *DKZ* 3 (1886): 316; H. Herzfeld, *Johannes von Miquel*, 2 (Detmold, 1938), p. 45.
74. *AMZ* 12 (1885): 561 ff. 14 (1887): 46; *ADK* pp. 51 ff.
75. Rohden, *Geschichte der Rheinischen Missions–Gesellschaft*, p. 510.
76. Hansemann to Neuendettelsau Mission, 18 January 1886, printed in Pilhofer, *Die Geschichte der Neuendettelsauer Mission in Neuguinea*, 1, pp. 58 ff. cf. *BRM* 43 (1886): 101; 57 (1886): 6; *KM* 18 (1886): 21, 25 ff.
77. *BRM* 43 (1886): 101 f. 165, 305; 44 (1887): 10 f, 163 f, 259; 57 (1886): 4 ff.; *AMZ* 14 (1887): 47; *MB* 62 (1887): 8.
78. *BRM* 44 (1887): 10–12; *AMZ* 14 (1887): 85 ff.
79. The missionaries paid reduced fares on ships and reduced prices for goods from the stores of the NGC. Land for the establishment of mission stations was made available free of charge. B. Schulze, "Der Diskonto–Ring und die deutsche Expansion 1871–1890" (phil. diss., Leipzig, 1965), p. 114.
80. *BRM* 44 (1887): 164. 235.
81. Schlatter, *Geschichte der Basler Mission 1815–1915*. 3. p. 221.
82. *BRM* 44 (1887): 11.
83. Firth "The New Guinea Company, 1885–1899". pp. 6 f., 11 f., 14 c.f. *BRM* 53 (1896): 55,336: 67 (1910): 133 *JbRM* 75 (1904): *68*; *AMZ* 23 (1896): 307; Schellong, *Alte Dokumente aus der Südsee*, pp. 89 ff. 103.
84. *AMZ* 23 (1896): 306.
85. *BRM* 61 (1904): 422; 67 (1910): 268; *JbRM* 74 (1903): 60; 76 (1905): 83.
86. Rohden, *Geschichte der Rheinischen Missions–Gesellschaft*, pp. 510 ff.
87. *BRM* 44 (1887): 357 ff.
88. If the culprit could not be caught, then the NGC transformed the punishment for a crime against whites or coloured workers automatically into a collective one. The regulation on punishment of the NGC foresaw for this case expressively "reprisal by damaging the property of the settlement where the act was commited". Schulze, "Der Diskonto–Ring", p. 115.
89. *BRM* 44 (1887): 359 f.; 47 (1890): 133 f.; *JbRM* 58 (1889): 57; *AMZ* 16 (1889): 81; 23 (1896): 304, 408; *KM* 19 (1887): 91; Rohden, *Geschichte der Rheinischen Missions–Gesellschaft* pp. 512 ff.; Schellong, *Alte Dokumente aus der Südsee*, pp. 151 ff.
90. A. Bonn, *Ein Jahrhundert Rheinische Mission* (Barmen, 1928), p. 89. The mission territory of the Barmen mission remained limited to the villages and islands of Astrolabe Bay. In 1887 the first station was founded in Bogadjim, in 1889 another followed on Siar, then in 1896–97 the station at Bongu. The fourth station was founded in 1890 on Dampier Island and had to be abandoned in 1896; it was re-opened only in 1912. In 1902 Ragetta was founded as an auxiliary of Siar and in 1906 a station was set up on Nobonob. *JbRM* 58 (1887): 45; 61 (1890); 57; 77 (1906): 91

ff.; *BRM* 46 (1889): 239 ff 54 (1897): 104; 63 (1906): 93; 69 (1912): 138; 75 (1918): 55 ff.; *AMZ* 30 (1903): 19.
91. *BRM* 45 (1888): 269; *JbRM* 59 (1888): 49; *AMZ* 23 (1896): 408; P. Lawrence, *Road Belong Cargo*, (Melbourne, 1964), pp. 35, 63 ff.; F. Steinbauer, "Die Cargo–Kulte" (theol. diss., Erlangen, 1971), pp. 118 ff.
92. The NGC set up its station of Stephansort in the immediate neighbourhood of the mission station of Bogadjim. *JbRM* 59 (1888): 49 ff.; *BRM* 47 (1890): 134; 75 (1918): 123.
93. Memorandum Fabri, August 1888, RKA 6924, pp. 7–9. c.f. the very restrained publicly expressed attitude: Fabri, *Kolonialpolitik*, pp. 9 ff.
94. Firth, "The New Guinea Company, 1885–1899", p. 3.
95. *AMZ* 18 (1891): 530; 22 (1895): 545; 23 (1896): 305.
96. *75 Jahre Rheinische Missionsarbeit 1828–1903* (Barmen, 1903), p. 195.
97. *BRM* 44 (1887): 197; 47 (1890): 134; 61 (1904): 424, 426; 62 (1905); 111; 75 (1918): 123; *JbRM* 59 (1888): 49 ff.; *AMZ* 21 (1894): 548; 32 (1896): 358.
98. *BRM* 50 (1893): 339, 341; *ARM* 21 (1894): 231.
99. *BRM* 50 (1893): 341–43.
100. *BRM* 50 (1893): 208; *JbRM* 62 (1891): 61 *AMZ* 21 (1894): 231. 548.
101. *JbRM* 62 (1891): 59; *AMZ* 18 (1891): 529; 23 (1896): 41 ff; *MB* 66 (1891): 83 ff.
102. *BRM* 61 (1904): 418 ff.; *JbRM* 75 (1904): 65 ff.; *AMZ* 35 (1908); 34 ff.; Steinbauer. "Die Cargo–Kulte", pp. 122 ff.
103. *BRM* 61 (1804): 421 ff.; 62 (1905): 9 ff.; 111, 1 *JbRM* 75 (1904): 66 ff.; 76 (1905): 82.
104. *BRM* 69 (1912): 262 ff.; 70 (1913): 25; *MB* 88 (1913): 10.
105. *BRM* 75 (1918): 73.
106. *MB* 61 (1886): 11; *AMZ* 23 (1896): 77.
107. *BRM* 45 (1888): 269; 46 (1889): 172; 49 (1892): 133; 64 (1907): 115; *JbRM* 59 (1888): 48 ff.; 63 (1892): 70 ff.; *AMZ* 28 (1902) 7 ff.; *MB* 78 (1903): 2. On the three stations of the Rhenish Mission there were three different languages to be mastered. *AMZ* 21 (1894): 548.
108. *BRM* 63 (1906): 217.
109. Ibid., pp. 94, 115.
110. *BRM* 62 (1905): 278; 63 (1906): 94, 115.
111. Ibid.
112. *BRM* 70 (1913): 26, 135.
113. *BRM* 63 (1906): 96.
114. Ibid., pp. 94, 126.
115. *AMZ* 23 (1896): 77.
116. *BRM* 49 (1892): 113 ff.; 53 (1896): 336: 63 (1921): 110. *AMZ* 23 (1896): 366; 35 (1908): 29: Bonn, *Ein Jahrhundert Rheinische Mission,* pp. 92 ff.
117. *JbRM* 74 (1903): 59; *BRM* 60 (1903): 143.
118. *BRM* 63 (1906): 181; *AMZ* 33 (1906): 489; *MB* 81 (1906): 67 ff.
119. *BRM* 68 (1911): 244, 246: 69 (1912): 107 ff.; 137 c.f. Bonn, *Ein Jahrhundert Rheinische Mission*, pp. 92, 93 ff. The numbers of members of the Rhenish Mission congregation in New Guinea were: 94 (1909); 107 (1910), 83 (1911), 81 (1911), 81 (1912) and 94 (1913). *JbRM* 80 (1909): 154; 81 (1910): 156; 82 (1911): 160; 83 (1912): 168; 84 (1913): c.f. Lawrence, *Road Belong Cargo*, pp. 52 f.
120. *JbRM* 85 (1914): 76; 89 (1918): 72; Bonn, *Ein Jahrhundert Rheinische Mission*, p. 98.
121. See particularly the reports on the behaviour of the Siar and Ragetta people who returned at the beginning of 1915: *BRM* 72 (1915): 106, 179, 27; 73 (1916): 30 ff., 185; 75 (1918): p. 126.
122. *JbRM* 91 (1920): 83.

123. *BRM* 77 (1920): 13 ff; 758 (1921): 165 ff.; *JbRM* 91 (1921): 43; Kriele, *Geschichte der Rheinischen Mission*, pp. 345 ff.; Pilhofer, *Die Geschichte der Neuendettelsauer Mission in Neuguinea.* 2, pp. 25 ff.
124. *BRM* 68 (1911): 15–17.
125. *BRM* 75 (1918): 46–48.
126. *BRM* 78 (1921): 181.

# PART 4

# Archival and Bibliographical Sources

15

# A Guide to Archival Sources Relating to Germany in the Pacific and Far East, 1870-1914

PAUL M. KENNEDY

The following guide to the whereabouts and contents of archival holdings relating to the German presence in the Pacific and Far East in the period 1870 to 1914 has been compiled as an aid to future scholars who wish to research in these fields. For reasons of economy, I have concentrated upon original documentary materials—governmental records, private correspondence, missionary and commercial sources—and have not ventured to list those libraries and institutes which possess collections of published works and newspapers upon the themes in question. I have also omitted to provide sections upon the archives of the individual German states, such as those in Dresden, Karlsruhe, Munich and Stuttgart, since the details they possess of overseas affairs for this period are usually of a second-hand nature, having been communicated to them by the imperial government in Berlin for the purposes of information and, occasionally, consultation. The exceptions made to this rule are the archives of the Hansa cities of Hamburg and Bremen, because of their early consular representation in the Pacific and Far East and their continued and growing interest in those regions after the founding of the second Reich; and the archives (at Merseburg) of the Prussian government itself, not only because of its own very noticeable activity in the Far East in the 1860s, but also because of its special constitutional position inside Germany after 1871. On the other hand, I have not confined this guide to strictly German sources, believing that much valuable information upon German activities in the Pacific and Far East can be found in the correspondence of the governments, individuals and institutions of other nations.

In compiling this guide, I have endeavoured to check the accuracy of all the facts contained below, and to give as comprehensive a description as possible in the space allowed. Any mistakes or major omissions which may be noticed by the reader will be gratefully received. It should be pointed out here that access requirements often greatly differ, depending upon the country and archive concerned; not all have the space for researchers of the Public Record Office in London or the National Archives in Washington, nor do all possess the attitude of those depositories that access to the country's records is to be regarded more as a right than as a privilege. The listing of the following sources, and more particularly of those papers in private hands, in no way implies that they are all completely open for research. Inquiries must be made at the addresses concerned and, with regard to the German archives at least, it is advisable to apply in advance for a place.

Outline of countries covered

1. German Democratic Republic
   - (a) Potsdam
   - (b) Merseburg
2. Federal Republic of Germany
   - (a) Bonn
   - (b) Koblenz
   - (c) Freiburg
   - (d) Hamburg
   - (e) Bremen
   - (f) Missionary records
   - (g) Company records
   - (h) Papers in private hands
3. West Berlin
4. United Kingdom
   - (a) London
   - (b) Outside London
5. United States of America
   - (a) Washington
   - (b) Outside Washington
6. France
7. Italy

8. Australia
   - (a) Canberra
   - (b) Sydney
   - (c) Brisbane
   - (d) Melbourne

9. New Zealand
   - (a) Wellington
   - (b) Auckland

10. New Guinea

11. Samoa

12. Fiji

13. Former German Island Territories

14. Hawaii

15. Japan

*1. German Democratic Republic*

a Potsdam
Deutsches Zentralarchiv I, *15 Potsdam, Berlinerstrasse 98–101.*

The most important sources for the study of Germany in the Pacific and Far East lie in the Central Archives, Division I, in Potsdam. A published guide, edited under the collective leadership of H. Lötzke and H. S. Brather, *Uebersicht über die Bestände des Deutschen Zentralarchivs Potsdam* (Berlin, 1957), gives a general survey of its contents, but more detailed information can be obtained only from the specific catalogues in the archives. The records of the Colonial Division of the Foreign Office, which in 1907 became a separate Colonial Office, contain an enormous load of some 920 volumes for the Pacific region itself, collected and catalogued in *Kolonial-Findbuch* no. 3 (German Pacific Colonies). These are most conveniently subdivided along numerous thematic lines so that the researcher may go straight to those files relating to his particular subject, be it native affairs, international relations, economic developments, etc. A typescript copy of this catalogue can be consulted at the university libraries of Oxford (Rhodes House) and Papua and New Guinea. In addition, another list of Colonial Office records in Potsdam relating to the Pacific area has been prepared and published: M. C. Jacobs, "German Colonial Archives: New Guinea and Samoa in the Deutsches Zentralarchiv", *Journal of Pacific History* (cited hereafter as *JPH*) 6 (1971): 151–61; this also mentions many volumes filed in separate divisions and therefore outside those of *Findbuch* no.3, but it does not include some of the major political sub-divisions within it, e.g., Reichskolonialamt volume nos. 3011–67, *Allgemeine Verhältnisse auf den Samoa-Inseln*, September 1885–October 1917 (56 volumes). These gaps will be made up by a further list, to be published in a future issue of *JPH*. Through the intercession of Professor Jacobs, the Potsdam archives authorities have permitted the National Library of Australia, Canberra, and the Mitchell Library, Sydney, to obtain microfilm copies of all these files relating to Australasia; the microfilms may be consulted in those libraries, but a reproduction is not permitted. Certain files, chiefly relating to New Guinea, have also been obtained on microfilm by Dr Firth for the university library of Papua and New Guinea, while some volumes relating to missionary activities in the Pacific will soon be deposited in Rhodes House.

The Deutsches Zentralarchiv possesses further the records of the former German embassy in China, a total of around 4400 volumes covering the years 1862–1945, much of it relating to economic matters.[1] Details of this useful series may be obtained from the two special catalogues in the archives itself, which also contains certain records from former German consulates in the Far East and Pacific.

A third, and very important section for the study of German activities in those regions consists of the records of the Commercial (*Handels-Politische*) Section of the Foreign Office—around 22,000 volumes covering the years before 1920.[2] (About 1,000 volumes from this section fell into Western hands in 1945 and have found their way to the Bundesarchiv, Koblenz, but by far the greater part is in Potsdam.) They are arranged under certain broad themes, such as *Handel* and *Schiffahrt*, and then further sub-divided into various regional and topical files. For such questions as the negotiation of commercial treaties, overseas investments, the subvention of steamship lines and the trade reports of German consular representatives abroad, these records are invaluable. Volumes upon the economic development of Kiautschou and the laying of German cables in the Pacific and East Indies can be found in this section.

Further ministries of the imperial German government have material in their records relating to the Pacific and Far East; none is as important or extensive as those mentioned above but many may be useful for specific purposes and are thus included here. They are: Reichskanzlei, Reichsamt des Innern, Reichsschatzamt (important for tariff questions), and Reichs-Postamt, each with special archival catalogues, although a general ides of their holdings may once again be obtained from the published *Uebersicht ...*

Finally, this depository contains the private papers of certain firms, including a few files of the Jaluit-Gesellschaft zu Hamburg and of the Neuguinea Compagnie; and the private papers of certain officials who played a role in German overseas policy in this period, the most important of which are those of Heinrich von Kusserow, first councillor for colonial affairs in the Foreign Office, 1874–84, and Paul Kayser and Gerhard von Buchka, directors of the Colonial Division of the Foreign Office for the years 1890–96 and 1898–1900 respectively. Another "non-official" source lies in the records of German pressure groups and organizations, such as the Pan-German League and the German Colonial Society, each possessing extensive holdings upon overseas and colonial affairs.

b Merseburg

Deutsches Zentralarchiv II, *42* Merseburg *1, Weisse Mauer 48.*

The Central Archives of the German Democratic Republic, Division 2, possesses the greater part of the records of the ministries of the Prussian government, formerly housed in the Geheimes Preussisches Staatsarchiv (the present Berlin-Dahlem depository holding the remainder of this material); some idea of its contents may be obtained from the pre-war publication: E. Müller and E. Posner, eds, *Uebersicht über die Bestände des Geheimen Staatsarchivs zu Berlin-Dahlem* (Leipzig, 1935). It is a less important source of information upon the Pacific and Far East for the period covered in this symposium than the Potsdam division, although the same could not be said of the years before 1870, for here lie the records relating to Prussia's colonization attempts in the Far East. Nevertheless, various branches of the Prussian government did receive useful material upon later affairs in those regions also, particularly upon commercial relations, and many references can be found in the files of the Ministerium für Handel und Gewerbe, Finanzministerium, and Geheimes Zivilkabinett. Important, too, are the records of the Prussian representative in Hamburg, e.g. the series *Rep.* 81 Gesandschaft Hamburg Kolonialakten Südsee nr. 10, thirteen volumes covering the years 1876–94.

The Merseburg archives also contain the private papers of "Welt-Marschall" Graf Alfred von Waldersee, the commander-in-chief of the international force organized to suppress the Boxer uprising of 1900.

### 2. *Federal Republic of Germany*

a Bonn
Politisches Archiv des Auswärtigen Amtes, *53* Bonn *1, Adenauerallee 99–101.*

The Foreign Office of the German Empire, founded in 1871, was sub-divided into a variety of sections dealing with commercial, legal, personal, colonial and other matters, but the most important and prestigious one always remained Abteilung 1A, the Political Department. It is the records of this department which, having survived the war almost intact, now lie in the archives of the German Foreign Ministry in Bonn. The contents of this very extensive collection may be found listed in the excellent published guide, *A Catalogue of the Files and Microfilms of the German Foreign Ministry Archives 1867–1920* (The American Historical Association Committee for the Study of War Documents, Oxford, 1959). This catalogue, which is used for ordering files in the archives itself, also gives details of those records which were filmed in the various programmes undertaken during their post-war stay in England, and provides information upon the reading or copying of such files n the Introduction. The series relating to *Asien* and to *Australien u. Südsee* contain the greater part of the material upon German policy and activities in the areas covered in this symposium; but other files also have relevant documents, and a careful use of the catalogue's subject index is recommended.

This depository also possesses the records of many of the German embassies and consulates abroad which were later returned to Berlin. For scholars unable to use the Reichskolonialamt material at Potsdam, these embassy files are particularly valuable since they contain copies of the drafts and reports relating to colonial affairs which were transferred from the Political Department to the Colonial Department, and thence to the Colonial Office. Only a small part of the embassy records was microfilmed and listed in the above-mentioned *Catalogue*; but complete lists of these files can be consulted in the Foreign and Commonwealth Office Library, Cornwall House, Stamford Street, London S.E.1. Certain of the unfilmed and unlisted records, such as the nineteen volumes concerning Samoa in the files of the German embassy in London, have since been filmed by the Australian Joint Copying Project. The Foreign Ministry Archives in Bonn are at present recataloguing these embassy and consulate records in order to make available for more general use the correspondence which is not already duplicated in the Political Department files themselves.

Of the private papers held in the Bonn archives, only those of Baron Friedrich von Holstein (privy councillor in the Political Department, 1878–1906) appear to have detailed references to events in the Pacific and Far East. Photostat copies of the Holstein papers are available in the Foreign and Commonwealth Office Library, London, and in the National Archives, Washington.

b Koblenz

Bundesarchiv, *54* Koblenz *1, Am Wöllershof 12.*

Although the Federal Archives in Koblenz are the main depository of the German Federal Republic, they contain fewer records relating to the Pacific and Far East for the years 1870–1914 than do certain other archives in Germany, due simply to historical circumstances. A guide to its holdings has been published: F. Facius, H. Booms, and H. Boberach, eds, *Das Bundesarchiv und seine Bestände* (Schriftenreihe des Bundesarchivs, vol.10, Boppard, 1961; 2d edit., 1968), and there are more specialized catalogues in the archives. The records of the Commercial Department of the Foreign Office, a small part of which has found its way here, possess much material upon the economic development of Shantung province in China; while the records of the Reichsschatzamt also contain certain files relating to the regions covered in this book.

Also to be noted are several entries in the *Kleine Erwerbungen* series, including no. 86, *Deutschtum in China*; and no. 340, R 101 F, which consists of copies of Reichskolonialamt documents upon the acquisition of German colonies in Africa and the Pacific.

More important for the researcher interested in Germany in the Pacific and Far East before 1914 is the extensive collection of private papers in the Bundesarchiv, which specializes in this field; it has incidentally produced an excellent guide to all known German private papers in: W.A. Mommsen, ed., *Verzeichnis der schriftlichen Nachlässe in den deutschen Archiven und Bibliotheken*, vol. 1, (Schriftenreihe des Bundesarchivs, vol.17, Boppard, 1971). The most notable private collection here is that of Wilhelm Solf (governor of German Samoa, 1900–11), to which are appended the papers and memoirs of a Herr von Wolffersdorff, an employee of the Deutsche Handels- und Plantagen-Gesellschaft in Samoa in the 1880s and later a police officer for the municipality of Apia.

There are also private collections which refer to China, the Philippines, Samoa and New Guinea, chiefly from a diplomatic viewpoint. These include the papers of Fürst Bernhard von Bülow (foreign secretary, 1897–1900, and chancellor, 1900–1909); Baron Oswald von Richthofen (director of Colonial Department of the Foreign Office, 1896–97, under-secretary of state, 1897–1900, and foreign secretary, 1900–1906); Fürst Chlodwig zu Hohenlohe-Schillingsfürst (chancellor, 1894–1900); and Fürst Philipp zu Eulenburg-Hertfeld (ambassador in Vienna, 1894–1902, and the kaiser's best friend). The Federal Archives have recently acquired copies on microfilm of the main political records of the Bismarck archives at Friedrichsruh (see section 2h).

### c Freiburg

Bundesarchiv-Militärarchiv, *78* Freiburg, *Wiesentalstrasse 10.*

The Military Archives section of the Federal Archives, the holdings of which are briefly summarized in: F.C. Stahl, "Die Bestände des Bundesarchiv-Militärarchivs", *Militärgeschichtliche*

*Mitteilungen* (1968), pp.139–44, possesses with only a few exceptions due to losses in wartime the complete records of the various departments of the imperial German navy—almost 8,000 *Fächer*, which are in fact bundle numbers, each usually comprising four to eight volumes of original documents. These bundles are listed in numerical order in thirteen unpublished catalogues. The largest amount of information upon events in the Pacific and Far East in this period is contained in the series of reports to Berlin from the squadron commanders or the individual ships captains, e.g. Fach 623, *Die Entsendung von Kriegsschiffen nach Australien und den Südsee-Inseln*, seven volumes. But there is also a great deal of material in the volumes relating to immediate audiences with the kaiser, newspaper clippings, operational planning, station records (especially of the Cruiser Squadron and the Australia station), colonies in general and administrative matters; among the latter are the files of the naval administration of Kiautschou—a very important collection indeed.

After these records had been seized by the Allies in 1945, a considerable number of the more important volumes of the central naval departments, including some upon the Pacific and Far East, were microfilmed by the British Admiralty on behalf of the universities of Cambridge and Michigan; see the privately mimeographed *Catalogue of Selected Files of the German Naval Archives Microfilmed at the Admiralty, London, for the University of Cambridge and the University of Michigan*, Project 1 (1959) and Project 2 (1964). These microfilms can be read (or ordered) in both universities and there are also copies in the Naval Historical Branch of the Ministry of Defence in London and in the National Archives in Washington. Further microfilming of the volumes dealing particularly with the areas covered in this book was undertaken by the British Admiralty on behalf of the Australian government and the University of Hawaii respectively; the latter project is entirely duplicated in the larger Australian series. See the mimeographs *List of German Naval Files Microfilmed in the Admiralty, London, for the University of Hawaii* (1959), and *List of German Naval Files Microfilmed in the Admiralty, Tondon, for Australia* (1959). These too can be found in London, as well as in Hawaii, Canberra and Sydney; many are also in Washington. Finally, the largest filming project of all was undertaken by the United States Office of Naval Intelligence in the late 1940s, concentrating chiefly upon the

German naval records of the two world wars; it includes many, though not all, of the files which were filmed in the four later programmes. Apart from some confidential material relating to World War II, these films have now been transferred to the National Archives, Washington. None of these projects completely covers the naval records pertaining to the Pacific and Far East, and a further list of relevant volumes—chiefy upon Australasia—was drawn up by Dr Kennedy and Mr Hempenstall in 1971; it is hoped that these might also be microfilmed for the Australian Joint Copying Project in the near future.

The Bundesarchiv-Militärarchiv also possesses certain private collections containing material relating to the Pacific and Far East; in all cases this is due to the fact that the officers concerned held important commands in those regions at some time. These include the papers of Grand-Admiral Alfred von Tirpitz; Admiral Eduard von Knorr; Vice-Admiral Otto von Diederichs; Admiral George von Müller; Rear-Admiral Otto Groos; and Admiral Oskar von Truppel (Governor of Kiautschou, 1906–11).

## d Hamburg

Hamburg possesses no records of central government ministries but, as the German city with the greatest commercial interest in colonial affairs before 1914, does contain in a variety of depositories a large amount of material upon German activities and interests in the regions concerned.[3]

The Staatsarchiv, 2000 Hamburg 36, ABC-Strasse 19, is the most important of these archives, holding as it does the records of the city administration. The latter include the files of the Hamburg Senate, the highest governing body, which communicated its views directly to the imperial government and to the Bundesrat; the Commission for Reich and Foreign Affairs; the Deputation for Trade, Shipping and Commerce, representing the commercial interests; the Hanseatic embassy in Berlin and the Hamburg plenipotentiary to the Bundesrat, both reporting upon the imperial government's attitude; and the Hamburg postal authorities, which contain material on Hamburg's shipping connections with the Pacific. The Senate records include those concerning the establishment of a Hamburg consulate in Samoa in 1861, and further consular correspondence and documents up to 1877.

While the above series contain information primarily upon official Hamburg attitudes to German policy in the Pacific and Far East, the company records deposited here provide evidence of Hamburg's commercial activity, especially in the islands. The most important are those of the Deutsche Handels- und Plantagen-Gesellschaft der Südsee-Inseln zu Hamburg (1878–1917), which include detailed balance sheets as well as minutes of directors' meetings; the Jaluit-Gesellschaft zu Hamburg (1887–1914); and the Société commerciale de l'Océanie (1876–1935), a Hamburg firm active in French Oceania. Microfilm copies of the last-named are also available at Oxford (Rhodes House), Canberra (National Library), Sydney (Mitchell Library), Wellington (Alexander Turnbull Library) and Hawaii (University Library). Little remains of the records of J.C. Godeffroy & Sohn, which were apparently destroyed in the last war, though there is a Godeffroy family archive left. Other family archives are those of Eduard Hernsheim, containing reminiscences of his commercial activities in the Pacific 1874–1892; Alfred Friedrich Tetens, another early trader, which contains an account of his voyages for J.C. Godeffroy & Sohn into the Caroline Islands in the 1860s; and the Lorenz-Meyer family, which possessed interests in the Far East and Southeast Asia.

The Hamburgisches Weltwirtschaftsarchiv, 2000 Hamburg 1, Neuer Jungfernstieg 9, although primarily a library, possesses miscellaneous copies of official and company papers relating to the Pacific up to the end of World War I.

The Commerzbibliothek, 2000 Hamburg 1, Rathaus, contains certain consular shipping returns, including those for Apia (Samoa) for the years 1872–76, and also the protocols of the Chamber of Commerce.

The Handelskammer (Chamber of Commerce) itself, located at 2000 Hamburg 1, Adolphusplatz, holds the records of this very influential pressure group, with its links to the Hamburg Senate and to the Reichstag. The records to note here are the petitions and memoranda to and from colonial organizations and the imperial government grouped under such classifications as *Kolonialpolitik*, *Kolonialwesen*, etc.; and also those of the *Ostasiatischer Verein*.

The offices of the Hamburg-Amerika-Linie, housed on the Ballindamm, contain the records of the former Deutsch-

Australische Dampfschiffs Gesellschaft, in particular business reports and minutes of board meetings.

Finally, the Museum für Völkerkunde, 2 Hamburg 13, Rothenbaumchaussee 64a, besides incidentally possessing a large collection of contemporary colonial literature, anthologies, travelogues, etc., also holds the diary of Richard Parkinson, a planter and ethnographer in New Guinea at the turn of the century.

### e Bremen

Staatsarchiv Bremen, *2800* Bremen *1, Präsident-Kennedy-Platz 2.*

The records of Bremen's consular service in the Far East before 1870, which was much more extensive than Hamburg's, remain largely intact and include reports from Bremen consuls in the Dutch East Indies, China and Japan. For the colonial period the most important records are those of the Senate itself and of the Hanseatic embassy in Berlin. There are series here in Bremen's interest in the German colonies and on the imperial postal steamer line which Norddeutscher Lloyd ran from Bremen to the Far East and Pacific from 1886 to 1914.[4] Almost all relevant private and company papers have been destroyed, however, leaving only those of H.H. Meier, founder of Norddeutscher Lloyd; and a fragmentary collection concerning the Deutsche Südsee-Phosphat AG, which mined phosphate in the western Carolines from 1909 to 1914.

### f Missionary records

The records of the various German-based missionary societies which operated in the Pacific and Far East all appear to have remained in private hands, often in small towns, and it is for this reason that they have been listed together in a separate section.

At 44 Münster, Kapuzinerstrasse 27–29, are found the archives of the Kapuziner Mission (Rheinisch-Westfälische Provinz). They contain the records of the mission's activities in Micronesia from the 1880s into the period of Japanese rule, and include meticulously kept official and private diaries, proceedings of mission conferences and correspondence with both local administrations in the islands and with Berlin. This is a particularly revealing source for Ponape, not only in the

German period but also for the Spanish era, for which there are translated mission diaries; the actual German records themselves do not begin until 1903 when the (German) Capuchins took over mission activities from the Spanish.[5]

Mission records also exist at 44 Münster, Warendörferstrasse 14, the home of the Herz Jesu Mission, also known as the Hiltruper Missionare. This is not a large depository, for the greater part of the archives of the Sacred Heart Mission lie in Rome (see section 7), but the German branch was active in the Gazelle Peninsula in the New Guinea colony, and in the Marshall Islands. Consequently there is a small number of relevant documents here, chiefly personal diaries of mission sojourns in New Britain and the Marshalls from the 1890s onward.

Other important sources are the archives of the Vereinigte Rheinische Mission (formerly the Rheinische Missions-Gesellschaft) at 56 Wuppertal-Barmen, Rudolfstrasse 137–39. This society was active in southern China in the provinces of Kwangtung and Fukien. The mission also operated in Astrolabe Bay on the northeastern coast of New Guinea from 1887 until World War I. The detailed records of the latter region include not only annual reports from the eight main stations established up to 1912, but also frequent correspondence from missionaries in the field, special reports from visiting missionary inspectors and the proceedings of local missionary conferences. There are in addition some plantation and station records, together with fragmentary correspondence with colonial authorities during the German era. Finally, there are certain private papers, not normally available to external researchers.[6]

Even larger sources are the main archives of the Evangelisch-Lutherische Missionsanstalt at 8806 Neuendettelsau. Missionaries of the Neuendettelsau Lutheran Mission arrived in New Guinea in 1886 and for most of the period of German rule they represented the main foreign influence in the coast and hinterland regions of the Huon Peninsula and the Huon Gulf; the extensive records are being catalogued on a card-index at the archives and are an indispensable source for a history of that part of New Guinea.[7]

At the Society of the Divine Word Mission Seminary, 5205 St Augustin, Arnold-Janssen-Strasse 30, there are only published materials, since the main archives are in Rome (see again section 7). Some of these scarce publications are ethnological and anthropological works by missionaries in the period of German rule, however, and this source is worth mentioning here. The Divine Word missionaries operated along the northern coast of Kaiser Wilhelmsland.

The main German Protestant missions in the Shantung area of China were the Allgemeiner evangelisch-protestantischer Missionsverein (the so-called Weimar Mission), which changed its name in 1929 to the Ostasienmission and now has its headquarters at 69 Heidelberg, Schröderstrasse 14; and the Berliner Gesellschaft zur Beförderung der evangelischen Mission unter den Heiden (the so-called Berlin Missionary Society), with its headquarters at 1 Berlin 41, Handjerystrasse 19–20. The educational activities of these missions in the German colony and surrounding sphere were of particular importance. Other missions to note are the Hildesheimer Blindenmission, 32 Hildesheim, Neustädter Markt 37, which operated in Hong Kong, and the three societies which operated in central China in connection with the famous China Inland Mission: these were the Barmer Allianz China Mission (Allianz-Mission-Barmen, 56 Wuppertal 11, Falkenhaynstrasse 11), the Deutscher Zweig der China-Inland-Mission, known after 1906 as the Liebenzeller Mission (7267 Bad Liebenzell, Postfach 21), and the Kieler-China-Inland Mission (Nordelbisches Zentrum für Weltmission und kirchlichen Weltdienst, 2 Hamburg 52, Agathe-Lasch-Weg 16). Finally, there are the records of the closely-associated Basler Mission, which operated in Canton; its address is Evangelische Missionsgesellschaft, Ch-4000 Basel, Missionstrasse 21, Switzerland. Brief details of all these societies may be obtained from W. Oehler, *Geschichte der deutschen evangelischen Mission*, 2 vols. (Baden-Baden, 1949–1951).

### g Company records

Most of the records of German companies which operated in the Pacific and Far East appear either to have found their way into public archives, or to have been destroyed during World War II, or to be as yet undiscovered by the historian. One worthy of mention, however, is the Hausarchiv Sal. Oppenheim jr. & Compagnie, 5 Köln, Untersachsenstrasse 4. The archives of this banking house contain a fragmentary collection of correspondence and documents concerning the New Guinea

Company 1884–1914. (The New Guinea Company records themselves, apart from those in Potsdam, appear to have been lost.)

### h Papers in private hands

Quite a number of collections of unofficial correspondence remain in family archives or simply in private hands; for a full list of those known to the Bundesarchiv, see the abovementioned publication, *Verzeichnis der schriftlichen Nachlässe ...* Among those containing references to the Pacific and Far East are the papers of the three German ambassadors in London between 1873 and 1912, although the use of all three is at present subject to restrictions: the Münster papers at 3201 Schloss Derneburg, Hildesheim, which may soon be transferred to the Niedersächsisches Hauptstaatsarchiv in Hanover; the Hatzfeldt papers, an enormous collection now being arranged and edited by Oberstudienrat G. Ebel at 3501 Haste, microfilm copies of which are being made for the Auswärtiges Amt Archiv in Bonn; and the Metternich papers, being arranged by Professor A. Thimme at Durbach, near Offenburg. The papers of Fürst Otto von Bismarck-Schönhausen (chancellor, 1871–1890) and of his son Herbert (foreign secretary, 1885–90), are both held at Schloss Friedrichsruh, 2055 Friedrichsruh-Aumühle, although microfilm copies have recently been acquired by the Bundesarchiv. There are many references in this enormous family collection to German policy in the Pacific, fewer to the Far East itself.

### *3. West Berlin*

*Geheimes Staatsarchiv Preussischer Kulturbesitz, 1* Berlin *33, Archivstrasse, 12–14.*

The contents of this archive are fully listed in H. Branig, W. Bliss and W. Petermann, *Uebersicht über die Bestände des Geheimen Staatsarchivs in Berlin-Dahlem*, pt 2 (Cologne/Berlin, 1967), although researchers should note that in recent years certain records relating to Reich affairs have been transferred to the Bundesarchiv. The records of the Prussian Ministry of Foreign Affairs, which maintained relations with the states *inside* the German Empire until 1918, include copies of German consular reports dealing with the German colonies 1885–89, the

Australian colonies 1888–1900, China 1874–1900, Hawaii 1875–89 and the Philippines 1886–95. Some files of the ministry for the years before 1870 are also kept here, but the most relevant for the Pacific and Far East regions are to be found at Merseburg.

This Berlin depository contains one important private collection, that of Heinrich Schnee (imperial judge and acting governor in New Guinea and Samoa, 1898–1902). Of the others, the papers of Graf Leo von Caprivi (chancellor, 1890–95) are very fragmentary, but some interesting material upon official German attitudes during the Russo-Japanese war of 1904–5 can be gleaned from the papers of Professor Theodor Schiemann (Professor at the Humboldt University, leader-writer for the *Kreuz-Zeitung*, and friend of Kaiser Wilhelm II, Bülow and Herbert Bismarck). Also worth looking at is the collection of private papers of Kaiser Wilhelm II himself, in the *Brandenburg-Preussisches Hausarchiv*, rep.53.

### 4. *United Kingdom*[8]

#### a London

i) The Public Record Office, Chancery Lane, London WC2.

This institution, probably the largest collection of state documents in the world, contains a great deal of information upon German activities in the Pacific and Far East as reported by British government officials. There is a general published guide to government records: *Guide to the Records of the Public Record Office*, vol.2, *State Papers and Departmental Records* (London, 1963), and some useful published handbooks, of which the one dealing with the Foreign Office records is particularly impressive (PRO Handbook no.13, *The Records of the Foreign Office, 1782–1939*): but researchers will need to use the more detailed catalogues and indices in the Public Record Office itself to obtain a full picture of the material available. As is to be expected, the records of those departments (Foreign Office, Colonial Office, Admiralty) which have had most to do with overseas affairs possess the largest amount of information upon the German presence, e.g. Admiralty series 1 (General Correspondence, In-Letters), 116 (Secretary's Case-Books), 50,

122 and 123 (Station journals and correspondence), Foreign Office series 17 (China), 58 (Pacific Islands) and 371 (Political, post-1905), and Colonial Office series 225 (Pacific Islands) and 422 (Papua). Important, too, are those volumes in the Foreign Office series 64 (Prussia and Germany), relating to Anglo-German boundary disputes in the Pacific. There are also some interesting documents in the records of the Cabinet Office, including those of the Committee of Imperial Defence.

A number of private collections provide useful information upon German policy in the Pacific and Far East. These include the papers of Sir Edward Malet and Sir Frank Lascelles, who were ambassadors to Germany in the years 1884–95 and 1895–1908 respectively; Sir Ernest Satow, ambassador to Japan, 1895–1900, and to China, 1900–1906; the second Earl of Granville, the fifth Marquis of Lansdowne and Sir Edward (later Lord) Grey, foreign secretaries for the years 1880–85, 1900–1905 and 1905–1916 respectively; Sir Francis (later Lord) Bertie, assistant under-secretary at the Foreign Office, 1894–1903, and Beilby Alston of the Far Eastern Department; and Sir John Jewell Jordan, minister to China, 1906–20.

ii) The British Museum, Great Russell Street, London WC2

The Manuscripts Division of the British Museum possesses an enormous number of private papers, of which the following are the most relevant here: Sir Arthur Gordon, governor of Fiji 1875–80 but titular high commissioner for the western Pacific until 1883; William Gladstone, prime minister, 1868–74, 1880–85, 1886 and 1892–94; Arthur J. Balfour, prime minister, 1902–5; the first Marquis of Ripon, colonial secretary, 1892–95; and Sir Charles Dilke, parliamentary under-secretary at the Foreign Office, 1880–82, and president of the Local Government Board, 1882–85. Many others have occasional references to German activities in the Pacific and Far East; details of these, and of any later acquisitions, may be discovered in the various *Catalogues of the Manuscript Collections* or in *The British Museum Quarterly*.

iii) Further records in London

The papers of the first Marquis of Curzon, parliamentary under-secretary at the Foreign Office, 1895–98, and viceroy of India, 1899–1905, are of some value here; they are housed at the India Office Library, Foreign and Commonwealth Office,

Blackhall Road, London SW2. The National Maritime Museum, Greenwich, London SE10, possesses the papers of Admiral Sir Cyprian Bridge (c-in-c, Australia station, 1894–98) and Vice-Admiral Sir Thomas Jerram (c-in-c, China station, 1913–15), both of whom followed German naval activity in those regions very closely. The library of the Royal Commonwealth Society, Northumberland Avenue, London WC2, contains the papers of Wilfred Powell, explorer in New Britain and later (1885–86) British consul in Samoa, and E.G. Cantrell, a planter in German Samoa in the years 1910–14. The records of Unilever Ltd., Unilever House, Blackfriars, London EC4, contain material upon the company's activities in the German Pacific colonies and dealings with German firms there, while further information may emerge from the records of the great Far Eastern firm, Jardine, Matheson & Co., now held at Cambridge University Library, West Road, Cambridge.

Very useful insights may also be obtained from the archival collections of British missionary societies. The London Missionary Society, Livingstone House, Carteret Street, London SW1, possesses a vast amount of missionary reports and miscellaneous documents relating to the Pacific islands, New Guinea and the Far East, together with certain private papers and diaries, such as those of J.R. Newall, who was active in Samoa before and during the period of German rule. More information about the role of this mission is to be found in the *History of the London Missionary Society*, vols 1–2 (covering 1795–1895) by R. Lovett, and vol.3 (covering 1895–1945) by N. Goodall. The Baptist Missionary Society, 93–97 Gloucester Place, London W1, has a considerable amount of records relating to the activities of their missionaries in Shantung and the northern part of China in this period. The Methodist Missionary Society, 25 Marylebone Place, London NW1, does not appear to have had mission stations in the German sphere of China, while its records relating to the Pacific itself peter out after 1880, since that area was by then being supervised by the Australasian Conference of the Methodist Church. The Church Missionary Society, which operated throughout China, has an extensive archive at Salisbury Square, London EC4.

The British and Foreign Bible Society, Bible House, 146 Queen Victoria Street, London EC4, houses the records of that society and also of the London Secretaries' Association. Both organizations took a great interest in missionary work all over the globe, and the archives of the former are particularly extensive. The United Society for the Propagation of the Gospel in Foreign Parts has a very large archive at 15 Tufton Street, Westminster, London SW1, which includes much material from its missions upon affairs in the Pacific; the society also operated in the Shantung province of north China. An idea of the extent of those activities, and of the usefulness of the records, may be gained from C.F. Pascoe, *Two Hundred Years of the S.P.G. ... 1701–1900* (London, 1901), and from H.P. Thompson, *Into All Lands [S.P.G. 1701–1950)* (London, 1951). Possessing traditional links with the SPG is the Society for Promoting Christian Knowledge, whose activities were extended into Melanesia in 1872 and into Polynesia in 1884; its records are housed at Holy Trinity Church, Marylebone Road, London NW1.

b Records outside London

First to be mentioned should be the extensive and well-indexed Royal Archives at Windsor Castle, Berkshire. The National Library of Scotland, George IV Bridge, Edinburgh, contains the papers of the fifth Earl of Rosebery (foreign secretary, 1886 and 1892–94, prime minister, 1894–95), and also those of the Church of Scotland with its missionary reports. Christ Church College, Oxford, possesses the enormous collection of the third Marquis of Salisbury (foreign secretary, 1878–80, 1885, 1887–92, 1895–1900, prime minister, 1885, 1886–92 and 1895 –1902), and Birmingham University Library, PO Box 363,

The Navy Department material is in Record Group 45 (Naval Records Collection of the Office of Naval Records and Library) and Record Group 80 (General Records of the Navy Department), the various sub-divisions of which contain the reports of American naval commanders of the Pacific and Asiatic squadrons together with those of the central naval authorities. The Bureau of Navigation records (Record Group 41) contain a certain amount of information upon German shipping in the Pacific and Far East. The interesting records of the General Board of the Navy, a strategic advisory body which collected material upon the German "threat" and prepared a war plan against it,[9] is not in the National Archives but in the nearby United States Navy Yard.

### ii) The Library of Congress, Manuscript Division, Washington, DC *20540*

The Manuscript Division of the Library of Congress, housed in a separate building opposite the main library, possesses a vast collection of the private papers of American presidents, cabinet members, politicians and officials, many of which contain references to the German presence in the Pacific and Far East, and especially to their rivalry over Samoa, the Carolines, China and the Philippines. To list all of these papers would unreasonably extend the size of this section: the depository holds, for example, the papers of every president in the period 1870–1914 with the exception of Rutherford B. Hayes (which are to be found at the Hayes Memorial Library, Fremond, Ohio), and every secretary of state with the exception of Robert Bacon. German-Americans such as Carl Schurz, naval leaders such as Admirals George Dewey and A.T. Mahan, diplomats such as Henry White, expansionist politicians such as J.T. Morgan, all have their papers here. Researchers looking for specific collections in this depository are advised to consult P.M. Hamer, *Guide to Manuscripts and Archives in the United States* (New Haven, 1961), pp.85–121, or the Library of Congress' own publication *National Union Catalogue of Manuscript Collections* (Washington, 1959f.). Both have a subject index, and provide a national survey of private collections.

### b Papers outside Washington

Many American diplomats and State Department officials who were involved in Pacific and Far Eastern affairs have left their papers to a variety of depositories, especially to the libraries of their own universities. Delaware University Library possesses the collection of G.H. Bates, American special commissioner to Samoa in 1886 and member of the Samoan Berlin Conference delegation; the Willard Straight papers are in the Collection of Regional History, Cornell University Library, Ithaca, New York, as are those of Andrew D. White, ambassador in Berlin; those of W.W. Rockill are in the university library at Harvard; Brown University Library, Rhode Island, contains some further correspondence of Secretary of State John Hay; the papers of Navy Secretary John D. Long and Senator Henry Cabot Lodge are housed with the Massachussetts Historical Society, Boston.

Birmingham 15, that of Joseph Chamberlain (colonial secretary, 1895–1903), both of which contain material relating to German policy in the Pacific and Far East. There may also be further documents of this sort in the papers of the second Earl of Selborne (parliamentary under-secretary at the Colonial Office, 1895–1900, first lord of the Admiralty, 1900–1905), recently acquired by the Bodleian Library, Oxford. The papers of the fifteenth Earl of Derby (foreign secretary, 1874–78, colonial secretary, 1880–85) in the Liverpool City Libraries, Record Office and Local History Department, William Brown Street, Liverpool, have some cabinet notes upon the New Guinea crisis of 1884–85. Many other collections contain incidental material upon the theme of this book. The National Registry of Archives, Quality House, Quality Court, Chancery Lane, London WC2, possesses a fine card-index and many catalogues relating to all known private collections of British persons of major and minor historical interest.

## 5. *United States of America*

### a Washington, DC

i) The National Archives, Washington, DC *20408*
This enormous and superbly-run depository houses the greater part of the records of the various departments of the United States government; its contents are briefly described in the published *Guide to the Records in the National Archives* (Washington, 1948, now being revised). With regard to material relating to the German presence in the Pacific and Far East before 1914, the files of the State Department and Navy Department are the most important. The former, located chiefly in Record Group 59, include correspondence with the American embassy in Berlin and the German embassy in Washington, together with reports from and instructions to the various American embassies and other posts in the Pacific and Far East. This latter material is reproduced, often with additional miscellaneous correspondence (some of great interest), in Record Group 84, which comprises the returned records of the American Foreign Service Posts abroad. Finally, useful information may also be found in Record Group 43, which has files relating to "U.S. Participation in International

Conferences, Commissions and Expositions". Virtually all of these State Department records can be ordered on microfilm.

The Houghton Library, Harvard University, has on deposit a substantial part of the records of the American Board of Commissioners for Foreign Missions.[10] They include, among many others, the letters and reports of the North China Mission, together with the Micronesia Mission papers of missionary activities in the Caroline and Marshall groups; these latter records have been copied on microfilm for the Pacific Manuscripts Bureau in Canberra. It is possible that the Congregational Library, 25 Beacon Street, Boston, may still have some records of this board. The archives of the Presbyterian Foreign Missions Board, which operated in Shantung province, are located at the United Mission Library, 475 Riverside Drive, New York, as are those of the Methodist Board of Missions. Further missionary records relating to the Far East are housed in the Historical Foundation of the Presbyterian and Reformed Churches, Montreat, North Carolina, and with the Presbyterian Historical Society, 425 Lombard Street, Philadelphia, Pennsylvania. Other American missionary societies which worked in China were the American Lutheran Church (Board of World Missions, 422 S. Fifth Street, Minneapolis) and the Southern Baptist Convention (Foreign Mission Board, 3806 Monument Avenue, Richmond, Virginia). Finally, the useful Missionary Research Library at 3041 Broadway, New York, has annual reports from these boards, plus some mission station reports from Shantung.

The Baker Library of Harvard University possesses many company papers, including those of American firms which traded in the Far East and Pacific regions. The Peabody Museum of Salem, Massachusetts, has a large collection of papers relating to maritime trade in those regions.

Trinity College Library, Hartford 6, Connecticut, has certain papers from the German Legation at Peking for the period 1868–1904.

### 6. *France*

The French archives, though less frequently used than their British and American counterparts for material upon German activities in the Pacific and Far East, contain much of interest in this field. The records of French colonial services in the

Archives du ministère de la France d'outre-mer may be dealt with first;[11] they are housed in a section of the Archives nationales at 27 rue Oudinot, Paris 7. With regard to the Pacific, this archive contains mainly material upon the internal administration of the French colonies, but the following file number may be noted: Nouvelle-Calédonie, 6:232 (Relations avec l'extérieur) *1884–1903 Colonies allemandes*. Other incidental material may be found in the records of the regional administrations of the French Overseas Territories at the Depôt des archives d'outre-mer, 13 Aix-en-Provence.

Far more important are the Archives du ministère des affaires etrangères, 3 Quai d'Orsay, Paris 7, with its detailed archival coverage of relations with Germany and of affairs in the Pacific and Far Eastern regions. All three main subdivisions "Correspondance Diplomatique", "Mémoires et Documents" an "Correspondance Consulaire et Commerciale" contain material in such relevant series as *Asie*, *Océanie*, *Extrême-Orient* and *Chine*. This depository also possesses the private papers of many prominent statesmen and diplomats, including Théodore Delcassé, Gabriel Hanotaux and Paul Cambon.

The French military records for this period, which are probably not so important a source for this study, are housed in the Château de Vincennes under the control of the Service historique de l'armée. Far more valuable are the naval records, which are however dispersed along chronological lines, with the pre-1870 material housed mainly at the Archives nationales, 60 rue des Francs Bourgeois, Paris 3, certain post-1870 records deposited at the Section d'outre-mer in the rue Oudinot, and records still held by the Service historique de la marine at 3 avenue Octave-Gréard, Paris 7. The naval records are very comprehensive and contain many ships' reports as well as intelligence information, strategic assessments, etc. Since the Ministère de la marine only lost its colonial and commercial responsibilities in the 1880s, the records are even more informative than one might at first imagine; especially useful are the exchanges of views with the Foreign Ministry in the series *Correspondance Générale*.

The Archives nationales possesses a vast collection (either original or on microfilm) of family papers, company records, collections in private hands and other categories of documents, and its catalogues should also be consulted.[10] Finally, the

Bibliothèque nationale has the papers of Eugène Étienne, under-secretary for the colonies 1887–88 and 1889–92, and leader of the French colonial party.

### 7. *Italy*

Rome forms an important archival centre, for here are to be found the headquarters of many of the various Roman Catholic missions which operated in the German territories in the Pacific and Far East. The archives of the Sacred Congregation of Propaganda, Palazzo di Propaganda Fide, Piazza di Spagna, should be noted first, since this body supervised all Roman Catholic missions on behalf of the pope and therefore received documents from all over the globe, including the areas of interest to this study. The largest number are in the series "Scritture riferite nei Congressi, Oceania" (17 vols, 1816–92) and "Scritture riferite nei Congressi, Cina e regni adiacenti" (36 vols, 1798–1892), and in the successor series after the 1892–98 archival reorganization, but others are to be found in the "Acta", "Scritture riferite nelle Congregazioni Generali" and "Lettere".

The Society of Mary (Marist Fathers) has many interesting files in its archive in the via Allessandro Poerio 63. In the Pacific region Marist fathers were active in the Territory of New Guinea, the Solomons, Samoa and Tonga, and often composed long reports or memoirs upon the political affairs of the islands, e.g. J. Forestier's account of the Samoan civil war of 1898–99 in the Vicarial series ON, 260, or the whole series of unpublished island histories which are kept separately in numbered boxes.[12] Certain of these records relating to Roman Catholic missions in the northern Solomons and Samoa have been microfilmed for the Pacific Manuscripts Bureau in Canberra.

The headquarters and archives of the German Herz Jesu Mission, mentioned in section 2 (f), are located at the following address: Missionari del SC, Via Asmara 11, 00199 Rome. There is a splendid catalogue of the Pacific holdings of this depository in: J. Bertolini, "L'Océanie dans les Archives générales des Missionaires du Sacré-Coeur", *Journal de la Société des Océanistes*, tome 25, no.25 (December 1969), pp.359–82, with details of missionary records from New Guinea, New Britain, the Solomons and the Marshalls. The Sacred Heart Mission was also active in China.

Similarly, the Society of the Divine Word headquarters, Collegio del Verbo Divino, via dei Verbiti 1, 00153 Roma, contains the original records of the German (St Augustin) missionaries, which were referred to in section 2 (f), although it is worth remarking that it was not until *after* World War I that they took over from the Steyler missionaries—another branch of the Society of the Divine Word, and so named because it was based not in Germany but across the Dutch border at Steyl. The Steyler mission operated also in Shantung, where the murder of two of their number in 1897 provided the occasion for the German government's acquisition of Kiautschou. By 1914 they had built up a flourishing organization in the colony and its surrounds; and they were also active in northern New Guinea, as mentioned earlier. Many Steyler records relating to China and New Guinea have been lost, but multi-volume histories of the missions in both regions are being prepared; they will contain much information upon archival sources.[13]

## *8. Australia*

### General note

The archives and libraries of Australia and New Zealand, on account of the widespread interest which those two countries have taken in the Pacific and Far East, possess an enormous variety of records relating to the history of the regions covered in this book. Many of these have been copied from the originals in Germany, Britain and elsewhere; they will not be listed here. Scholars particularly interested in Pacific history will be aware of the activities of the Pacific Manuscripts Bureau, Research School of Pacific Studies, The Australian National University, Box 4, PO, Canberra, ACT 2600. This organization, headed by Mr Robert Langdon, seeks to locate and film for its sponsoring libraries unpublished manuscripts relating to the Pacific islands, and also issues a newsletter (*Pambu*) with details of recent discoveries and acquisitions of manuscripts. A Joint Copying Project, which arranges for the sharing of the costs of copying such records, works in close connection with the bureau. The same School of Pacific Studies publishes annually the *Journal of Pacific History* (vol.1, 1966), which includes reports upon archival holdings of all kinds relating to the Pacific.

Similarly, *Historical Studies: Australia and New Zealand* (published by the University of Melbourne, 1940f.), has devoted space to notes upon the accession of manuscripts. Finally, all scholars interested in archival holdings in the South Pacific (including New Zealand) will benefit from reading the fine survey by R.W. Winks, "Archives and Libraries in the South Pacific Islands", *News from the Center*, vol.5 (Spring, 1969), pp.19–40.

a Canberra

i) Commonwealth Archives Office, PO Box *358, Kingston, ACT 2604*

First to be mentioned here should be the originals of German records relating to the administration of the former German possessions in the Pacific. They include the surviving files upon German New Guinea which have been transferred to Canberra from the Papua and New Guinea Archives. This collection consists of a large number of boxes containing the records both of the Herbertshöhe central offices and of the various local administration posts in German New Guinea, and dealing mainly with court cases, customs, finance, registrations, native labour, shipping and postal communications.

Another important collection held at this depository is the two record series G1 and G2, still under the general title "Kaiserliches Gouvernement von Deutsch Neu Guinea", which is somewhat deceptive since there are very few files relating to German New Guinea itself, but a great many upon the Pacific island groups which were under the administrative control of the governor's office at Herbertshöhe. There are, in fact, over 200 boxes of files about the Marshalls, Carolines, Marianas, Palaus and Nauru as well as many other topics, which probably makes this the most important collection of records outside Potsdam upon German Micronesia.

The second group of records consists of documents of the Commonwealth government relating to Pacific affairs. Understandably, there are very few for the years before federation, and even in the 1900–1914 period this material is slight in regard to the German colonies; only with the question of their disposal does the documentation become adequate. Nevertheless, there are some files in the governor-general's department, and a whole series upon the Pacific islands in the prime minister's department.[14] Among the records of the Public Trustee and the Custodian of Expropriated Property are the papers and account-books of several German or German-Australian firms which fell into Australian hands in 1914: these include The Stevedoring and Shipping Co., Lohman & Co., Stephens and Noelle, and G. Hardt & Co. Ltd. The records of the Commonwealth Defence and Navy Departments and committees—held not here but at the Victorian branch in Melbourne—contain a number of relevant pre-war files upon the German presence in the Pacific.

The Commonwealth Archives also possess, once again held at Melbourne, the records of the British Phosphate Commissioners. These include files of the Pacific Islands Co. and the Pacific Phosphate Co., both of which operated in the German colonies. There are many references in this correspondence to the Jaluit-Gesellschaft zu Hamburg, with which they both had connections.

ii) The National Library of Australia, Parkes Place, Canberra, ACT *2600*

This depository possesses the largest collection of private papers of Australian statesmen and officials, details of which are published in the *Guide to Manuscripts Relating to Australia* or (for many collections here) the library's own roneo indices which scholars may obtain upon request. They include the papers of governor-generals such as Lord Tennyson, Lord Denman and Sir Ronald Munro-Ferguson, prime ministers such as Sir Edmund Barton, Alfred Deakin, J.C. Watson, Andrew Fisher and Joseph Cook, ministers of external affairs such as W.M. Hughes, Littleton Groom and Patrick McM. Glynn, New Guinea administrators such as Sir William MacGregor and Sir Hubert Murray, and publin servants such as Atlee Hunt (secretary to the Department of External Affairs, 1901–16); yet apart from the latter collection a general conclusion would be that mention of the German presence in the pre-war years is only incidental and fragmentary in all these papers. The same is true of the small collection of the papers of Sir John Thurston (high commissioner of the western Pacific, 1888–97), but it does possess the originals or copies of a large number of missionary letters and journals which are of more value to this survey.[15] Of these, perhaps the most important is the history of the Lutheran Mission in German New Guinea, written by John Flierl between 1910 and 1915 (MS 3399).

iii) Australian National University, Department of Pacific History, Canberra, ACT *2600*

The papers of John T. Arundel (businessman, head and manager of several firms operating in the Pacific) are of importance here, revealing some interesting aspects of British political and commercial attitudes towards Germany in the Pacific.

The Pacific Manuscripts Bureau, although not a depository itself, has acquired the originals or copies of some interesting documents for deposit in its sponsoring libraries; scholars wishing to inquire about current holdings should write to Mr Langdon.

b Sydney

i) The Mitchell Library, Public Library of New South Wales, Macquarie Street, Sydney, NSW *2000*

This depository, together with the Dixson Library and the Public Archives of New South Wales which are housed at this address also, possesses either as copies or in original form one of the largest collections of manuscripts upon the Pacific region. The Mitchell's holdings include the papers of politicians such as Sir Henry Parkes (prime minister of New South Wales, 1872–75, 1878–82, 1887–90); notes upon German activities in Samoa in 1886 by W.L. Rees, a lawyer resident there; the papers of James Lyle Young, a merchant who played a part in Steinberger's downfall in Samoa, then became manager of the Jaluit-based German firm of A. Capelle & Co. before moving to Tahiti in 1882; the diaries for the period 1887–97 of a German woman, Mrs Davies; the papers of the Rev. Shirley Baker, "uncrowned king" of Tonga; the journals and letters of the Rev. George Brown, missionary in Samoa and the Solomons, of the Rev. Ernest E. Crosby, missionary in Tonga, and a whole host of other private missionary papers. Also held here are the archives of the Methodist Church of Australasia, Department of Overseas Missions, which include reports from German-administered territories. The letters and records of the Taimua-Faipule government of Samoa of 1876–77 have found their way here, too.

The Dixson Library also possesses a collection of the papers of the Rev. Shirley Baker. More important, perhaps, are the records of the New South Wales government housed here in the Public Archives of New South Wales. These contain certain material (often selectively published already) upon the Pacific region, including New Guinea, a brief description of which can be found in: M. Saclier, "Records relating to the Pacific in the Archives Office of New South Wales", *JPH* 2 (1967): 174–76.

ii) Burns Philp & Co. Ltd, *7 Bridge Street, Sydney, NSW 2000* The records of this famous Australian firm, which probably had the largest and most extensive trading interest in the Pacific in the pre-war years, are in the head office at the above address, where they are in the process of being organized. They should offer valuable insights into the economic life of the German Pacific colonies, although they are not large and there is probably more at the Fiji branch offices (now microfilmed by Pacific Manuscripts Bureau).

c Brisbane

Queensland State Archives, Annerley Road, Dutton Park, Brisbane. This important state archive contains a great deal of material upon the Pacific in the files of such departments as the Governor's Office, the Colonial Secretary's Office, the Premier's Department, etc. Information upon the German presence can be found in the papers relating to New Guinea, the labour trade, and defence. The holdings of this depository have been briefly described in: R.C. Sharman, "The Queensland State Archives", *JPH* 4 (1969):pp.166–74.

The nearby Oxley Memorial Library, which is part of the State Library of Queensland, holds the diaries of Captain William Hamilton relating to his labour trade voyages in the 1880s and to the later Hamilton Pearling Company in New Guinea.

d Melbourne

i) Archives of the Congregational Union of Victoria, Independent Hall, Collins Street, Melbourne.

A series of letter-books covering the outgoing correspondence of the Australasian representatives of the London Missionary Society for the period 1886–1912 are held here. According to a brief guide to this material, there are many letters upon New Guinea.[16]

ii) University Archives, University of Melbourne, Parkville, Victoria *3052*.

These archives collect the papers of Australian companies and may hold some relevant material from those which traded in the Pacific.

*9. New Zealand*

a Wellington

i) National Archives of New Zealand, *85 The Terrace, Wellington 1*

This depository contains much material relating to German activities in the Pacific, but it need only be briefly summarized here since it has recently been described in more detail in: J. Hornabrook, "The National Archives of New Zealand", *JPH* 3 (1968): pp.181–91.

By far the most important are the records of the successive governments of Samoa, which were transferred to Wellington for safekeeping. These include the only surviving files of the Tamasese-Brandeis regime of 1887–88 and of the Malietoa government of 1891–1900, with details of Samoan affairs and with come court cases going as far back as 1874; the records of the British consulate in Samoa for the years 1847–1916, covering a large variety of topics, together with the papers of Thomas Trood, British vice-consul at Apia, 1900–1916; and a much smaller amount of material from the German consulate for the years 1879–99. Here, too, are the records of the German administration of western Samoa for the period 1900–1914; although there are gaps, these records are extensive and relate to native affairs, land settlements, court cases, finance and customs, census returns, foreign affairs, etc. Finally, there are the records of the British Military Occupation and of the New Zealand Administration, which contain references to the pre-1914 period.

The National Archives also possess the bulk of the original files of the Australia station of the Royal Navy, with frequent references to Anglo-German naval relations in the Pacific and to events in New Guinea, the Solomons, Samoa and Tonga, chiefly in the years 1880–1900. They have been briefly described in: L. Cleland, "Royal Navy—Australia Station", *JPH*: 1 (1966): pp.183–84.

This depository houses the extensive records of the Governor's Office and of the Prime Minister's Office, together with the private papers of that most imperialistically-minded premier, Richard John Seddon. The latter contain little original material, but the former two groups have many papers relating to the German presence in the Pacific, no doubt due to New Zealand's preoccupation with foreign threats in this region in the nineteenth century.[17]

Finally, there are the files of the Island Territories Department, which, however, contain nothing upon Germany apart from the account-sheets of certain German firms, and a few pages from the diary of Dr E. Schultz, the governor of Samoa, relating to the occupation of the group in 1914.

ii) The Alexander Turnbull Library, PO Box *8016*, Wellington

Among the many papers held by this library are those of Edwin W. Gurr, a New Zealand lawyer who played a prominent part in Samoan local politics before 1900; Sir Robert Stout, who as prime minister of New Zealand (1884–87) shared Seddon's views about German expansion in the Pacific; Coleman Philipps, a publicist and adventurer who sought to turn the dreams of a New Zealand Pacific empire into reality; William Gilbert Muir, who was for a brief period British consul in Samoa; George Westbrook, a customs officer and trader in Samoa before and during the German administration; and a variety of papers relating to the Rev. Shirley Baker, his dealings with the Germans in Tonga and the official charges against him by the Weslyan missionary commissioners.

b Auckland

The Auckland Public Library, Box *4138, Auckland*

This depository houses the papers of Sir George Grey, colonial administrator and prime minister of New Zealand (both before our period and in 1877–79). Since he agitated so persistently for British or New Zealand expansion in the Pacific, there are frequent references in this collection to the German activities there.

### *10.* New Guinea

The Papua and New Guinea Archives, Port Moresby, New Guinea. Almost all local records relating to the administration of German New Guinea appear to have been destroyed, apart from those now resting in Canberra which are described in section 8, (a) i, of this survey. The Port Moresby Archives do, however, possess the records of the administration of Papua, which may contain references to the neighbouring German territory. The holdings of this relatively new depository are surveyed in: K.A. Green and M. Helai, "The Papua and New Guinea Archives", *JPH*: 6 (1971): pp.164–69.

### *11.* Samoa

The vast majority of the records relating to the German presence in the Samoan group has been transferred to the National Archives of New Zealand (see section 9, (a) i. Nevertheless, at the time of writing, some material remains in the group, including the bulk of the surviving files of the Land Commission and Supreme Court, housed at the Public Record Office, Apia; these, too, will be transferred to Wellington for safekeeping in the near future. The Marist Archives at Mulivai contain some papers from, and unpublished memoirs of, the German period, together with a collection of even earlier documents relating to the Steinberger regime in Samoa, 1873–75 (copies of which are in the Mitchell Library, Sydney).

The records of the administration of American Samoa, held at Pago Pago, are only of value—and then incidentally—for the period after 1900.

### *12.* Fiji

The Central Archives of Fiji and the Western Pacific High Commission, Suva, are, as the person who has to date made most use of them has pointed out. "of transcendent value for the study of Pacific history from 1875 onward",[18] even though their contents are partly duplicated by files in the Public Record Office, London. These Fiji records have been briefly described in: A.L. Diamond, "The Central Archives of Fiji and the Western Pacific High Commission", *JPH*, 1 (1966): pp.204–11. Those relating particularly to the German presence in the Pacific include the records of the High Commission itself; of the deputy commissioner (and British consul) at Samoa, and of the agent and consul at Tonga; and of the Fiji Lands Commission, which after the British annexation of 1874 considered all the land claims, including those of many Germans.

The Central Archives has also been presented with the private papers of the Hennings family; these were Germans who were active as merchants and planters in the Lau group and Levuka, and who also held office in the Fijian government before annexation.[19]

### *13*. The Former German Island Territories (Marshalls, Marianas, Carolines, Palaus, Nauru)

The surviving records relating to the German administration of the Pacific island territories are held in Canberra and described in section 8, (a) i. As far as I know, there are no other local records for these groups, which is no doubt due to the ravages of two world wars.

### *14*. Hawaii

The Public Archives of Hawaii, Honolulu 13, contain the records of the Hawaiian native government in the period before the American annexation of 1898; they include documents from the Foreign Office and Executive Files and the Military Department upon relations with Germany and upon the Hawaiian mission to Samoa in 1886, which so annoyed Bismarck. These records are briefly described in: A.C. Conrad, "The Archives of Hawaii", *JPH* 2 (1967): pp.191–197, and have been extensively used by R.S. Kuykendall in his monumental work, *The Hawaiian Kingdom*, 3 vols, (Honolulu, 1957–67).

### *15*. Japan

The records of the Nihon Gaiko bunsho shitsu (Japanese Foreign Ministry) and Senshi shitsu (Japanese Defence Ministry) are both housed in Tokyo, and contain large amounts of material upon relations with Germany, part of which is now being printed. Considerable microfilming of these records was done by the Americans after 1945, and copies of these programmes are now deposited in the Library of Congress. There are two guides: C.H. Uyehara, *Checklist of archives in the Japanese Ministry of Foreign Affairs, 1868–1945* (Washington, 1954); and J. Young, *Checklist of Microfilm Reproductions of Selected Archives of the Japanese Army, Navy and other Government Agencies, 1868–1945* (Washington, 1959).

The Kensei shiryo shitsu (National Diet Library) in Tokyo holds the papers of many Japanese statesmen, including Kaoru Inoue and Aritomo Yamagata, whose roles in German-Japanese relations have been examined by Professor Miyake in this book.

Scholars might also like to note the useful guide by H. Webb, *Research in Japanese Sources* (published for the East Asia Institute of Columbia University, New York, 1965).

1. For a more precise breakdown, see H. Lötzke, "Quellen zur Wirtschaftsgeschichte in der Epoche des Imperialismus im Deutschen Zentralarchiv Potsdam", *Jahrbuch für Wirtschaftsgeschichte*, 1961, pt. 1, 249–50. The records relating to the pre-1900 period have been very thoroughly exploited in H. Stoecker, *Deutschland und China im 19. Jahrhundert. Das Eindringen des deutschen Kapitalismus* (Berlin, 1958).
2. See I. Schmidt, "Der Bestand des Auswärtigen Amts im Deutschen Zentralarchiv Potsdam. Pt. 1: 1870–1920", *Archivmitteilungen* 12.Jg.: 71–79.
3. Further details of the archives of the Hansa cities are included in the bibliographies of the following studies: E. Böhm, *Ueberseehandel und Flottenbau. Hanseatische Kaufmannschaft und deutsche Seerüstung 1879–1902* (Düsseldorf, 1972); H.Washausen, *Hamburg und die Kolonialpolitik des deutschen Reiches 1880 bis 1890* (Hamburg, 1968); and D.Kersten, "Die Kriegsziele der Hamburger Kaufmannschaft im ersten Weltkrieg" (phil. diss., Hamburg, 1963).
4. A fuller list of these records is available in Böhm, *Ueberseehandel und Flottenbau*, pp.366–67; and in D.Glade, *Bremen und der Ferne Osten* (Bremen, 1966).
5. See generally, F.X.Hezel, "Catholic Missions in the Caroline and Marshall Islands", *JPH* 5(1970): 213–27. It is also worth mentioning at this point the study by R.Streit and J.Dindinger, *Bibliotheca Missionum ... Einundzwanzigster Band Missions-Literatur von Australien und Ozeanien, 1525–1950* (Freiburg, 1955), which gives details of all Roman Catholic missionaries to the South Seas and of their writings.
6. In connection with the activities of this Rhenish mission in New Guinea, see the contribution by K.Bade in this volume.
7. Use has been made of them in D.G.Philhofer, *Die Geschichte der Neuendettelsauer Mission in Neuguinea*, 3 vols. (Neuendettelsau, 1961–63).
8. For manuscripts in Britain relating to the Pacific area, there is now a most valuable new guide: P.Mander-Jones, ed., *Manuscripts in the British Isles relating to Australia, New Zealand and the Pacific* (Canberra, 1972).
9. These State and Navy Departments' reactions to Germany's activities in the Pacific and Far East have been carefully described in W.R.Braisted,

*The U.S. Navy in the Pacific, 1897–1909* (Austin, Tex. 1958),...*1909–1922* (Austin, Tex. 1971). This rivalry has also been analysed at length in A. Vagts, *Deutschland und die Vereinigten Staaten in der Weltpolitik*, 2 vols (London, 1935).

10. M.A. Walker, "The Archives of the American Board for Foreign Missions", *Harvard Library Bulletin* 4 (1952) 52–68.
11. In this connection, see: E. Taillemite, "Inventaire du fonds Océanie (Polynésie francaise) conservé aux archives du Ministére de la France d'Outre–Mer", *Journal de la Société des Océanistes* 15 (1959): 267–320; idem., "Les archives de la France d'Outre–Mer", *Gazette des Archives* (July, 1957): 7–23; E. Scarr, "French Government Archives", *JPH*, (1970): 176–94.
12. Marist records relating to the Pacific in general have been described in: H.M. Laracy, "The Archives of the Marist Fathers–an untapped Source of Material on the History of the Pacific", *JPH* 2 (1968): 165–71, with an addendum in 5 (1970): 158–59.
13. See R.A. Norem, "German Catholic Missions in Shantung", *Chinese Social and Political Science Review* 19 (1935): 45–64; and F. Bornemann, "Die Angliederung von Kiaochow (Tsingtao) an das Vikariat Süd–Shantung", *Zeitschrift für Missionswissenschaft und Religionswissenschaft*, no. 3 (1970): 81–100.
14. Use has been made of them, for example, in: P. Biskup, "Foreign Coloured Labour in German New Guinea: a Study in Economic Development", *JPH* 5 (1970): 85–107.
15. See the list in *JPH* 1 (1966): 187–88.
16. N. Gunson, "The Out–Going Correspondence of the Australasian Representatives of the London Missionary Society 1886–1912", *JPH* 6 (1971): 161–63.
17. Well analysed, using these records, in A. Ross, *New Zealand Aspirations in the Pacific in the Nineteenth Century* (Oxford, 1964).
18. D. Scarr, *Fragments of Empire: A History of the Western Pacific High Commission 1877–1914* (Canberra, 1967), p. 341.
19. These have been used in: D. Scarr, "Creditors and the House of Hennings", *JPH* 7 (1972): 104–23.

# 16

JOHN A. MOSES

# A Select Bibliography Relating to Germany in the Pacific and Far East, 1870-1914

In venturing to compile a bibliography on the subject covered by this symposium the problem of selection had to be squarely confronted. Indeed, anything approaching a complete bibliography would have far exceeded the size of this present volume. However, to adopt the view of "all or nothing" would have been too easy and hardly very helpful to students seeking bibliographical guidance. The result is, then, that those items have been included which proved of greatest usefulness to the contributors themselves and so, in a real sense, this bibliography represents the bulk of the secondary and printed material which they themselves consulted in preparing their work. The editor wishes to acknowledge their cheerful co-operation. Every effort has been made to ensure that the more relevant works have been included while obscure and peripheral material has been avoided, though, of course that is no guarantee that such titles have not found their way into this list. The editors will be glad to have their attention drawn to publications which have been overlooked.

The problem of subdividing the bibliography also had to be confronted. The first suggestion to make an "area division", i.e. listing material which related to separate areas such as Samoa, New Guinea, Kiautschou, etc., proved to be totally impracticable because much of the colonial history of these places is closely interrelated, and in any case, authors often wrote about them collectively. It seemed, therefore, most useful to divide the material up under the heading of Books, Dissertations, Articles and Other Published Material. The word "books" had to be chosen instead of, say, "monographs", because among them are examples of travel literature or *Reiseberichte*, which may or may not lay claim to scholarly pretensions but which, nevertheless, include valuable material for the student of the area. "Other Published Materials" include the titles of German periodicals and newspapers devoted to colonial matters as well as published bibliographies, government papers such as white papers and memoranda (which are often held by libraries as well as archives) and the newspapers and letters published by various mission organizations.

Another important factor in the selection was that of language. The bulk of the material has come from writers in the English and German languages, but Japanese scholars, too, for example, have been and are researching in the area. But due to the impracticability of including original titles in languages other than the major European ones, only translations have been listed.

Mention ought to be made of the fact that writers listed here often wrote on other aspects of German colonization in the Pacific, and for reasons of space, not all their works have been included. It may be that readers will miss titles which they feel should have been given here. Students seeking further information should therefore be aware that the work of a particular author listed here may not be the only material of relevance to this topic which he produced. In this sense the present bibliography can only claim to have encompassed the more significant writers on the subject and not necessarily *all* their relevant scholarly production.

Books

Allen, G.C., and Donnithorne, A.G. *Western Enterprise in Far Eastern Economic Development*. London, 1954.

Anderson, P.R. *The Background of Anti-English Feeling in Germany 1890–1902. Washington,* 1939.

Bachmann, J. *Von Kiautschou bis Kreta. Ein Beitrag Zur Erforschung des deutsch-englischen Verhältnisses um die Jahrhundertwende*. Berlin, 1929.

Backhaus, E. *Die Arbeiterfrage in der deutschen Südsee. Eine wirtschaftlich-juristische Kolonialstudie*. Berlin, n.d.

Baessler, A. *Südsee-Bilder*. Berlin, 1900.

Bahse, M.F. *Die Wirtschafts- und Handelsverhältnisse der Fidschi-, Tonga- und Samoainseln*. Leipzig, 1881.

Beasley, W.G. *The Modern History of Japan*. London, 1963.

Behme, F., and Krieger, M. *Führer durch Tsingtau und Umgebung*, Berlin, 1906.

Behrmann, W. *Im Stromgebiet des Sepik. Eine deutsche Forschungsreise in Neuguinea*. Berlin, 1922.

Beresford, Lord Charles. *The Break-Up of China*. London, 1899.

Bergmann, G. *De, Arbeitstag eines Pioniers der Rheinischen Neu-Guinea Mission im Spiegel seiner Briefe*. Barmen, 1922.

Bigelow, P. *Die Völker im kolonialen Wettstreit*. Berlin, 1902.

Binder-Kriegelstein, E. *Die Kämpfe des deutschen Expeditionskorps in China und ihre militärischen Lehren*. Berlin, 1902.

Bley, B. *Die Herz Jesu Mission in der Südsee*. Hiltrup, 1924.

Blum, H. *Neu-Guinea und der Bismarck-Archipel. Eine wirtschaftliche Studie*. Berlin, 1900.

Böhm, H. *Überseehandel und Flottenbau. Hanseatische Kaufmannschaft und deutsche Seerüstung 1879–1902*. Hamburg, 1972.

Bohner, Th. *Die Woermanns. Vom Werden deutscher Grösse*. Berlin, 1935.

Bonhard, O. *Geschichte des Alldeutschen Verbandes*. Leipzig/Berlin, 1920.

Braisted, W.R. *The United States Navy in the Pacific 1897–1909*. Austin, 1958.

———.*The United States Navy in the Pacific 1909–1922*. Austin, 1971.

Brandt, M. von. *Ostasiatische Fragen*. Berlin, 1897.

———.*China und seine Handelsbeziehungen zum Auslande, mit besonderer Berücksichtigung der deutschen*. Berlin, 1898.

——— *33 Jahre in Ostasien. Erinnerungen eines deutschen Diplomaten*. 3 vols. Leipzig, 1901.

Brenninkmeyer, L. *Fünfzehn Jahre beim Bergvolk der Baininger*. Düsseldorf, 1928.

Brookes, J.I. *International Rivalry in the Pacific Islands 1800–1875*. Berkeley/Los Angeles, 1941.

Brown, G. *Pioneer Missionary and Explorer. An Autobiography*. London, 1908.

Brücke, O. *Die Entwicklung und weltwirschaftliche Bedeutung der Kopra—und Kokosölproduktion und Konsumtion*. Nuremberg, 1930.

Buchner, M. *Aurora colonialis*. Munich, 1914.

Bülow, Fürst Bernhard von. *Denkwürdigkeiten*. Vol. 1. Berlin, 1930.

Burger, F. *Die Küsten—und Bergvölker der Gazellehalbinsel*. Stuttgart, 1913.

———.*Land und Leute auf den südöstlichen Molukken, dem Bismarckarchipel und den Salomon-Inseln*. Berlin, 1914.

———.*Urwald und Urmenschen. Reisen und Abenteuer auf den melanesischen Inseln*. 2d ed. Leipzig, 1928.

Burnell, F.S. *Australia versus Germany: the Story of the Taking of German New Guinea*. London, 1915.

Cayley-Webster, H. *Through New Guinea and the Cannibal Countries*. London, 1898.

Cecil, L. *Albert Ballin. Business and Politics in Imperial Germany 1888–1919*. Princeton, 1967.

Churchward, W.B. *My Consulate in Samoa*. London, 1887.

Class, P. *Die Rechtsverhältnisse der freien farbigen Arbeiter in den deutschen Schutzgebieten Afrikas und der Südsee*. Ulm, 1913.

Clyde, P.H. *The Far East. A History of the Impact of the West on Eastern Asia*. New York, 1955.

Colquhon, A.R. *The Mastery of the Pacific*. New York, 1904.

Colwell, J., ed. *A Century in the Pacific*. London, 1914.

Coppius, A. *Hamburgs Bedeutung auf dem Gebiete der deutschen Kolonialpolitik*. Berlin, 1905.

Cordier, H. *Histore des Relations de la Chine avec les Puissances occidentales 1860–1900*. 3 vols. Paris 1901–2 (German transl. Hu Schöng, *Der Imperialismus and Chinas Politik*. Berlin, 1959).

Coulter, J.W. *The Pacific Dependencies of the United States*. New York, 1957.

Cowan, C.D., ed. *The Economic Development of South-East Asia. Studies in Economic History and Political Economy*. Studies in Modern Asia and Africa, 3. London, 1964.

Cowan, J. *Samoa and its Story*. Wellington, 1914.

Danks, B. *A Brief History of the New Britain Mission*. Sydney, 1899.

Darden, T.F. *Historical Sketch of the Naval Administration of the Government of American Samoa 1900–1951*. f1. Washington, 1952.

Davidson, J.W. *Samoa mo Samoa: The Emergence of the Independent State of Western Samoa*. Oxford, 1967.

Dawson, W.H. *The German Empire*. 2 vols. London, 1919.

Deane, W., ed. *In Wild New Britain. The Story of Benjamin Danks, Pioneer Missionary, from his Diary*. Sydney, 1933.

Deeken, R. *Manuia Samoa! Samoanische Reiseskizzen und Beobachtungen*. Berlin/Oldenburg/Leipzig, 1902.

———.*Die Karolinen*. Berlin, 1912.

———.*Die Landwirtschaft in den deutschen Kolonien*. Berlin, 1914.

Dehio, L. *Deutschland und die Weltpolitik im 20. Jahrhundert*. Munich, 1955.

Dernburg, B. *Zielpunkte des deutschen Kolonialwesens*. Berlin, 1907.

Deutsche Kolonialgesellschaft. *Erörterungen der Rassenfrage in den deutschen Schutzgebieten*. submitted to German Reichstag, Berlin, 1909.

*Die Diskonto-Gesellschaft 1851–1901. Denkschrift zum 50 jährigen Jubiläum*. Berlin, 1901.

Dittmar, H.G. *Die deutsch-englischen Beziehungen in den Jahren 1898–99*. Stuttgart, 1938.

Djang, Feng Djen. *The Diplomatic Relations between China and Germany since 1898*. Shanghai, 1936.

Dulles, F.R. *America in the Pacific*. Boston/New York, 1932.

Easton, S.C. *The Rise and Fall of Western Colonialism*. New York, 1964.

Ebert, P. *Südsee-Erinnerungen*. Leipzig, 1924.

Ehler, O.E. *Samoa, die Perle der Südsee*. 2d ed. Berlin, 1895.

Eisenstein, Richard, Freiherr von und zu. *Reise nach Siam, Java, Deutsch-Neu-Guinea und Australasien*. Vienna, 1904.

Ellison, J.W. *Opening and Penetration of Foreign Influence in Samoa to 1880*. Oregon, 1938.
Epstein, A.L. *Matupit, Land, Politics and Change among the Tolai of New Britain*. Canberra and London, 1969.
Epstein, T.S. *Capitalism, Primitive and Modern. Some Aspects of Tolai Economic Growth*. Manchester, 1968.
Eyck, E. *Bismarck and the German Empire*. London, 1960.
Fabri. F. *Bedarf Deutschland der Kolonien? Eine politisch-ökonomische Betrachtung*. Gotha, 1879.
———.*5 Jahre deutscher Kolonialpolitik*. Gotha, 1889.
Fieldhouse, D.K. *The Colonial Empires*. London/New York, 1966.
Finsch. O. *Samoafahrten. Reisen in Kaiser-Wilhelmsland und Englisch-Neu-Guinea in den Jahren 1884–85 an Bord des deutschen Dampfers Samoa*. Berlin, 1888.
Fischer, D. *Unter Südseeinsulanern. Das Leben des Forschers Mikloucho Maclay*. Leipzig, 1955.
Fischer, K. *Kolonien auf dem grünen Tisch—Deutschlands Weg nach Übersee*. Berlin, 1938.
Fischer, M. *Szetschaun. Diplomatie und Reisen in China während der letzten 3 Jahre der Kaiserzeit. Aus den Papieren des Gesandten. Mit einem Anhang: 40 Jahre deutscher China-Politik*. Munich/Vienna, 1968.
Fletcher, C.B. *The New Pacific: British Policy and German Aims*. London, 1917.
———.*Stevenson's Samoa: The Case Against Germany in the Pacific*. London, 20.
Flierl, J. *Forty Years in New Guinea, Memoirs of Senior Missionary J. Flierl*. Iowa, 1927.
Florack, F. *Die Schutzgebiete, ihre Organisation in Verfassung und Verwaltung*. Berlin, 1905.
Fox, F. *Problems in the Pacific*. London, 1912.
Fox, J.W., and Cumberland, K.B. *Western Samoa: Land, Life, and Agriculture in Tropical Polynesia*. Christchurch, 1962.
Francke, O. *Die Grossmächte in Ostasien von 1894 bis 1914*. Brunswick, 1923.
Franzius, G. *Kiautschou. Deutschlands Erwerbung in Ostasien*. Berlin, 1899.
Freytag, A. *Die Missionen der Gesellschaft des Göttlichen Wortes*. Steyl, 1912.
Friedjung, H. *Das Zeitalter des Imperialismus 1884–1914*. 3 vols. Berlin, 1919–22.
Fritz, G. *Ad majorem Dei gloriam: die Vorgeschichte des Aufstandes von 1910/11 in Ponape*. Leipzig, 1922.
Frommund, B. *Deutsch-Neuguinea, eine Perle der Südsee*. Hamburg, 1926.
Galster, K. *England, Deutsche Flotte und Weltkrieg*. Kiel, 1925.
Gareis, K. *Deutsches Kolonialrecht*. Berlin, 1902.

Gartzke. *Der Aufstand in Ponape und seine Niederwerfung durch S.M. Schiffe 'Emden', 'Nürnberg', 'Cormoran', und 'Planet'.* Berlin, 1911.

Genthe, S. *Samoa: Reiseschilderungen.* Berlin, 1908.

Giese, F. *Kleine Geschichte der deutschen Flotte.* Berlin, 1966.

Gilson, R.P. *Samoa 1830 to 1900: The Politics of a Multi-Cultural Community.* Melbourne, 1970.

Glade, D. *Bremen und der Ferne Osten.* Veröffentlichungen aus dem Staatsarchiv der Freien Hansestadt Bremen, vol. 34. 1966.

Gnielinski, S. von. *Struktur und Entwicklung Papuas und des von Australien verwalteten ehemals deutschen Gebietes der Insel Neu-Guinea.* Hamburger Geographische Studien, no.9, 1958.

Godshall, W.L. *Tsingtau under Three Flags.* Shanghai, 1929.

Gooch, G.P. *Before the War, Studies in Diplomacy.* vol.1. Oxford, 1936.

Grapow, M. von. *Die deutsche Flagge im Stillen Ozean.* Berlin, 1915.

Grattan, C.H. *The United States and the Southwest Pacific.* Cambridge, Mass., 1961.

———. *The Southwest Pacific to 1900.* Ann Arbor, Mich., 1963.

———. *The Southwest Pacific since 1900.* Ann Arbor, Mich., 1963.

Gray, J.A.C. *Amerika Samoa: A History of American Samoa, and its U.S. Naval Administration.* Annapolis, 1960.

Gröner, E. *Die deutschen Kriegsschiffe, 1815–1945*, 2 vols. Munich, 1966–68.

Grote, G. *Untersuchungen zur deutschen Kolonialpolitik um die Jahrhundertwende.* Berlin, 1940.

Grotewold, Ch. *Unser Kolonialwesen und seine wirtschaftliche Bedeutung.* Stuttgart, 1911.

Grunzel, J. *Die kommerzielle Entwicklung Chinas in den letzen 25 Jahren.* Leipzig, 1891.

Hackett, R.F. *Yamagate Aritomo in the Rise of Modern Japan 1838–1922.* Cambridge, Mass., 1971.

Hagen, B. *Unter den Papuas. Beobachtungen und Studien über Land und Leute, Tier- und Pflanzenwelt in Kaiser Wilhelmsland.* Wiesbaden, 1899.

Hagen, M. von. *Bismarcks Kolonialpolitik.* Stuttgart/Berlin, 1921.

Hager, C. *Kaiser-Wilhelmsland und der Bismarck-Archipel.* Leipzig, 1886.

———. *Die Marshall-Inseln in Erd- und Völkerkunde, Handel und Mission.* Leipzig, 1886.

Hahl, A. *Deutsch-Neuguinea.* Berlin, 1936.

———. *Gouverneursjahre in Neuguinea.* Berlin, 1937.

Haller, C. *Die Phosphat-Gesellschaften der Südsee*, 2d ed. Mannheim/Leipzig, 1911.

Hallgarten, G.W.F. *Imperialismus vor 1914.* 2d rev. and extended ed. 2 vols. Munich, 1963.

Hallmann, H. *Der Weg zum deutschen Schlachtflottenbau.* Stuttgart, 1933.

Hammann, O. *The World Policy of Germany, 1890–1912*. London, 1927.

Hanke, A. *Die Rheinische Mission in Kaiser-Wilhelmsland*. 3d rev. ed. Barmen, 1908.

Harms, O. *Deutsch-Australische Dampfschiffs-Gesellschaft, Hamburg. Ihre Gründung und Entwicklung bis zum Krieg*. Hamburg, 1933.

Hassert, K. *Deutschlands Kolonien*. Leipzig, 1894.

———.Die neuen deutschen Erwerbungen in der Südsee: Karolinen-, Marianen- und Samoa Inseln. Leipzig, 1902.

Haushofer, K. *Geopolitik des Pazifischen Ozeans*. Berlin, 1924.

Heide, P. [a.d.] *Die Missionsgesellschaft von Steyl*. Steyl, 1900.

Heilborn, A. *Die deutschen Kolonien. Land und Leute*. Berlin, 1906.

Helfferich, E. *Zur Reform der kolonialen Verwaltungsorganisation*. Berlin, 1905.

———.*Die Niederländischen-Indischen Kulturbanken*. Jena, 1914.

———.*Ein Leben*, vols 1–3. Hamburg, 1948 (printed as MS).

———.*Zur Geschichte der Firmen Behn, Meyer & Co., gegründet in Singapore am 1. November 1840 und Arnold Otto Meyer gegründet in Hamburg am 1. Juni 1857*. Hamburg, 1957.

Helfferich, E., and Witthoeft, F. *Deutsche Wirtschaftspolitik in Südost-Asien*. Hamburg, 1910.

Henderson, W.O. *Studies in German Colonial History*. Chicago, 1962.

Hernsheim, F. *Südsee-Erinnerungen [1875–1880]*. Berlin, 1883.

Herrfurth, K. *Fürst Bismarck und die Kolonialpolitik*. Berlin, 1909.

Hertz, R. *Das Hamburger Seehandelshaus J.C. Godeffroy und Sohn*. Hamburg, 1922.

Hesse-Wartegg, E. von. *Schantung und Deutsch-China*. Leipzig, 1898.

———.*Samoa, Bismarck-Archipel und Neu-Guinea. Drei deutsche Kolonien in der Südsee*. Leipzig, 1902.

Hessler, G. *Deutsch-Kiautschou—Kurze Beschreibung von Land und Leuten*. Berlin, 1898.

Hieke, E. *Die Reederei M. Jebsen A.G., Apenrade*. Hamburg, 1953.

Hoffman, A. *Lebenserinnerungen eines Rheinischen Missionars*, 2 vols. Wuppertal-Barmen, 1948–49.

Hoffman, H. von. *Einführung in das deutsche Kolonialrecht*. Leipzig, 1911.

Hoffmann, R.J.S. *Great Britain and German Trade Rivalry 1875–1914*. Philadelphia, 1933.

Hohenlohe-Schillingfürst, C.v. *Denkwürdigkeiten*, vols 1 and 2. Stuttgart/Leipzig, 1907.

Holland, H.E. *Samoa, a Story that Teems with Tragedy*. Wellington, 1918.

Hubatsch, W. *Die Aera Tirpitz*. Göttingen, 1955.

———.*Der Admiralstab und die Obersten Marinebehörden in Deutschland, 1848–1945*. Frankfurt, 1958.

Hughes, E.R. *The Invasion of China by the Western World.* London, 1937.

Huntington, S.P. *The Soldier and the State, The Theory and Politics of Civil-Military Relations.* Toronto, 1957.

Hu Sheng. *Imperialism and Chinese Politics.* Peking, 1955.

Hüskes, J., ed. *Pioniere der Südsee.* Hiltrup, 1932.

Ibbeken, R. *Das aussenpolitische Problem. Staat und Wirtschaft in der deutschen Reichspolitik 1880–19141.* Schleswig, 1928.

Idditti, S. *The Life of Marquis Shigenobu Okuma, a Maker of New Japan.* Tokyo, 1940.

Indra, K.R. *Südseefahrten. Schilderungen einer Reise nach den Fidschi-Inseln, Samoa und Tonga.* Berlin, 1903.

Interstate Commission of Australia. *Report on South Pacific Trade.* Melbourne, 1918.

Irwin, G. *Nineteenth-Century Borneo. A Study in Diplomatic Rivalry.* The Hague, 1955.

Jacob, E.G. *Deutsche Kolonialpolitik in Dokumenten.* Leipzig, 1938.

Japikse, N. *Die politischen Beziehungen Hollands zu Dcutschland in ihrer historischen Entwicklung.* Heidelberg, 1925.

Jerussalimski, A.S. *Die Aussenpolitik und die Diplomatie des deutschen Imperialismus Ende des 19.* Jahrhunderts. Berlin, 1954.

Kade, E. *Die Anfänge der deutschen Kolonial-Zentralverwaltung.* Forschungen zur Kolonialfrage, vol 2. Würzburg-Aumühle, 1939.

Kajima, M. *A Brief Diplomatic History of Modern Japan.* Tokyo, 1965.

Kausch, O. *Deutsches Kolonial-Lexikon. Allgemeine Übersicht über die deutschen Kolonialgebiete.* Berlin, 1903.

Kautsky, K. *Sozialismus und Kolonialpolitik.* Berlin, 1907.

Keesing, F.M. *Modern Samoa.* London, 1934.

Kennedy, P.M. *The Samoan Tangle: A Study in Anglo-German-American Relations 1878–1900.* Dublin/New York/St Lucia, Qld, 1974.

Kerst, G. *Jacob Meckel, sein Leben, sein Wirken in Deutschland und Japan.* Göttingen, 1970.

Keysser, Ch. *Anutu im Papualand.* 3d ed. Neuendettelsau, 1958.

———. *Das bin bloss ich.* Neuendettelsau, 1966.

Kienitz, E. *Zeittafel zur deutschen Kolonialgeschichte.* Munich, 1941.

Kiernan, E.V.G. *British Diplomacy in China 1880–1885.* Cambridge, 1939.

Kirchoff, A. *Die Südseeinseln und der deutsche Südseehandel.* Heidelberg, 1880.

Kleintitschen, A. *Die Küstenbewohner der Gazellehalbinsel.* Münster, 1907.

Koch, P. *Geschichte der deutschen Marine.* Berlin, 1902.

Kolisch, O., ed. *Die Kolonialgesetzgebung des Deutschen Reichs mit dem Gesetze über die Konsulargerichtsbarkeit.* Hanover, 1896.

Königk, G. *Die Berliner Kongo-Konferenz 1884–1885. Ein Beitrag zur Kolonialpolitik Bismarcks.* Essen, 1938.

Koschitzky, M.v. *Deutsche Colonialgeschichte.* 2 vols. Leipzig, 1887–88.

Koskinen, A.A. *Missionary Influence as a Political Factor in the Pacific Islands.* Helsinki, 1953.

Kotze, S. von. *Aus Papuas Kulturmorgen. Südsee-Erinnerungen.* Berlin, 1905.

Kraft, H.H. *Chartergesellschaften als Mittel zur Erschliessung kolonialer Gebiete.* Hamburg, 1943.

Krämer, A. *Die Samoa-Inseln. Entwurf einer Monographie, mit besonderer Berücksichtigung Deutsch-Samoas.* 2 vols. Berlin, 1910.

Krämer, K.R. *Hawaii, Ost-Mikronesien und Samoa. Meine zweite Südseereise 1897–1899 zum Studium der Atolle und ihrer Bewohner.* Berlin, 1906.

Krausnick, H. *Holsteins Geheimpolitik in der Aera Bismarck 1886–1890.* Hamburg, 1924.

Krieger, M. *Neu-Guinea.* Berlin, 1899.

Kriele, E. *Das Kreuz unter den Palmen, Die Rheinische Mission in Neu-Guinea.* Barmen, 1927.

Kruck, A. *Geschichte des Alldeutschen Verbandes 1890–1939.* Wiesbaden, 1954.

Kubary, J.S. *Ethnographische Beiträge zur Kenntnis des Karolinen-Archipels.* Berlin, 1889.

Kubicek, R.V. *The Administration of Imperialism: Joseph Chamberlain at the Colonial Office.* Durham, NC, 1969.

Kuczynski, J. *Studien zur Geschichte des deutschen Imperialismus.* Vol. 1: *Monopole und Unternehmer-Verbände.* Berlin, 1948; vol. 2: *Propagandaorganisationen des Monopolkapitalismus.* Berlin, 1950.

Kuhn, H. *Die deutschen Schutzgebiete Erwerb, Verwaltung und Gerichtsbarkeit.* Berlin, 1913.

Kunze, G. *Im Dienst des Kreuzes auf ungebahnten Pfaden.* No. 2, 3d ed. Barmen, 1925.

Kurze, G. *Samoa, Land, Leute und Mission,* Berlin, 1900.

Langer, W.L. *The Diplomacy of Imperialism 1890–1902.* New York, 1951.

Latourette, K.S. *A History of Christian Missions in China.* London, 1929.

Lawrence, P. *Road Belong Cargo. A Study of the Cargo Movement.* Melbourne, 1964.

Lehmann, J. *Die Aussenpolitik und die Kölnische Zeitung während der Bülow-Zeit 1897–1909.* Leipzig, 1937.

Lepsuis, I.; Thimme, F.; and Mendelsohn-Bartholdy, A. *Die Grosse Politik der Europäischen Kabinette: 1871–1914.* 40 vols. Berlin, 1922–27.

Lettenbaur, J.A. *Morgen, Mittag und Abend. Schattenrisse zur Zeit- und Völkergeschichte von einem deutschen Auslandsvertreter.* Stuttgart/Berlin, 1927.

Lignitz, von. *Deutschalnds Interessen in Ostasien und die gelbe Gefahr.* Berlin, 1907.
Linckens, H. *Streiflichter aus der Herz Jesu Mission.* Hiltrup, 1921.
Loehnis, H. *Die europäischen Kolonien. Beiträge zur Kritik der deutschen Kolonialprojekte.* Bonn, 1881.
Louis, W.R. *Great Britain and Germany's Lost Colonies, 1914–1919.* Oxford, 1967.
Lovett, R. *The History of the London Missionary Society 1795–1895.* London, 1899.
Luettich, G. *Bundesrat und Reichstag bei der Kolonialgesetzgebung.* Münster, 1914.
Luke, Sir Harry. *Britain in the South Seas.* London, 1945.
———.*Islands of the South Pacific.* London, 1962.
MacMurray, J. van Antwerp. *Treaties and Agreements With and Concerning China, 1894–1919.* 2 vols. New York/London, 1921.
Mander, L.A. *Some Dependent Peoples of the South Pacific.* New York, 1954.
Mansergh, N. *The Coming of the First World War. A Study in the European Balance 1878–914.* London, 1949.
Mantey, von. *Deutsche Marinegeschichte.* Charlottenburg, 1926.
Marder, A.J. *The Anatomy of British Sea Power: A History of British Naval Policy in the Pre-Dreadnought Era 1880–1905.* Hamden, Conn. ed. 1964.
Marquardt, C. *Zur Lösung der Samoafrage.* Berlin, 1899.
———.*Der Kampf um und auf Samoa.* Berlin, 1899.
Martin, K.L.P. *Missionaries and Annexations in the Pacific.* Oxford, 1924.
Mastermann, S.R. *The Origins of International Rivalry in Samoa 1845–1884.* London, 1934.
Mathies, O. *Hamburgs Reederei 1814–1914.* Hamburg, 1924.
Maudsley, A.P. *Life in the Pacific Fifty Years Ago.* London, 1930.
McArthur, N. *Island Populations of the Pacific.* Canberra, 1968.
Meusel, A. *Beiträge zur Geschichte des deutschen Imperialismus von 1890–1914*, pt 1. Berlin, 1951.
Meyer, H. *Das Deutsche Kolonialreich. Eine Länderkunde der deutschen Schutzgebiete*, vol. 2. Leipzig/Vienna, 1909–10.
Michalik, G. *Probleme des deutschen Flottenbaus.* Breslau, 1931.
Mirbt, C. *Mission und Kolonialpolitik in den deutschen Schutzgebieten.* Tübingen, 1910.
Mohr, H. *Katholische Orden und deutscher Imperialismus.* Berlin, 1965.
Moon, P.T. *Imperialism and World Politics.* New York, 1926.
Moors, H.J. *With Stevenson in Samoa.* Boston, 1910.
Morrell, W.P. *Britain in the Pacific Islands.* Oxford, 1960.
———.*The Great Powers in the Pacific.* London, 1963.
Morse, H.B. *The International Relations of the Chinese Empire.* 3 vols. London/New York, 1910 and 1918.

Mosolff, H. *Die Chinesische Auswanderung [Ursachen, Wesen und Wirkungen] unter besonderer Berücksichtigung der Hauptauswanderungsgebiete und mit einem ausführlichen Bericht über die chinesische Arbeiterbeschaffung für Samoa unter der deutschen Verwaltung*. Rostock, 1932.

Müller, G. *Land und Leute im Bismarck-Archipel.* Berlin, 1895.

Müller, G.A. v. *Der Kaiser ... Aufzeichnungen des Chefs des Marinekabinetts über die Ära Wilhemls II.* Berlin/Brankfurt/Zürich, 1965.

Müller-Jabusch, M. *Fünfzig Jahre Deutsch-Asiatische Bank 1890–1939.* Berlin, 1940.

Münch, H. *Adolph von Hansemann.* München/Berlin, 1932.

Nadel, G.H., and Curtis, F. eds. *Imperialism and Colonialism.* New York, 1964.

Naval Intelligence Division of the Admiralty. *Pacific Islands*, vols 1–3. Geographical Handbook Series. London, 1943–45.

Neale, R.G. *Britain and American Imperialism 1898–1900.* St Lucia, Qld, 1965.

Neill, S. *Colonialism and Christian Missions.* New York, 1966.

Neuhauss, R. *Deutsch-Neu-Guinea.* 3 vols. Berlin, 1911.

———.*Unsere Kolonie Deutsch Neu-Guinea.* Weimar, 1914.

Norem, R.A. *Kiaochow Leased Territory.* Berkeley, 1936.

Noske, G. *Kolonialpolitik und Sozialdemokratie.* Stuttgart, 1914.

Nussbaum, M. *Vom "Kolonialenthusiasmus" zur Kolonialpolitik der Monopole. Zur deutschen Kolonialpolitik unter Bismarck, Caprivi, Hohenlohe.* Berlin, 1962.

Oliver, D.L. *The Pacific Islands.* Cambridge, Mass., 1951.

Osborn, F. *The Pacific World.* New York, 1944.

Overell, L. *A Woman's Impression of German New Guinea.* London, 1923.

Parkinson, C.N. *British Intervention in Malaya 1867–1877.* Singapore, 1960.

Parkinson, R. *Im Bismarck-Archipel. Erlebnisse und Beobachtungen auf der Insel Neu-Pommern.* Leipzig, 1887.

———*30 Jahre in der Südsee.* Edited by G. Ankermann. Stuttgart, 1907.

[The]Parliament of the Commonwealth of Australia. *Interim and Final Reports of Royal Commission on Late German New Guinea.* 1920.

Parnaby, O.W. *Britain and the Labour Trade in the Southwest Pacific.* Durham, NC, 1964.

Paul, C. *Die Missionen in unseren Kolonien. Vierter Teil: Die deutschen Südsee-Inseln.* Dresden, 1908.

Peekel, G. *Religion und Zauberei auf dem mittleren Neu Mecklenburg.* Münster, 1910.

Peters, E. *Der Begriff sowie die staats- und völkerrechtliche Stellung der*

*Eingeborenen in den deutschen Schutzgebieten nach deutschem Kolonialrechte*. Göttingen, 1906.

Pfeil, Joachim Graf von. *Studien und Beobachtungen aus der Südsee*. Brunswick, 1899.

*Plangzungs-Betriebe auf Samoa. Auskunft über das Schutzgebiet, herausgegeben von dem Pflanzerverein*. Apia, 1910.

Pilhofer, G. *Die Geschichte der Neuendettelsauer Mission in Neuguinea*. 3 vols. Neuendettelsau, 1961–63.

Pitcairn, W.D. *Two Years Among the Savages of New Guinea*. London, 1891.

Pitt, D. *Tradition and Economic Progress in Samoa*. Oxford, 1970.

Prager, E. *Die deutsche Kolonialgesellschaft 1882–1907*. Berlin, 1908.

Presseisen, E.L. *Germany and Japan, A Study in the Totalitarian Diplomacy 1933–1941. The Hague,* 1958.

———.*Before Aggression, Europeans Prepare the Japanese Army*. Arizona, 1965.

[*Die*] *Preussische Expedition nach Ostasien*, from official sources. 4 vols. Berlin, 1864ff.

Prothero, G.W., ed. *Foreign Office* [*Great Britain*] *Historical Section Handbooks*. London 1920. No. 42: *German Colonisation*; no. 71: *Kiachow and Wei-hai-wei*; no. 139: *Discoveries and Acquisitions in the Pacific*; no. 146: *Former German Possessions in Oceania*.

Prowazek, S. von. *Die deutschen Marianen. Ihre Natur und Geschichte*. Leipzig, 1913.

Pullen-Burry, B. *In a German Colony, or Four Weeks in New Britain*. London, 1909.

Reed, S.W. *The Making of Modern New Guinea, with Special Reference to Culture Contact in the Mandated Territory*. Memoirs of the American Philosophical Society, vol. 18. Philadelphia, 1943.

Remer, C.F. *Foreign Investments in China*. Shanghai, 1933.

Rich, M. *Friedrich von Holstein*. 2 vols. Cambridge, 1965.

Rich, M., and Fischer, M.H., eds. *The Holstein Papers*. 4 vols. Cambridge, 1955–63.

Richthofen, Freiherr F. von. *Schantung und seine Eingangspforte Kiautschou*. Berlin, 1898.

———.*Deutschalnd in Ostasien*. Berlin, 1898.

———.*Tagebücher aus China*. Edited by E. Tiessen. 2 vols. Berlin, 1907.

Riedel, O. *Der Kampf um Deutsch-Samoa. Erinnerungen eines Hamburger Kaufmannes* Berlin, 1938.

Riesenberg, S. *The Native Policy of Ponape*. Washington, 1968.

Ritter, G. *Bismarcks Verhältnis zu England und die Politik des neuen Kurses*. Berlin, 1924.

———.*Staatskunst und Kriegshandwerk, vol 2: Die Hauptmächte Europas und das Wilhelminische Reich 1890–1914*. Munich, 1960.

Robson, R.W. *The Pacific Islands Handbook*. New York, 1945.
Röhl, J.C.G. *Germany Without Bismarck*. London, 1967.
Rohrbach, P. *Kulturpolitische Grundsätze für die Rassen- und Missionsfragen*. Berlin-Schöneberg, 1909.
———.*Das deutsche Kolonialwesen*. Leipzig, 1911.
Romilly, H.H. *Letters from the Western Pacific and Mashonaland 1878–1891. London,* 1893.
Roskoschny, H. *Die Deutschen in der Südsee*. Leipzig, 1885.
Ross, A. *New Zealand Aspirations in the Pacific in the Nineteenth Century*. Oxford, 1964.
Rothfels, H. *Bismarcks englische Bündnispolitik*. Berlin/Leipzig, 1924.
Rowe, N.A. *Samoa under the Sailing Gods*. London/New York, 1930.
Rowley, C.D. *The Australians in German New Guinea, 1914–1921*. Melbourne, 1958.
Rutherford, N. *Shirley Baker and the King of Tonga*. Melbourne, 1971.
Ryden, G.H. *The Foreign Policy of the United States in Relation to Samoa*. New Haven, 1933.
Sack, P.G. *Land Between Two Laws. Early European Land Acquisition in New Guinea*. Canberra, 1973.
Salesius, D.O. *Die Karolineninsel Jap. Ein Beitrag zur Kenntnis von Land und Leuten in unseren deutschen Südsee-Kolonien*. Berlin, 1906.
Salisbury, R.F. *Vunamami. Economic Transformation in a Traditional Society*. Berkeley and Los Angeles, 1970.
*Samoa, Handbook of Western*. Wellington, 1925.
Sass, J. *Die deutschen Weissbücher zur auswärtigen Politik 1870–1914*. Berlin/Leipzig, 1928.
Scarr, D. *Fragments of Empire. A History of the Western Pacific High Commission 1877–1914*. Canberra, 1967.
Schack, F. *Das deutsche Kolonialrecht in seiner Entwicklung bis zum Weltkriege*. Hamburg, 1923.
Schäfer, D. *Kolonialgeschichte*. Berlin, 1906.
———.*Deutschland und England in See- und Weltgeltung*. Leipzig, 1915.
Schanz, M. *Australien und die Südsee an der Jahrhundertwende*. Berlin, 1901.
Schellong, O. *Alte Dokumente aus der Südsee*. Königsberg, 1934.
Schieber, C.E. *The Transformation of American Sentiment towards Germany, 1870–1914*. Boston/New York, 1923.
Schmack, K. *J.C. Godeffroy* & Sohn, Kaufleute zu Hamburg. Hamburg, 1938.
Schmidlin, J. *Die Katholischen Missionen*. Münster, 1913.
———.*Rechtszustände der Eingeborenen in der deutschen Südsee*. Berlin, 1914.
Schmidt, R. *Aus kolonialer Frühzeit*. Berlin. 1922.
Schnee, H. *Bilder aus der Südsee. Unter den kannibalischen Stämmen des Bismarck-Archipels*. Berlin, 1904.
———.*Unsere Kolonien*. Leipzig, 1908.
———.*German Colonization, Past and Future*. London, 1926.

Schnee, H. ed. *Deutsches Kolonial-Lexikon*. 3 vols. Leipzig, 1920.

Schoen, W. von. *Deutschlands Kolonialweg: Die Geschichte unserer Schutzgebiete*. Berlin, 1939.

Scholefield, G.H. *The Pacific, its Past and Future, and the Policy of the Great Powers from the Eighteenth Century*. London, 1919.

Schrameier, W. *Die Grundlagen der wirtschaftlichen Entwicklung in Kiautschou*. Berlin, 1903.

———.*Aus Kiautschous Verwaltung. Die Land-, Steuer- und Zollpolitik des Kiautschougebietes*. Jena, 1914.

Schramm, P.E. *Deutschland und Übersee*. Brunswick/Berlin/Hamburg/Kiel, 1950.

Schrecker, J.E. *Imperialism and Chinese Nationalism*. Cambridge, Mass., 1971.

Schreiner, A. *Zur Geschichte der deutschen Aussenpolitik 1871–1945*, vol. 1. Berlin, 1952.

Schüddekopf, O.E. *Die britische Marinepolitik 1880–1918*. Hamburg, 1938.

———.*Die Stützpunktpolitik des Deutschen Reiches 1890–1914*. Berlin, 1941.

Schuemacher, K. *Europäische Zollbeamte in China und ihr Einfluss auf die Förderung unseres Aussenhandels*. Karlsruhe, 1901.

Schultz, E. *Die wichtigsten Grundsätze des samoanischen Familien- und Erbrechts*. Apia, 1905.

Schultz-Ewerth, E. *Erinnerungen an Samoa*. Berlin, 1926.

Schultz-Ewerth, E., and Adam, L., eds. *Das Eingeborenenrecht*. 2 vols. Stuttgart, 1929–30.

Schulze-Hinrichs, A., ed. *Weltmachtstreben und Flottenbau*. Witten, 1956.

Schütze, W. *Kolonialpolitik und Kolonialinstitut in Hamburg*. Hamburg, 1909.

Schwabe, K., ed. *Die deutschen Kolonien*. 2 vols. Belin, 1910.

Seelbach, F. *Grundzüge der Rechtspflege in den deutschen Kolonien*. Berlin, 1904.

Shineberg, D. *They Came for Sandalwood. A Study of the Sandalwood Trade in the South-West Pacific 1830–1865*. Melbourne, 1967.

Seimes, J. *Hermann Roessler and the Making of the Meiji State with his Commentaries on the Meiji Constitution*. Tokyo, 1966.

Siewert, W. *Die Stützpunktpolitik der U.S.A.* Berlin, 1942.

Solf, W.H. *Eingeborene und Ansiedler auf Samoa*, printed as MS 1908.

———.*Kolonialpolitik. Mein politisches Vermächtnis*. Berlin, 1919.

Sontag, R.J. *Germany, England, Background to the Conflict 1848–1894*. New York, 1938.

Spellmeyer, H. *Deutsche Kolonialpolitik im Reichstag*. Stuttgart, 1931.

Spiess, G. *Die preussische Expedition nach Ostasien*. Berlin/Leipzig, 1864.

Spoehr, F.M. *White Falcon: The House of Godeffroy and its Commercial and Scientific Role in the Pacific*. Palo Ato, Calif., 1963.

Springborn, A. *Englands Stellung zur deutschen Welt- und Kolonialpolitik in den Jahren 1911–61914*. Forschungen zur Kolonialfrage, vol. 4. Würzburg-Aumühle, 1939.
Stegmann, D. *Die Erben Bismarcks*. Cologne/Berlin, 1970.
Steinberg, J. *Yesterday's Deterrent: Tirpitz and the Birth of the German Battle Fleet*. London, 1965.
Steinberg, S. *Vom Schiffsjungen zum Wasserschout. Erinnerungen aus dem Leben des Capitäns Alfred Tetens, gegenwärtig Wasserschout und Vorstand des Seemannsamtes der Freien und Hansestadt Hamburg*. Hamburg, 1889.
Stevenson, R.L. *A Footnote to History: Eight Years of Trouble in Samoa*. London, 1892.
———. *Vailima Letters*. London, 1895.
Stoecker, H. *Deutschland und China im 19. Jahrhundert*. Berlin, 1958.
Stolberg-Wenigerode, Graf Otto zu. *Deutschland und die Vereinigten Staaten von Amerika*. Berlin/Leipzig, 1933.
Strausz-Hupé, and Hazard, H.W., eds. *The Idea of Colonialism*. New York, 1958.
Stuemer, W., and Duems, E. *50 Jahre Deutsche Kolonialgesellschaft 1882–1932*. Berlin, 1932.
Suchan-Galow, E. *Die deutsche Wirtschaftstätigkeit in der Südsee vor der ersten Besitzergreifung 1884*. Hamburg, 1940.
Takekoschi, Y. *Prince Saionji*. Translated by N. Kozaki. Kyoto, 1933.
Tansill, C.C. *The Foreign Policy of Thomas F. Bayard 1885–1897*. New York, 1940.
Tappenbeck, E. *Deutsch Neuguinea*. Berlin, 1901.
Taylor, A.J.P. *Germany's First Bid for Colonies 1884–85*. London, 1938.
Teng, Ssu-yü, and Fairbank, J. eds. *China's Response to the West, A Documentary Survey 1839–1923*. Cambridge, Mass., 1954.
Tetens, A. *Among the Savages of the South Seas. Memoirs of Micronesia 1862–1868*. London, 1958.
Thauren, J. *Die Missionen der Gesellschaft des Göttlichen Wortes in den Heidenländern. Die Missionen in Neu-Guinea*. Steyl, 1931.
Tirpitz, A. von. *Erinnerungen*. Leipzig, 1919.
Townsend, M.E. *The Origina of Modern German Colonialism 1871–1885*. New York, 1921.
———. *The Rise and Fall of Germany's Colonial Empire 1884–1914*. New York, 1930.
Tripp, B. *My Mission to Samoa*. Iowa, 1911.
Troost, E. *Samoanische Eindrücke und Beobachtungen*. Berlin. 1901.
Turner, G. *Samoa a Hundred Years Ago and Long Before*. London, 1884.
Vagts, A. *Deutschland und die Vereinigten Staaten in der Weltpolitik*. 2 vols. London, 1935.
Veur, P.W. van der. *Search for New Guinea's Boundaries. From Torres Straits to the Pacific*. Canberra and the Hague, 1966.
Vié, M. *Le Japon Contemporain*. Paris, 1971.

Vietor, J.K. *Die wirtschfatliche und kulturelle Entwicklung unserer Schutzgebiete*. Berlin, 1913.

Vietsch, E. von. *Wilhelm Solf, Botschafter zwischen den Zeiten*. Tübingen, 1961.

Vogel, H. *Eine Forschungsreise im Bismarch-Archipel*. Hamburg, 1911.

Volz, B. *Unser Kolonien, Land, Leute*. Leipzig, 1891.

Ward, J.M. *British Policy in the South Pacific 1786–1893*. Sydney, 1948.

Ward, R.E. ed. *Political Development in Modern Japan*. Princeton, 1968.

Washausen, H. *Hamburg und die Kolonialpolitik des deutschen Reiches 1880 bis 1890 Hamburg,* 1968.

Watson, R.M. *History of Samoa*. Wellington, 1918.

Wawn, W.T. *The South Seas Islanders and the Queensland Labour Trade*. London, 1893.

Weber, Th. *Ländereien und Plantagen der D.H.P.G. der Südsee-Inseln zu Hamburg*. Hamburg, 1885.

Wegener, G. *Deutschland im Stillen Ozean*. Bielefeld/Leipzig, 1903.

Wehler, H.-U. *Bismarck und der Imperialismus*. Köln/Berlin, 1969.

Weicker, H. *Kiautschou. Das deutsche Schutzgebiet in Ostasien*. Berlin, 1907.

Wenckstern, A. von. *Heimatpolitik durch Weltpolitik: Reden zur Flottenvorlage 1900*. Leipzig, 1900.

Wendland, W. *Im Wunderland der Papuas. Ein deutscher Kolonialarzt erlebt die Südsee*. Berlin-Dahlem, 1939.

Werner, B. von. *Ein deutsches Kriegsschiff in der Südsee*. Leipzig, 1889.

———.*Deutschlands Ehr im Weltenmeer*. Berlin, 1902.

Werner, E. *Kaiser-Wilhelmsland. Beobachtungen und Erlebnisse in den Urwäldern Neuguineas*. Freiburg i. Br., 1911.

Werner, L. *Der Alldeutsche Verband 1890–1918*. Berlin, 1935.

Wertheimer, M.S. *The Pan-German League 1890–1914*. New York, 1924.

Wilda, J. *Reise auf S.M.S. "Möwe". Streifzüge in Südseekolonien und Ostasien*. Berlin, 1903.

Willoughby, W.W. *Foreign Rights and Interest in China*. 2 vols. Baltimore, 1927.

Witte, E. *Revelations of a German Attaché: Ten Years of German-American Diplomacy*. New York, 1916.

Wohltmann, F. *Pflanzung und Siedelung auf Samoa. Erkundungsbericht an das kolonial-wirtschaftliche Komitee zu Berlin*. Berlin, 1904.

Wolf, M.L. *Botschafter Graf Hatzfeldt. Seine Tätigkeit in London 1885–1901*. Munich, 1935.

Wolferstan, B. *The Catholic Church in China 1860–1907*. London, 1909.

Wolff, M.J. *Die Disconto-Gesellschaft*. Berlin, 1930.

Wright, S.F. *China's Struggle for Tariff Autonomy 1843–1938*. Shanghai, 1938.

Young, W.A. *Christianity and Civilisation: the Influence of Missionaries upon European Expansion in the Pacific in the Nineteenth Century*. Oxford, 1922.

Zache, H. *Vertreter der Kolonien im Reichstag*. Hamburg, n.d.
Zieschank, F. *Ein Jahrzehnt in Samoa [1906–1916]*. Leipzig, 1918.
Zimmermann, A. *Geschichte der deutschen Kolonialpolitik*. Berlin, 1918.
———. *Geschichte der preussisch-deutschen Handelspolitik, aktenmässig dargestellt*. Oldenburg/Leipzig, 1892.
———. *Weltpolitisches. Beiträge und Studien zur neueren Kolonialbewegung*. 2d ed. Berlin, 1931.
Zöller, H. *Deutsch-Neuguinea und meine Ersteigung des Finisterre-Gebirges*. Stuttgart/Berlin/Leipzig, 1891.
Zühlke, H. *Die Rolle des Fernen Ostens in den politischen Beziehungen der Mächte 1895–1905*. Berlin, 1929.

*Articles*

Aydelotte, W.O. "Wollte Bismarck Kolonien". In *Deutschland und Europa. Festschrift für Hans Rothfels*, edited by W. Conze. Düsseldorf (1951).
Beazley, R.C. "Das deutsche Kolonialreich. Grossbritannien und die Verträge von 1890". *Berliner Monatshefte* 9 (1931).
———."Britain, Germany and the Portuguese Colonies 1898–1899". *Berliner Monatshefte* 14 (1936).
———."Samoa: eine deutsch-englische Kolonialverständigung". *Berliner Monatshefte* 15 (1937).
Becker, W. "Die deutsch-russische Krise bei der Erwerbung von Kiautschou". *Zeitschrift für Politik* (1926).
Behrsing, S. "Huang Tsun-Hsien und Berlin". *Ostasiatische Studien*, Berlin (1959).
———."The Memoirs of Lü Hai-huan, Chinese Minister to Berlin, 1897–1901". *Mitteilungen des Instituts für Orientforschung* 7, no. 3, Berlin (1960).
———."Zum Besuch der chinesischen Studienkommission in Deutschland im Jahre 1906". In *Studia Sino-Altaica. Festschrift für Erich Haenisch zum 80. Geburtstag*, edited by H. Franke. Wiesbaden (1961).
Berghahn, V. "Zu den Zielen des deutschen Flottenbaus unter Wilhelm II". *Historische Zeitschrift* 210 (1970).
Biskup, P. "Dr. Albert Hahl—Sketch of a German Colonial Official". *Australian Journal of Politics and History* 14 (December 1968).
———."Foreign Coloured Labour in German New Guinea. A Study in Economical Development". *Journal of Pacific History* 5 (1970).
Blum, H. "Das Wirtschaftsleben der deutschen Südseeinsulaner". *Preussische Jahrbücher* 98 (November 1899).
Boie, F. "Weltmachtstreben und Flottenbau: Marine-Fragen". *Marine-Rundschau* (1957).

Bülow, F. von. "Kiautschou". *Beiträge zur Kolonialpolitik und Kolonialwirtschaft* 1 (1899–1900).

Cheng, Chung-kuei. "The Financial Phases of China's Foreign Trade". *Chinese Social and Political Science Review* 10 (1926).

Clark, D.K. "Manifest Destiny and the Pacific". *Pacific Historical Review* 1 (1932).

Corris, P. "'Blackbirding' in New Guinea Waters, 1883–84". *Journal of Pacific History* 3 (1968).

Costenoble, H.L.W. "Die Behandlung der Eingeborenen und anderen farbigen Arbeiter und 'die Frauenfrage' in den Kolonien", *Der Tropenpflanzer* 6 (1909).

Couper, A.D. "The Island Trade. An Analysis of the Environment and Operation of Seaborne Trade Among Three Island Groups in the Pacific". *A Report* submitted to the ANU (March 1967). (Copy in the Library of the Royal Geographical Society, London.)

———."Protest Movements and Proto-Co-operatives in the Pacific Islands". *Journal of the Polynesian Society* 7, no. 3, (September 1968).

Daniels, E. "Amerikanischer Imperialismus und deutsche Vorkriegspolitik". *Preussische Jahrbücher* 188 (1922).

Deeken, R. "Die Arbeiterfrage in Samoa". *Zeitschrift für Kolonialpolitik. Kolonialrecht und Kolonialwirtschaft* 13 (1911).

Dempwolff, O. "Die Erziehung der Papua zu Arbeitern". *Koloniales Jahrbuch* 11 edited by G. Meinecke (1898).

Denby, C. "Kiaochou—German Colonial Experiment". *Forum* 29 (March-August 1900).

Ehrmann, H.M. "Imperialismus und internationale Beziehungen 1890–1902". *Berliner Monatshefte* 14 (1936).

Ellis Barker, J. "The Absorption of Holland by Germany". In *The Nineteenth Century and After*, London, no. 60 (1906).

Ellison, J.W. "The Partition of Samoa: A Study in Imperialism and Diplomacy". *Pacific Historical Review* 8 (1939).

Fecht, O. "Die Wahrung wirtschaftlicher und politischer Belange in Ostasien durch die Norddeutsche Bundesmarine. Nach unveröffentlichten Akten des Marinearchives". *Marine-Rundschau*, nos 6–8 (1937).

Firth, S.J. "The New Guinea Company 1885–1899: A Case of Unprofitable Imperialism". *Historical Studies* 15 no. 59 (October 1972).

Flierl, J. "Die eingeborenen Stämme in der Umgegend von Finschhafen auf Neu-Guinea". *Koloniale Rundschau*, 1909, edited by E. Vohsen, Berlin.

———."Zur Mischehenfrage". *Koloniale Rundschau* 1910, edited by E. Vohsen, Berlin.

Forke, A. "Aus alten Briefen eines Konsulatsbeamten in China". *Ostasiatische Rundschau* 6 (1941).

Franke, B. "Handelsneid und Grosse Politik in den englisch-deutschen Beziehungen 1871–1914". *Zeitschrift für Politik* (1939).

Franke, O. "Eisenbahnbau und Eisenbahnpol tik in China". *Marine-Rundschau* (1906).

Gadow, R. "Flottenstützpunkte". *Militärwissenschaftliche Rundschau* 4 (1936).

Grabowski, F. "Erinnerungen an Neu-Guinea". *Ausland* (1890).

Groos, O. "Stand und Bedeutung der maritimen Stützpunkte im Bereich des Stillen Ozeans". *Nauticus* (1939).

Guyot, Y. "German designs on Holland and Belgium". *The North American Review*, no. 184, New York (1907).

———."Le Pangermanisme, la Hollande et la Belgique". *The Nineteenth Century and After*, no. 60, London (1906).

Hahl, A. "Rechtsgewohnheiten und Sitten der Eingeborenen auf Ponape". *Ethnologisches Notizblatt* (1900).

———."Über die Entwicklung von Neuguinea". *Jahrbuch über die deutschen Kolonien* 5, edited by Karl Schneider (1912).

Hanneken, W.v. "Eine Kolonie in der Wirklichkeit. Illusionsfreie Betrachtungen eines ehemaligen Stationsvorstehers im Schutzgebiet der Neu-Guinea-Compagnie". *Die Nation* 13 (1895–96).

Henderson. W.O. "The German Colonial Empire". *History*, no. 20 (September 1935).

Hennig, R. "Die deutsch-niederländische Telegraphenallianz im fernen Osten". *Grenzboten* 65, no. 2 (1906).

Hildebrand, G. "Die Stellung der Sozialdemokratie zur Kolonialpolitik". *Koloniale Rundschau* (1911).

Hoffmann, A. "Sprache und Sitten der Papua Stämme an der Astrolabe Bai". *Verhandlungen des deutschen Kolonialkongresses 1905*, Berlin (1905).

Hoffmann, H. von. "Die Verordnung des Gouverneurs von Deutsch-Neu-Guinea betreffend das Eherecht unter den Eingeborenen". *Zeitschrift für Kolonialpolitik* 7 (1905).

Hubatsch, W. "Ziele und Wirkungen der deutschen Flottenpolitik um 1900". *Marine-Rundschau* (1960).

Ide, H.C. "Our Interests in Samoa". *North American Review* (August 1897).

———."The Imbroglio in Samoa". *Norther American Review* (June 1899).

———."Über die Theilnahme SMS *Iltis* und des deutschen Landungskorps an den Kämpfen um die Takipu-Forts". *Marine-Rundschau*, Berlin (1900tɪ).

Jäckel, H. "Die Neu-Guinea-Compagnie". *Zeitschrift für Kolonialpolitik, Kolonialrecht und Kolonialwirtschaft* 11 (1909).

Jacobs, M.G. “Bismarck and the Annexation of New Guinea”. *Historical Studies, Australia and New Zealand* 5 (November 1951).

———.“The Colonial Office and New Guinea 1874–1884”. *Historical Studies, Australia and New Zealand* 5 (May 1952).

———.“German Colonial Archives: New Guinea and Samoa in the Deutsches Zentralarchiv”. *The Journal of Pacific History* 6 (1971).

———.“German New Guinea”. In P. Ryan, ed. *Encyclopaedia of Papua and New Guinea*, Melbourne (1972).

Jerussalimski, A.S. “Das Eindringen der deutschen Monopole in China an der Wende vom 19. zum 20. Jahrhundert”. *Zeitschrift für Geschichtswissenschaft* 8 (1960).

———.“Der deutsche Imperialismus und die diplomatische Vorbereitung der internationalen Intervention in China im Jahre 1900” in *Die Volksmassen: Gestalter der Geschichte. Festgabe für Leo Stern zu seinem 60. Geburtstag*. Berlin (1962).

Kehr, D. “Die deutsche Flotte in den neunziger Jahren und der politisch-militärische Dualismus des Kaiserreichs”. *Archiv für Politik und Geschichte* (1927).

———.“Soziale und finanzielle Grundlagen der Tirpitzschen Flottenpropaganda”. *Die Gesellschaft* (1928).

Kennedy, P.M. “Anglo-German Relations in the Pacific and the Partition of Samoa, 1885–1899”. *Australian Journal of Politics and History* 17, no. 1 (April 1971).

———.“German Colonial Expansion in the Late Nineteenth Century: has the “Manipulated Social Imperialism” been antedated” *Past and Present*, no. 54 (February 1972).

———.“Bismarck's Imperialism: The Case of Samoa, 1880–1890”. *Historical Journal* 15 (June 1972).

Keysser, Ch. “Mission work among primitive peoples in New Guinea”. *International Review of Missions*, London (1924).

Klein, F. “Zur China-Politik des deutschen Imperialismus im Jahre 1900”. *Zeitschrift für Geschichtswissenschaft* 8 (1960).

König, B. von. “Die Eingeborenen-Besteuerung in unseren Kolonien”. *Verhandlungen des deutschen Kolonialkongresses 1910*, Berlin (1910).

Krausnick, H. “Botschafter Graf Hatzfeldt und die Aussenpolitik Bismarcks”. *Historische Zeitschrift* 167 (1943).

Krieger, M. “Über Handel und Verkehr auf Neuguinea”. *Zeitschrift für Kolonialpolitik, Kolonialrecht und Kolonialwirtschaft* 1 (1899–1900).

.“Über die Handelsunternehmungen in unseren Südsee-Kolonien”. *Beiträge zur Kolonialpolitik und Kolonialwirtschaft* 1 (1899–1900).

Kusserow, H. von. “Zur Samoafrage”. *Beiträge zur Kolonialpolitik und Kolonialwirtschaft* 1 (1899–1900).

Langen, E. "Deutsch-Samoa". *Jahrbuch über die deutschen Kolonien* 5, edited by Karl Schneider (1912).

———."Wie wandelt sich Samoa und seine Bevölkerung?". *Jahrbuch über die deutschen Kolonien* 6, edited by Karl Schneider (1913).

Livermore, S.W. "The American Naval-Base Policy in the Far East 1850–1914". *Pacific Historical Review* 13 (1944).

Miyake, M. "Die Achse Berlin-Rom-Tokio im Spiegel der japanischen Quellen". *Mitteilungen des Österreichischen Staatsarchivs* 21 (1969).

Moses, J.A. "The German Empire in Melanesia" in *The History of Melanesia*, Canberra-Port Moresby (1969).

———."The Solf Regime in Western Samoa—Ideal and Reality". *The New Zealand Journal of History* 6, no. 1 (April 1972).

Neuhauss, R. "Die 25 jährige Tätigkeit der Neuendettelsauer Mission in Deutsch-Neu-Guinea". *Koloniale Rundschau* (1911).

Newbury, C.W. "Aspects of French Policy in the Pacific 1853–1906". *Pacific Historical Review* 27 (1958).

Norem, R.A. "German Catholic Missions in Shantung". *Chinese Social and Political Science Review* 19 (1935).

O'Connor, P. "The Problem of Indentured Labour in Samoa under the Military Administration". *Political Science* 20, no. 1 (July 1968).

"[Die] Overbeck'sche Expedition nach Borneo". *Österreichische Monatsschrift für den Orient* 4 (1878).

Penfield, W.S. "The Settlement of the Samoan Cases". *American Journal of International Law* 7 (1913).

Poschinger, H. von. "Denkschrift des Geheimen Kommerzien Rat A. von Hansemann über die Zielpunkte der deutschen Kolonialpolitik". *Neues Bismarck Jahrbuch* 1 (1911).

Prager, E. "Der Reichstag und Deutschlands Südseepolitik". *Beiträge zur Kolonialpolitik und Kolonialwirtschaft* 1 (1899–1900).

Quinn, P.E. "The Diplomatic Struggle for the Carolines". *Pacific Historical Review* 14 (1945).

Reinecke, E. "Deutsch Samoa". *Beiträge zur Kolonialpolitik und Kolonialwirtschaft* 2 (1900–1901).

———."Die wirtschaftliche Entwicklung Samoas". *Beiträge zur Kolonialpolitik und Kolonialwirtschaft* 4 (1902–3).

Rohrbach, P. "Deutsch-China". *Jahrbuch über die deutschen Kolonien* 2 (1909).

Roloff, G. "Die Bündnisverhandlungen zwischen Deutschland und England 1898–1901". *Berliner Monatshefte* 7 (1929).

Rowley, C.D. "Native Officials and Magistrates of German New Guinea—1897–1921". *South Pacific* 7 (January–February 1954).

———.The Promotion of Native Health in German New Guinea". *South Pacific* 9 (1956–58).

Salisbury, R.F. "Early Stages of Economic Development in New Guinea". *Journal of the Polynesian Society* 71 (September 1962).

Scarr, D. "Recruits and Recruiters. A Portrait of the Labour Trade". In J.W. Davidson and D. Scarr, editors. *Pacific Islands Portraits*, Canberra (1970).

Schnee, P. "Unsere schwarzbraunen Landsleute in Neu-Guinea". *Beiträge zur Kolonialpolitik und Kolonialwirtschaft* 1 (1899–1900).

Schüddekopf, O.E. "Die deutsche Flottenpolitik von 1890–1914 und ihr Einfluss auf die Deutsch-englischen Beziehungen". *Internationales Jahrbuch für Geschichtsunterricht* (1951).

Schumacher, H. "Eisenbahnbau und Eisenbahnpläne in China". *Archiv für Eisenbahnwesen*, Berlin (1900).

Schumpeter, J. "Zur Soziologie der Imperialismen". *Archiv für Sozialwissenschaft und Sozialpolitik* 46, Tübingen (1918–19).

Shippee, L.B. "Germany and the Spanish-American War". *The American Historical Review* 30 (July 1925).

Sieveking, H. "Die Anfänge des Hauses Behn, Meyer & Co. in Singapore 1840–1856". *Vierteljahreschrift für Sozial- und Wirtschaftsgeschichte* 35 (1942).

———."Das Haus Behn, Meyer & Co. in Singapore unter der Leitung Arnold Otto Meyers während der Krise von 1857 und in neuem Aufstieg". *Vierteljahresschrift für Sozial- und Wirtschaftsgeschichte* 36 (1944).

Stengel, C. von. "Die Eingeborenenfrage und die Regelung der Rechtsverhältnisse in den deutschen Schutzgebieten". *Zeitschrift für Kolonialpolitik, Kolonialrecht und Kolonialwirtshcaft* 12 (1910).

Stoecker, H. "Der Eintritt Preussens und Deutschlands in die Reihe der in China bevorrechteten Mächte". *Zeitschrift für Geschichtswissenschaft* 5, no. 2 (1957).

Stoecker, H. ed. "Dokumente zur deutschen Politik in der Frage der Industrialisierung Chinas (1889–1894)". *Zeitschrift für Geschichtswissenschaft* 5, no. 31 (1957).

Strandmann, H. Pogge von. "Domestic Origins of Germany's Colonial Expansion under Bismarck". *Past and Present*, no. 42 (February 1969).

Tarling, N. "British Policy in the Malay Peninsula and Archipelago 1824–1871". *Journal of the Malayan Branch Royal Asiatic Society* 30, pt 3 (1957).

"Tätigkeit der Linienschiffsdivision in Ostasien". *Marine-Rundschau*, Berlin (1901).

Thurnwald, R. "Dic eingeborenen Arbeitskräfte im Südseeschutzgebiet". *Koloniale Rundschau* 2 (October 1910).

———."Drei Jahre im Innern von Neu-Guinea, 1913–15". *Städtisches Museum für Völkerkunde Leipzig-Jahrbuch* (1915 and 1917).

Treue, W. "Die Jaluit-Gesellschaft". *Tradition.* Zeitschrift für

Firmengeschichte und Unternehmer-Biographie 7, nos 2–3 (April 1962).

Viator. "Deutschtum und deutscher Handel in Südostasien". *Deutsche Tageszeitung*, nos 10, 6 (1912) appendix Zeitfragen.

Vormann, F. "Beitrag zur Psychologie, Soziologie und Geschichte der Monumbo-Papua, Deutsch-Neuguinea". *Anthropos* 5 (1910).

Watters, R.F. "The Transition to Christianity in Samoa". *Historical Studies, Australia and New Zealand* 8 (1959).

Wegener, E. "Weltmachtstreben und Flottenbau: Die Frage an die Geschichte". *Marine-Rundschau* (1957).

Wehler, H.-U. "1889: Wendepunkt in der americanischen Aussenpolitik. Die Anfänge des modernen Panamerikanismus—die Samoakrise". *Historische Zeitschrift* 201 (1965).

Wiltgen, R. "Catholic Mission plantations in mainland New Guinea". In *The History of Melanesia*, Canberra (1969).

Wolff, E. "Der 'farbige Orstvorsteher' im Schutzgebiet Deutsch Neuguinea". *Zeitschrift für Kolonialpolitik, Kolonialrecht und Kolonialwirtschaft* 6 (1904).

———. "Das Recht am Grund und Boden im Schutzgebiet von Deutsch Neuguinea". *Zeitschrift für Kolonialpolitik* 8 (1906).

*Dissertations*

Backen, H. "Die Karolinen-Frage 1885". phil, diss., Cologne, 1963.

Bade, K.-J. "Revolution—Depression—Expansion: Friedrich Fabris 'konialpolitische Episode'. Ein Beitrag zur Geschichte der deutschen Kolonialbewegung in der Bismarckzeit". phil. diss., Erlangen, 1971.

Bünemann, R.J.P. "The Anglo-German 'Colonial Marriage', 1885–1894". B.Litt. thesis, Oxford, 1955.

Burgsdorff, C. von. "Die Entwicklung der kolonialen Rechtspflege". jur.diss., Leipzig, 1911.

Clement, W. "Die amerikanische Samoapolitik und die Idee des Manifest Destiny". phil.diss., Marburg, 1949.

Donner, H. "Der Karolinenstreit". jur.diss., Würzburg, 1930.

Firth, S.J. "German Recruitment and Employment of Labourers in the Western Pacific before the First World War". D.Phil. thesis, Oxford, 1973.

Foerster, R. "Politische Geschichte der Preussischen und Deutschen Flotte bis zum ersten Flottengesetz von 1898". phil.diss., Leipzig, 1928.

Ganz, A.H. "The Role of the Imperial German Navy in Colonial Affairs". Ph.D.diss., The Ohio State University, 1972.

Göpfert, H. "Die Eingeborenenlandschaft von Morobe (Neuguinea) und ihre Wandlung unter dem Einfluss der Mission". phil.diss., Hamburg, 1956.

Gördes, H. "Die Arbeiterfrage in der deutschen Südsee unter Berücksichtigung der englischen Fidschi-Inseln. Ein Beitrag zur Lehre von der Volkswirtschaft in tropischen Ländern". phildiss., Erlangen, 1915.

Hannemann, E.F. "Village Life and Social Change in Madang Society". M.A. thesis, University of Chicago, 1945.

Hartwig, E. "Zur Politik und Entwicklung des Alldeutschen Verbandes von seiner Gründung bis zum Beginn des ersten Weltkrieges 1891–1914". phil.diss., Jena, 1966.

Hasse, H. "Kiautschou. Sein Erwerb, Verlust und seine Bedeutung". phil.diss., Rostock, 1921.

Hausotter, E. "Li Fengbao, der zweite chinesische Gesandte in Berlin (1878–1884). Eine Darstellung seiner Karriere und eine kommenteirte Übersetzung seines Tagebuches". phil.diss., Humboldt University, Berlin, 1969.

Herkner, W. "Drei Systeme kolonialer Herrschaft auf Samoa". jur.diss., Erlangen, 1951.

Holzer, S. "Der Karolinenstreit, eine völkerrechtliche Studie". jur.diss., Würzburg, 1930.

Hövermann, O. "Kiautschou. Bedeutung und Recht seiner Erwerbung". jur.diss., Bonn, 1913.

Ibbeken, R. "Das aussenpolitische Problem Staat und Wirtschaft in der deutschen Reichspolitik 1880–1914. Untersuchungen über Kolonialpolitik, internationale Finanzpolitik, Handelsverträge und die Bagdadbahn". phil.diss., Munich, 1928.

Irmer, A.J. "Die Erwerbung von Kiautschou, 1894–1898". phil.diss., Bonn, 1930.

Jäckel, H. "Die Landgesellschaften in den deutschen Schutzgebieten". diss., Halle, 1909.

Kennedy, P.M. "The partition of the Samoan Islands, 1898–1899". D.Phil. thesis, Oxford, 1970.

Klauss, K. "Die Deutsche Kolonialgesellschaft und die deutsche Kolonialpolitik von den Anfängen bis 1895". phil.diss., Humboldt University, Berlin, 1966.

Lackner, H. "Koloniale Finanzpolitik im Deutschen Reichstag von 1880–1919". diss., Königsberg, 1939.

Laracy, H.M. "Catholic Missions in the Solomon Islands 1845–1966". Ph.D. thesis, Australian National University, Canberra, 1969.

Lincoln, A. "Cleveland, Bismarck and Samoa". M.A. thesis, University of California, 1938.

Löding, W. "Die deutsch-englischen Bündnisverhandlungen 1898 bis 1901. Ihr Verlauf auf Grund der deutschen und der englischen Akten". phil.diss., Hamburg, 1929.

Mann, P. "Die Bedeutung Kiautschous und seine wirtschaftliche Entwicklung unter deutscher Verwaltung". jur.diss., Freiburg, 1923.

Meyer, G. "Das Eindringen des deutschen Kapitalismus in die niederländischen und britischen Kolonien in Südostasien von den Anfängen bis 1918". phil.diss., Berlin, Humboldt University, 1970.

Meyer, J. "Die Propaganda der deutschen Flottenbewegung 1897–1900". phil.diss., Bern. 1967.

Michelis, A.A. "Niederländisch-Indien und die politischen, wirtschaftlichen und finanziellen Beziehungen Deutschlands zu Holland und seinen Kolonien". diss., Frankfurt/Main, 1922.

Möller, M. "Deutschlands Chinapolitik vom Einspruch von Shimonoseki bis zur Erwerbung von Kiautschou". phil.diss., Münster, 1927.

Müller, F. "Die Kolonialpolitik des Deutschen Reiches und die deutsche Sozialdemokratie". Phil.diss., Tübingen, 1923.

Oncken, D. "Das Problem des Lebensraumes in der deutschen Politik vor 1914". diss., Freiburg i.Br. 1948. MS.

Pehl, H. "Die deutsche Kolonialpolitik und das Zentrum (1884–1914)". phil.diss., Frankfurt, 1934.

Pierard, R.V. "The German Colonial Society, 1882–1914". phil.diss., State University of Iowa, 1964.

Reinhardt, H.D. "Tirpitz und der deutsche Flottengedanke in den Jahren 1892–1898". phil.diss., Marburg, 1964.

Schlieper, H.C. "Niederländisch-Indien als Absatzmarkt". diss., Munich, 1934.

Schulze, B. "Der Disconto-Ring und die deutsche Expansion 1871–1890. Ein Beitrag zum Verhältnis Monopol: Staat". phil.diss., Leipzig, 1965. MS.

Schwarze. F. "Das deutsch-englische Abkommen über die portugiesischen Kolonien vom 30.8.1898". phil.diss., Göttingen, 1931.

Smidl. J.F. "British, German and United States Rivalry in the Samoan Islands". M.A. thesis, University of Chicago, 1925.

Spellmeyer, H. "Bismarcks parlamentarische Kämpfe um seine Kolonialpolitik". phil.diss., Bonn, 1930.

Strandmann, H. Pogge von. "The Kolonialrat, its Significance and Influence on German Politics 1890–1906". D.Phil. thesis, Oxford, 1970.

Strohschneider, G. "Die Stellungnahme der Hamburger Presse als Ausdruck der öffentlichen Meinung zu den Anfängen der Bismarckschen Kolonialpolitik". phil.diss., Hamburg, 1956.

Stuhlmacher, W. "Bismarcks Kolonialpolitik, dargestellt nach den Aktenveröffentilchungen des Auswärtigen Amts". phil.diss., Halle, 1924.

Thacker, J.W. "The Partition of Samoa". Ph.D. thesis, South Carolina, 1966.

Treue, W. "Der Erwerb und die Verwaltung der Marshall-Inseln. Ein Beitrag zur Geschichte der Jaluit-Gesellschaft". phil.diss., Berlin, 1940.

Ueberhorst, P. "Die Arbeiterfrage in den deutschen Kolonien". jur.diss., Münster, 1926.

Voigt, W. "Die Entwicklung der Eingeborenenpolitik in den deutschen Kolonien. Ein Beitrag zur Bekämpfung der kolonialen Schuldlüge". phil.diss., Giessen, 1927.

Weck, P.A. "Deutschlands Politik in der Samoa-Frage". phil.diss., Leipzig, 1934.

Westphal, G. "Der Kolonialrat 1890–1907. Ein Beitrag zur Geschichte der Herausbildung des deutschen imperialistischen Kolonialsystems". phil.diss., Humboldt University, Berlin, 1964.

Wood, C.L. "Die Beziehungen Deutschlands zu China (eine historische Betrachtung in politischer und ökonomischer Hinsicht vom 19. Jahrhundert bis zum Jahre 1934)". diss., Heidelberg, 1934.

### *Other Published Material*

*Adressbuch für Deutsch-Neuguinea, Samoa und Kiautschou*, vols 1–14, Berlin, 1901–14.

*Amtsblatt für das Schutzgebiet Deutsch-Neuguinea* , vols 1–6, published by Kaiserl. Gouvernement, Rabaul, 1909–1914.

*Amtsblatt für das Schutzgebiet Kiautschou*, vols 1–15, published by Kaiserl. Gouvernement, Tsingtau, 1900–1914.

*The Australian Missionary Review*, monthly paper of the Australian Methodist Society, vol. 1 (1891), Sydney.

*Beiträge zur Kolonialpolitik und Kolonialwirtschaft*, I–V (1899/1900–1903), continued as *Zeitschrift für Kolonialpolitik* ... (1904–12) and *Koloniale Monatsblätter* (1913–14).

*Berichte der Rheinischen Missionsgesellschaft*, vols 41–71 (1889–1914) Barmen.

Carlson, A.R. *German Foreign Policy, 1890–1914 and Colonial Policy to 1914: A Handbook and Annotated Bibliography*, Metuchen N.J., 1970.

*The Chronicle*, Monthly Magazine of the London Missionary Society, Series 3, vol. 1 (1892), London.

*Denkschriften* (papers presented to the German Reichstag)

By KA: *Die Entwicklung unserer Kolonien*, Berlin, 1892.

*Denkschrift betr. Den Übergang der Landeshoheit über das Schutzgebiet der Neu Guinea-Kompagnie auf das Reich.* In

Haushalts-Etat des Schutzgebietes 1896–97. Nachtrag and Haushalts-Etat 1899.

*Denkschrift betr. die Inselgruppen der Karolinen, Palau und Marianen.* Anlage zum zweiten Nachtrag zum Etat der Schutzgebiete auf das Rechnungsjahr 1899. No. 395.

*Denkschrift über die Errichtung eines Reichskolonialamts* 1890–1907, Anlagen nos 1–5, Berlin, 1907.

By RKA: *Denkschrift über die Arbeitsverhältnisse im Schutzgebebiet Deutsch Neu-Guinea.* September 1913.

*Denkschrift über die Ausgestaltung der Verwaltungsorganisation im Schutzgebiet Neu-Guinea*, in Haushalts-Etat für das Schutzbegiet, 1913.

By Reichs-Marine-Amt: *Denkschrift betr. die Entwicklung des Kiautschou-Gebiets.* 11 vols, Berlin, 1899–1910.

*Deutsche Kolonialzeitung.* Organ der Deutschen Kolonialgesellschaft, Berlin, 1884–1914.

*Deutsches Kolonialblatt. Amtsblatt für die Schutzgebiete des Deutschen Reiches*, published by Kolonial-Abtheilung des Auswärtigen Amts [from 1907: *Amtsblatt für die Schutzgebiete in Afrika und in der Südsee*, published by Reichskolonialamt vols 1–25 (1890–1914)]

*Deutsche Wacht. Zeitschrift für Handels- und Kolonialpolitik, Volkswirtschaft und Völkerrecht*, Batavia, no. 1. 1915–8. 1922. (Organ of "Deutscher Bund" in Batavia).

*Jahrbuch über die deutschen Kolonien*, ed. by K. Schneider, vols 1–7, Essen, 1908–14.

*Jahresberichte der Rheinischen Missionsgesellschaft*, vols 55–85, Barmen, 18 84–1914.

*Kirchliche Mitteilungen aus und über Nord Amerika, Australien und Neuguinea*, published by Neuendettelsauer Mission, vols 19–42, 1887–1910. Neuendettelsau (continued as *Neuendettelsauer Missionsblatt*).

*Koloniale Monatsblätter. Zeitschrift für Kolonialpolitik, Kolonialrecht und Kolonialwirtschaft* edited by Deutsche Kolonialgesellschaft, vols 15–16 (1913–14). [Until 1913: *Zeitschrift für Kolonialpolitik* ... ]

*Koloniale Reichstagsreden*, 3 vols. Berlin, 1902–7.

*Koloniale Rundschau. Zeitschrift für Kolonialwirtschaft, Völker- und Länderkunde.* [Until 1923: *Monatsschrift für Interessen unserer Schutzgebiete*], Leipzig, formerly Berlin.

*Koloniales Jahrbuch.* edited by G. Meinecke, vols 11, Berlin, 1888–98.

*Koloniale Zeitschrift.* vols 1–15, edited by Fr. Kolbe [from 1913, organ of Deutschnationaler Kolonialverein], Berlin, 1900–1914/15.

[*Die deutsche*] *Kolonialgesetzgebung*, Berlin 1884–1914.

[*von der Heydt*] *Kolonialhandbuch. Jahrbuch der deutschen Kolonial—und Überseeunternehmungen.* edited by F. Mensch and J. Hellman, 7 vols., Berlin/Leipzig/Hamburg, 1907–13.

[*Die Deutsche*] *Kolonialliteratur*. compiled by Max Brose. Special issue of *Zeitschrift für Kolonialpolitik, Kolonialrecht und Kolonialwirtschaft*, published by Deutsche Kolonialgesellschaft, Berlin. First issue covered 1884–95, thereafter annually, to 1914.

*Die Deutsche Kolonialpolitik, Aktenstücke*, 3 vols., Berlin, 1902–7.

*Kolonial-politische Korrespondenz*, edited by Gesellschaft für Deutsche Kolonisation, vols 1–3, Berlin 1885–87.

Leeson, Ida. *Bibliography of Bibliographies of the South Pacific*, London/Melbourne/New York, 1954.

*Mitteilungen aus den deutschen Schutzgebieten* (quarterly publication with *Deutsches Kolonialblatt*), edited by Freiherr v. Danckelmann; from 1912–14 edited by H. Marquardsen, Berlin.

*Nachrichten über Kaiser-Wilhelmsland und den Bismarck Archipel*, published by Neuguinea Compagnie, Berlin, 1885–98.

*Neuguinea Compagnie. Geschäftsberichte der Direktion*, Berlin, 1885–1914.

Reichskolonialamt (until 1907–KA) *Jahresbericht über die Entwicklung der deutschen Schutzgebiete in Afrika und der Südsee 1894-95–1908-09*, Berlin, 1896–1910.

Reichskolonialamt: *Die deutschen Schutzgebiete in Afrika und der Südsee. Amtliche Jahresberichte*, vols 1909/10–1912/13. [See *Jahresberichte*.]

Reichskolonialministerium: *Deutsche und französische Eingeborenenbehandlung*, Berlin, 1919.

*Samoanische Zeitung*, vol. 1, no. 1 (1900)–vol. 15, no. 52 (1914), edited by Emil Luebke, Apia.

*Samoanisches Gouvernements-Blatt*, published by Kaiserl. Gouvernement, Apia, 1892–1914 (formerly *Samoa Royal Gazette*).

[*Das*] *Staatsarchiv*, 1899–1900, vols 62–63, pp.264–81, *Die Vorgänge auf Samoa, Anfang* 1899.

*Stenographische Berichte über die Verhandlungen des Reichstages*, 6. Legislaturperiode, 1. Session 1884–85, vol. 5, no. 63, pp.197–231, *Deutsche Interessen in der Südsee I.*

Ibid., no. 115, pp.418–55, *Deutsche Land-Reklamationen auf Fidji.*

Ibid., vol. 6, no. 167, pp.687–728, *Deutsche Interessen in der Südsee II.*

Ibid., 7. Legislaturperiode, 4. Session 1889–89, vol. 5, no. 110, pp.557–94, *Sammlung von Aktenstücken, betreffend Samoa.*

Ibid., no. 138, pp.874–90, *Samoa* (cont.).

Ibid., vol. 6, no. 210, pp.1234–36, *Samoa* (cont.).

Ibid., no. 214, pp.1359–1362, *Samoa* (cont.).

Ibid., 8. Legislaturperiode, 1. Session 1890–91, vol. 1. Anlageband, no. 64, pp.5571, *Samoa* (cont.)

Ibid., 2. Session 1892–93, vol. 1. Anlageband, no. 79, pp.456–541, *Samoa* (cont.).

*Steyler Missionsbote*, monthly paper of SVD mission, vol. 41 (1914) Steyl.

Taylor, C.R.H., *A Pacific Bibliography*, 2d ed. Oxford, 1965.
[*Drucksachen zu den*] *Verhandlungen des Bundesrats des Deutschen Reiches*, 1879, 2, no. 96, *Weissbuch vom 22. Mai 1879 zum Freundschaftsvertrage zeischen dem Deutschen Reiche und Samoa vom 24. Januar 1879*. Ibid., 1880, vol. 1, no. 69, *Weissbuch zur Samoavorlage vom 4. April 12880.*
*Verhandlungen des deutschen Kolonialkongresses 1902*, Berlin, 1902; ... *1905*, Berlin, 1905; ... *1910*, Berlin, 1910.
*Verordnungsblatt für das Kiautschougebiet*. supplement to *Marineverordnungsblatt*, published since 1903 by Reichsmarineamt, Berlin.
*Zeitschrift für Kolonialpolitik, Kolonialrecht und Kolonialwirtschaft*, 6–14, 1904–12, Berlin; 15–16, 1913–14: *Zeitschrift für Kolonialrecht*, as part of *Koloniale Monatsblätter*.

# Index